Defenders of the Norman Crown

To my family and friends, with love.

Defenders of the Norman Crown

Rise and Fall of the Warenne Earls of Surrey

Sharon Bennett Connolly

PEN & SWORD HISTORY

First published in Great Britain in 2021 and reprinted in 2023 by
Pen & Sword History
An imprint of
Pen & Sword Books Ltd
Yorkshire – Philadelphia

ISBN 9 781 39901 636 0

A CIP catalogue record for this book is
available from the British Library.

Typeset by Mac Style
Printed in the UK on paper from a sustainable source by CPI Group
(UK) Ltd, Croydon, CR0 4YY

Pen & Sword Books Limited incorporates the imprints of Atlas,
Archaeology, Aviation, Discovery, Family History, Fiction, History,
Maritime, Military, Military Classics, Politics, Select, Transport, True
Crime, Air World, Frontline Publishing, Leo Cooper, Remember
When, Seaforth Publishing, The Praetorian Press, Wharncliffe Local
History, Wharncliffe Transport, Wharncliffe True Crime and White
Owl.

For a complete list of Pen & Sword titles please contact

PEN & SWORD BOOKS LIMITED
47 Church Street, Barnsley, South Yorkshire, S70 2AS, England
E-mail: enquiries@pen-and-sword.co.uk
Website: www.pen-and-sword.co.uk

Or

PEN AND SWORD BOOKS
1950 Lawrence Rd, Havertown, PA 19083, USA
E-mail: Uspen-and-sword@casematepublishers.com
Website: www.penandswordbooks.com

Contents

Acknowledgements

Writing my fourth book, the second for Pen & Sword, has been an incredible experience and I would like to thank everyone who has helped and encouraged me throughout the process. I would like to thank the staff at Pen & Sword, especially my editors Claire Hopkins and Danna Messer for giving me the opportunity to write this book and for their continuous support, Paul Wilkinson for the stunning cover and Laura Hirst for her incredible work on the technical side, turning my Word document into the book you see before you.

I would particularly like to thank Amy Licence, whose help, advice and friendship has been invaluable to me in my journey to become an author. I am also grateful to my fellow authors, Kristie Dean and Annie Whitehead, who have offered advice and encouragement throughout. And thank you to: Bev Newman, for the discussions on the Poynings and the Warenne affinity; Catherine Hanley for helping me resolve the age of Isabel, the fourth countess, and the issue of the confusing numbering of the earls; Rich Price for his invaluable work on King John's letters; and Elizabeth Chadwick for all the little Warenne-related chats we've had over the years. Thanks also go to some amazing historians, including Louise J. Wilkinson, Ralph V. Turner, Richard Cassidy, Simon Forder, Michael Jones, James Wright and David Santiuste for helping me with all my little queries about various aspects of the Warenne family and their associates.

Writing can be a lonely experience, you spend your time reading books for research, or sitting, staring at the computer screen, trying to think of something to write. But social media has changed all that, there are always friends just a 'click' away to give you a diversion or encouragement. I would therefore like to thank the readers of my blog, *History ... the Interesting Bits. com* for their wonderful support and feedback. A special thank you goes, too, to my friends in the online community, whose amusing anecdotes and memes have given me that boost when I needed it, particularly Karrie Stone, Tim Byard-Jones, Karen Clark, Geanine Teramani-Cruz, Anne Marie Bouchard, Harry Basnett, Derek Birks and every one of my Facebook friends and Twitter followers. Also, the online author community has proved invaluable to me. So, I would like to extend a special 'thank you' to Darren Baker, Matthew Lewis, Dan Spencer, Julian Humphreys, Nathen Amin, S.J.A. Turney, Tony Riches, Sarah Bryson, Matthew Harffy, Dr Janina Ramirez, Giles Kristian, Justin Hill, Mary Anne Yard, Paula Lofting, Samantha Wilcoxson, Lynn Dawson, Jacqueline Reiter, Stephanie Churchill and Prue Batten for all your support and encouragement with this book and the previous ones.

And thank you to the various historical sites I have visited, including the British Library, Doncaster Museum, Conisbrough Castle, Lewes Castle and Priory, Sandal Castle, Castle Acre Castle and Priory, Pevensey Castle, Lincoln Castle and Cathedral, and all the wonderful staff who have been happy to talk about all things Warenne. I am grateful to Conisbrough residents Brenda Houlbrook and Peter Henderson for bringing to my attention the story of the mysterious knight who is buried in St Peter's churchyard, Conisbrough; and to my cousin Andrea Houlbrook for going out especially during the coronavirus lockdown to take a photograph of St Peter's Church for this book. I also have to thank my friend Andrea Raee, who took a photograph of the Warenne tomb at Southwark Cathedral and has kindly allowed me to use it in the book, as the lockdown prevented my planned field trip to the cathedral. And my gratitude goes to Trinity Church, Southover and the Dean and Chapter of Southwark Cathedral for graciously allowing me to use photographs taken within their churches. I must also thank the Sussex Archaeological Society for their support and encouragement in this project – and wish them 'happy 175th birthday'. The Society were founded in 1846, shortly after the discovery of the tomb of Gundrada de Warenne, during the excavations for the new railway line in Lewes.

I would like to include some 'thank yous' to those who supported the release of my previous books, *Heroines of the Medieval World*, *Silk and the Sword: The Women of the Norman Conquest* and *Ladies of Magna Carta: Women of Influence in Thirteenth Century England*. Particular thanks have to go to Sasha and Gill at Lindum Books in Lincoln for hosting my author talks and being a huge support of this local author. I am grateful to Victoria, Nicola, Marian and everyone at Gainsborough Old Hall, for hosting my book signings and being my place of refuge when I need to get away from the computer. And to Gavin, Liam and the staff at Conisbrough Castle – who are always happy to talk about the Warennes.

A thank you must also go to my friends closer to home, particularly Sharon Gleave, Jill Gaskell, Di Richardson, Helen Walker, Bernadette

Blaevoet-Fletcher and all my local friends, for their wonderful support and for dragging me out for a coffee every once in a while.

I reserve a special thanks to my family, especially my niece, Jessica, for her drawing of Conisbrough Castle, for me, as a souvenir. And my sister, Suzanne, whose support has been incredible and very much appreciated, and my brother Stephen. And to my mum and dad for all their love and encouragement, and for their own passion for history. A huge thank you also goes to my research assistant and son, Lewis Connolly, who has travelled to various wonderful places with me in the process of making this book a reality and has turned into a fabulous sounding-board for my ideas and arguments, as well as a source for numerous Warenne-related jokes – mainly about rabbits! And to my husband, James, thank you for putting up with all the history talks. I could not have done it without all of you.

I will always owe a debt of gratitude to the great historians throughout history – to the present day – who have gallantly edited and translated the great chronicles of the medieval era, so that they are accessible and readable for all of us who have an interest in the period, but very little understanding of Latin. Every effort has been made to ensure the accuracy of this book. However, any errors that may occur are entirely my own.

Foreword

I have had a personal interest in the Warennes for as long as I can remember. Writing the story of the family is a work that I have always wanted to do, but never expected to get the chance: I am immensely grateful to Pen & Sword for giving me the opportunity.

Growing up close to the Warenne castle at Conisbrough in South Yorkshire, you would expect to know their story intimately. Except you don't. As a child, I regularly visited Conisbrough Castle. I have fond memories of summer picnics in the outer bailey, rolling down the hills and sneaking past the man in his little hut to get into the inner bailey without paying (sorry about that). We even went on a primary school trip to the castle. It was only a few miles from my school, not far enough to justify a coach, so we all marched down to the nearest bus stop, got on the 224 Doncaster bus that stopped down the hill from the castle. I can still remember my poor teacher handing the unfortunate bus driver thirty 2*p* pieces to pay our fares. It is hard to find anyone in South Yorkshire who didn't go to Conisbrough Castle on a school trip at some point.

However, in those days the history of the castle mainly focused on the fact it was the inspiration for the Saxon stronghold of the eponymous hero's father in Sir Walter Scott's novel, *Ivanhoe*. Scott is said to have been driving by in a carriage, on his way to Scotland, when he saw the castle and decided it was the perfect setting for a Saxon lord's home – quite ironic, considering the fact it had been a Norman stronghold since the Conquest, although it had previously belonged to the unfortunate King Harold II, defeated and killed at the Battle of Hastings. The stories I heard growing up were of secret tunnels, running either to the church a few hundred yards away, to Tickhill or to Doncaster, both some miles away; the first would have been a difficult undertaking but the latter two, requiring several miles of tunnelling, would have been highly unfeasible for medieval miners.

Little was made of the family that had once owned Conisbrough Castle and built the magnificent hexagonal keep. Years later, after graduating, I volunteered there for several months, helping out in the gift shop and giving guided tours to the many local schools who still regularly arrange an annual trip to Conisbrough Castle. This was the early 1990s and, as a tour guide, I still mentioned *Ivanhoe* but more was said of its history. The name

Conisbrough could be a derivation of Cyngesburgh, meaning King's Burh, though it is not known to which king the name refers, possibly one of the kings of Northumbria of the seventh or eighth century. Burhs were defensive forts developed to offer protection to the population from Viking attack. King Alfred the Great later developed a system of burhs throughout Wessex to provide protection for his people; this was then expanded by his children, Edward the Elder and Æthelflæd, Lady of Mercia, spreading the system north into Mercia, East Anglia and beyond.

Conisbrough also has a legendary history. According to Geoffrey of Monmouth, in his *Historia Regum Britanniae* (History of the Kings of Britain), Conisbrough was founded as 'Conan's Burg' by a British leader called Conan. It was said to have later belonged to Ambrosius Aurelianus, a candidate for the legendary King Arthur. As Geoffrey of Monmouth says, Ambrosius captured the Saxon leader Hengist, once a mercenary for Vortigern, at the battle of 'Maisbeli', and brought him to his stronghold at Conisbrough. Hengist was then beheaded on Ambrosius' orders and buried at the entrance to the castle of 'Cunengeburg', that is Conisbrough.[1] A small hill, locally called Hengist's Mound, is in the grounds of the outer bailey (though Gavin Smithies, the castle's manager, assures me it is a Victorian rubbish dump). At the time of the Norman Conquest, Conisbrough was in the hands of the king himself, Harold II, although there is no suggestion that he ever visited. And when Harold died at Hastings, Conisbrough became the property of the new king, William the Conqueror. William in turn passed the town and castle to one of his loyal battle commanders, William de Warenne.

When I was giving guided tours around the castle, the story of the Warenne family focused on the man who built Conisbrough Castle between 1170 and 1180, Hamelin de Warenne, half-brother to King Henry II and husband of Countess Isabel de Warenne, only child of the third Earl Warenne.

The story of the Warennes is a personal journey that has spanned my whole life. It is also the story of one of the greatest families of medieval England.

P.S. I must also give a nod to living through history. I started writing this foreword while visiting Conisbrough Castle in March 2020. I finished it at home, during 'lockdown' as the dreadful Coronavirus runs its course. I had planned to visit the castle again before completing the book, but that has proved impossible. Though the castle itself stands as a reminder that it has stood through over 800 years of history. It has stood witness to the dreadful effects of invasion, war, famine and plague and its survival is, in itself, a promise of better days to come.

Stay safe.

Sharon Bennett Connolly,
May 2020

Introduction

Ingland during the medieval period was ruled by a king who had supreme executive power over his people. The king had the final say on all government policy. One man cannot rule a country alone, however; he needs the help of his senior barons, both as administrators on a national and local level, as ambassadors on the international stage and as military generals and a source of manpower in times of war. Feudal society in England flowed from the king down, with an understanding that mutual need and reliance would maintain the natural order of society. Although this did not always work, a king basically gave his protection to his barons, who in turn gave their administrative and military service; the common man was, in turn protected and governed by his lord in return for providing the services the manor needed to function. The English earls were an integral part of this system, their influence spreading as far and wide as their landholdings.

From the time of the Norman Conquest to the death of the seventh and last earl, the Warenne family was at the heart of English politics and the establishment, providing military and administrative support to the Crown. In the years following 1066 William I de Warenne, who became the first Earl of Surrey in 1088, was the fourth richest man in England and the richest not related to the royal family – he ranks at number 18 in MSN.com's Top 20 Richest People of All Time. The earls of Surrey were at the centre of the major crises of medieval England, from the Norman Conquest itself to the deposition of Edward II and accession of Edward III. Strategic marriages forged links with the leading noble houses in England and Scotland, from the Marshals, the FitzAlans, the d'Aubignys and Percys to the Scottish and English royal families themselves. Indeed, it is from Ada de Warenne, daughter of the second earl, married to the oldest son of the king of Scots, that all the leading competitors for the Scottish throne, after the death of Margaret, Maid of Norway in 1286, are descended. Queen Elizabeth II, herself, can trace her own lineage back to Ada and, through Ada, to the second earl of Warenne and Surrey. Furthermore, Ada's own great-great-niece, Isabella de Warenne, daughter of John de Warenne, the sixth earl, was married to the winning competitor, John Balliol, King of Scots from 1292 to 1296.

William I de Warenne was rewarded for his support of King William II in the 1088 rebellion with the earldom of Surrey. However, the earls thereafter were as often referred to as the earls of Warenne – or the familial Earl Warenne, rather than earls of Surrey. The earldoms of Sussex and Strathearn (Scotland) were later added to these titles. As they appear to have preferred the simple familial title of Earl Warenne, that is how I have chosen to refer to them throughout the book, except when establishing their titles. The Warenne extensive lands spanned the country from Lewes on the south coast to their castles of Conisbrough and Sandal in Yorkshire, with their family powerbase in East Anglia, where they built a magnificent priory, castle and medieval village at Castle Acre. The family mausoleum was at St Pancras Priory in Lewes, founded by the first earl and his wife, Gundrada, burial place of all but two subsequent earls and numerous other family members, as well as several earls of Arundel and their countesses.

For almost 300 years the Warenne earls of Surrey were some of the most influential men in the country, but the family died out rather ingloriously, with the seventh – and last – earl's marital difficulties. Despite a prestigious marriage to a granddaughter of the king of England, John de Warenne, 7th Earl Warenne, died with no legitimate son to succeed him, though he had numerous acknowledged illegitimate children to whom he had given the family name.

The first earl is one of the few people identified as being present at the Battle of Hastings. The second earl had a complicated relationship with Henry I and supported King Stephen against Matilda. The third earl died on Crusade, leaving only a daughter to succeed him. Countess Isabel de Warenne, the richest heiress in England, married first a king's son and then a king's brother. The fifth Earl Warenne was cousin to King John, but briefly joined the cause of the French invader, the Dauphin Louis, during the Magna Carta crisis. The sixth earl was a staunch supporter of Edward I and guardian of Scotland after the deposition of King John Balliol. The seventh earl was renowned for his marriage difficulties, but was also a keen supporter, for the most part, of Edward II. Each earl, and his family, has a colourful story in their own right, and adds their own dimension to the Warenne family's story. And while each Warenne earl brings his own characteristics to the family story, the Warenne women, daughters and wives of the various earls, are also an integral part of the history, with several of them making names for themselves through politics, dynastic ambition and their own marriages.

Just a mention about the numbering of the Warenne earls of Surrey, which can cause confusion. Depending on which sources you read, there were either seven or eight earls. This arises from the fact that the fourth earl was, in fact, a countess – Isabel (b.c. 1135, d. 1203). Countess Isabel married twice, though she had no children with her first husband. The subsequent numbering differs due to the fact that Isabel's husbands are either counted as the fourth and fifth earls, or both are seen as the fourth earl. As they held the title only by right of their wife, and Isabel survived both husbands, I have chosen to count them based on Isabel being the fourth countess and therefore William and Hamelin are, in this book, both numbered as the fourth earl, with Isabel and Hamelin's son, William, becoming the fifth earl on his father's death.

It is also necessary to point out that family name traditions may cause confusion. Five of the eight men who used the title earl of Surrey were named William, two were named John and one Hamelin. We also have several Isabels and Isabellas in the family, as well as a number of Gundradas, Elas and Avas. I have endeavoured to make sure that each individual is clearly identified, using their full title and comital number or relationship wherever possible.

The Warenne story is one of drama, tragedy, glory and ambition that was consigned to history with the death of John II de Warenne, the seventh and last Earl of Warenne, Surrey, Sussex and Strathearn. The dynasty founded by William and Gundrada in the turmoil of the Norman Conquest would continue to serve the Crown until John's death in 1347.

Chapter One

The Warenne Origins

As with most families, the origins of the Warenne family are shrouded in the sands of time and the distance of over a thousand years. Given that the family hailed from Normandy, it is likely that they had Scandinavian ancestry, just like the majority of Normans, including their duke, William (known as William the Bastard, or William the Conqueror). Duke William was descended from the famous Rollo, the first Norse, or Viking, ruler of Normandy. William was the illegitimate son of Robert I the Magnificent, who was duke of Normandy from 1027 until his death in Nicaea in 1035, whilst returning from pilgrimage to Jerusalem. Before departing on this pilgrimage, Robert had named William, then only 7 or 8 years old, as his heir, despite the question mark over his birth.

Several studies were written in the eighteenth, nineteenth and twentieth centuries in an attempt to establish the Warenne family's origins, and its relationship to the duke of Normandy.[1] The family name is probably derived from the hamlet of Varenne, situated just south of Arques in northern France and thirteen miles from Bellencombre. The village is situated on the river of the same name, Varenne (previously known as Guarenne). Varenne was part of the Warenne lands in the *département* of Seine-Inférieure, Normandy. William de Warenne, the first earl of Surrey, was a younger son of Rodulf, or Ralph, de Warenne. The correct form of Rodulf's name, as it appears in the twelfth century manuscript of the cartulary of the Holy Trinity at Rouen, is 'Rodulfus', rather than 'Radulfus', which appears in the same manuscript, but was a distinctly different name at the time.[2]

Rodulf was a minor Norman lord with lands in the Pays de Caux; his first wife, Beatrix, was the mother of William and his older brother, another Rodulf, and possibly an unnamed sister. Although William de Warenne's ancestry is far from clear, it seems likely that his mother Beatrix was a niece of Duchess Gunnor. As the wife of Duke Richard I of Normandy, Gunnor was the mother of Emma of Normandy and the great-grandmother of Duke William of Normandy. Emma of Normandy was wife of both Æthelred II and King Cnut, kings of England; she holds the distinction of being the only woman to have been crowned queen of England twice, with two different husbands. Emma was the mother of Harthacnut and Edward the Confessor, also kings of England, and great-aunt of Duke William, later king of England. If Beatrix's familial link to Duchess Gunnor is true, it would mean that William de Warenne was a second cousin, once removed, of the victorious duke of Normandy, later to be known as William the Conqueror. The two families were certainly related in some way, as Anselm, Archbishop of Canterbury, would later forbid a marriage between William de Warenne's son, another William, and an illegitimate daughter of Henry I on the grounds of consanguinity (meaning the couple was too closely related by blood to be allowed to marry).[3]

In 1782 Rev John Watson wrote a two-volume biography of the Warenne earls of Surrey for Sir George Warren, to demonstrate the knight's descent from the Warenne earls. Watson tried to establish the origins of the Warennes, but his family trees are confusing, and his sources are not cited. He claimed that the Warennes were descended from Herfastus through a daughter who married Walter de Saint Martin. This daughter supposedly gave birth to William de Warenne, Earl of Varenne in Normandy, who in turn married a daughter of Rafe de Torta, a Danish nobleman who was protector of Normandy in the time of Duke Richard I. This William de Warenne was, supposedly, the father of William I de Warenne. Although there are no sources mentioned, it seems likely that Rev Watson got his information from the chronicler Robert de Torigny.[4] There was no mention of Rodulf, who is clearly identified in the cartulary of the Holy Trinity of Rouen as being the father of William de Warenne and his older brother: '*filii eorum Rodulfus et Willelmus*'.[5]

It was suggested by Robert de Torigny, in his additions to the *Gesta Normannorum Ducum* of William of Jumièges, that William de Warenne was the brother of another Norman baron, Ralph de Mortemer.[6] However, de Torigny's genealogies are also rather confusing and it seems more likely that the two lords were cousins, as described by Orderic Vitalis, rather than brothers.[7] Both are said to be descended from Hugh, who later joined the church and became bishop of Coutances. William's father, Rodulf de Warenne, has been described as '*filius episcopi*', as was Roger de Mortemer, Ralph's father. It was, apparently, the cartulary of the abbey of the Holy Trinity of the Mount at Rouen which first corrected the misunderstanding that William and Ralph were brothers and that both were the 'sons of Walter de St Martin'.[8] The cartulary of Rouen's Abbey of the Holy Trinity describes Rodulf and Roger as co-heirs, implying they were brothers, in the abbey's purchase of 100 acres of woodland. The relevant charter can be dated to before 1055 as it is witnessed by Mauger, Archbishop of Rouen, who was deposed in that year. Duke William, Rodulf's wife Beatrix and Roger's two sons, William and Hugh, were also witnesses to the charter.[9]

William's father, Rodulf I de Warenne, who survived to a grand old age and died around 1074, is also mentioned in a charter of Robert I, Duke of Normandy, father of William the Conqueror which can be dated to sometime between 1030 and 1035, when Duke Robert left on a pilgrimage to the Holy Land, and confirmed the foundation of the Abbey of St Amand at Rouen.[10] The duke died on his return journey and was succeeded by his son, William. The charter describes the abbey lands: '*Qui locus circa ecclesiam extenditur usque ad vicum per quem ad portam Roddebecce itur et inde usque ad terram Willielmi de Tornebu. Iterum ab ista usque ad terram Radulfi de Warenna inde verro usque ad murum civitatis.*'[11] Briefly, the details of the charter give sufficient information of the landscape to suggest that Rodulf's lands must have been outside Rouen's existing city wall; it describes the land 'as far as the wall of the city that sweeps from there to the land of Ralph de Warenne.' The land was to the east of the city and close to Mount Saint Catherine, where the Abbey of the Holy Trinity stood.

In 1053, the year by which William of Normandy had married Matilda of Flanders, Rodulf, described as '*quidam miles de Warenna, Radulfus nomine*' ('a Warenne knight named Ralph'), gave all his land in Vascœuil, in the Eure *département*, to the Abbey of St Pierre de Préaux. This charter also granted high justice to the duke of Normandy, which suggests that Vascœuil was a part of the ducal demesne, another possible indication of a familial link between Rodulf, and his wife, and the ducal house. Rodulf's wife Beatrix gave her consent to the gift, with Rodulf's brother Godfrey being a witness on the charter.[12]

Sometime between May 1055 and 1059, Beatrix died and Rodulf married his second wife, Emma. Beatrix's last appearance in the charters was in 1055, as witness to the sale of lands to the Abbey of Holy Trinity in Rouen. However, in 1059 Rodulf and new his wife, Emma, sold four churches in the Pays de Caux, to the same abbey. Rodulf and Beatrix had at least three children. The oldest was Rodulf (or Ralph) II de Warenne, who inherited the greater part of the Warenne estates from his father. William de Warenne was the second son of the family. The feodary of Philip II Augustus, King of France, dated between 1210 and 1220 demonstrates that some of the Warenne estates, both in the Pays de Caux and near Rouen, by the dawn of the thirteenth century, formed part of the barony of Esneval. This suggests that Rodulf II had at least one child, and that his lands eventually passed through a daughter, an heiress, who married into the d'Esneval family.

These lands are shown to be in the hands of Robert d'Esneval in return of knights' fees in 1172.[13]

Rodulf I de Warenne also had a daughter, whose name is unknown, though whether her mother was Beatrix or Emma is undetermined as she does not appear as a witness on any charters, unlike her brothers. This daughter was married to Erneis de Coulances and had two sons, Richard and Roger. Richard became lord of Coulances and a benefactor of the Abbey of St Evroul; he had fifteen children by his wife, Adelaisa and died on 15 September 1125. Roger, also named Roger de Guarenna and described by Orderic Vitalis as nephew of William Earl of Surrey, became a monk at St Evroul in 1081, spending forty-six years there.[14]

Another branch of the Warenne family may have descended from Roger, son of Ralph (or Rodulf) de Warethnæ, who held lands near Arques and was himself witness to a charter in favour of the Abbey of St Wandrille sometime before 1045. There is no extant evidence of a familial link, but it is possible, given that Roger and Rodulf were of the same generation, that they were cousins and that Rodulf is likely to be the Rodulf referred to as Rodulf Warethna in an entry in the Holy Trinity cartulary, undated but probably around 1060, in which Hugh de Flamanville sold to the abbey tithe and land in Emanville, Motteville and Flamanville.[15]

William's birth, as you might expect, is shrouded in the fog of time; a younger son of the minor nobility does not tend to get a mention until he does something remarkable or becomes someone notable. He was considered to be still young in the mid-1050s, so may have been born sometime in the late 1020s or early 1030s. By the middle of the 1050s, despite his relative youth, William was considered a capable and experienced enough soldier to be given joint command of a Norman army. His first recorded military action is in the campaign against the king of France, Henry I, who invaded Normandy in 1052. King Henry had been an ally of Duke William, supporting him during his minority; he had aided the young duke against an army of rebel Norman barons, led by William's cousin, Guy of Burgundy, at the Battle of Val-ès-Dunes in 1047. In 1052, however, the French king turned against his former protégé and led an alliance of French barons against him, invading Normandy. While Duke William faced the army of the French king to the west of the river Seine, William de Warenne was among the Norman lords, under the leadership of Count Robert of Eu, who faced a second French army. This force, commanded by King Henry's brother, Odo, had invaded eastern Normandy and began a campaign which was intended to devastate the countryside, looting, destroying crops and damaging property. The two forces came face-to-face at the Battle of Mortemer in 1054. The French army had been scattered to pursue their depredations and proved an easy target for the Norman forces. After several hours of fierce fighting, and heavy French losses, the Normans proved victorious, even taking prisoner Guy, Count of Ponthieu, one of the French commanders.[16] When news of his brother's defeat reached King Henry, he withdrew his remaining forces back into France.

William's own kinsman, Roger, had also fought on the side of the Normans in the battle. He took possession of the castle of Mortemer after the battle and took its name for his own, being known afterwards as Roger (I) de Mortemer. However, in the same year Roger fell foul of Duke William, when he played host for several days to one of the duke's enemies, a Frenchman known as Count Ralph III the Great, before providing the count with an escort back to his own lands. The fact that Count Ralph happened to be the father-in-law of Roger de Mortemer proved an inadequate excuse for Duke William, who exiled Roger from Normandy and confiscated all his possessions. As a consequence, William de Warenne was rewarded for his services against the French, with some of the Mortemer lands, including the castle of Mortemer itself. Years later, Orderic Vitalis would refer to this in the deathbed speech he ascribes to Duke William, by then King William, in 1087. In it, the king recalls giving the castle of Mortemer to William de Warenne, Mortemer's cousin; '*Castrum tanem Mortui Maris, in quo inimicum meum salvavit, illi jure, ut reor, abstuli; sed Guillelmo de Guarenna, consanguineo ejus, tironi legitimo dedi.*'[17] When Duke William eventually forgave Roger de Mortemer and restored him to his estates, William de Warenne was able to hold on to the castles of Mortemer and Bellencombre. Mortemer would later be returned to Roger's son, Ranulph, though still within the Warenne barony. Bellencombre would become the capital of the Warenne estates in Normandy. At about the same time, Warenne received more rewards from the lands of William, count of Arques, confiscated in 1053.[18]

William's father, Rodulf I de Warenne, appears to have survived well beyond the Norman Conquest of England; he is recorded in 1074 as having made a gift of a church and tithe in the Pays de Caux to the Abbey of Holy Trinity in Rouen. The charter is witnessed by Rodulf, his wife and his sons: '*Signum ipsius Rodulfi. Signum Emmæ uxoris ejus. Signum Rodulfi filii eorum. Signum Willelmi fratris ejus*' ('Signed Rodulf our son and William his brother').[19] This is the last mention of Rodulf I and he is likely to have died shortly afterwards.

By this time William I de Warenne was a wealthy lord in his own right, with extensive lands in England and Normandy.

Chapter Two

William de Warenne and the
Norman Conquest

B y the time of the Norman invasion of England, William de Warenne
was a trusted companion to William, Duke of Normandy. After his
involvement in the 1054 Battle of Mortemer and assumption of the
Mortemer lands following Roger de Mortemer's banishment, which included
the castles of Mortemer and Bellencombre, William became a lord in his
own right, independent of the Warenne dominions of his father and, later,
his brother. When the king and Mortemer reconciled shortly afterwards,
Mortemer's lands were restored to him, except Mortemer and Bellencombre,
which remained in William de Warenne's possession; Bellencombre was
about fifteen miles west of Mortemer and became the capital of the Warenne
honour in Normandy. William also held lands at Offranville, just west of
Dieppe and eighteen miles north-west of Bellencombre, and Louvetot; it
is possible the latter, Louvetot, was William's Warenne inheritance as a
younger son, as it is some distance from his other Norman holdings but just
west of the Warenne lands in the Pays de Caux.[1]

Although there seems to have been some confusion as to whether William
was the son of Beatrix, the first wife of Rodulf de Warenne, or Emma, his
second wife, the latter seems highly unlikely. It is known that Beatrix was
still living in 1053, when she witnessed a charter to the Abbey of the Holy
Trinity in Rouen, which would mean that William would not have been
born when the Battle of Mortemer, in which he is said to have taken part,
was fought. Moreover, if he were the son of Emma, he would have been too
young to play a significant role in the campaigns of 1066 and the Norman
Conquest of England, nor would he have been rewarded as substantially
as he was by a grateful William the Conqueror. William de Warenne is
noted in the cartulary of the Abbey of the Holy Trinity, in around 1060,
as having joined his brother in signing a charter and placing it on the altar,
which would suggest he was an adult by then, although it was not unheard
of for children to take part in such events.[2] While William's involvement
in the 1054 Mortemer campaign could be explained away as the faulty

memory of a dying man, seeing as the evidence for this is from William the Conqueror's deathbed speech, William de Warenne's participation in the Norman Conquest is vouched for by the chroniclers William of Poitiers and Orderic Vitalis.[3]

William de Warenne was one of William the Conqueror's most loyal knights, and one of the few men who it is known, beyond doubt, was with the Norman duke at the Battle of Hastings. He was one of the duke's closest friends and supporters from the early 1050s onwards. The duke's confidence in him is demonstrated in the fact he was among the barons consulted during the planning of the invasion of England in 1066:

> Among the laity, the leading barons were Richard, count of Evreux, son of Archbishop Robert; Count Robert, son of William count of Eu; Robert, Count of Mortain, half-brother of Duke William; Raoul de Conches, son of Roger de Tosny, the Normans' standard-bearer; William, son of Osbern, the duke's cousin and grand seneschal; William de Warenne; Hugh d'Ivry, chief cupbearer; Hugh de Grandmesnil; Roger de Mowbray; Roger de Beaumont; Roger de Montgomery; Baldwin and Richard, sons of Gislebert, count of Brionne and several others, proud of their military reputations and enjoying great influence by their merit and the wisdom of their opinions. They would not have yielded neither virtue nor wisdom to the Roman senate and applied themselves equally to the constancy of their work and in triumphing over the enemy by their genius and courage.[4]

William's expedition to England arose from his claim that Edward the Confessor had promised the crown to him during his visit to England in 1051, a visit recorded by the *Anglo-Saxon Chronicle*: 'Then soon came Duke William from beyond the sea with a great retinue of Frenchmen, and the king received him and as many of his companions as it pleased him, and let him go again.'[5] If Edward did offer William the succession in 1051, it would have been to spite his most powerful noble, and father-in-law, Earl Godwin. At that time, his relationship with the Godwin family was at its lowest point and he owed a debt of gratitude to the Normans for sheltering him throughout the 1020s and 1030s, when England was ruled by the Danes. It may also be that Edward was trying to tempt the young duke away from too close an alliance with Flanders, a country that had frequently harboured fugitives from English justice, by dangling the English crown in front of the ambitious duke. Moreover, in 1064, when Harold found himself as a guest at the court of the duke of Normandy, the English earl is said to have sworn on holy relics that he would support Duke William's claim to the English throne when the time came. That Edward changed his mind on his deathbed, and named Harold as his successor in January 1066, may have been forced on the dying king when it became apparent that the English would not be willing to accept the Norman as their king.

Before leaving for England on his expedition of conquest in September 1066, Duke William spent the summer preparing for war. William mounted a propaganda campaign that was intended to rally his vassals to his cause, foment dissension among his enemies and gain him the support of Europe, in general, and the pope, in particular. His military preparations included building ships, gathering men and arms, and organising the administration of his duchy for what could be a prolonged absence. The duke's wife, Matilda of Flanders, supported her husband's proposed invasion of England and promised a great ship for William's personal use; called the Mora, the ship had a mast topped with a cross. The Mora's stern bore the head of a lion, while the figurehead on the prow was a statue of a small boy, whose right hand pointed to England and left hand held a horn to his lips. It also flew the pope's flag as a sign that the expedition had the blessing of God and the papacy. According to Elisabeth Van Houts, the ship's name derives from 'Morini', the name of the ancient people of Flanders and was a reminder of Matilda's origins.[6]

By the end of August 1066 all was ready and Duke William simply needed to wait for a favourable wind that would carry him and his army across the English Channel. In the meantime, King Harold had faced and defeated an army led jointly by Harald Hardrada, King of Norway and Denmark, and his own brother, Tostig, the former earl of Northumberland. Both Harald and Tostig had defeated a combined force of the brothers Edwin and Morcar, the earls of Mercia and Northumberland, respectively, on 20 September, at Fulford Gate, but were defeated and killed in the fighting at the Battle of Stamford Bridge, five days later; both battle sites are on the outskirts of York. News of the Norman landing on the south coast of England, at Pevensey, reached Harold just days after his victory at Stamford Bridge. The English king gathered his household troops and marched south to meet the new threat. According to Orderic Vitalis, Harold spent six days in London on his way south, possibly waiting for his army to assemble from throughout the southern shires.[7]

Duke William would have been waiting on the southern shores around Pevensey and Hastings, anxious for news, not only of Harold's army, but of who his opponents may be. It seems likely that he knew of Harald

Hardrada's expedition, but he would not have yet known of the outcome of the subsequent battles. William of Poitiers related that the duke eventually heard the news from Robert fitz Wimarc, a Norman living in England, who advised Duke William to stay behind his fortifications as Harold was heading south to confront him after having successfully dealt with the forces of Hardrada and Tostig.

Messages were exchanged between the two leaders, setting out their opposing claims to the throne, with William claiming that Edward the Confessor had made him his heir, with oaths sworn and hostages exchanged, and reminding Harold of his own promise to uphold the duke's claim during his stay in Normandy. Harold in turn responded with Edward the Confessor's death-bed nomination of himself as his heir. Each, in turn, offered terms to avoid conflict, with William offering that Harold could retain his earldom of Wessex if he were to accept the duke as king.[8] Harold, rather disingenuously, offered that William could return to Normandy unmolested if he paid compensation for the substantial damage to the area his army had already caused; the Bayeux Tapestry itself shows Norman soldiers setting a house alight, with a woman and child fleeing the flames.

Before his army was fully mustered, Harold marched his troops to meet the Norman threat. According to William of Poitiers, 'the furious king was hastening his march all the more because he had heard that the lands near to the Norman camp were being laid waste.'[9] Although Harold had hoped to take Duke William by surprise, the duke had received news of the arrival of the English king's army and had his men stand ready throughout the night of 13 October, in anticipation of a night time raid that never happened. The next morning, the duke marched to confront Harold, who was drawn up seven miles to the north-west of Hastings at a place that had no obvious name, the *Anglo-Saxon Chronicle* merely states the English were at 'the grey apple tree'.[10] Instead of Harold achieving surprise, the *Chronicle* goes on to say that 'William came upon him [Harold] unexpectedly, before his army was set in order.'[11]

On the morning of 14 October 1066, before the two armies joined battle, William addressed his troops:

> What I have to say to you, ye Normans, the toughest of nations, does not spring from any doubt of your valour or uncertainty of victory, which never by any chance or obstacle escaped your efforts. If, indeed, once only you had failed of conquering, it might be necessary to inflame your courage by exhortation. But how little does the inherent spirit of your race require to be roused![12]

The long harangue, as told by Henry of Huntingdon, has William relating much of the story of Normandy. It closes with:

> Is it not shameful, then, that a people accustomed to be conquered, a people ignorant of the art of war, a people not even in possession of arrows, should make a show of being arrayed in order of battle against you, most valiant? Is it not a shame that this King Harold, perjured as he was in your presence, should dare to show his face to you? It is a wonder to me that you have been allowed to see those who by a horrible crime beheaded your relations and Alfred my kinsman, and that their own accursed heads are still on their shoulders. Raise, then, your standards, my brave men, and set no bounds to your merited rage. Let the lightning of your glory flash, and the thunders of your onset be heard from east to west, and be the avengers of the noble blood which has been spilled.[13]

When battle commenced, the English were arrayed on foot, on the hilltop, Harold taking his place at the centre of the line. The Normans were at the base of the hill, the men formed up in three lines; the first line was made up of archers, the second of men-at-arms, probably carrying swords, and the third of cavalry. The English had no cavalry, they traditionally fought on foot. For several hours, the Normans tried to break through the English lines, the effectiveness of their cavalry neutralised by the fact they were fighting uphill. The turning point came when a rumour ran through the Norman army that William had been killed. The Normans began to flee, the English in pursuit, and the invaders were only steadied by William standing in front of his army, taking off his helmet and showing himself to his men. The Normans then turned themselves about and attacked the English, with renewed vigour. The *Anglo-Saxon Chronicle* tells how the battle ended:

> The English being crowded in a confined position, many of them left their ranks, and few stood by him [Harold] with resolute hearts; nevertheless he made a stout resistance from the third hour of the day until nightfall, and defended himself with such courage and obstinacy, that the enemy almost despaired of taking his life. When, however, numbers had fallen on both sides, he, alas! fell at twilight. There fell, also, his brothers, the earls Gyrth and Leofwine, and almost all the English nobles.[14]

Orderic Vitalis gives us a muster roll of the prominent Normans present for the battle and a wonderful description of Duke William's own part in it:

Among those to be found at the battle are noted Eustace, Count of Boulogne; William, son of Richard, Count of Evreux; Geoffrey, son of Rotrou, Count of Martaigne; William, son of Osbern; Robert Tiron, son of Roger de Beaumont; Haimeric, lord of Troarn; Hugh the Constable; Walter Giffard; Raoul de Tosny; Hugh de Grandmesnil; William de Warenne and several other knights of great military reputation and whose names should be given an honourable place in history, among those of the most famous warriors. Every time, Duke William surpassed them in bravery and prudence; not only did he skillfully direct his army, halting their panicked flight, reviving their courage, sharing their danger, often rallying them to him so that they could push forwards together. During the fighting, three horses fell from under him. Each time he intrepidly dismounted and did not delay in avenging the deaths of his horses. In his anger he battered shields, helmets and breastplates. With his own shield he knocked down the English soldiers....[15]

Following his victory at Hastings, William made his way to London, albeit by a circuitous route and not without opposition, where he was crowned on Christmas Day, 1066. The duke may have wanted to delay the coronation, so that he and Matilda, his wife, could be crowned together, but he was persuaded that his immediate consecration as king would help to subdue the people and establish his authority over the country. William de Warenne was one of the many beneficiaries of the lands and titles handed out to Duke William's loyal Norman supporters in the years immediately after the Conquest. He was rewarded with vast swathes of land throughout the country. Although they were not all acquired in 1066, by the time of the Domesday survey Warenne's lands extended over thirteen counties; stretching from Conisbrough in Yorkshire to Lewes in Sussex with more than half of his property located in Norfolk. Of these, the most important was the majority share of the rape of Lewes, on the south coast, along with manors in Norfolk, Suffolk and Essex. Conisbrough came a little later as did Castle Acre, in Norfolk, which had previously been held by Frederic, the brother of Warenne's wife, Gundrada. His territories were acquired over the course of the reign of William I and elevated him to the highest rank of magnates. By 1086, he was the fourth richest man in the kingdom, after the king; his riches only surpassed by the king's half-brothers and his own kinsman, Roger de Montgomery.[16]

Shortly after the Conquest, William de Warenne was given the rape of Lewes in Sussex, which probably stretched from the River Adur in the west to the River Ouse in the east, and indeed beyond the Ouse to the north. At Lewes, William ordered the construction of a castle on the top of the hill with two mottes, rather than the usual one; St Pancras Priory would be built at the base of the hill. The administration of the area was reorganised before 1073, with William giving seventeen manors to William de Braose, to create a new rape to the west of Lewes and twenty-eight of his manors in the east were added to the count of Mortain's rape of Pevensey. William was compensated for these losses with new lands in East Anglia.[17] William also received the honour of Conisbrough in South Yorkshire, previously owned by the last Anglo-Saxon king, Harold II Godwinson. Conisbrough was an ancient manor; its name probably derived from the term 'king's burgh', it guarded a ford on the River Don. The manor probably passed to William following the 1068 campaigns in northern England, known as the Harrying of the North. Other land handed to William de Warenne, that had previously belonged to King Harold, included Kimbolton and two manors in Lincolnshire.[18] William de Warenne's most important lands, however, were in Norfolk, in eastern England, where he was the largest landowner in the shire. His lands in East Anglia centred on Castle Acre, where William built a stone manor house protected by a bailey, but no motte (the mound of earth on which Norman castles were normally built). The motte at Castle Acre was added later, probably for protection during the civil war between King Stephen and Empress Matilda.[19]

The Norman Conquest of England was not without problems. Duke William was able to return to Normandy for a time in 1067, taking many English nobles with him as hostages and to guard against them inciting unrest in England while he was away. However, he had to return to his new kingdom within months, when Exeter, encouraged by King Harold's mother, Gytha, rose against him. The city submitted after a short siege, but it was not until 1068 that William thought that the country was safe enough for him to bring his wife, Matilda, from Normandy, for her coronation. Matilda was crowned Queen of England in Westminster Abbey, by Archbishop Ealdred of York, on 11 May 1068. The *Anglo-Saxon Chronicle*, as usual, was economical with the details, simply recording; 'And soon after that the Lady Matilda came here to the land, and Archbishop Aldred consecrated her queen in Westminster on Whit Sunday.'[20] The coronation ceremony included a crowning and anointing with holy oil. The wording of the coronation ceremony was changed slightly for Matilda, making queenship more constitutional than customary. The inserted phrases included: '*regalis imperii ... esse participem*' ('the queen shares royal power') and '*laetatur gens*

Anglica domini imperio regenda et reginae virtutis providential gubernanda' ('the English people are blessed to be ruled by the power and virtue of the Queen').[21]

Sometime in the years either side of the Conquest, William de Warenne married Gundrada. Gundrada's parentage has long been a subject of debate among historians. Her story throughout history has been coloured by the belief, now thought to be a mistaken one, that she was the daughter of Queen Matilda. Many historians from the eighteenth to the twentieth centuries accepted this as fact and obviously started their research from this false assumption, without looking deeper into the origins of the story.

For many years Gundrada was believed to be the fifth and youngest daughter of William the Conqueror and his wife, Matilda of Flanders. In 1878 Sir George Duckett wrote an article for the Cumberland and Westmorland Archaeological Society arguing that the foundation charter for Lewes Priory 'expressly states Gundrada to have been the *Queen's Daughter'*, the wording within the charter being; *'pro salute dominæ meæ Matildis Reginæ matrix uxoris mea'*.[22] This statement in the priory's second founding charter, issued in the reign of King William II Rufus, appeared to contradict the claims by Orderic Vitalis, a near contemporary, that *'Guillelmo de Guarenna qui Gundredam sororem Gherbodi conjugem* [William de Warenne's wife Gundrada, sister of Gerbod] *habitat, dedit Surregiam.'*[23] In 1846 Thomas Stapleton wrote a paper for the *Archaeological Journal* proposing that Gundrada was Matilda's daughter from an earlier, undocumented marriage, to Gerbod, advocate of Saint-Bertin, thus explaining her also being a sister to Gerbod, Earl of Chester.[24] In this theory, it was proposed that Gundrada was not a daughter of the king, but his stepdaughter. This notion neatly ties in with Orceric Vitalis identifying Gundrada as 'Sister of Gherbode, a Fleming, to whom King William the First had given the City and Earldom of Chester.'[25] E.A. Freeman, in his six-volume *The History of the Norman Conquest of England,* published between 1867 and 1879 stated, 'For a long while, Gundrada was looked on as a daughter of William himself, but there is no doubt that she and her brother Gerbod were the children of Matilda by her first husband.'[26]

Disputing the suggestion of Matilda's marriage to Gerbod, historian W.H. Blaauw observed that not one of the Norman chroniclers 'dropped the smallest hint of any husband or child, or consequently any such divorce on the part of Matilda previous to her marriage with the King.'[27] Duckett goes on to say that the Norman chroniclers, indeed, said quite the opposite; each of them attesting that Matilda was a young, unmarried girl at the time of her betrothal to William of Normandy. However, Duckett then goes on to conclude that this can only mean that Gundrada was the daughter of both Matilda and William of Normandy, and that Gerbod of Chester was her foster-brother, rather than actual brother.[28] The claim was also made in a charter in which the king gave to the monks of St Pancras the manor of Walton in Norfolk, on the foundation of the priory. In the charter the king distinctly names '*Guilelmi de Warenna, et uxoris suæ Gundredæ filiæ meæ*' ('William de Warenne and his wife Gundrada, my daughter').[29]

St Pancras was founded as a Cluniac monastery by William and Gundrada and it may be that the monks got carried away with the idea of their foundress having royal blood; royal links could prove financially lucrative when a monastery was looking for benefactors, and would help a monastery stand out among the many vying for patronage. However, it may also be that there was a simple error when copying the charter from the original. For whatever reason, the claims by St Pancras Priory at Lewes have caused controversy throughout the ensuing centuries. Other suggestions have included that Gundrada was an adopted daughter, raised alongside William and Matilda's own children who were of a similar age. Alternatively, due to her Flemish origins, it has been argued that the confusion arose as she had joined Matilda's household at an early age; an assertion supported by Matilda's gift to Gundrada of the manor of Carlton in Cambridge – a manor Gundrada later gave to Lewes Priory. In 1888, writing in the *English Historical Review*, E.A. Freeman returned to the subject and used the priory's original charter to conclude that there was no familial relationship between Gundrada and William the Conqueror. In it, while the king and William de Warenne, both, mention Gundrada, neither refer to her as being related to the king or queen. Freeman stated, 'there is nothing to show that Gundrada was the daughter either of King William or of Queen Matilda; there is a great deal to show that she was not.'[30]

It now seems more likely that Gundrada was a Flemish noblewoman, the sister of Gerbod who would be, for a brief time, earl of Chester. Historian Elisabeth van Houts argues that Gundrada was most likely a distant relative of Queen Matilda and the counts of Flanders, as asserted in her epitaph as 'offspring of dukes' and a 'noble shoot'.[31] Indeed, had her father been William the Conqueror, her epitaph would surely have referred to her as the offspring of kings. Even if she had been the daughter of Matilda by an earlier marriage, off-spring of kings would have still been appropriate, given that Queen Matilda was the granddaughter of King Robert II of France. Gundrada's father may also have been called Gerbod, or Gherbode. It is highly likely that this was the same Gerbod who was the hereditary advocate of the monastery of St Bertin; a title which in later generations will pass down through the Warenne family.[32] Another brother, Frederic, had lands in England even before the Conquest, when two people named Frederic and Gundrada are mentioned as holding four manors in Kent and Sussex. It would indeed be a coincidence if there were two other related people, named Frederic and Gundrada, very distinctive foreign names, in England at that time. The brothers, it seems, were deeply involved in the border politics between Flanders and Normandy; indeed, it is thought that Gerbod resigned his responsibilities in Chester in order to return to the Continent to oversee the family's lands and duties there. Frederic, along with the count of Flanders, was a witness to Count Guy of Ponthieu's charter to the Abbey of St Riquier in 1067.[33] The 'dukes' referred to in Gundrada's epitaph, although naturally assumed to be of Normandy, could well refer to a kinship with the house of Luxembourg, to which Queen Matilda's paternal grandmother, Orgive, belonged. Moreover, Frederic was a familial name within the house of Luxembourg. This kinship with Queen Matilda would also explain the queen's gift to Gundrada, of the manor of Carlton, which is usually given as evidence that Gundrada belonged to the queen's household, an association which would be entirely consistent with kinship.[34]

Marriage between William de Warenne and Gundrada was a good match on both sides. Although William was a second son, he had acquired lands and reputation through his military skills. Warenne's lands in Normandy lay close to the border with Flanders, while Gundrada, with her politically astute brothers and links to England even before the Conquest, would have been an attractive proposition as a bride. Both Frederic and Gerbod appear to have joined the Norman expedition to England, with Frederic receiving, as reward, lands in Norfolk, Suffolk and Cambridgeshire, valued at over £100 a year; lands which had previously belonged to a rich Englishman named Toki.[35] Gerbod, in turn, was given the earldom of Chester, which he held until relinquishing it to return to Flanders in 1071.[36]

Chapter Three

William and Gundrada and the Foundation of a Dynasty

Throughout his career, William de Warenne acquired lands in numerous counties, sometimes by nefarious means. By the time of the Domesday Survey, he possessed manors across thirteen counties, including Sussex, Norfolk and Yorkshire. He held four castles: Reigate in Surrey, Conisbrough in Yorkshire, Castle Acre in Norfolk and Lewes in Sussex. The rape of Lewes, in Sussex, was probably William's first acquisition after the Conquest; it may have stretched from the river Adur in the west, as far as the Ouse in the east. The shire was divided into five territories, of which the rape was one; this included the town of Lewes, which was a prosperous port on the tidal estuary and divided between William and the king himself. The first castle erected there, whether by the king or William de Warenne, was probably to the south of the town, where William rebuilt the church of St Pancras and a large mound, which may have been the original motte, can still be seen today. This castle was abandoned in the 1070s, to make room for the new Cluniac priory of St Pancras, built by William and Gundrada. A new castle, still standing today, was built to the north of the town, with two mottes, one at each end of the bailey. With the town, castle and priory, all owned by William de Warenne, Lewes became the capital of the Warenne lands in England.[1] When the rapes were reorganised in or before 1073, in order to assign land to William de Braose, William de Warenne relinquished seventeen manors, receiving lands in East Anglia in compensation.

The last manors given to him were probably those of the great lordship of Conisbrough; this may have been after the suppression of the northern uprising of 1068, called the Harrying of the North. The uprising caused William the Conqueror to establish an increased Norman presence in Yorkshire and thus gain a tighter hold on the land and its people. Conisbrough had formerly belonged to the late king, Harold, and included twenty-eight towns and hamlets within its soke:

the lands which compose the honour of Coningsburgh do not lie contiguously, and a few only are in the vicinity of the castle (the caput baroniæ); most of them are on the south side of the river Don, and Hatfield was mostly reserved in demesne for the pleasures of the chace [sic], though separated from Coningsburgh itself by the lands of Geoffrey Alselin.[2]

The honour of Conisbrough included much of what is now South Yorkshire, including Dinnington and Greaseborough near Rotherham, Hoyland near Barnsley, Warmsworth, Kirk Sandal and Cusworth near Doncaster.[3] Guarding the main road between Doncaster and Sheffield, Conisbrough had command of the fords across the River Don. Fortifications already existed before William took possession of the area, but the new owner probably strengthened these; the construction of the stone keep and curtain wall we see today was started by Hamelin, the fourth earl, in the late twelfth century.

William de Warenne's most important and extensive lands, overshadowing both Lewes and Conisbrough, were in East Anglia, where he was the largest landowner in the shire, holding 139 manors.[4] The majority of his lands were located in the west of the county of Norfolk, complemented by lands in Suffolk and Essex as far as the Thames estuary and reaching into south-east Cambridgeshire. The centre of these Warenne lands was situated at Castle Acre, where William built a large stone manor house and a planned medieval village. The manor house would be fortified around the turn' of the century, and a Cluniac priory would be built at the opposite end of the village by the second earl. These lands were not all acquired at once; some had belonged to King Harold II and may have been awarded to William soon after the Norman Conquest, whereas others had belonged to an English thegn called Toki, which were then given to Frederic, Gundrada de Warenne's brother, after the Conquest. They passed to Gundrada on Frederic's death in 1070, and thus came into William's possession on his wife's death in 1085, though he will have had significant say in their administration before this.[5]

William de Warenne was involved in a number of disputes over his efforts to extend his influence in the regions in which he held lands. In Norfolk, William de Warenne is said to have asserted lordship over freemen who were not necessarily assigned to him. He had disputes with neighbouring landowners in Conisbrough over which properties were sokelands, in other words, which lands belonged to the honour of Conisbrough. In Essex he is said to have stolen lands from the bishop of Durham and the abbot of Ely; and in Sussex from the nuns of Wilton. With many of these disputes, details were recorded in the Domesday Book. Some acquisitions, however, were obtained peacefully, such as the manor of Whitchurch in Shropshire, which was left to him by his kinsman Roger de Montgomery.

William was an energetic and attentive landowner and improved the economy of most of his estates; more than tripling his sheep flock at Castle Acre and doubling the value of his Yorkshire estates in just twenty years (at a time when the county was recovering from the devastation of the Harrying of the North). In Bedfordshire, he won the allegiance of an English thegn named Augi, despite the king assigning him to another Norman lord; when Augi then died, William de Warenne claimed the land, rather than it passing to the successor to Augi's assigned lord. William did, however, share lands among some fifty of his supporters, many of whom had come over from Normandy with him. Although it appears he kept the largest four manors in Sussex for himself, he was not so choosy elsewhere, dividing much of his land in Norfolk among his supporters; he retained direct control over one manor in both Buckinghamshire and Oxfordshire, in addition to the core of Kimbolton and the entire honour of Conisbrough.[6]

By 1086 and the time of the Domesday Survey, the eastern shires accounted for half the value of the entire Warenne estates in England – more than half of that being in Norfolk itself. Sussex accounted for two-fifths of Warenne revenue, with Conisbrough, and various other estates scattered around the country, accounting for the final tenth. These scattered estates included single manors in Hampshire, Buckinghamshire, Huntingdonshire and Bedfordshire. Kimbolton, a couple of estates near Wallingford, two manors in south Lincolnshire and some fishermen in Wisbech completed the Warenne holdings.[7]

William de Warenne's brothers-in-law had also joined the expedition to conquer England. As a consequence, Frederic was rewarded with those lands previously belonging to a man named Toki, situated in Norfolk, Suffolk and Cambridgeshire and worth in excess of £100. However, Frederic was unable to enjoy his good fortune for long, as he was killed in the rebellion of Hereward the Wake in 1070. His lands, still known as 'Frederic's Fief' in 1086, were inherited by his sister, who retained control of them throughout her lifetime. One manor was given to the Abbey of St Riquier, possibly by Gundrada in memory of her brother. Gundrada's other brother Gerbod, known as Gerbod the Fleming, was given command of Chester and possibly made its earl but resigned his position in 1070 and returned to Flanders, which was in the midst of civil war after the death of Count Baldwin VI.

Gerbod's return home was essential to guarantee the safety of the family's lands and interests. The former earl of Chester's fate is uncertain, however; one report has him killed while another sees him imprisoned. His most likely fate comes from a third account, which claims that Gerbod accidentally killed his lord, Count Arnulf III, the nephew of Queen Matilda, at the Battle of Cassel in 1071. According to this last account, Gerbod travelled to Rome to perform penance for killing his young lord, but was prevented from his self-imposed mutilation by Pope Gregory VII. Instead, the pope sent him to Abbot Hugh at Cluny, who gave Gerbod absolution and admitted him to the order as a monk.[8] This would explain the Warenne attraction to the Cluniac order which led to the foundation of the Cluniac priory of St Pancras at Lewes. Although it is possible that Gerbod left two sons, Gundrada still inherited some of her brother's lands in Flanders, including the family interest in the Abbey of St Bertin, where they were hereditary advocates; this advocacy would eventually be passed on to Gundrada and William's second son, Rainald.

It seems likely that Gundrada, Frederic and Gerbod had an older brother, Arnulf II of Oosterzele-Scheldewindeke, who remained in Flanders when his siblings sought their fortunes in England. Arnulf inherited their father's extensive estates in northern Flanders but died childless in 1067. His lands eventually passed to two brothers, Arnulf III and Gerbod III, who, it appears, were the sons of Gerbod, former earl of Chester and then a monk at Cluny. The death of his brother, Arnulf II, may well have been Gerbod's reason for surrendering his earldom of Chester and returning to Flanders.[9]

In 1067 William de Warenne was one of four prominent Normans appointed to govern England during William the Conqueror's absence in Normandy. In the years following the Conquest, William continued to support the king and – subsequently – his son, William II Rufus, as a military commander for over twenty years. He features in the *Gesta Herewardi* as a villain, pursuing a personal feud against the English folk hero of the post-Conquest years, Hereward the Wake. William's hostility towards Hereward is understandable, given that the *Warenne Chronicle* states that Hereward; 'Among his other crimes, by trickery he killed Frederick, brother of Earl William of Warenne, a man distinguished by lineage and possessions, who one night was surrounded in his own house.'[10] Following Frederic's murder, according to the Chronicle, 'such discord arose between Hereward and William that it could not be settled by any reparation nor in any court.'[11] According to the *Gesta Herewardi*, Frederic was planning to capture or kill Hereward, who struck first by killing Frederic. Hereward had been an outlaw even before the Norman Conquest, when he was exiled for disobedience to his father. He returned from Flanders in 1067, after learning that his family lands had been taken over by Normans and his brother killed. After exacting revenge for his brother's death, by killing fifteen of the Normans believed to be responsible, Hereward briefly returned to Flanders, to allow things to cool down.

By 1070, he was back in England and killing Frederic. He joined the camp of rebels on the Isle of Ely, who were, on the whole, protected from attack by the marsh that surrounded them. Once Hereward was back in England, William de Warenne prepared to get his revenge; he attempted to ambush Hereward at a place called Earith. One of William's men tried unsuccessfully to bribe Hereward's men to betray him. William was unhorsed when Hereward fired an arrow at him; it rebounded from William's mail-coat, but the force of the shot saw William fall from his horse and rendered unconscious as he hit the ground.[12] The ambush having failed, William de Warenne then appears in the *Gesta Herewardi* with an angry outburst against the Norman knight Deda, who had given a eulogistic account of the rebels on the Isle of Ely. According to the *Liber Eliensis*, William 'flared up with weighty indignation, and alleged that he [Deda] had been inveigled by a bribe and was lying.'[13]

Although the *Gesta Herewardi* and *Liber Eliensis* may have exaggerated events a little to emphasise William de Warenne's actions as being dishonourable, by using ambushes and bribery to capture Hereward, the *Warenne Chronicle* corroborates the growing feud between them. The *Liber Eliensis*, the chronicle of the Abbey of Ely, had its own feud with William de Warenne, and so was not disposed to be kind to the Norman lord. The *Warenne Chronicle*, on the other hand, is less complimentary of Hereward, describing how when he could not take a castle by force he had 'pretended that he was dead,' and had ordered that he be 'carried in false mourning to the castle's church for burial by the unwary inhabitants. As soon as he could tell that he had been brought in by the men, fully armed he jumped from the bier and deceitfully subjugated the castle with its inhabitants.'[14] This story is not repeated elsewhere in the other chronicles which reference Hereward's story, and so may well be false or misrepresented, though it certainly serves to tell the reader exactly what the chronicle thought of Hereward the Wake.

When the Normans eventually managed to storm the rebel stronghold on the Isle of Ely, many rebels were killed and others, including Morcar, the former earl of Northumberland, were captured. Hereward, it seems, managed to escape capture and disappeared in the surrounding fenland with a small band of supporters. His eventual fate is open to conjecture, with stories having Hereward escaping to Scotland, pardoned by King William or killed by Norman knights whilst on the verge of making peace. The *Warenne Chronicle* claims that 'after many killings and insurrections, after many treaties made with the king and then violated rashly, one day he died wretchedly with all his allies, surrounded by enemies.'[15] Whatever his fate, Hereward the Wake disappears from the story around 1072. William de Warenne, on the other hand, continued to feature heavily in William the Conqueror's government of England.

When the king left England for Normandy again, in 1073, William de Warenne was named alongside Richard fitz Gilbert as chief justiciar of the kingdom. The two justiciars soon faced challenging times when not one, but two earls rose in revolt: the earls of Hereford and East Anglia rebelled, with the half-hearted assistance of the earl of Northumberland. The Revolt of the Earls arose out of the refusal of King William to sanction the marriage of Ralph de Gael, Earl of East Anglia, to Emma, sister of Roger de Breteuil, Earl of Hereford. The couple still married, without the king's permission. Ralph de Gael was summoned to answer for this act of defiance. In the meantime, the king had fallen seriously ill in Normandy and Earl Ralph seized the opportunity.[16] He and Breteuil, along with Waltheof, Earl of Northumberland, rose in revolt. Waltheof soon lost heart and confessed the conspiracy to Lanfranc, Archbishop of Canterbury. Lanfranc urged Breteuil to return to the king's peace and when he refused, Breteuil and his supporters were excommunicated. William de Warenne and the bishops of Bayeux and Coutances, Odo and Geoffrey, led a combined army that defeated the rebels at Fawdon in Cambridgeshire, 'but followed up their victory with unwarrantable cruelties', mutilating their prisoners afterwards.[17] Orderic Vitalis relates events:

A little time after, a sudden revolt erupted throughout England, the fruit of the conspiracy and opposition to the king's representatives spread far and wide. As a result, William de Warenne and Richard the Blessed, son of Count Gilbert, who the king had appointed principal justiciars to oversee affairs in England, summoned the rebels to them. They refused to obey the summons they received and striving to follow the course of their insolence, preferred to fight the king's men. William and Richard assembled the English army and brought the rebels to bloody battle in the camp called Fawdon. By God's grace they triumphed over the insurgents and, having captured all, whatever their condition, they cut off the right foot of each, so they were recognisable.[18]

Another army in Herefordshire was outmanoeuvred by Walter de Lacy, who came upon the insurgents as they attempted to cross the River Severn, neutralising the armed force without a battle being fought.[19] Ralph de Gael withdrew to Norwich Castle; he was besieged for three months before he managed to escape his attackers by boat, while the castle surrendered and was occupied by William de Warenne. Earl Ralph's lands passed to Alan Rufus (Alan the Red), the son of the count of Brittany who lived with, or married, Gunhild, the daughter of King Harold II and Edith Swanneck; Edith Swanneck's lands had made up the vast majority of Earl Ralph's barony in East Anglia and it is believed that Alan Rufus married Gunhild to strengthen his claim to her mother's lands.[20] The revolt of the Earls was the second conspiracy in which Earl Waltheof had had a hand. He had been forgiven for the first, but was not so lucky with this second one, despite his kinship with King William; Waltheof was married to Judith of Lens, the king's niece. Waltheof was 'condemned at London according to the laws of the English and the Danes.'[21] According to the *Warenne Chronicle*, Waltheof asked to be allowed to become a monk, but was refused by the king and when 'he had been beheaded, his body was carried to a certain church, which he had built in regions near the sea, and numerous miracles occur at his tomb up to the present day, so they say.'[22] After Waltheof's execution, his wife, Judith, had the body taken to his own foundation of Crowland Abbey, Lincolnshire, for burial.

As with so many nobles of the eleventh century, Gundrada and William were known for their piety. Either in 1077 or 1081–83 (the dates vary according to the sources) the couple set off on a pilgrimage to Rome. Unfortunately, they never actually made it as far as Italy, due to the outbreak of war between the pope, Hildebrand, and the Holy Roman Emperor. They did, however, reach the magnificent Abbey of St Peter and St Paul at Cluny in Burgundy, where Gundrada's brother was now a monk and they themselves were received into the fellowship of the monks. Although Abbot Hugh was absent at the time of their visit, the abbey at Cluny inspired the couple, they 'were so struck with the high standard of religious life maintained there that they determined to put their proposed foundation under Cluny, and accordingly desired the abbot to send three or four of his monks to begin the monastery. He, however, would not at first consent – fearing that at so great a distance from their mother-house they would become undisciplined.'[23]

It was only after William and Gundrada managed to gain the backing of the king that the abbot gave his consent and eventually sent a monk named Lanzo, to act as prior, with three other monks to found the community. William gave them the church of St Pancras at Lewes, which had recently been rebuilt in stone, and the land surrounding it. Their territory was extended by William de Warenne acquiring 'all the land and the island near

Lewes which is called Southye' for his monks, in return for, every Nativity of St John the Baptist, the delivery of 'ten arrows, barbed, shafted, and feathered'.[24] William and Gundrada were expecting to build a community to house twelve monks. All the churches on the vast Warenne estates were given to the priory, including endowments from the lands of Gundrada's brother Frederic in Norfolk. The priory was to pay a fixed sum of 50s a year to the abbey at Cluny, but the independence of the Lewes monks was severely restricted, with the right of appointing its prior and admitting new monks being solely the reserve of the abbot of Cluny.[25] A second priory, started by William but finished by his son, also William, was built on their lands at Castle Acre in Norfolk.

The Priory of St Pancras at Lewes was the first Cluniac house in England. The Cluniac order were unique in the church in that they had been granted exemption from excommunication by Pope Alexander II in 1061, declaring that anyone attempting to excommunicate the monks of Cluny would be 'accursed by our Lord and St Peter, and fit to be burnt in eternal fire with the devil and the traitor Judas, and to be cast down with the impious into the abyss and Tartarean chaos.'[26] The order had been founded in the year 910 by monks seeking to pursue a more austere lifestyle and a stricter interpretation of the Rule of St Benedict, laid down in the sixth century and the basis for medieval monastic life. Cluniac monks were renowned for the length and rigour of their church worship, the strict rules that governed them and their freedom from lay control and episcopal control, save for the pope. Their stringent rule contrasted with the order's love of art and decoration, as demonstrated in the magnificent façade of the Cluniac priory of Castle Acre in Norfolk.[27] Lanfranc, Archbishop of Canterbury, laid down eight general rules for the monastic communities in England to follow, including the Priory of St Pancras at Lewes. These were: that monks were to hold no property of their own; no monks were to leave the cloister without permission, and even then, only with good cause; silence was to be kept and the monks were to obey their prelates; they were never to murmur or blame, for any reason, even if their cause was just; they were to love one another, to make confession of all their sins and not to neglect the services of their church.[28]

As the first Cluniac priory in England, St Pancras was also the acknowledged chief among Cluny's establishments in the country, all of which were founded within 150 years of the Norman Conquest; it became one of the wealthiest monasteries in England. Although the *Warenne Chronicle* is also called the *Hyde Chronicle*, it is so called because it was discovered at Hyde Abbey in Winchester. Its origin before that is unknown, but it is entirely possible that the chronicle originated at St Pancras Priory in Lewes, which would explain the chronicler's extensive knowledge of the Warenne family. Not only did the priory receive gifts and grants from each successive earl of Warenne, but also from other quarters, including those who wished to be buried there and those wanting to become monks. Among the grants issued to the priory over the years were allowances of venison for sick monks, fishing rights, the monopoly of eels from the Warenne's Yorkshire properties and the right of taking wood three days a week from Pentecost (fifty days after Easter Sunday) to St Peter's day (29 June).[29] Of the Warenne earls of Surrey, all were buried at the priory at Lewes, except the third earl, who died on crusade in the Holy Land, and William of Blois, the first husband of Isabel de Warenne, the fourth countess, who was buried in France. In addition to the family members, Lewes Priory was the chosen final resting place for the rich and noble, including earls and countesses of Arundel, and members of the prominent Nevill, Maltravers and Bohun families.

Gundrada and William had three children together: William, Rainald and Edith. Their eldest son, William, would succeed his father as earl of Warenne and Surrey. He married Isabel de Vermandois as her second husband. Isabel had the blood of kings flowing through her veins; her father was Hugh Capet, younger son of King Henry I of France, and her mother was Adelaide de Vermandois, a descendant of the ancient Carolingian dynasty. Gundrada and William de Warenne had a second son, Rainald (or Reginald) de Warenne. While his brother William inherited the Warenne lands of England and Normandy, Rainald succeeded to the family's lands in Flanders, which had probably come into the Warenne holdings through his mother, Gundrada. Both William and Rainald retained the advocacy of Saint-Bertin, a hereditary post within their mother's family, until the late 1090s, as demonstrated by charter evidence.[30]

Rainald led the assault on Rouen in 1090, for William II Rufus, in the conflict between the king of England and his older brother, Robert, Duke of Normandy. Rouen had become a hotbed of insurgency, with rival factions vying for control of the city for either Duke Robert on one side and King William II on the other. Henry, supporting his oldest brother, Duke Robert, was already in Rouen, holding the castle for Normandy, as reinforcements arrived from Duke Robert, under the command of Gilbert de l'Aigle, crossing the Seine from the south on 3 November 1090. Rainald de Warenne, acting for King William arrived in the city at about the same time, coming from the castle at Gournay, to the north. He led 300 men-at-arms and entered the city by the west gate, without meeting resistance, the gate having been left open by Conan Pilatus, a rich Rouen citizen who was leading the king's faction within the city. The fighting seems to have mainly been in the streets of the city, among its own citizens, with rival factions taking advantage of the situation to gain revenge for real and perceived slights.

Few of Rainald de Warenne's men were killed and the Anglo-Norman troops fled the city in the early part of the fighting, hiding in the woods outside Rouen until nightfall, when they managed to effect their escape. The rival factions within Rouen accounted for most of the disorder and deaths. The leader of William II's supporters in the city, Conan, was captured and fell into Henry's custody. The story goes that Conan was hogtied, taken to the highest tour of Rouen's castle, and thrown from the battlements; the tower was henceforth known as Conan's Leap.[31] By 1105, Rainald de Warenne was fighting for Duke Robert against Henry, the youngest of the Conqueror's sons and now King Henry I of England, defending the castle of Saint-Pierre-sur-Dives for the duke. Rainald was captured by Henry the following year but had been freed by September 1106. There is no mention of Rainald ever having married, nor any children attributed to him. It is possible he died shortly after his release in 1106, but he was certainly dead by 1118, when his brother issued a charter in which he gave six churches to Lewes Priory for the repose of the souls of deceased family members, including Rainald.[32]

A third child was a daughter, Edith, who married Gerard de Gournay, son of the lord of Gournay-en-Bray. Edith's marriage portion was a manor in Mapledurham, Oxfordshire, where her father held seven hides at the time of Domesday, and which then passed down through the Gournay family. Gerard also supported William II Rufus against Duke Robert and took part in the Crusade of 1096. Edith later accompanied him on pilgrimage back to Jerusalem, sometime after 1104, where he died. Gerard was succeeded by their son, Hugh de Gournay. Edith and Gerard also had a daughter Gundreda, named after her grandmother, who would marry Nigel d'Aubigny and be the mother of Roger de Mowbray, a Norman magnate who fought with King Stephen and was captured at the Battle of Lincoln in 1141. It was due to his mother Gundreda that in 1142–43 Roger de Mowbray donated to the monks at Hood, the village of Old Byland, in Ryedale, Yorkshire, to which they then moved. Byland Abbey later becoming one of the three great abbeys of the north, alongside Fountains and Rievaulx. Although it is not certain, it is possible that Roger de Mowbray was buried there after his death in 1188. Edith later married Drew de Monchy as her second husband, with whom she had a son, Drew the Younger.[33]

An experienced military commander, William de Warenne fought almost to his last breath. In 1083–85 William fought with the king on campaign in Maine, France, where he was wounded at the siege of the castle of Sainte-Suzanne.[34] Following William the Conqueror's death in 1087, William de Warenne continued in service to the king's successor in England, his second son, William II Rufus. The Conqueror's eldest son had inherited the duchy of Normandy, whilst his youngest son, Henry, was given a large sum of money and lands in Buckinghamshire and Gloucestershire. According to Orderic Vitalis, William de Warenne was created earl of Surrey shortly before William the Conqueror's death. However, studies suggest the creation was made by William II Rufus shortly before Warenne's own death in 1088, after suffering a fatal wound at the siege of Pevensey. Unrest had followed William the Conqueror's death in 1087, with the late king's oldest sons, Robert and William, vying for supremacy. The barons chose their sides. William de Warenne declared for William II but his neighbour at Pevensey, the Conqueror's half-brother, Robert of Mortain, declared for Robert, now duke of Normandy. By 1088, the great revolt in favour of Robert led by his uncles Bishop Odo of Bayeux and Robert, Count of Mortain, had stalled, with only Pevensey holding out, hoping for relief from Duke Robert in Normandy. According to the *Warenne Chronicle* the shock of the rebellion prompted William II's actions:

> All of England was shaken by this news and King William was distressed by great worries. Seeing, therefore, that the magnates of his kingdom were wavering and that his army was melting away from him, making use of wise counsel, in friendship he raised William of Warenne, a warlike man, fierce in spirit, strong in body, and distinguished in reputation, to the honour of the earldom of Surrey, and he spent much and promised much.[35]

Unfortunately, William de Warenne, 1st Earl Warenne, was not to enjoy his new status for very long. Now possibly in his sixties, Warenne was actively involved in the siege at Pevensey. The castle withstood six weeks of attacks by both land and sea, although it never faced a direct assault, before the half-starved garrison was finally forced to surrender. William de Warenne was an early casualty in the skirmishes. He was wounded by an arrow from a crossbow bolt, shot from the castle walls, and died a short time later.[36] The date of his death is given as 24 June 1088 by the Lewes Cartulary; the cartulary of Lewes Priory, which recorded all the grants received by the priory, is the main documentary source for the history of the Warenne holdings in the eleventh and twelfth centuries.[37] The *Warenne Chronicle* relates his last days:

> At the siege of Pevensey William of Warenne was badly wounded in the leg by an arrow, and was carried to Lewes to the grief of everyone. When he realised that his death was imminent, he made his two sons his heirs according to the king's decree, namely William in England and Reginald [Rainald] in Flanders, and thus in peace he rested in the Lord. His body was received by the blessed father Lanzo and the whole congregation of St Pancras with due honour, and was buried inside the cloisters of the monastery next to his wife who had died a few years previously.[38]

Gundrada had died in childbirth at Castle Acre in Norfolk on 27 May 1085. The child probably perished with its mother, as Gundrada's three surviving children were approaching adulthood at the time of their mother's death. Gundrada died before her husband received his earldom, and so never bore the title of countess. She was buried in the chapter house of St Pancras Priory at Lewes, where her husband would be buried beside her three years later. Around 1145, when new monastic buildings were consecrated at St Pancras, Gundrada's bones were placed in a leaden chest and interred under a tombstone of black Tournai marble, 'richly carved in the Romanesque style, with foliage and lions' heads.'[39] The sculptor was trained at Cluny and would later work for Henry I's nephew, Henry of Blois, Bishop of Winchester and brother of King Stephen. The inscription on the tombstone, which runs along all four sides and down the middle, reads:

> Gundrada, offspring of dukes, glory of the age, noble shoot,
> brought to the churches of the English the balm of her character.
> As a Martha ...
> she was to the wretched; a Mary she was in her piety.
> That part of Martha [in her] died; the greater part of Mary survives.
> O, pious Pancras, witness of truth and justice,
> she makes you her heir; may you in your clemency accept the mother.
> The sixth day of the kalends of June, showing itself,
> broke the alabaster containing her flesh ...[40]

Following the dissolution of St Pancras Priory at Lewes in the sixteenth century, the tombstone was first moved to Isfield Church, to the north-east of Lewes and moved again in 1775 to the parish church of St John the Baptist at Southover in Lewes. The church is situated close to the grounds of the ruined priory and may once have been within the priory's precincts. The remains of Gundrada and William were discovered in two leaden chests in 1845 and finally laid to rest in the Gundrada chapel at the Southover church in 1847.[41]

William had married again after Gundrada's death. His second wife was a sister of Richard Guet; Guet was described as '*frater comitissae Warennae*' ('brother of Countess Warenne') when he gave the manor of Cowyck to Bermondsey Abbey in 1098.[42] Guet was a landowner in Perche, Normandy, but his sister's name has not survived the passage of time. All we know of her is that, a few days after her husband's death, she attempted to gift 100 shillings to Ely Abbey, who had been punished by William for their support of Hereward the Wake's rebels, and from whom he is said to have stolen land.[43] The monks refused the donation, apparently hoping that Warenne's departing soul had been claimed by demons.[44] It is conceivable that William's epitaph was written by Orderic Vitalis himself, who recreates it in volume iv of his *Ecclesiastical History*.[45] It reads:

Earl William, in this place your fame is kindled.
You built this house and were its generous friend:
This (place) honours your body, because pleasing was the gift
you gave so willingly to the poor of Christ.
The saint himself, Pancras, your heir, who guards your ashes,
Will raise you to the mansions of the blessed in the stars.
Saint Pancras give, we pray, a seat in heaven
To him who for your glory gave this house.[46]

The dynasty founded by William and Gundrada would continue to serve the Crown loyally – on the whole – until the death of John, the seventh and final Warenne Earl of Surrey, in 1347.

Chapter Four

The Second Earl and the Norman Kings

William de Warenne did not live long enough to enjoy his new earldom, dying within months, or possibly weeks, of attaining the honour, in June 1088. His wife, Gundrada, often referred to as Countess Gundrada, had died in childbirth three years before, and so was never, in fact, a countess. The first Warenne to properly make use of the dignity and earldom of Surrey, therefore, was their eldest son, also named William. William (II) de Warenne, 2nd Earl of Warenne and Surrey, would work to maintain the prestige of the family name and take it to even greater heights, holding the earldom for fifty years, until his death in 1138. As the great-great-nephew of Duchess Gunnor of Normandy, William was a distant kinsman of the Norman kings; he would serve both William II Rufus and Henry I, the sons of William the Conqueror, and be active during the early years of the Anarchy, supporting King Stephen against the rival claims of Empress Matilda, daughter and heir of King Henry I. William's ambitions saw him seek the hand in marriage of a Scottish princess, before his actual marriage to the granddaughter of a king of France. He would see his daughter marry a Scottish prince and two of his grandsons would sit on the throne of Scotland, though he did not live to see it.

It is believed that William de Warenne, the first earl, married Gundrada sometime around the Norman Conquest of 1066. This would make it plausible that William, the second earl, was born in the late 1060s or early 1070s, at the latest. It seems likely, therefore, that young William was in his late teens or early twenties at the time of his father's death in 1088. This theory is borne out by the fact that the second earl was among those barons fighting in Normandy in 1090, suggesting he was no minor and old enough to claim the rights and responsibilities of the earldom on his father's death. Of William's childhood, we know nothing. He was the son and heir of one of the richest nobles in England and Normandy, and one of the most experienced military leaders of the era. His father had fought in the pre-Conquest battles in Normandy, was known to have fought at Hastings, battled Hereward the Wake in England, thwarted a rebellion in the Midlands in 1074 and was appointed as justiciar of England when the

Conqueror was absent in Normandy. The second earl had a pretty impressive legacy to live up to.

As earl, William II de Warenne habitually used the style 'Willelmus comes [earl] de Warenna' on charters, the alternate 'Willelmus de Warenna comes de Sudreie' (or 'Surregie', 'Suthreie' or 'Sudreie'), as recognition of his Surrey earldom, appearing less often.[1] William and his brother, Rainald, are mentioned in a charter of their father of 1080, in which they are named as 'Willelmo et Reynaldo filiis et heredibus meis' ('William and Rainald, my sons and heirs').[2] According to both Orderic Vitalis and the Warenne (Hyde) Chronicle the first William de Warenne divided his lands between his two sons, William and Rainald, he 'made his two sons his heirs according to the king's decree, namely William in England and Rainald in Flanders.'[3] Although no mention is made of Normandy, it appears that the Warenne lands were split so that William inherited the patrimony – the lands of their father in England and Normandy – while Rainald inherited the lands in Flanders, the lands that had come to William de Warenne through his wife Gundrada. The fact the Regesta Regum Anglo-Nomannorum stipulates the Warenne's Norman holdings of Mortemer and Bellencombre passed to the second earl's son, William, the third Earl Warenne, supports this theory.[4]

From his father, the second earl inherited one of the largest estates in England at the time, with lands valued at about £1,165 a year and spread across thirteen counties, including vast estates in Sussex, Norfolk and Yorkshire.[5] As his parents before him, William continued to be a major benefactor to the priory of St Pancras at Lewes and also patronised the abbeys of St Evroult and St Amand, and the priories of Castle Acre, Wymondham, Pontefract and Bellencombre. Castle Acre Priory, built at the west end of the village of the same name, and close to the Warenne manor house, was founded in the 1080s by the first earl, but it is the second earl who gave the monks the land on which the priory now stands: 'two orchards up to my castle in which ... they have founded their church, because that same place in which they now live is too confined and highly unstable for the dwelling of monks.'[6] Building began in about 1090, the grant from the earl actually including 'Ulmar the mason of Acre' to work on building the new priory. The west front, which is still impressive to this day, has been described as 'one of the jewels of English Romanesque architecture and decoration.'[7] The town of Castle Acre itself is enclosed in a medieval precinct wall; the priory sits just outside the town wall. The planned medieval town stretches from the priory in the west to the castle in the east, access into the town from the north is through the twelfth-century Bailey Gate, while access from the south was through another gate, now lost.

The castle at Castle Acre was originally built as a manor house by the first earl and it was here that Gundrada died in childbirth in 1085. The manor house's conversion into a castle, according to archaeological examination, was already under construction at the time of Gundrada's death.[8] Unlike Conisbrough Castle, which still has its impressive cylindrical keep, Castle Acre has been robbed of its stone over the centuries and little more than the earthworks now remain. However, those earth works are still impressive and give the visitor a good impression of the size and extent of the castle in its heyday, with an inner bailey enclosing what would have been the square keep. This was then surrounded by a ditch with a bridge leading into the large outer bailey, surrounded by high earthen defences which were topped with stone walls and in turn surrounded by a moat or ditch. The second earl started the rebuilding project at the end of the eleventh century, but it seems likely that the castle was not completed until the 1160s, in the time of Isabel de Warenne, the fourth Countess Warenne.[9] Built as much to impress as it was a defensive structure, Castle Acre was the centre of the Warenne holdings in East Anglia and, indeed, England, being accessible to both their lands in the south and in the north.

William de Warenne, 2nd Earl Warenne, had a somewhat chequered career and was drawn into the power struggles of the three surviving sons of William the Conqueror; William Rufus, Robert Curthose and Henry. The second earl was not at court as frequently as his father had been, and only attested one or two royal charters during the reign of William II Rufus.[10] As King William's eldest son, Robert had been created Duke of Normandy on his father's death, while the English crown had gone to the Conqueror's second son, William II Rufus; the youngest brother, Henry, had been given estates and money, but no lands to govern. In 1090, William de Warenne could be found in Normandy fighting against the recalcitrant Robert de Bellême, in the sporadic warfare that marred the duchy in the early years of Duke Robert's rule. Orderic Vitalis talks of William and his brother, as well as Gundrada, though he appears to be unaware that their mother was deceased by this point (it may be that he had her confused with the first earl's second wife, who survived him): 'This count had as successors his sons William and Rainald with their mother Gundrada; these men stood out for a long time by their prowess and their power under the kings of England, William and Henry.'[11]

In 1088, Robert de Bellême, occasionally known as Robert de Talvas and later earl of Shrewsbury and count of Ponthieu, had launched a rebellion in England, in favour of Duke Robert's claim to the throne. The insurrection failed, with Bellême finding himself and his fellow conspirators besieged in Rochester Castle. William II Rufus negotiated a peaceful surrender and allowed Bellême to sail away to Normandy in the company of Henry, William the Conqueror's youngest son. On arriving in the duchy, Bellême was arrested and imprisoned at Neuilly l'Évêque, on the orders of Duke Robert. The duke had been persuaded by Bishop Odo of Bayeux that Bellême had changed sides and was now conspiring with King William. Bellême's father, Roger de Montgomery, Earl of Shrewsbury, then proceeded to Normandy and prepared his castles to oppose the duke. On Montgomery's orders, one of Bellême's castles, Saint-Céneri, held out until all their supplies ran out; once in possession of the castle a furious Duke Robert had Saint-Céneri's castellan blinded and its defenders mutilated. Montgomery then sued for peace with Duke Robert, the price of Bellême's freedom being the forfeiture of his castle of Saint-Céneri, already in the duke's hands.[12]

By 1090 Bellême was back in the duke's good graces and stirring up discontent against William II Rufus. In the same year, William de Warenne, the second Earl Warenne, could be found in Normandy, fighting against Bellême. As we have seen, the earl's brother, Rainald, was also caught up in the fighting, particularly at the flashpoint that was Rouen, the capital of the duchy. The whole duchy was suffering from the unrest engendered by Duke Robert's rule and King William took advantage of this, sending his agents into Rouen to stir up the populace. When a wealthy burgher named Conan took the lead in the support for King William, he agreed with the king to arrange the handover of the city in return for money and promises. In October 1090, messages were sent to the king's supporters in nearby castles, giving the day and time that the city's gates would be opened to them. Duke Robert received intelligence of the plot and called his supporters to defend the city. Henry, brother of both king and duke, heeded his oldest brother's call; his speedy response saw him joining his brother in the castle at Rouen days before the planned insurrection. The once-rebellious Robert de Bellême also marched to Duke Robert's aid.

On the appointed day, 3 November 1090, the king's force of 300 knights, led by Earl Warenne's brother, Rainald, gained access to the city through the west gate, opened by those within the city who were loyal to the king. Almost simultaneously, Gilbert de l'Aigle and a troop of horsemen in the service of Duke Robert, arrived at the south gate of Rouen. The citizens of the town chose their loyalties, with Conan's supporters eager to open the gates to Rainald's forces and to prevent Gilbert de l'Aigle's ducal forces from gaining access to the city, while a rival faction sought to support the duke, attacking their fellow citizens at the two gates. In the midst of the fighting, Duke Robert and Henry, together with their retinues, forced their way out of the castle. Henry joined in the fighting, while Duke Robert carried on riding, charging through the east gate and into the Normandy countryside. The duke took a boat across the river Seine before seeking refuge in the church of Notre Dame du Pré.

Back in Rouen, the duke's forces gained the upper hand, with Gilbert de l'Aigle's men forcing their way into the city to join forces with Henry's men. Battle raged through the streets, with the citizens taking the opportunity to settle old scores. According to Orderic Vitalis, 'the city resounded with cries of grief and terror ... The innocent and guilty alike were everywhere butchered, or captured or driven to flight.'[13] The tide turned in favour of the duke's forces, with William's men finding much greater resistance than expected, with a number of them being captured or killed. The survivors of Rainald de Warenne's force fled the city, concealing themselves in nearby woods until nightfall, when they could make their way back to their castles under cover of darkness. With the fighting in the city over, Robert returned victorious, though his flight had bruised his prestige; the duke claimed his advisors had insisted he leave the city, lest he be killed in the confusion of the mêlée that had raged through the streets.[14]

Henry, on the other hand, was the hero of the hour and as a reward, claimed the right to deal with the leading insurgent, Conan. The unfortunate burgher had been captured alive and, though he offered all his wealth as a ransom, Henry had other ideas. Conan was taken to the top of the castle's tower by Henry himself, according to Vitalis, who 'seizing him with both hands dashed him backwards from the tower window.'[15] The tower was ever after known as 'Conan's Leap'. The corpse was then dragged through the centre of Rouen behind a horse as a warning of the fate of all traitors. In 1096 Duke Robert gathered an army and left to join the First Crusade, mortgaging Normandy to his brother, King William, for 10,000 marks to pay for the enterprise. In 1100, he was returning home when news reached Duke Robert of the death of King William.

In the later 1090s William de Warenne, the second earl, had turned his mind to marriage and set his sights rather high. William was in search of a royal bride. The young woman in which he expressed an interest was Matilda (also known as Edith), daughter of Malcolm III Canmor, King of Scots, and his wife, the saintly Queen Margaret. Matilda not only had the blood of Scottish kings flowing through her veins, but also the blood of England's Anglo-Saxon kings; her mother Margaret was the daughter of Edward the

Exile, a grandson of King Æthelræd II the Unready, and a descendant of Alfred the Great. Born in the early 1080s, Matilda and her sister Mary had been raised and educated by their aunt, Christina, at the abbey of Romsey, though their father had apparently insisted that they were not destined for the religious life. Matilda and her sister had returned to Scotland in 1093, after their father's falling-out with William Rufus, but were brought back south in 1094, by their uncle Edgar, following Malcolm's demise in battle at Alnwick and Queen Margaret's own sad death just days later. Mary would eventually be married to Eustace III, Count of Boulogne, and was the mother of Matilda of Boulogne, wife of King Stephen. At some point after Matilda's return to England, William de Warenne sought Matilda's hand in marriage, although he was not the only one. As Orderic Vitalis says:

> Alain the Red, Count of Brittany, asked William Rufus for permission to marry Matilda, who was first called Edith, but was refused. Afterwards, William de Warenne, Earl of Surrey, asked for this princess; but reserved for another by God's permission, she made a more illustrious marriage. Henry, having ascended the English throne, married Matilda.[16]

Following the rebuff from King William, Earl William seems to have rarely appeared at court. A royal bride would have been a major asset for a man with Earl William's ambition, but a marriage alliance of the powerful Warennes with a descendant of the Scottish and Anglo-Saxon royal houses could have been perceived as a threat to the ruling Normans. Aware that William de Warenne was disappointed with the loss of his royal bride and then seeing her married to the new king, Henry attempted to make amends and win the earl's support by offering one of his illegitimate daughters as an alternative bride. Unfortunately, Anselm, Archbishop of Canterbury, opposed the marriage on the grounds of consanguinity – the bride and groom were distant cousins – and Earl William was once again disappointed. William, it seems, was quite bitter at having been thwarted in his plans to marry the Scottish princess, to the extent that he is credited with making up derogatory nicknames for the royal couple. He ridiculed Henry's studious approach to hunting by calling him 'stagfoot'; a reference to Henry's claim that he could tell the number of tines in a stag's antlers by examining the beast's hoofprint, although the nickname could also be applied to Henry's notorious womanising and the numerous illegitimate offspring that resulted.[17] In a dig at both Henry and Matilda, Earl William is believed to have been behind the Anglo-Saxon nicknames 'Godric and Goda', used by some of the Norman nobles as an insult and possibly an allusion to Henry's inclination towards his English subjects at the expense of his Norman ones.[18]

It probably came as no surprise to Henry, then, that when Robert, Duke of Normandy, invaded England on 20 July 1101, Earl William de Warenne was among the barons who flocked to the duke's side, having apparently been involved in some kind of anti-royal conspiracy for several months.[19] Many Anglo-Norman barons, holding lands in both England and Normandy, preferred to see the two territories under one ruler: Robert Curthose, Duke of Normandy. Earl William seems to have spent the year trying to decide which side to back. Although Orderic Vitalis places him firmly at the duke's side, charter evidence places him in King Henry's company for the confirmation of the possessions of St Pancras in Autumn 1101 and at Windsor with the king on the 1 and 2 September; although he had not been present for the treaty between Henry and Robert II of Flanders at Dover on 10 March 1101. On 29 August, King Henry authorised Roger Bigod to do justice against Warenne's men in Norfolk.[20] When it came to a showdown between the royal brothers at Alton, neither side was eager for battle and in the subsequent Treaty of Alton, the duke accepted an annuity of 3,000 marks to abandon his invasion and renounce his claims to the throne while King Henry in turn renounced his lands in Normandy, save for Domfront, where he had made a solemn vow to the inhabitants that he would never relinquish control. The brothers agreed to support each other, should either be attacked by a third party, and to be each other's heir if neither sired a son.[21]

Having been present at Alton to see the brothers come to terms, Earl William de Warenne was now left isolated and at Henry's mercy.[22] For violating his oath of homage to the king, and for the violence perpetrated by his men in Norfolk, Earl William's English estates were declared forfeit and he was effectively forced to cross the English Channel into exile. Arriving on his Norman estates, Earl William complained to Duke Robert of his sufferings and losses on the duke's behalf. The duke obviously felt some responsibility, as he set out for England to intercede with his brother for the earl. He arrived at Henry's court, uninvited and unwelcome, in 1103. Terrified and threatened with imprisonment by an angry brother, Duke Robert agreed to relinquish his annuity of 3,000 marks in return for the reinstatement of Earl William's English estates and titles.[23] William de Warenne's allegiance to Duke Robert, however, was now at an end. As Orderic Vitalis tells us, the earl, 'having thus recovered his father's inheritance ... learned wisdom from his misfortunes, and afterwards adhered faithfully to the king during the thirty-three years they lived together.'[24]

Restored to his lands but not yet to favour, Earl William probably received a frosty welcome at the English court; he seems to have kept a low profile – or was not welcome – and attested no royal charters between 1103 and 1107.[25] He did eventually regain the king's confidence, becoming a trusted member of the court and thereafter remained loyal to King Henry. William's brother, Rainald, on the other hand, having inherited the Warenne's Flemish lands and with no interests in England, threw in his lot with Duke Robert in Normandy. *The Warenne (Hyde) Chronicle* reports:

> Robert de Stuteville and Reginald [Rainald] of Warenne and many others who were furious at King Henry about their own eventual expulsion were equally allied with Count Robert [of Normandy], and hindered King Henry as much by greater hatred as by many more protests, rather than by inflicting harm.[26]

In 1105 Rainald de Warenne was among the supporters of Duke Robert who captured and imprisoned Robert fitz Hamon, a friend of King Henry, intending to ransom him. Henry saw fitz Hamon's capture as an opportunity to deal decisively with Normandy, though he claimed he was invading not out of ambition, but to protect the church and the poor people of Normandy. Henry invaded in the spring of 1106. Rainald de Warenne was captured by Henry's forces during a skirmish at the fortified Abbey of Saint-Pierre-sur-Dive.[27] The abbot had been plotting with Duke Robert to trap Henry, offering to hand over the castle, while sequestering Rainald de Warenne, Robert de Stuteville and their men within, ready to seize the king as soon as he entered. Suspecting treachery, Henry arrived at daybreak with a force of 700 men-at-arms and took the castle by surprise, capturing the duke's men and burning the castle to the ground.[28] The king then moved on to invest William of Mortain's castle at Tinchebrai in close siege. Mortain complained of this to Robert as his overlord. Aware of the need to demonstrate support for his barons, Duke Robert mobilised his forces and marched to raise the siege.

Arriving at Tinchebrai, the duke was faced with a much larger force commanded by his little brother, King Henry, who had travelled to Normandy with a full contingent of knights, which were, in turn, supported by additional forces from Maine. Several of Duke Robert's erstwhile allies were among Henry's forces, including Rotrou de Perche, who had married one of Henry's many illegitimate daughters. The king also had contingents from the Contentin, including his own town of Domfront, and from Brittany, led by Henry's brother-in-law, Count Alan, the widower of Henry and Robert's sister, Constance. In addition, Henry was supported by a large contingent of Anglo-Norman barons, including Robert de Beaumont, Earl of Leicester, William de Warenne, Earl of Surrey, Ralph de Tosny, who had turned against Duke Robert for failing to return Evreux to him, Robert de Grandmesnil and many others. Duke Robert's forces included William of Mortain, whose castle was being threatened, Robert de Bellême and Edgar the Ætheling, a friend and crusading companion of Duke Robert, who was the last scion of the House of Wessex which had ruled England until the death of Edward the Confessor. Edgar was also the uncle of Henry's wife, Queen Matilda.

The two sides were negotiating on the eve of battle, with Henry offering to take over the administration of the duchy for half of its revenues, leaving Robert as a figurehead with the remaining half of the duchy's revenues. Whether an insult was intended or not, Duke Robert took the offer as one and negotiations broke down.[29] On the 26, 27 or 28 September 1106 the two armies faced each other across the battlefield. According to the *Roman de Rou*, Duke Robert's vanguard 'attacked well' but was no match for Henry's army, which won the day 'with scarcely any bloodshed'.[30] William of Mortain, fought in the frontline of the duke's forces and was making headway into the king's line when he was attacked in his flank, by the combined force of men from Maine and Brittany, who are said to have charged so well that they 'broke the ducal army to pieces.'[31] The battle lasted less than an hour. Duke Robert was in the thick of the fighting but made little headway against his brother's forces. The battle of Tinchebrai effectively ended when the duke was captured by fellow crusader Gaudry Waldric, Henry's chancellor. William of Mortain and Edgar Ætheling were also taken prisoner. Robert de Bellême had been at the head of the reserve force and is said to have fled once he saw that the day was lost, it was reported he had 'received no blow, nor gave no blow.'[32] As a consequence, Bellême was blamed for the defeat by both Duke Robert and William of Mortain, who felt he had let them down badly.

Robert Curthose, Duke of Normandy, was to spend the remainder of his days as his little brother's prisoner, while King Henry went on to conquer the whole of Normandy. Rainald de Warenne, captured by the king's forces in the spring of 1106, was released either shortly before or shortly after the battle, the sources vary. Orderic Vitalis claims that William de Warenne served as one of King Henry's chief commanders at Tinchebrai and that Rainald was released shortly before the battle. Grateful for his brother's release, Earl William urged his men to fight the king's cause with the utmost determination.[33] According to the *Warenne (Hyde) Chronicle*, however, Rainald was not released until after the battle, when he was 'reluctantly handed back to his brother, who pleaded for him to Henry.'[34] Whichever is correct, the result was the same, Rainald was now free. With his greatest rival now in his hands, Henry could afford to be charitable. In 1109 Earl William was present '*in concilio totius Anglie*', a council of all the nobles of England at Nottingham and on 17 May the following year, he was at Dover with King Henry as a surety for the performance of the treaty with Robert, Count of Flanders.[35]

Robert Curthose's young son, William Clito, was not perceived as a threat by Henry. He was, after all, still only a child. He was given into the custody of Duke Robert's son-in-law, Elias of Saint-Saens, to be raised and educated. By 1110, however, William Clito was old enough to embroil himself in Norman conspiracies against Henry I, involving the king of France, the count of Anjou and some of Henry's own barons. On hearing of the conspiracy, Henry ordered the arrest of Clito, but the young prince evaded capture and escaped Normandy with his guardian, Elias of Saint-Saens. As a rival claimant to Normandy and England and a focal point for disaffected and dissatisfied barons, William Clito would be a thorn in Henry's side for many years to come. For the moment, though, with the young prince in exile, Henry seized the castle of Saint-Saens, just three miles from the Warenne castle of Bellencombre. As Orderic Vitalis says, Henry 'gave it [Saint-Saens] to his kinsman, William of Warenne, to the end that William would adhere faithfully to the king and firmly resist the king's enemies.'[36] Earl William was in Normandy at the time, where he was serving in the capacity of judge in the Norman ducal court of 1111; he is named among the justices in a case in which Urse, Abbot of Rouen, recovers a tenement in the city.[37] The proximity to Bellencombre meant that Saint-Saens fit neatly into the other Warenne holdings in Normandy. It also meant that William de Warenne would be a loyal and valuable vassal in Normandy, intent on holding onto his new property, which would surely be confiscated were William Clito to ever get a foothold in the duchy; the young pretender would want to return the castle to his faithful brother-in-law, Elias de Saint-Saens.

Despite very rocky beginnings, William de Warenne, 2nd Earl of Warenne and Surrey, had now become an ardent royalist and an active member of King Henry's court. Having attested only one or two charters for William II Rufus, and none for Henry I between 1103 and 1107, the earl witnessed sixty-nine of Henry's charters in total, a clear indication of his new-found loyalty and industry in favour of King Henry.[38] Moreover, in the reign's sole surviving pipe roll, Earl William is recorded as receiving the third highest geld exemption of any magnate in England, at £104 8*s* 11*d*, which demonstrated the extent of not only his holdings and wealth, but also his place in the king's favour.[39] At some point no later than 1121, William de Warenne's lands in Yorkshire were increased with the grant of the extensive manor of Wakefield, which had been in the king's hands at the time of the Domesday Survey. Before 1130, however, the Warenne holdings of Kimbolton in Huntingdonshire and Dean in Bedfordshire had passed to the custody of William Meschin, possibly as the subject of an exchange for the lands at Wakefield.[40]

Chapter Five

The Second Earl and the Last
of the Norman Kings

William de Warenne stood steadfast in his support of King Henry during the crucial years of 1118 and 1119, when Normandy was again seething with rebellion and a French army had crossed the border and was roaming to the southeast of Rouen, almost unhindered. Although there still appears to have been some question mark over his loyalty, or, at least, William felt there was. On the eve of the Battle of Brémule, fought between King Henry and Louis VI of France on 20 August 1119, when Henry wavered in his belief in the support of his magnates and ordered his army to return to Rouen, William de Warenne is credited with making a rousing speech declaring his loyalty to the king of England:

> My lord king, your reverence has for a long time held me and my relatives unjustly suspect, although no one has been able to convict me of treason or perjury. And so now that I see you under pressure of greater need than you have been in your entire life, since the king of the French, so exasperated and hasty with pride, hurries to meet you with his own troops, today I expose myself and my relatives on your behalf to death against him, so that you may certainly consider me to be the most faithful to you, and whatever you may have heard said by slanderers, you will know that it is fictitious and false. Therefore halt the army and arrange the battle-lines against him in such a manner, that I, placed in the first line with my men, will take him on and I will receive the weight of the whole battle on myself. For although by the custom of ancient lordship he is our lord, because he attacks us unjustly and refuses to receive the justice offered by us, rush against him boldly with all fear set aside.[1]

According to the Warenne chronicler, Earl William's fellow magnates were roused by shame and fear to offer their own assurances to the king. Henry, reassured of the support of his leading magnates, ordered the battle-lines be drawn up and prayed, 'Most holy Virgin Mary, do not allow me, your unworthy servant, to be given today to my enemies as a disgrace.'[2] Henry formed his men into four lines of battle, with William de Warenne in the first line, alongside Dreux of Mouchy-la-Châtel – though it is unclear whether this was/ William's brother-in-law or nephew of the same name – Walter Giffard and 'Roger, son of Richard, and various other relatives'.[3] The second line also included the forces of Henry's counts and magnates, while the third line was comprised mainly of foot-soldiers, in a dense wedge formation, and it was in this line that Henry placed 'both his sons and faithful knights'.[4] Robert and Richard, two of Henry's illegitimate sons, were in this third line, along with the king's only legitimate son and heir, William, who was about 16 years old and about to take part in his first battle. Henry placed himself in the fourth line, along with several of his most powerful magnates.

Seeing that Henry intended to fight, the French army, led by Louis VI and William Clito, formed up to face Henry's army. The French king was 'frenzied with indignation and anger, for, puffed up with arrogance, he thought that Henry would in no way dare to presume such things, and he roused up his men and, impatient of delay, he quickly rushed to meet him with all impetuosity and without order or proportion.'[5] The French charge broke through the first line of Henry's defences but was stopped at the second line. Henry of Huntingdon describes the confrontation:

> The battle raged fiercely; the lances were shivered, and they fought with swords. At this time William Crispin twice struck King Henry on the head and though his helmet was sword-proof, the violence of the blow forced it a little into the king's forehead, so that blood gushed forth. The king, however, returned the blow on his assailant with such force that though his helmet was impenetrable, the horse and its rider were struck to the ground and the knight was presently taken prisoner in the king's presence. Meanwhile, the infantry with whom the king's sons were posted not being yet engaged, but waiting for the signal, levelled their spears, and charged the enemy. Upon which the French were suddenly daunted, and broke their ranks, and fled.[6]

Although the war was not over, Brémule proved to be a turning point and Henry embarked on a process of reconciliation with his disaffected Norman barons. However, while Richer de l'Aigle and Eustace de Breteuil, Henry's son-in-law, accepted the proffered olive branch, Stephen of Aumale still held out and tried to persuade Charles of Flanders to join him. King Henry moved his army to Eu, and prepared to besiege Stephen, but sent William de Warenne to negotiate with the recalcitrant baron. As the *Warenne*

(Hyde) Chronicle says: 'And so, while King Henry sought peace more than dissension, he sent Earl William of Warenne with a few men to the castle of the enemy to negotiate peace with them.'[7] Without further recourse to violence, Stephen of Aumale submitted and Normandy was finally at peace.

In all the years of unrest with Normandy, Earl William de Warenne had remained a bachelor. Having been rebuffed by Matilda of Scotland and barred from marrying an illegitimate daughter of King Henry by the Archbishop of Canterbury, William's marriage prospects appear to have dried up. With peace now achieved in Normandy, it seems that the earl was finally ready to settle down. Unfortunately, the object of his affections was Isabel de Vermandois, wife of Robert de Beaumont, Earl of Leicester. Isabel was the mother of no less than nine children, including the redoubtable twins, Waleran and Robert de Beaumont, who would both make names for themselves in the period known as the Anarchy, when Empress Matilda tried to wrest the throne from King Stephen.

Also sometimes known as Elisabeth, Isabel had the blood of kings flowing through her veins; her father was Hugh Capet, Count of Vermandois by right of his wife, a younger son of King Henry I of France and Anne of Kiev. Her mother was Adelaide de Vermandois, a descendant of the ancient Carolingian dynasty. Isabel was one of her parents' nine surviving children, four boys and five girls. As with many medieval women, there are no images of Isabel, not even a description of her appearance. Her life can be pieced together, somewhat, through her marriages and through her children. From her birth, as the granddaughter of the king of France, Isabel was a valuable prize on the international marriage market. As a result, her childhood proved to be depressingly short. By 1096 a marriage was mooted between Isabel and Robert de Beaumont, Count of Meulan and Earl of Leicester, he was 46 years old. Robert de Beaumont was a seasoned warrior and courtier, with lands in both England and Normandy. He had fought alongside William the Conqueror at the Battle of Hastings and was with William II Rufus when he was killed in a hunting accident in the New Forest. A loyal supporter of Henry I, he would fight for his king at the Battle of Tinchebrai in 1106 and received the earldom of Leicester in 1107.

The marriage was originally opposed by the church. Not only were the prospective couple related within the prohibited degrees, but also, Isabel was not yet 12, the minimum legal age that a girl could marry. Before leaving on the First Crusade, however, Isabel's father was able to persuade Pope Urban to issue a dispensation and the marriage went ahead in 1096. The fact their first child was not born until 1102 suggests that, despite her father's haste in arranging Isabel's marriage, her husband at least gave the young girl time to mature before taking her to his bed. Isabel gave Robert nine children; the first was a daughter, Emma, born in 1102. Twin boys followed in 1104; Waleran and Robert de Beaumont, earls of Worcester and Leicester, respectively. The brothers were active supporters of King Stephen during the conflict with Empress Matilda, but while Robert would come to terms with Matilda's son, the future Henry II, in 1153, Waleran was distrusted due to his support of Louis VII of France. Another daughter, Isabel, was a mistress of Henry I before being married to Gilbert de Clare, 1st Earl of Pembroke. Through her son Richard de Clare, 2nd Earl of Pembroke, she would be the grandmother of Isabel de Clare, wife of the great knight and regent for Henry III, William Marshal.

Isabel's marriage to Robert de Beaumont seems to have ended in scandal and controversy. The chronicler Henry of Huntingdon reported that she was seduced by William de Warenne, 2nd Earl Warenne, saying of Robert that 'when he was at the height of his fame, it happened that another count stole his wife, by intrigue and violent treachery.'[8] It is hard to blame a young woman of 30 in an arranged marriage to a man more than twice her age, for looking elsewhere for love and comfort, although William de Warenne himself must have been around 50 and still twenty years Isabel's senior. It seems that Earl William hatched a plot to kidnap Isabel – possibly with her approval – after Robert de Beaumont refused to grant his wife a divorce. It was claimed that the adultery of his wife with another earl had made the end of Robert de Beaumont's life all-the-more miserable, 'he passed into the shadows of grief, and never again experienced happiness or cheerfulness'.[9] Beaumont died on 5 June 1118, in England.[10] Huntingdon records the aged warrior's death, saying:

> Robert, earl of Mellent [Meulan], the greatest politician among all those who had dwelt at Jerusalem , and chancellor of King Henry exhibited his folly at the end; for when he would neither at the persuasion of his priests, give up the lands which he had appropriated, nor make the confession which it was his duty to do, he fell away and died, as it was, of inward weakness. Well then it was said, 'The wisdom of this world is foolishness with God.'[11]

Such rumours of adultery, however, may be little more than gossip, or a later invention, arising from the haste in which Isabel de Vermandois was married to Earl William de Warenne following her husband's demise. The marriage was arranged, or at least sanctioned, by the king, possibly at the instigation of Earl Warenne, though this is by no means proof of any relationship prior to the marriage.[12] Earl Warenne was now a faithful adherent of King Henry and badly in need of a wife, having been active on the political stage for thirty years and still with no heir to succeed him. Indeed, the death of his brother, Rainald, leaving no heirs, sometime before 1118, may have prompted Earl William to consider the future of the earldom with more of a sense of urgency. It is thought he may have been the father of two illegitimate sons, Rainald *blundus* and Rainald *brunus*, who appear as brothers of the third earl in a charter of Stephen son of Richard de Scalers, giving the church of Caxton to Lewes Priory; though nothing else is known of them.[13] Isabel and William appear to have married very soon after Robert de Beaumont's death, given that their first child, a son also named William, was born in 1119: he would become the third Earl Warenne on his father's death in 1138.

At least four more children followed, including two sons. Reginald de Warenne would marry the heiress to the barony of Wormegay: he was a trusted administrator of the Warenne lands for his brother, the third earl, and will be discussed in a later chapter. There is little information on a third son, Ralph de Warenne, beyond the charter evidence, which certainly demonstrates that Ralph was an integral member of the family and supported both his father and brother as earls. He is mentioned as a joint donor, alongside his older brother, William, in charters issued by his parents granting lands to Lewes Priory and to Castle Acre Priory and granting lands in Normandy and England to the priory of Bellencombre in Normandy. In the grant to Lewes Priory the brothers are named as *'Willelmus et Radulfus filii nostri'* ('William and Ralph, our sons').[14] The fact William and Ralph are included in the charters, but not Reginald, suggests that Ralph was the second son and Reginald the third and youngest son. Ralph was also a witness, again with his older brother William, to his father's charter to Longueville priory, in which the earl confirms the grant, of a tenant to the priory, by William of Trubleville. In the witness list, he is named as *'Radulfo filiis eorum'* ('Ralph son of the earl').[15] Ralph's appearance in charters continues into his brother's tenure as earl, from 1138. In a charter issued in 1147, he appears above his brother Reginald, again possibly indicating his seniority in age. In this charter, Ralph is witness to his oldest brother's confirmation of grants to Lewes Priory, which included 'in Yorkshire the church of Conisbrough with its other churches, chapels, lands and tithes, and the churches of Wakefield and Dewsbury.'[16]

An endearing story involving Ralph comes amid his brother's preparations to go on crusade. Earl William (III) de Warenne joined the Second Crusade, led by his cousin, King Louis VII of France, in 1147. Before leaving for the Holy Land, the earl held a dedication ceremony for the new church at Lewes Priory, in which he confirmed 'to Lewes priory all of its lands of his fee, undertaking to acquit it of danegeld and all other services due to the king; and the gift of tithe corn, etc, from all his demesne lands and a full tenth penny of all his rents in England.'[17] The earl endowed the priory, in which his father and grandparents were buried, and where his mother would soon be laid to rest, with the tenth penny of his rents and 'giving it seisin thereof by hair from his own head and that of Ralph de Warenne his brother, cut with a knife by Henry, bishop of Winchester, before the altar.'[18] It is not hard to imagine how moving a ceremony this must have been, two brothers kneeling before the altar to have their hair cut by the bishop of Winchester, Henry of Blois, the brother of King Stephen. The scene is made all the more poignant in hindsight, knowing that the third earl never returned from the crusade on which he was about to embark. Ralph appears as witness in at least two more of his brother's charters, the confirmation of land to Castle Acre Priory and a grant to the Templars of 40s yearly from the earl's rents of Lewes; in them he is named as Radulfo de Warenna.[19] Beyond this, nothing more appears to be known of him, though it is interesting to think that there may be a lock of his hair in an archive somewhere, folded into a charter; or maybe it was discarded many years ago, the story of its provenance unknown to the finder. Given that the third brother, Reginald, did not take part in the hair cutting ceremony, and did not join his brother, the third earl, on crusade, it may be that Ralph de Warenne did accompany his brother. Certainly, he seems to disappear from the records at this stage, and nothing more is heard of him; it is possible, though only conjecture on my part, that he also perished in the Holy Land.

William and Isabel also had two daughters. Ada de Warenne, whose story will be told in the next chapter, fulfilled her father's royal ambitions when she married Henry of Huntingdon, heir to the Scottish throne. Two of Ada's sons became kings of Scotland; Malcolm IV and William the Lion. Another daughter, Gundreda, is described as 'uterine sister' of Waleran de Beaumont, Isabel de Vermandois' son by her first marriage.[20] Gundreda is a clear demonstration of how well Countess Isabel's two families integrated. Gundreda married Roger de Beaumont, a cousin of her Beaumont half-siblings. Roger had become earl of Warwick on his father's death in 1119 and must have been some years older than his wife, who cannot have been born before 1119, the same year her husband succeeded to his earldom. Gundreda and Roger had two sons and two daughters. Their sons, William and Waleran, would each, in turn, succeed to their father's earldom. Waleran married Margery de Bohun, daughter of Humphrey de Bohun and Margaret of Hereford. Their eldest son, Henry, would succeed as fifth earl of Warwick.

Of the daughters of Gundreda and Roger, Margaret was named after her paternal grandmother, Margaret, daughter of Geoffrey, Count of Mortagne, and wife of Roger's father, Henry, Earl of Warwick. Gundreda was named for her mother, or more likely her maternal great-grandmother, the wife of the first Earl Warenne. She would later marry Hugh Bigod, 1st earl of Norfolk, as his second wife. The couple had two sons, Hugh and William. After the death of her husband in 1177, the younger Gundreda attempted to claim the earldom for her eldest son, Hugh, to the exclusion of the late earl's son, Roger Bigod, by his first wife. This failed and Roger became the second earl; he married Ida de Tosny, the former mistress of King Henry I and mother of the king's illegitimate son William Longespée, Earl of Salisbury. Following the death of Hugh Bigod, Gundreda married Roger de Glanville, she died sometime between 1200 and 1208. She is remembered as the foundress of Bungay Priory in about 1188.[21]

Roger de Beaumont vacillated during the period known as The Anarchy, initially supporting King Stephen before briefly changing his allegiance to Empress Matilda in the summer of 1141, following the king's capture at the Battle of Lincoln. On Stephen's release, Roger once again joined the king's faction and remained loyal thereafter, though he appears to have been little thought of, and Stephen made sure that Warwick castle was put in the hands of a royal garrison. Of Roger and the castellan of Oxford, the *Gesta Stephani* said they were 'feeble men, rejoicing more in pleasure than in resolution of mind.'[22] Henry of Huntingdon, writing in the 1120s, said the earl was 'debased in spirit.'[22] Such descriptions are borne out when hearing of the manner of Roger de Beaumont's death. The earl of Warwick was with the royal court when news reached it that his wife, Countess Gundreda, had tricked the garrison of Warwick castle into surrendering to the supporters of Henry of Anjou, the future King Henry II.

The earl apparently died from the shock of hearing of his wife's actions on 12 June 1153. Although the *Gesta Stephani* admitted that he could hardly be to blame for his wife's perfidy, the unfortunate, now-dead earl, did not escape the scorn of being a man who could not manage his wife.[24] Gundreda went on to marry William de Lancaster, Lord of Kendal, son of Gilbert de Lancaster by his second wife. There is no mention of children from this marriage, and William's heir was his son by his first wife, also named William. A charter from sometime before 1156, in which William gave the manor and church of Cokerham to the abbey of St Mary de Pré, Leicester, declares that the grant is made with the assent of Gundreda his wife and of William his son and heir.[25] In 1156 or later, William granted common of pasture throughout his fee in Lonsdale and Amounderness. This grant was issued 'with the assent of William his son and heir and of Gundreda his wife, for the souls of Gilbert his father, Goditha his mother, Jordan his son, and Margaret daughter of the countess, the first two witnesses being William his son and heir and Gundreda daughter of the countess.'[26] The inclusion of Margaret and Gundreda as daughters of the countess are clearly Gundreda's two daughters by Roger, Earl of Warwick. Also evident is that, by the time of the charter, Margaret had died but the younger Gundreda was still living and acted as a witness. The elder Gundreda died sometime after 1166, when she is recorded as holding Walton in dower of her son William, Earl of Warwick.[27]

Marriage and children must have been a welcome change of pace for Earl William, after the many years of war and politics. On his marriage to Isabel, William assumed the Vermandois coat of arms as his own and the blue and gold checks became known as the 'Warenne chequer', possibly as a way to highlight his wife's illustrious ancestry as a member of the French royal family. That is not to say, however, that politics did not infringe upon the lives of the Warenne family. In 1120 a national tragedy occurred which was to have far-reaching consequences for England and Henry I. The king of England and his wife, Queen Matilda, had two children who survived childhood. Matilda had been sent to the German imperial court at the age of 8, where she was to marry Emperor Henry II of Germany when she turned 12 in 1114. Her brother, William, was raised to succeed his father, King Henry I. Harking back to the Anglo-Saxon kings, William was given the soubriquet 'the ætheling', meaning throne-worthy, to highlight his position as heir to the throne. According to William of Malmesbury, William was trained for his future role 'with fond hope and immense care.'[28]

In 1115, according to the *Anglo-Saxon Chronicle*, Henry had arranged for the Norman barons to do homage and swear fealty to William as their future duke, in an attempt to counter the claims of William Clito. A similar ceremony was arranged in England in 1116, for all the great men and barons of England to swear fealty to William as the king's heir. The *Warenne (Hyde) Chronicle* referred to William as '*rex Norman-Anglorum, ut putabatur futurus*' (assumed to be the future king of the Norman-English).[29] On 1 May 1118 William's mother, Queen Matilda, died at Westminster and was laid to rest in Westminster Abbey. It is from this point that William took on more responsibility, acting as regent whenever the king was away in Normandy. In December 1118 Henry's troops defeated the Angevins, under Fulk of Anjou, at Alençon. To counteract the defeat, William and Matilda of Anjou were married, with Count Fulk settling Maine on them as their marriage gift, thus deserting the cause of the French king. Inevitably, this had given Louis VI one more reason to support William Clito in his attempts to conquer Normandy in 1118 and 1119. As we have seen, on 20 August 1119, 16-year-old William was with his father at the Battle of Brémule. Henry won the fight against the forces of Louis VI of France and William Clito. During the battle, William had captured the palfrey of his cousin, William Clito, which he chivalrously returned at the end of the battle.[30]

In the same year William witnessed a charter at Rouen, in which he was described as '*dei gratia, rex designatus*' ('by the grace of God, king designate'). And continuing his education in diplomacy, in November 1119, William accompanied his father to a meeting with Pope Calixtus II; the pope was William's second cousin once removed.[31] At the turn of the year, it must have seemed to Henry that his dynasty – and the future of England – was secure in the hands of his son; at the age of 16 he was experienced in warfare and diplomacy and married to 12-year-old Matilda, who brought with her the county of Maine as her marriage portion. In 1120 peace was finally achieved with France, with William being created Duke of Normandy by his father, and paying homage for the duchy to King Louis; a precedent that would be used by future English kings, in order to avoid a king paying homage to a fellow king for part of his holdings. William, in turn, then received the homage of the Norman barons. Accompanied by his father, wife and several of his half brothers and sisters, it must have been a time of great rejoicing and festivities.

Indeed, when the large party prepared to cross the Channel, to return to England, it seems that a number of them were still celebrating. While Henry made the crossing in his own ship, taking with him several nobles and his daughter-in-law, the prince took the offer of a newly built ship, the *Blanche Nef* – or *White Ship* – which its owner, Thomas FitzStephen, claimed would guarantee a swift, safe passage. William the Ætheling was accompanied by many of the young nobles of the great families of England, including his half-sister, Matilda, and half-brother, Richard of Lincoln. His cousin, Stephen of Blois, perhaps concerned at the level of inebriation of the crew, chose to disembark at the last moment, and took another ship. A decision that was to not only save his life but also be of great significance in the future, when this same Stephen would successfully challenge the claim of William's sister, Empress Matilda, to the English throne.

Most of the passengers and crew were still drunk from celebrating when the ship finally left the harbour of Barfleur, in the dark, on the evening of 25 November 1120. Orderic Vitalis described the scene:

> At length he gave the signal to put to sea. Then the rowers made haste to take up their oars and, in high spirits because they knew nothing of what lay ahead, put the rest of the equipment ready and made the ship lean forward and race through the sea. As the drunken oarsmen were rowing with all their might, and the luckless helmsman paid scant attention to steering the ship through the sea, the port side of the White Ship struck violently against a huge rock, which was uncovered each day as the tide ebbed and covered once more at high tide. Two planks were shattered and, terrible to relate, the ship capsized without warning. Everyone cried out at once in their great peril, but the water pouring into the boat soon drowned their cries and all alike perished.[32]

As the ship went down, William was ushered into a small boat and was being rowed to safety when he is said to have heard the cries of his half-sister, Matilda. The 17-year-old prince insisted on rowing to her aid, but the little boat was overwhelmed by those trying to make it to safety, and capsized, taking everyone with it. There was only one survivor, a butcher from Rouen; over 300 souls were lost – drowned – and only a handful of bodies were ever recovered. With the sinking of the *White Ship* Henry I lost his son, England and Normandy lost their next ruler and the certainty that comes with a stable succession. As a consequence, Louis VI renewed his support of William Clito, who continued to be a thorn in Henry I's side until his death fighting in Flanders in 1128. Henry himself, in the hope of producing another son, married again in 1121 to Adeliza of Louvain. Unfortunately, the marriage proved childless and Henry spent the final years of his reign trying to secure the throne for his daughter, Matilda. Matilda had returned to Henry's court following the death of her husband in 1125 and was married again, in 1128, to Geoffrey, Count of Anjou, in the hope that the union would strengthen her claim to the throne. In the end, however, despite the fact Henry had made the barons of England swear fealty to Matilda as his successor, Henry's nephew, Stephen, claimed the throne on the old king's death in 1135; thus ushering in almost twenty years of warfare that defined The Anarchy.

Although he is not mentioned specifically William, 2nd Earl Warenne, would have been among those asked to swear their support of Matilda's

claim to the throne, along with all the nobles of Henry's court. He was one
of the earls present at Henry I's deathbed on the night of 1 December 1135
at Lyons-la-Foret. William de Warenne also had both his oldest son and
stepsons, Waleran and Robert de Beaumont, with him when the king died.
William was one of the five earls who escorted the royal corpse to Rouen for
embalming with a large escort and 'the nobles acting as bearers in turn.'[33]
Fearful of his corpse being ignominiously abandoned, as had happened with
his father William the Conqueror, the dying king had prevailed upon these
earls to swear an oath, administered by the archbishop of Rouen, that they
would not leave his body unattended until it was buried.[34] In the meantime,
it seems that Stephen of Blois had prepared well for the king's death and had
been forming alliances that would see him accede to the English throne in
place of the king's daughter, Matilda. As he was escorting the king's body
through Normandy, William de Warenne was also smoothing the way
for Stephen. Within two days of Henry's death, and as Stephen entered
London, Earl William had been delegated to assume command of Rouen,
Normandy's capital, and its surrounding province, the Pays de Caux. As the
king's body was moved to Caen, to await transportation to Reading Abbey
in England, the English magnates were working out their next move, their
minds firmly on the next reign rather than the last.

In March 1136, the nobles gathered at Stephen's Easter court at
Westminster. Forming their own significant faction, Earl William de
Warenne, his stepson Waleran, Count of Meulan and his son-in-law, Roger,
Earl of Warwick, who was also Count Waleran's cousin, were all present.
With their significant landholdings in both England and Normandy –
Count Waleran was the biggest Norman landholder after the duke – Stephen
needed the support of the Beaumont twins and their wider family, including
the ageing Earl Warenne. The earl was again with Stephen at Oxford shortly
afterwards when he attested the king's charter of liberties for the church. He
may have retired to his estates sometime after mid-1136, when he is last seen
attesting royal charters, during Stephen's campaign against Exeter.[35]

Involvement in the major events of the forthcoming conflict, later to be
remembered as a time 'when Christ and his Saints slept', however, was to fall
on the next generation.[36] Probably in his early 70s and having been one of
the leading magnates of England and Normandy for fifty years, William de
Warenne, 2nd Earl Warenne died in 1138, around 11 May.[37] He was buried
at his father's feet at St Pancras Priory, Lewes.

Although a narrative account in the Lewes Cartulary states that she died
on 13 February 1131, Isabel de Vermandois outlived her husband by almost

ten years, dying around 1147 or 1148. Isabel was also buried at Lewes Priory, close to her husband. After the earl's death, Isabel made a number of gifts in his memory. With the consent of her son, the third earl, Isabel gave the church of Dorking to Lewes Priory.[38] In another charter of 1138, or shortly after, the third earl confirmed 'the gift of Ordric de Barcombe with all his holding which countess Isabel, his mother, made to Lewes priory for buying a lamp for the burial-place of William his father.'[39] Although her life was tinged with scandal, Isabel of Vermandois raised two families who lived in harmony, together, through one of the harshest periods of English history. She has had a major influence on the history of England and Scotland. As the great matriarch of the twelfth century, from Isabel are descended the greatest families of England and all Scottish monarchs from Malcolm IV, the Maiden down to Queen Elizabeth II herself.

Having inherited an earldom that was no more than a few months old, William de Warenne, the second earl of Warenne and Surrey, took it to great heights. With his hand on the helm for fifty years, Earl William was at the centre of Norman and English politics and successfully negotiated his way through the quagmire that was the struggle for the succession between William the Conqueror's three surviving sons, even though he did not always choose the winning side. When he died, he left the earldom with more land than he had inherited and even greater prestige, having married a member of the French royal family. Just a year after his death, his daughter Ada would marry the heir to the Scottish throne; the second earl's royal ambitions were fully realised when two of his grandsons, Malcolm IV and William the Lion, in turn, sat on the throne of Scotland.

Chapter Six

Ada de Warenne, Queen Mother of Scotland

Ada de Warenne was probably born in the mid-1120s. She was the youngest daughter of William de Warenne, 2nd Earl Warenne and Isabel de Vermandois. Through her mother, she was a great-granddaughter of King Henry I of France and through her father she was a distant cousin of the Norman kings of England. Ada had three brothers, William and Reginald, who were the third earl Warenne and Baron of Wormegay, respectively, and Ralph de Warenne. Her one sister, Gundreda, would marry Roger de Beaumont and become countess of Warwick. Through her mother's first marriage to Robert de Beaumont, Earl of Leicester, Ada had nine further half-siblings, including Waleran de Beaumont, Count of Meulan, Robert de Beaumont, 2nd Earl of Leicester and Hugh de Beaumont, 1st Earl of Bedford, known as Hugh le Poer, because he was the younger brother rather than because of his financial situation. She also had six half-sisters, one of whom became a nun, while another was the mistress of King Henry I; with the exception of the nun, of course, all of Ada's half-sisters made good marriages. Ada's niece, Isabel de Warenne, heiress to the earldom of Warenne and Surrey, would marry William of Blois, the younger son of King Stephen and, following his death, Hamelin, half-brother of Henry II of England.

When her father died, in 1138, it was Waleran de Beaumont, twenty years Ada's senior, who became the head of the large Beaumont/Warenne family. As is almost always the case with medieval women, we know nothing about Ada's childhood. We can, however, assume that she was taught the skills needed by a noblewoman, such as needlework, dancing, music and the management of a noble household. Her mother, who had raised two separate broods of noble children, would have ensured that Ada had all the skills required to take on the responsibilities of a noblewoman. As distant kin to the Norman kings of England and the Capetian kings of France, Ada's family connections were of the highest quality, which made her a valuable commodity on the marriage market. The first mention of her in the chronicles, therefore, is on the arrangements for her marriage. Ada's proposed bridegroom was Prince Henry of Scotland. Born about 1115, Henry was probably eight to ten years older than Ada.

Henry was the only surviving son of King David I of Scotland and his queen, Matilda (or Maud), widow of Simon (I) de Senlis, who had died in 1113. Matilda was the daughter of Waltheof, Earl of Northumbria, and Judith, a niece of William the Conqueror.[2] Henry's older brother, Malcolm, was tragically killed when a toddler; he was reportedly murdered by a Scandinavian monk in his father's service, who is said to have savagely attacked the child with his artificial iron hand. Needless to say, the murderous monk was executed: David ordered that he be torn apart by wild horses.[3] King David was the youngest son of Malcolm III Canmor and his second wife, Margaret of Wessex, great-granddaughter of Æthelred II (the Unready) and a descendant of King Alfred the Great of Wessex. Queen Margaret was canonised as Saint Margaret in 1249–50 and was named the patroness of Scotland in 1673. King David's sister, Matilda (also known as Edith), was the wife of King Henry I of England and had, rather ironically, been sought as a bride by Ada's father William, the second Earl Warenne in the 1090s. David had succeeded his older brother, Alexander I, as King of Scots on 23 April 1124, when Henry was about 9 years old.

On his marriage to Matilda, David acquired lands in Northampton, Bedford, Cambridge and Huntingdon, as well as lands stretching from South Yorkshire to Middlesbrough, which would become known as the honour of Huntingdon.[4] By the first treaty of Durham, agreed in February 1136, David's son, Henry, was given Doncaster and the lordship of Carlisle, in addition to his mother's inheritance, the honour and earldom of Huntingdon. He paid homage for these lands to King Stephen at York. At Stephen's Easter court that same year, Henry sat at the king's right hand, his royal birth giving him precedence ahead of the English earls. This precedence and the confirmation of lands assigned to the Scottish prince infuriated Earl Ranulf of Chester, who had wanted Carlisle for himself, and Simon (II) de Senlis, Henry's own half-brother, who maintained a rival claim to the Huntingdon lands. The two barons withdrew from the court in disgust.[5] As the grandson of Earl Waltheof, Henry also demanded he be granted the earldom of Northumberland. When Stephen refused to relinquish it, Scottish raids into Northumberland were renewed. David ostensibly argued that he was supporting his niece, Empress Matilda, in her struggle with Stephen over the English crown, though his actual motives were far from selfless. He had been quick to seek peace with Stephen, who was married to another of his nieces, in 1136 and to back the empress now was accompanied by a strong dose of self-interest.

With Stephen occupied in the south, committed to dealing with the empress's formidable brother, Robert of Gloucester, David crossed the river

Tees with a Scottish army in July. He sent two Scottish barons to lay siege to Wark Castle, while he headed further south. Eustace fitz John, deprived of Bamburgh Castle by King Stephen, but still in control of Alnwick, chose to add his own forces to those of King David. The army intended to march past Bamburgh, leaving the stronghold unmolested; until the garrison believing themselves impregnable, taunted the Scots from the safety of the walls. The Scots promptly attacked, broke down the barricades and killed everyone in the castle. Bernard de Balliol was sent north by King Stephen and he and Robert de Bruce, ancestor of the king of Scots of the same name, were tasked with discussing terms with the Scots; if the Scottish forces went home, then Prince Henry would be given the earldom of Northumberland. David rejected the offer.[6]

The defence of the north fell to Thurstan, Archbishop of York since 1115 and nearing his seventieth year, a move which would prevent baronial squabbling over seniority. Thurstan marched his English army to Northallerton, in Yorkshire, just thirty miles north-west of York. On 22 August 1138, in the centre of the English army, a ship's mast, displaying the banners of St Peter, St John of Beverly and St Wilfrid of Ripon, was secured to a cart at the top of a hill. Above the emblems of the saints a banner read 'Body of the Lord, to be their standard-bearer and the leader of their battle.'[7] It is from this pious display that the ensuing battle, the Battle of the Standard, would get its name. The presence of the apostle and two Yorkshire saints, and a contingent of Picts among the Scottish army, led to the sense, among the English, that they were on a noble crusade. According to Henry of Huntingdon, the bishop of Durham then gave a rousing speech, before the bishops and priests retreated from the field:

Rouse yourselves, then, gallant soldiers, and bear down on an accursed enemy with the courage of your race and in the presence of God. Let not their impetuosity shake you, since the many tokens of our valour do not deter them. They do not cover themselves with armour in war; you are in the constant practice of arms in time of peace, that you may be at no loss in the chances at the day of battle. Your head is covered with the helmet, your breast with a coat of mail, your legs with greaves and your whole body with shield. Where can the enemy strike you when he finds you sheathed in steel ... It is not so much the multitude of a host, as the valour of a few which is decisive. Numbers, without discipline, are an hindrance to success in the attack and to retreat in defeat. Your ancestors were often victorious when they were but a few against many....[8]

As the English soldiers shouted out 'Amen! Amen!' in response to the bishop's speech, the Scottish army advanced with their own battle cry of 'Alban! Alban!' on their lips. The men of Lothian had been granted the vanguard and 'bore down on the English mailed knights with a cloud of darts and their long spears.'[9] The English proved to be a wall of steel, their ranks impenetrable, while the lightly-armoured Scots had no protection against the cloud of arrows and English swords: 'The whole army of English and Normans stood fast around the Standard in one solid body.'[10] According to chronicler Henry of Huntingdon, the men of Lothian were put to flight when their chief fell, pierced by an arrow. Fighting along the line continued until, having seen what befell the men of Lothian, the remainder of the Scots army began to falter as panic set in.

Seeing that the battle was lost, men began to flee, in small numbers at first, but soon the greater part of the army was in retreat. King David had chosen the greatest of the Scottish knights as his personal guard, who remained steadfast almost to the last. Once they saw the battle was lost, however, they persuaded the king to call for his horse and retreat, rather than risk death or capture. Henry of Huntingdon reserves praise for his namesake, Prince Henry, King David's

> brave son, heedless of what his countrymen were doing, and inspired only by his ardour for the fight and for glory, made a fierce attack, with the remnant of the fugitives on the enemy's ranks ... But this body of cavalry could by no means make any impression against men sheathed in armour, and fighting on foot in a close column; so that they were compelled to retire with wounded horses and shattered lances, after a brilliant but unsuccessful attack.[11]

Henry of Huntingdon reports 11,000 Scottish dead, while the English had few casualties, with Gilbert de Lacy's brother the only English knight to fall on the field of battle.

On 9 April 1139, a peace treaty was concluded between King Stephen and David of Scotland. Primarily negotiated by Stephen's wife, Queen Matilda – King David's own niece – the contents of the agreement were kept secret for almost a year, an indication that Stephen knew they would be hard for his barons to swallow. The terms were, indeed, extremely favourable to the defeated Scots. All the lands that Prince Henry had held in 1138 were returned to him, save for the castles at Bamburgh and Newcastle, for which he was recompensed with two towns of equal value in the south. Furthermore, Henry was confirmed as earl of Huntingdon and created earl of Northumbria, a title which encompassed Northumberland, Durham, Cumberland, Westmoreland and the parts of Lancashire north of the Ribble.[12] It was agreed that English law would remain in force in these regions, but that the barons within the earldom were permitted to do homage to Prince Henry, saving only their allegiance to King Stephen. In return, King David and his son promised a permanent peace and provided four hostages. Although the text of the treaty is now lost, it seems likely that the prince's marriage to Ada de Warenne, sister of the third Earl Warenne and half-sister of the Beaumont twins, was included in the terms of the Treaty of Durham.

Shortly after the treaty was signed, Prince Henry joined King Stephen's court for a time, accompanying Stephen on campaign, which came with some risk. Whilst Stephen's forces besieged Ludlow, 'this Henry was dragged from his horse by an iron hook, and nearly taken prisoner, but was gallantly rescued from the enemy by King Stephen.'[13] It was not all fighting, however, and it was probably during his stay with Stephen's court that Henry married his bride. Orderic Vitalis claims that the marriage was a love match; however, the timing clearly suggests that the union was a consequence of the 1139 treaty of Durham, perhaps with the intention of drawing Henry into Stephen's corner by allying him in marriage to his staunchest supporters, the Beaumont twins.[14] On her marriage, which took place sometime between the conclusion of the treaty of Durham and Henry's return to Scotland, Ada became Countess of Huntingdon and Northumbria and Lady of Haddington and Crail. Although she would never become queen, before her death, she would also be recognised as Queen Mother of Scotland as the mother of Malcolm IV and William I, both kings of Scots. It was not until after Michaelmas (19 September) 1140 that Ada and Prince Henry returned to Scotland. A disgruntled Ranulf, Earl of Chester, angry that the Scottish prince had been given both Carlisle and Cumberland – lands that he nursed claims to – apparently planned to ambush the prince on his journey north. Queen Matilda got wind of the plan and in order to thwart the recalcitrant earl she persuaded her husband, the king, to accompany the Scottish heir and his party to the border.[15] This event caused the frustrated earl of Chester to break with Stephen and pursue his own aims, which would lead to the Battle of Lincoln in 1141 and Stephen's capture by Matilda's forces; but we will discuss the events at Lincoln, in which Ada's brothers played a part, in greater detail in a later chapter.

While the marriage was part of the peace treaty, it failed to seal a lasting peace between the two kingdoms and relations with England remained fractious. This probably came as no surprise to anyone at the time, given the unrest engendered by Stephen's seizure of the English crown and Empress Matilda's determination to win it back. It would have been remiss of the Scots not to take advantage of England's woes to advance their own aims. That is not to say, however, that the marriage in itself was not successful. Ada appears to have taken to her new role as the wife of Scotland's future king, settling into a life of duty as a wife, mother, feudal landholder and religious benefactor. She is most frequently styled 'Ada comitissa regis Scottorum' ('countess of Scots').[16]

As David I's wife, Queen Matilda, had died in 1131, Ada was the first lady of the Scottish court although her public role was severely limited by her frequent pregnancies throughout the first decade of her marriage. She appeared as a witness on three of her husband's charters between 1139 and 1142, at Jedburgh, Selkirk and Huntingdon.[17] King David's relationship with King Stephen broke down permanently in 1141, when the English king gave the earldom of Huntingdon to Prince Henry's older, half-brother, Simon de Senlis, along with the lands in the midlands that comprised the honour of Huntingdon.[18] Henry had been involved in the government of Scotland, alongside his father, since 1144; he was recognised as 'rex designatus' or 'king-designate'. He shared his father's policies of modernisation in Scotland, helping to transform it into a European-style kingdom. The prince's lands in Northumberland, north of the Ribble and the Tees, were ruled by Henry as part of an extended Scottish-Northumbrian realm.[19] Henry issued coins in his own name at Bamburgh, Carlisle and Corbridge and endowed numerous religious houses within the region, demonstrating a sensitivity to local interests. He stood sponsor for the knighthood of Empress Matilda's son, Henry Plantagenet, which was performed by King David at Carlisle on 22 May 1149. With an eye on cross-border relations, Henry even held out an olive branch to the earl of Chester, offering to marry one of his daughters to the earl's son as a resolution to their differences, though the wedding never came about. In 1150 Henry and his father co-founded a Cistercian house at Holmcultran, Cumberland, for monks from Melrose Abbey. It was to be one of the prince's last major acts. The prince had fallen seriously ill in 1140 but was supposedly cured at the intervention of a visitor to the Scottish court, the Irish reformer, St Malachy. However, he may have suffered a recurrence of this illness when he died on 12 June 1152, probably at Peebles, still relatively young at the age of 37. He left his wife, Ada, still only in her late twenties, a widow with five young children. 1152 was a year of tragedy for Ada, moreover, as the couple's sixth child, Matilda, not yet 7 years old and possibly only a baby, died shortly after her father.[20]

By all accounts, it appears that Henry would have made an impressive Scottish king and continued his father's work in advancing Scotland's interests. Chroniclers boasted of his kingly qualities and he was greatly mourned on both sides of the Anglo-Scottish border. Henry and Ada's eldest son, 12-year-old Malcolm, became David I's heir and their second son, William, was given his father's earldom of Northumbria. Shortly after Henry's death, King David took 9-year-old William to Northumberland to receive the homage of the barons. Ada was to spend twenty-six years as a widow and it is in this period that her dedication to her estates and people, and to Scotland, shines through. Through her own cosmopolitan outlook, Ada is credited with encouraging European values and norms within the society of the Scottish nobility.

Ada did not forget her Warenne roots and encouraged knights from the great Warenne honours in England and Normandy, as well as from Northumberland, to settle in Scotland. It seems likely that Ela, who married Duncan (II), Earl of Fife, was a daughter of Reginald de Warenne, Baron of Wormegay, and therefore one of Ada's nieces. Ada's great-nephew, the grandson of her half-brother, Robert, Earl of Leicester, had joined the church and found great favour in Scotland, he became chancellor of Scotland and was elected as bishop of St Andrews in 1189. Ada must also have kept one eye on English affairs, following the exploits of her brothers and half-brothers in the contest for the English throne. Her family losses included her mother's death in 1147, the same year that her brothers William, Earl Warenne, and Waleran, Count of Meulan and Earl of Worcester, left England to take part in the Second Crusade. Waleran would survive the expedition and return home; his younger half-brother, William, was not so fortunate. He died in battle in the Holy Land in 1148.

Ada's chief dower estates were the burghs and shires of Haddington and Crail, with lands also in Tynedale at Whitfield, near Hexham, and in the honour of Huntingdon, at Harringworth and Kempston. It seems likely that Ada's main residence was in Haddington, where she is still well thought of to this day, and where she founded a priory for Cistercian nuns sometime before 1159.[21] It was in her widowhood, as the dowager countess of Northumbria and queen mother of Scotland, that Ada's own patronage and interests come to the fore. Although they do not give the full picture of the countess and her holdings, her numerous surviving charters shed light on Ada's lands and responsibilities. Haddington is proved to have been Ada's main place of residence after the death of her husband; she refers to it as 'my burgh of Haddington.'[22] Her charters included grants of land, varying in size from half a carucate to a full toft, to various religious houses, including Dunfermline Abbey, Kelso Abbey, Dryburgh Abbey and Newbattle Abbey, Bearford. St Andrews Cathedral Priory benefited greatly from Ada's largesse, receiving land in Crail, a full toft from her burgh at Haddington and 'one silver merk annually in Pitmilly for the soul of Earl Henry, for building the new church and for lighting, to be paid by Malise.'[23] Further common pastureland held by Malise in Pitmilly was to be granted to St Andrews Cathedral Priory and their hospital.[24] Grants to Hexham Priory in Northumberland included 'all Whitfield except the lands of Robert son of William (of Dilston) and Joel of Corbridge, by the same boundaries of which she held it of Earl Henry and King William afterwards, and wasteland which she and Robert the chaplain through her cultivated and populated; for a rent of 6 pounds of pepper yearly at Michaelmas.'[25]

Although the majority of her endowments were to Scottish religious houses, Ada also confirmed gifts to convents in England, including Wardon Abbey and Nuneaton Priory, founded by Ada's half-brother Robert, Earl of Leicester, which was to receive 20 *solidi* rent annually; this latter was confirmed by Pope Alexander III, who referred to Ada as *'Ade comitisse Scotie'* (countess Scotland).[26] The cathedral at Durham received a sum of money for Ada's health, following a bout of illness.[27] It is notable that these gifts were not to religious houses that were traditionally in the Warenne sphere of influence. Ada supported fourteen religious houses, in total, ten of which were in Scotland. These houses covered almost the full spectrum of religious groups, with donations to the Benedictines, the Tironensian monks, the Augustinian and Arrouaisian canons, the Cistercian monks and nuns, the Premonstratensian canons, Fontevriste nuns and a hospital.[28]

Several grants were made to individuals, including Ada's chaplain, Robert, who received grants of land in Whitfield, comprising land 'to be held of Hexham priory in fee.' In another, a man named William Carpenter received a grant of one toft and common pasture in Crail. While Alexander de St Martin, Ada's chief baron and the sheriff of Haddington, was granted the land of Athelstaneford 'by the same boundaries by which King David gave the same land to him.'[29] As an example of Ada's continued patronage, one grant is a confirmation to Matthew, the son of her chaplain, Robert, of the land at Whitfield, 'to be held as it was before the war.'[30] The war referred to is most likely that of 1173–74, in which King William was captured by the English (more of that in the next chapter). Two of Ada's charters were witnessed by her youngest son, referred to as 'David, my son'; he was the only one of her children to witness her charters. And while Alexander de St

Martin witnessed no less than twelve charters, other witnesses included Ela, Countess of Fife and Thorald, archdeacon of Lothian. Other vassals who appeared as witnesses in Ada's charters were from such prominent families as the Giffards and Balliols.[31]

The charters demonstrate not only the size of Ada's landholdings, but also the breadth of her patronage, both to individuals and to the church. The number of charters in her own name also suggests that Ada maintained a hands-on approach to the management of her estates and the distribution of her patronage. We can be certain that, as the queen mother of Scotland, Ada had her own household, which included her chaplain, Robert, and a clerk named William, although we know little else of its composition. Her grants to religious foundations were a demonstration of her piety, but also an expected social obligation. She had clearly embraced her life and family in Scotland, choosing to patronise institutions associated with her new home, rather than the Cluniac foundations of her Warenne birth family.

Ada and Henry had three sons, two of whom became kings of Scots; Malcolm IV and William I. Their youngest son, David, was the fifth Scottish earl of Huntingdon. Although David never became king of Scots, he was to have great influence on the Scottish succession in later generations. During his brother Malcolm's reign, in 1163 David was sent to England as a hostage, but returned to Scotland in 1165, following Malcolm's death and the accession of his remaining brother, William. Until William married and produced a son and heir, David was seen as the heir to the Scots throne. He married Matilda of Chester, the granddaughter of Ranulf de Gernons, Earl of Chester; the same Ranulf who had been denied Carlisle and Cumberland in favour of Prince Henry, and who had attempted to ambush Prince Henry and Ada on their return to Scotland in 1140. It is through the daughters of David and Matilda that Robert the Bruce (grandfather of Robert the Bruce, King of Scots) and John Balliol (later John, King of Scots) both based their claims as competitors to the Scots throne in the 1290s. They were two of the thirteen competitors who vied for the crown following the extinction of the senior royal line with the death of 8-year-old Margaret, known as the Maid of Norway, granddaughter and heir of Ada's great-grandson, Alexander III.

Ada and Henry also had three daughters.

The eldest daughter, Ada, was born around 1142. In August 1162, she was married to Florent III (or Floris), Count of Holland and was given the county of Ross in Scotland as her marriage gift. Ada died sometime after 1206; she and Florent had between eight and ten children, including two sons, Dirk and William, who each became count of Holland, in turn. It was through his descent from Ada that Florent (or Floris) V, Count of Holland, also claimed his place as one of the competitors to the Scottish throne in 1292. The count claimed that his descent from Ada, older sister of David, should give him precedence over David's daughters and their descendants. He also claimed that David had relinquished his rights to the Scottish crown in return for lands in Garrioch in north-east Scotland, and that William I had then settled the succession on Ada. Unfortunately, Count Florent was unable to produce any written evidence to support his claims and failed to secure the nomination of King Edward to become king of Scots.[32]

A second daughter, Margaret, was born around 1145. In 1160 she married Conan IV, Duke of Brittany, and was the mother of the duke's sole surviving heir, Constance, Duchess of Brittany. Constance was to marry, as her first husband, Geoffrey Plantagenet, third surviving son of Henry II and Eleanor of Aquitaine. Constance's son – and Margaret's grandson – Arthur, Duke of Brittany, was cruelly murdered by, or on the orders of, his uncle, King John of England. His sister, Eleanor, was to be a perpetual prisoner of the English Crown from her capture in 1203 to her death in 1241, aged 57. Duke Conan died in 1171, leaving Margaret a widow at the age of 26. Sometime between the duke's death, in February 1171, and Easter 1175, Margaret was married to Humphrey III de Bohun of Trowbridge, hereditary Constable of England in the service of King Henry II. Humphrey died in 1181, leaving a daughter, Matilda, and son, Henry, who was to become the first Bohun Earl of Hereford.

As we have seen, a third daughter, Matilda, died in the same year as her father, 1152, whilst still only a young child.

It was Ada's two oldest sons, Malcolm and William, who would guide the kingdom and people of Scotland in the second half of the twelfth century and, indeed, into the dawn of the thirteenth century and problems with a resurgent England under the Plantagenets.

Chapter Seven

Warenne Blood on Scotland's Throne

Henry and Ada's eldest son, Malcolm, was born between 23 April and 24 May 1141. He was later known as Malcolm the Maiden, due to his youth, religious devotion and the fact he remained unmarried.[1] He had become his grandfather's heir following his father's death, at which time he had been placed into the custody of Duncan, Earl of Fife, and taken on a progress around Scotland north of the Forth, following the old Celtic tradition of showing the heir to the people of the kingdom. When King David I died less than twelve months after his son, Henry, on 24 May 1153, he was succeeded by his grandson, Malcolm, then aged 12 – possibly even on his twelfth birthday – as Malcolm IV. The accession of Malcolm surpassed all the ambitions of his Warenne grandfather, William de Warenne, the second earl, who had sought a royal bride for himself. The earl had not lived to see his daughter marry the heir to the Scottish throne but, had he lived, he would have seen Malcolm's accession as the culmination of his aspirations for his family. The chronicles make no mention of Ada playing a part in the politics of Scotland during her eldest son's kingship. She did appear at court often and was present for many of the important occasions; she was also a witness to no less than sixteen of Malcolm's charters. Ada did, moreover, take great interest in the futures of her children, arranging the marriages of her two surviving daughters and working hard to persuade her son to marry. The chronicler, William of Newburgh, relates a story of the lengths Ada had to go to in order to encourage her reluctant son to choose a bride. Ada went so far as to present her son with a young woman of noble birth, in his bed. Not wishing to cause an argument with his mother, Malcolm did not send her away and allowed the lady to spend the night in his royal bed; while he slept on the floor, wrapped in his cloak. Ada, it seems, was relentless in her attempts to persuade Malcolm to marry, until the young king tired of her constant nagging and begged her to hold her peace.[2]

While William of Newburgh makes it sound as if Ada was pushing for grandchildren, or tempting her son to lose his innocence, Ada's constant attempts to discuss marriage with Malcolm had a political motive as much as a personal one. She was well aware of the importance of royal marriage, not just for the continuation of a dynasty and political alliance, but also for the strength and stability of the monarchy itself. Ada, moreover, was not the only one eager to see the young king settle down with a wife. The Scottish *curia regis* (royal council) continued to pressure Malcolm to find a bride, even after his mother had given up. Arnold, Bishop of St Andrews encouraged Malcolm to follow the example of his recently married sisters. The king, however, was no more swayed by the archbishop and his royal council than he was by his mother. It seems that he was eager to hold onto the highest ideals of Christian knighthood and remain chaste.[3] Malcolm's relative youth may also have led him to believe that he had many years ahead of him and plenty of time before he needed to settle down and raise a family.

Malcolm's kingship faced several challenges. In November 1154, the young king was faced with a revolt from Somerled, Earl of Argyll. The unrest was to continue for several years, with Somerled only suing for peace in 1159 having been deprived of his chief supporters, the MacHeths, father and sons, who had been reconciled with the king in 1157.[4] Malcolm's greatest challenge, however, was his larger neighbour, England. While David I had taken advantage of the civil war in England during Stephen's turbulent reign, the accession of Henry II in 1154 changed the political landscape entirely. In 1157 the two kings met at Chester, where Malcolm performed homage 'in the manner in which his grandfather had been the man of old King Henry.'[5] This homage suggests that Malcolm was accepting that he was a vassal of Henry II, as his grandfather had been a vassal of Henry I. He was also forced to resign his lordship of Northumberland, Cumberland and Westmorland, although the honour of Huntingdon was returned to the Scots king and his brother and heir, William, was given the lordship of Tynedale.

In 1159 Malcolm, his brother and others joined Henry II and the English army on an expedition to Toulouse; it gave Malcolm the chance to be knighted honourably in the field. The Scots contingent joined Henry II at Poitiers on 24 June and Henry knighted Malcolm at Périgueux a few days later.[6] The expedition met with initial success and the army overran the county of Toulouse before laying siege to the city itself. However, the siege had to be abandoned when King Louis VII of France intervened in support of the count of Toulouse. By the end of the year, Henry and Malcolm were back in Limoges, crossing to England shortly afterwards. Malcolm returned to Scotland in 1160 and to a revolt of six earls led by Feterth, Earl of Strathearn, angry at the king's expedition with the English army. Mediation by the clergy led to an uneasy peace and their abandoning of besieging Malcolm at Perth. Unrest then arose in Galloway and Malcolm made several forays into the region before the end of the year, when Fergus, lord of Galloway, submitted to the king.[7] It was the last major unrest by any Scottish earls for not only Malcolm's reign, but also for that of his brother, William I.

Malcolm was again summoned to meet Henry II in 1163. Despite falling ill at Doncaster, he was still expected to complete the journey to Henry's court and arrived at Woodstock at the end of June. It seems Henry wanted to assert his supremacy over Britain, as a group of Welsh rulers had also been called to attend the English king. On 1 July, Malcolm renewed his oath to Henry and handed over hostages, the most senior of whom was his own youngest brother, David, soon to be made earl of Huntingdon.[8] Homage given, Malcolm returned to Scotland, where he faced a revolt led by Somerled, Lord of the Isles, who was later killed in an attempted raid on Glasgow in 1164.[9] Malcolm appears to have never fully recovered from the illness he suffered in Doncaster in 1163 and frequently complained of pains in his head and feet. He planned a pilgrimage to Santiago de Compostela, to pray for healing, but was unable to undertake it. He died at Jedburgh on Thursday 9 December 1165, aged 24: he had reigned for twelve years and six months and was buried among his ancestors at Dunfermline Abbey.

We do not have Ada's response to the death of her first-born son, but it cannot have been easy for her, only in her 40s herself and already a widow of thirteen years. Malcolm was succeeded by his brother William, later known as William the Lion. William had succeeded his father as earl of Northumbria in June 1153, when he was about 11 years old. He lost the earldom, however, when his brother, Malcolm IV surrendered the northern counties of England to Henry II; he was given lands in Tynedale, worth £10 per annum, in compensation. This loss of Northumbria was never forgotten and was to colour William's future dealings with the English Crown throughout his reign. William was probably knighted in 1159, when he accompanied his brother Malcolm on an expedition to Toulouse. In 1163, he was in attendance on Malcolm in a meeting with King Henry II at Woodstock, where the Scots king did homage to the English king. William ascended the Scottish throne on Malcolm's death on 9 December 1165, aged about 23; his coronation took place at Scone on Christmas Eve, 24 December, the same year. In appearance and demeanour, William was more like his Warenne ancestors than Malcolm had ever been. He had even used the Warenne surname when earl of Northumberland.[10] Ada appears to have been less influential at court during the reign of her second son. He had ascended the throne as a grown man, who had already seen war, rather than a boy, as Malcolm had been. She witnessed only five of William's charters in the thirteen years between his accession and her death, and none after 1173.[11] Her advancing years and occasional illnesses may have been the reason, rather than any loss of regard on her son's part.

In 1166 William travelled to Normandy to meet with King Henry II and, although we do not know what they spoke of, it was reported that they parted on bad terms.[12] Nevertheless, in 1170 William and his brother David were at the English court, where David was knighted. They attended Henry II's council at Windsor on 5 April 1170 and were in London on 14 June, when Henry's eldest son, also Henry, was crowned king of England in his father's lifetime. He would be known as the Young King, rather than Henry III, and died in 1183, six years before his father. Both William and his brother David performed homage to the Young King after the coronation.[13] In 1173 when the Young King and his brothers, Richard and Geoffrey, rebelled against their father, the younger Henry promised that he would return the northern counties of England to the Scots king, and the earldom of Huntingdon with Cambridgeshire to the king's brother, David, in return for their support in the rebellion. William considered the offer, consulting his barons in the summer of 1173. It was decided to ask Henry II to return Northumbria, and to renounce homage if he refused. Henry II refused, and William joined the Young King's rebellion.

William formed an alliance with Louis VII of France and Count Philippe of Flanders, who both promised mercenaries would be sent to England in support. This was the start of the long Scottish tradition of alliances with France, against England, which would become known as the Auld Alliance. On 20 August 1173, the Scottish forces moved south, to Alnwick, Warkworth and Newcastle. Although they devastated the countryside, the Scots were unable to take the castles. They moved on to Carlisle, in the west, but having again failed to take the castle, they pulled back to Roxburgh after receiving news that a new English force was advancing. This force, under Ranulf de Glanville, the justiciar, burned Berwick. A truce was agreed until 13 January 1174, before the English returned south to deal with an invasion from Flanders. The truce was later extended to 24 March 1174, after a payment of 300 marks by the bishop of Durham to King William.[14]

At the end of the truce, the Scots, accompanied by Flemish mercenaries, again advanced into England. While David joined the rebels at Leicester, the king ravaged the Northumberland coast and besieged both Wark-on-Tweed (on the Northumberland-Scotland border) and Carlisle castles, but failed to take either. The castles at Appleby and Brough surrendered to them, but they were resisted at Prudhoe Castle, near Newcastle, from where they moved north to Alnwick after hearing of an approaching English army. On 13 July, while much of the Scottish army was spread out in raiding parties, the Scots were the victims of a surprise attack. King William's horse was killed, the king trapped underneath.

William surrendered to Ranulf de Glanville and was taken south, with his feet bound by a rope passed under his horse's belly, as a humiliation. He was taken first to Newcastle and then to Northampton, where he appeared before Henry II on 24 July.[15] He was sentenced to imprisonment at Falaise in Normandy and the price of his freedom was to submit himself, his kingdom and the castles of Berwick, Roxburgh and Edinburgh to King Henry II.[16] This must have been a hard time for Ada, seeing her son defeated, captured, humiliated and imprisoned. More heartache was to follow when Ada's younger daughter, Margaret, dowager Duchess of Brittany and Countess of Richmond, after her brother's capture, was imprisoned at Rochester castle and then moved to Rouen. Some of Ada's own household were also affected: her associates Jordan the Fleming, Ralph de Vere and William de Mortemer had all been involved in the fighting. Vere and Mortemer were captured.[17]

The Convention of Falaise on 1 December 1174 also granted that 'the church of Scotland shall henceforward owe such subjection to the church of England as it should do.'[18] It was a humiliating treaty for the Scots, which also required twenty Scottish noble hostages, including Ada's son, David, and kinsman Duncan (II), Earl of Fife. Ada's retainers Hugh Gifford, William de la Hay and William de Mortemer were also counted among the hostages to be handed to the English in return for their king's freedom.[19] King William arrived back in Scotland in February 1175, having spent two months in England until the handover of the Scottish castles had been completed. David returned with his brother and their sister, Margaret, was also released to marry Humphrey de Bohun; their son was born the next year. Ada must have rested more easily with her children freed and her daughter settled once again in marriage. She may have been already ailing, however, as she died in 1178, although where and of what she died has gone unrecorded. She had spent forty of her 55 years in Scotland, first as the wife of Scotland's heir and then as mother to two of her kings. Although there is no surviving eulogy for Ada, she is remembered in charters of donations to religious houses by her children, her household and her vassals.[20]

William returned from England to a revolt in Galloway, which he managed to quash, but in 1179 the king of Scots was forced to go north, to answer the threat of Donald Ban Macwilliam, grandson of Duncan II, who was gaining support for a challenge to the throne and a return to the royal line of Duncan. William built two new castles at Redcastle and Dunskeath and confirmed to his brother David the earldom of Lennox and lordship of Garrioch, thus controlling the roads to Moray and Ross. Things quietened down for a time, but in April 1181, when the king and David were in Normandy Donald Ban Macwilliam led an uprising in Moray and Ross, apparently gaining full control of the two earldoms. One royal retainer, Gillecolm the Marischal, surrendered the castle of Auldearn and then joined the rebels.[21]

The king was also faced with unrest in Galloway, where Gilbert of Galloway had failed to pay the money he had owed to Henry II since his earlier uprising. Gilbert died on 1 January 1185 and shortly after King William invaded Galloway, alongside Gilbert's nephew Roland, son of Uhtred of Galloway, who had been murdered by Gilbert, his own brother, in 1174. On 4 July 1185 William and his allies defeated the main force of Gilbert's followers and in July 1186, King William presented Roland to King Henry at Carlisle. By 1190 Roland had been granted the lordship of Galloway by King William while Gilbert's son, Duncan, was made lord of Carrick.[22] As a result, Galloway remained at peace well into the thirteenth century, until the death of Roland's son, Alan, in 1234. With Galloway subdued, in 1187 King William was finally able to quash the rebellion in the north, leading his considerable army as far as Inverness. On 31 July, at the now-lost site of 'Mam Garvia', Roland of Galloway faced the rebels in battle where over 500 of them were killed, including Donald Ban Macwilliam, whose head was sent to the King.

The overlordship of Henry II caused additional problems for King William in the Scottish church; the archbishops of York and Canterbury both claimed the homage of the Scottish clergy. William also had a long-running dispute with the papacy, with five successive popes, in fact, over the appointment of a bishop of St Andrews, with neither approving of the other's candidate. The English king sided with the popes on the matter and in 1181 King William was excommunicated by the archbishop of Canterbury; the Scottish people, as a whole, were subsequently excommunicated by the bishop of Durham. Within two years, however, the papacy and the Scots king were on such good terms that the pope sent William the Golden Rose as a tribute to 'a king of exceptional religious zeal'.[23] On 13 March 1192 Pope Celestine III issued the papal bull, *Cum universi*, recognising the Scottish church as a 'special daughter' of the apostolic see and subject to Rome without an intermediary. Thereby denying the claims to superiority of both York and Canterbury.[24]

Unusually for a king in this period, by 1180 William had been on the throne for fifteen years and was still unmarried, a fact which must have irked

Ada until the day she died. Given the lengths she had gone to in order to get Malcolm to marry, one cannot imagine that she had been any less persuasive with William. Unlike Malcolm's chaste lifestyle, however, William had several illegitimate children, including a daughter, Isabella, who was married to Robert de Brus, heir to the lordship of Annandale, in 1183. Another daughter, Ada, was married to Patrick, Earl of Dunbar and a son, Robert of London was endowed with royal lands. In spite of these children, until he married, William's heir was his younger brother, David. With this in mind, in 1184, William was at King Henry's court to discuss a possible marriage with Henry's granddaughter, Matilda of Saxony. The match was forbidden by the pope on the grounds of consanguinity; both Matilda and William were descendants of Malcolm III and St Margaret. In May 1186, during a council at Woodstock, King Henry suggested Ermengarde de Beaumont as a bride for King William.

Ermengarde was the daughter of Richard, Vicomte de Beaumont-sur-Sarthe, who was himself the son of Constance, one of the many illegitimate daughters of King Henry I of England. With such diluted royal blood, she was hardly a prestigious match for the king of Scots, but he reluctantly accepted the marriage after consulting his advisers. The wedding took place at Woodstock on 5 September 1186, with King Henry hosting four days of festivities; Edinburgh Castle was returned to the Scots as part of Ermengarde's dowry.[25] Although we do not know Ermengarde's birth date, at the time of the marriage, she was referred to as 'a girl', suggesting that she may have only just reached the age of 12, the legal age to marry for girls.[26] King William agreed to provide Ermengarde with £100 of rents and forty knights' fees in Scotland, for the financial maintenance of her household; she also had dwellings and lands at Crail and Haddington, lands which had previously been held by William's mother, Ada de Warenne.[27] After the wedding, King William accompanied King Henry to Marlborough whilst the Scottish queen was escorted to her new home by Jocelin, Bishop of Glasgow, and other Scottish nobles. Between 1187 and 1195 Queen Ermengarde gave birth to two daughters, Margaret and Isabella. A son, the future Alexander II, was finally born at Haddington on 24 August 1198, the first legitimate son born to a reigning Scottish king in seventy years; a contemporary remarked that 'many rejoiced at his birth'.[28] A third daughter, Marjorie, was born sometime later.

On the death of King Henry II in 1189, King William again went south, and met with the new king, Richard I, at Canterbury, where he did homage for his English lands. Desperate for money for his crusade, on 5 December 1189,

Richard abandoned his lordship of Scotland in the quitclaim of Canterbury; King William was released from the homage and submission given to Henry II, the castles of Roxburgh and Berwick were returned and the relationship between the kingdoms reverted to that in the time of Malcolm IV. The cost to the Scots was to be 10,000 marks, but Scotland was independent once again.[29] Richard, however, refused to sell Northumberland back to William; instead, he sold a life-interest in the earldom to the bishop of Durham. The Scots king remained on good relations with King Richard, paying 2,000 marks towards his ransom in 1193 and meeting him at Nottingham in April 1194, where William asked for two favours.

The first favour was a request to be granted an honourable escort and daily subsistence allowances during his visits to the English court: this was granted but not put into effect until the reign of King John. For the second favour, William asked to be granted the earldom of Northumberland, the lordships of Cumberland and Westmorland and the earldom of Lancaster, last held by the Scots in the 1140s. This second favour was, unsurprisingly, refused by Richard.[30] The Scots king carried one of the three swords of state at Richard's solemn crown-wearing at Winchester on 17 April 1194. Two days later, the bishop of Durham surrendered the earldom of Northumberland; William offered 15,000 marks for it and Richard made a counteroffer saying that William could have the earldom but not its castles, which William refused. The matter remained unresolved.

In the spring of 1195 King William fell gravely ill at Clackmannan, causing a succession crisis, the sum of his legitimate children being one, possibly two, daughters at this time – and no son. The Scottish barons appear to have been divided, between recognising William's oldest legitimate daughter, Margaret, as his heir, or marrying Margaret to Otto, Duke of Saxony, grandson of Henry II, and allowing Otto to succeed to the throne. The earl of Dunbar led a faction who claimed that both solutions were contrary to the custom of the land, so long as the king had a brother who could succeed him.[31] In the event, the discussion was moot as the king recovered from his illness and three years later the queen gave birth to Alexander, the much-desired son and heir. For the last years of the century, William was again occupied with unrest in the north. Before going on campaign in October 1201, he had the Scottish barons swear fealty to his son, Alexander, now 3 years old, a sensible precaution, given that he was approaching his sixtieth birthday.

Relations with England had changed in 1199, with the accession of King John. During the reign of King Richard, William had agreed with the justiciar, William Longchamp, and backed Arthur of Brittany as the king's heir. John may well have remembered this. Soon after John's accession, King William asked for the return of Northumberland. The two kings met at Lincoln in 1200, with William doing homage for his English lands and John asking for the discussion over Northumberland to be deferred until Whitsun 1201. John kept putting the matter off until the two kings finally met for formal talks at York from 9 to 12 February 1206 and again from 26 to 28 May 1207, although we have little record of what was discussed. William was confirmed in his lands in Tynedale and John granted Arbroath Abbey trading privileges in England.[32] However, John appears to have been prevaricating, suggesting another meeting in October 1207, which the Scots rejected. The dispute over Northumberland remained unresolved. In the meantime, the death of the bishop of Durham meant John took over the vacant see and set about building a castle at Tweedmouth. The Scots, seeing this as a direct threat to Berwick, destroyed the building works and matters reached a crisis point in 1209.

After many threats, and with both sides building up their armies, the two kings met at Norham, Northumberland, in the last week of July and first week of August 1209. The Scots were in a desperate position, with an ailing and ageing king, and a 10-year-old boy as heir, whilst the English, with their Welsh allies and foreign mercenaries, had an army big enough to force a Scottish submission. The subsequent treaty, agreed at Norham on 7 August, was humiliating for the Scots. They agreed to pay 15,000 marks for peace and to surrender hostages, including the king's two eldest legitimate daughters, Margaret and Isabella. As a sweetener, John promised to marry the princesses to his sons; although Henry was only 2 years old at the time and Richard was just 8 months, whilst the girls were probably in their mid-to-late teens. John would have the castle at Tweedmouth dismantled, but the Scots would pay an extra £4,000 compensation for the damage they had caused to it. The king's daughters and the other Scottish hostages were handed into the custody of England's justiciar, at Carlisle on 16 August.[33] How the girls, or their parents, thought about this turn of events, we know not. Given John's proven record of prevarication and perfidy, King William may have hoped that the promised marriages would occur in good time but may also have expected that John would find a way out of the promises made.

There is no mention of Queen Ermengarde being present for the treaty at Norham, although she did act as mediator in 1212, when her husband was absent, in negotiations with King John at Durham. A contemporary observer described the Scottish queen as 'an extraordinary woman, gifted with a charming and witty eloquence.'[34] It seems likely that King John was not immune to the queen's charms, as he did not ask for more hostages and agreed that the Scottish heir, Alexander, would be knighted and one day marry an English princess. Alexander was knighted at Clerkenwell on 4 March 1212.[35] King William I, later known as William the Lion, died on 4 December 1214, aged about 72, having reigned for a total of forty-nine years, almost to the day. He was succeeded by Alexander, his only legitimate son, who was proclaimed king at Scone on 6 December 1214, aged just 16.

King Alexander II sided with the English barons in their struggle against the tyranny of King John, making an alliance with the northern barons, who agreed to press for a decision on the future of Alexander's sisters, and a resolution of the lordship of the northern counties.[36] He raided the northern English earldoms, exploiting the unrest in England to renew Scottish claims to these counties, besieging Norham in October 1215 and receiving the homage of the leading men of Northumberland on 22 October 1215.[37] In the summer of 1216 Alexander took the castle and town of Carlisle and in September the Scots king marched his army the length of England, from Scotland to Dover to pay homage to the dauphin, Louis, for his English lands. Following John's death in October 1216 and the defeat of the French rebel army at Lincoln in May 1217, Alexander's position in England became precarious. England's status as a papal fief saw Alexander and Scotland put under interdict. The Scots king surrendered Carlisle Castle at Berwick on 1 December 1217 and submitted to Henry III at Northampton later in the same month.[38] With King Alexander's submission, there followed an unprecedented almost eighty years of unbroken peace between England and Scotland. In June 1221, Alexander married Henry III's sister, Joan, in York Minster, with a hope that the Scottish succession was now secured. The marriage remained childless, however, and Alexander remarried after Joan's death in 1238. His second wife, Marie de Coucy, gave birth to a son, two years after their marriage in 1239. He would succeed his father as Alexander III in July 1249, ensuring that the Warenne blood would continue in the Scottish royal family for years to come.

It is hard to assess Ada's contribution to Scottish history beyond her securing the Scottish succession for generations, and her own patronage of religious houses, particularly the nunnery at Haddington, which she founded shortly before her death in 1178. She is believed to be buried in the Haddington area, although the exact location of her grave is lost to history. It is interesting to note that in 1198 her grandson, the future Alexander II, would be born in her old palace at Haddington, after her dower-lands were passed on to Queen Ermengarde. As the surviving information from her charters show, Ada de Warenne, Countess of Huntingdon and Northumbria, spent her entire adult life, forty years, in service to her family, her adopted country and her friends. The dignity by which she bore herself, both as a wife and a widow, is clearly indicated by the foundations she patronised and the contributions made by all three of her sons, to Scotland and its history. She fully deserved the title and accolade of queen mother of Scotland.

Chapter Eight

The Crusading Earl

The year before the treaty of Durham had decided Ada de Warenne's future, Ada and her brothers and sister had grieved the death of their father William, the second earl of Warenne and Surrey. At the time of his death in 1138, William had been earl for half a century. He had fought for William II Rufus, for and against Henry I and was a staunch supporter of King Stephen. He had increased the family's lands and influence, adding the honour of Wakefield to his extensive holdings and building Castle Acre Priory in Norfolk. He had also increased the family's prestige by marrying Isabel de Vermandois, the granddaughter of Henry I, King of France, and his wife, Anne of Kiev. At his death, the second earl had left the earldom in a strong, robust state, with three sons to ensure its continued existence and prosperity. The marriage of his daughter, Ada, to the heir to the Scottish throne in 1140, as a condition of the peace treaty between England and Scotland, was an indication of the heights to which the family had risen and a vindication of the ambitions that the second earl had harboured for himself and his family. It was up to his son, another William, to continue the earl's hard work.

William (III) de Warenne, the third Earl Warenne was born in 1119, a year after his parents' marriage. He was the eldest of five children. His two brothers, Reginald and Ralph, appear frequently in his story, suggesting a close family bond. Of his sisters, Ada, as we have seen, married Prince Henry of Scotland, and was the mother of two Scottish kings. Gundreda de Warenne married Roger de Beaumont, Earl of Warwick, who was a cousin of Gundreda's half-brothers, the famous Beaumont twins, Waleran and Robert. Waleran and Robert de Beaumont were the oldest sons of Isabel de Vermandois by her first husband, Robert de Beaumont, Count of Meulan and Earl of Leicester. Isabel had nine children with her first husband and five more with Earl Warenne. Interestingly, the two families appear to have got on rather well together. William III can often be found in the company of one or both of his older half-brothers, such as at the deathbed of Henry I, at Lyons-la-Forêt in 1135; William was there alongside his father, the second earl, and oldest half-brothers, the twins Waleran de Beaumont, Count of Meulan, and Robert de Beaumont, Earl of Leicester.[1]

As a child, from 1130, William appeared as witness or co-grantor of several of his father's grants and charters, alongside his brother, Ralph. The two boys are described as '*filii nostri Willelmus ... et Radulfus*' ('my sons William and Ralph').[2] The grants included land and rents in Norfolk and 'the priory church of Kingston [Sussex] and an acre of land; and the stalls which Alwin of Winchester held. Also confirmation of a hide of land in Rottingdean [Sussex], which William de Pierrepont held.'[3] Both of these grants were to the Warenne foundation of Lewes Priory in Sussex, where the first earl and his wife, Gundrada, were buried. In the summer of 1138, William may have been the witness and guarantor – though it is unclear whether this was William or his father – in an important charter in which his brother-in-law, Roger, Earl of Warwick, settled the marriage arrangements for his daughter with the chamberlain, Geoffrey de Clinton.[4]

As with all young lords of the time, William de Warenne would have been trained in arms from an early age. Young William's military career, however, had a rather unimpressive start. He was among the young men described by Orderic Vitalis as 'hot-headed youths', who deserted King Stephen during his unsuccessful attempt to take Normandy in 1137.[5] The king's army was in disarray and riven by factions, with William of Ypres and Robert of Gloucester practically at each other's throats. The result was the army – and its leaders – melting away and heading home even before a battle was fought. The duchy had been overrun by Count Geoffrey of Anjou, husband of the rival for Stephen's throne, Empress Matilda. The following year, William's father, the second earl, died and the young man, 19 years old at the most, was now Earl Warenne, his new status confirmed by the king himself. In the same year, he was in Normandy again, this time with his older brother Waleran, Count of Meulan. He was at Rouen with Waleran on 18 December 1138, when they were both witnesses to an agreement arising out of a plea of 1111, in which his father, the second earl had acted in a judicial capacity.[6] The brothers then proceeded to the court of their second cousin, Louis VII of France, on an embassy for King Stephen.[7]

At some point, possibly in the late 1130s, William was married to Ela (or Adela) de Talvas. Ela was the youngest daughter of William de Talvas, Count of Ponthieu, and his wife Ela, daughter of Odo Borel, Duke of Burgundy. Ela's paternal grandfather was Robert de Bellême, the man who had been blamed for the Norman defeat by Henry I at Tinchebrai, having fled the field with his men when he saw the battle was lost.[8] He was later captured by Henry I and imprisoned for the rest of his life, his lands seized. Ela's father, Count William, had the lands returned to him in 1119, but they were again seized by Henry I in 1135. As a consequence, Count William allied himself with Count Geoffrey of Anjou when he invaded Normandy after Henry's death and Stephen claimed the English throne ahead of Geoffrey's wife, Empress Matilda. Ela and William de Warenne would have only one child, a daughter, Isabel, who succeeded her father on his death, as Countess of Warenne and Surrey.

William de Warenne, 3rd Earl Warenne, appears to have been back in England by 1139, along with his half-brother, Waleran. In that year, or early 1140, the young earl appears as a witness, as *'Willelmus comes de Warenna'* on King Stephen's confirmation charter to Alcester Abbey. He would have also been involved in the arrangements for the marriage of his sister, Ada, to Henry of Scotland; the couple married sometime between the signing of the 1139 treaty of Durham and 1140, when the prince returned to Scotland after spending several months in attendance on King Stephen. As Earl Warenne, William was also in attendance at Stephen's court, at this time, where he was witness to at least twelve of the king's charters between 1139 and 1147. This began a career of loyal, if not always distinguished, service to the king whose reign would be marred by civil war. In 1140, William de Warenne was one of four earls in attendance on the king at Norwich and it was at this court that the king gave Thetford, the second town in Norfolk, to Earl William.[9] William already had extensive lands in Norfolk, radiating from his substantial holdings at Castle Acre, which included a castle, a planned village and the Cluniac priory. The earl was a useful counterbalance to the ambitions of Hugh Bigod, Earl of East Anglia. The Bigods and Warennes had a long-standing rivalry which they could trace back to the early days of the Norman Conquest; they had vied for dominance of the county for almost 100 years and had found themselves on opposite sides in previous succession disputes

William was in attendance on King Stephen in early 1141, when news reached the king that Ranulf de Gernons, the disgruntled earl of Chester, had captured Lincoln Castle. Disappointed in his aspirations to Carlisle and Cumberland after they were given to Prince Henry of Scotland, Ranulf had turned his sights on Lincoln Castle, which had been held by his mother, Lucy of Bolingbroke, Countess of Chester. Countess Lucy had died around 1138, leaving her Lincolnshire lands to her son by her second marriage, William de Roumare. Her lands elsewhere had been left to Ranulf de Gernons, who was the son of her third marriage, to Ranulf le Meschin, Earl of Chester. It seems that in late 1140 Ranulf and his half-brother had contrived to gain possession of Lincoln Castle by subterfuge. As the story goes, the two brothers waited until the castle garrison had gone hunting before sending their wives to visit the castellan's wife. A short while after, Earl Ranulf appeared at the castle gates, wearing no armour and with only three attendants, supposedly to collect his wife and sister-in-law. Once allowed inside, he and his men overpowered the small number of men-at-arms left to guard the castle and opened the gates to his brother. The two brothers took control of the castle and, with it, the city of Lincoln.

The citizens of Lincoln appealed to the king, who had promptly arrived outside the castle walls by 6 January 1141 and began his siege. Earl Ranulf escaped from the castle and returned to his lands in Chester in order to raise more troops. He also took the opportunity to appeal to his father-in-law for aid. Ranulf's father-in-law was Robert, Earl of Gloucester, the illegitimate son of Henry I and brother of Empress Matilda. A very capable soldier, Earl Robert commanded Matilda's military forces and his daughter, Maud of Gloucester, was still trapped inside Lincoln Castle. If the need to rescue his daughter was not enough motivation to persuade Robert to intercede at Lincoln, Ranulf also promised to switch his allegiance, and his considerable resources, to Empress Matilda.[10] Robert marched to Lincoln, meeting up with his son-in-law along the way. The earls' forces arrived on the outskirts of Lincoln on 1 February, crossed the Fossdyke and the River Witham and arrayed for battle. Their rapid approach caught Stephen unawares. Outnumbered, Stephen was advised to withdraw his forces, until he could muster enough men to make an even fight of it.

Stephen, perhaps remembering the destruction of his father's reputation after his flight from Antioch, refused to withdraw. He would stand and fight. Before battle, King Stephen attended a solemn mass in the cathedral; according to Henry of Huntingdon, who claimed Bishop Alexander of Lincoln as his patron, and may well have been present, the service was replete with ill omens. As the king 'placed in the hands of Bishop Alexander the taper of wax, the usual royal offering, it broke, betokening the rupture of the kings. The pix [pyx] also, which contained Christ's body snapt its fastening, and fell on the altar while the bishop was celebrating; a sign of the king's fall from power.'[11] After mass, the king led his forces through Lincoln's West Gate, deploying them on the slope leading down to the Fossdyke. He formed his army into three divisions, with mounted troops on each flank and the infantry in the centre. On the right flank were the forces of Waleran de Meulan, William de Warenne, Simon de Senlis, Gilbert of Hertford, Alan of Richmond and Hugh Bigod, Earl of Norfolk. The left was commanded by William of Aumale and William of Ypres, Stephen's trusted mercenary captain, who led a force of Flemish and Breton troops. The centre comprised the shire levy, which included citizens of Lincoln, and Stephen's own men-at-arms, fighting on foot around the royal standard.[12]

The opposing army also deployed in three divisions, with 'the disinherited', those deprived of their lands by King Stephen, on the left. The infantry, comprising of Earl Ranulf's Cheshire tenants and other levies, and dismounted knights were in the centre under Earl Ranulf himself. The cavalry, under the command of Earl Robert of Gloucester formed the right flank. The Welsh mercenaries ill-armed but full of spirits' were arrayed on the wings of the army.[13] Before the battle, Earl Ranulf addressed his father-in-law and fellow barons, saying,

> Receive my hearty thanks, most puissant earl, and you, my noble fellow-soldiers, for that you are prepared to risk your lives in testimony of your devotion to me. But since it is through me you are called to encounter this peril, it is fitting that I should myself bear the brunt of it, and be foremost in the attack on this faithless king, who has broken the peace to which he is pledged. While I, therefore, animated by my own valour, and the remembrance of the king's perfidy, throw myself on the king's troops ... I have a strong presage that we shall put the king's troops to the rout, trample under foot his nobles, and strike himself with the sword.[14]

Earl Robert of Gloucester responded to Ranulf and addressed the army, according to Henry of Huntingdon:
while standing on an eminence, he spoke to this effect:

> It is fitting that you should have the honour of the first blow, both on account of your high rank and your exceeding valour ... The king has inhumanely usurped the crown, faithless to the fealty which he swore to my sister, and by the disorder he has occasioned caused the slaughter of many thousands; and by the example he has set of an illegal distribution of lands, has destroyed the rights of property ... There is one thing, however, brave nobles and soldiers all, which I wish to impress on your minds. There is no possibility of retreat over the marches which you have just crossed with difficulty. Here, therefore, you must either conquer or die, for there is no hope of safety in flight. The only course that remains is, to open a way to the city with your swords. If my mind conjectures truly, as flee you cannot, by God's help you will this day triumph ... You. Victorious, will see the citizens of Lincoln, who stand in array nearest their walls, give way before the impetuosity of your

attack and, with faint hearts, seek the shelter of their houses ... There is Alan of Brittany in arms against us, nay against God himself; a man so execrable, so polluted with every sort of wickedness that his equal in crime cannot be found ... Then, we have opposed to us the Earl of Mellent [Meulan], crafty, perfidious; whose heart is naturally imbued with dishonesty, his tongue with fraud, his bearing with cowardice ... slow in advance, quick in retreat, the last in fight, the first in flight. Next, we have against us Earl Hugh, who not only makes light of his breach of fealty against the empress, but has perjured himself most blatantly a second time; affirming that King Henry conferred the crown on Stephen, and that the king's daughter abdicated in his favour. Then we have the Earl of Albemarle [Aumale], a man singularly consistent in his wicked courses, prompt to embark in them, incapable of relinquishing them; from whom his wife was compelled to become a fugitive, on account of his intolerable filthiness. The earl also marches against us, who carried off the countess just named; a most flagrant adulterer, and a most eminent bawd, a slave to Bacchus and no friend to Mars; redolent of wine, indolent in war. With him comes Simon, earl of Northampton, who never acts but talks, who never gives but promises, who thinks that when he has said a thing he has done it, when he has promised he has performed ... So of the rest of Stephen's nobles: they are like the king; practised in robbery, rapacious for plunder, steeped in blood and all alike tainted with perjury ... If you are of one mind in executing the divine judgement, swear to advance, execrate retreat, and in token of it, unanimously raise your hands to heaven.[15]

Earl Robert's speech spared no criticism of King Stephen's noble commanders. By process of elimination, we can surmise that Earl William de Warenne is the unnamed earl who carried off the wife of the earl of Aumale and is dismissed as a drunken womaniser who was 'indolent in war'. Though Warenne had had little success in conflict, thus far, we can still believe that this harangue is somewhat of an exaggeration and I could find no further details of the earl's supposed abduction of the countess of Aumale, whose own identity is also a mystery. It should be pointed out that Earl Warenne was still relatively young, being no more than 21 years old at the time of the battle; he had managed to achieve quite a reputation in a very short time if Robert of Gloucester was referring to him.

Henry of Huntingdon reports speeches from both sides, exhorting the men to battle and insulting the opposing commanders. As his voice 'was not clear' Baldwin fitz Gilbert was deputed to speak for King Stephen. Henry of Huntingdon again takes up the story:

Placed on a commanding spot where the eyes of all were directed to him, after arresting their attention by a short and modest pause, he thus began: -

All ye who are now about to engage in battle must consider three things: first, the justice of your cause; secondly, the number of your force; and thirdly, its bravery: the justice of your cause that you may not peril your souls; the number of your force that it may not be overwhelmed by the enemy; its valour, lest, trusting to numbers, cowardice should occasion defeat. The justice of your cause consists in this, that we maintain, at the peril of our lives, our allegiance to the king, before God, against those of his subjects who are perjured to him. In numbers we are not inferior in cavalry, stronger in infantry. As to the valour of so many barons, so many earls, and of our soldiers long trained to war, what words can do it justice? Our most valiant king will alone stand in place of a host. Your sovereign, the anointed of the Lord, will be in the midst of you; to him, then, to whom you have sworn fealty, keep your oaths in the sight of God, persuaded that he will grant you his aid according as you faithfully and steadfastly fight for your king, as true men against the perjured, as loyal men against traitors....[16]

Baldwin fitz Gilbert's speech goes on to describe Earl Robert of Gloucester as having 'the mouth of a lion and the heart of a hare', saying he is 'loud in talk, but dull in action.'[17] Earl Ranulf of Chester is described as 'a man of reckless audacity, ready for a plot, not to be depended on in carrying it out, rash in battle, careless of danger; with designs beyond his powers aiming at impossibilities....'[18] The speech is just as scathing for the rest of the rebel army, announcing, 'For the other nobles and knights, they are traitors and turncoats, and I would that there were more of them, for the more there are the less are they to be feared.'[19] The harangue ends with the exhortation, 'Lift up your hearts, and stretch out your hands, soldiers, exultingly, to take the prey which God himself offers to you.'[20]

According to Henry of Huntingdon, the armies mobilised before Baldwin fitz Gilbert's speech ended. The rebels were the first to advance, 'the shouts of the advancing enemy were heard, mingled with the blasts of their trumpets, and the trampling of the horses, making the ground to quake.'[21] The ranks of the 'disinherited' moved forward with swords drawn, rather than lowered lances, intent on close quarter combat. This left flank of the rebel army fell upon Stephen's right flank, 'in which were Earl Alan, the Earl of Mellent [Meulan], with Hugh, the Earl of East Anglia [Norfolk], and Earl Symon, and the Earl of Warenne, with so much impetuosity that it was routed in the twinkling of an eye, one part being slain, another taken prisoner and the third put to flight.'[22] Faced with the ferocity of the assault and the very real prospect of death, rather than being taken prisoner and held for ransom, the earls fled the field with the remnants of their men. It was every man for himself as Stephen's right wing disintegrated in panic.

The left wing of the royal army appeared to have greater success, at least initially. The men of William of Aumale, Earl of York and the mercenary captain, William of Ypres, rode down the earl of Chester's Welsh mercenaries and sent them running, but 'the followers of the Earl of Chester attacked this body of horse, and it was scattered in a moment like the rest.'[23] Other sources suggest that William of Ypres and William of Aumale fled before coming to close quarters with the enemy.[24] Either way, William of Ypres' men were routed and he was in no position to support the king and so fled the field, no doubt aware that he would not be well-treated were he to be captured. Stephen's centre, the infantry, including the Lincolnshire levies and the king's own men-at-arms, were left isolated and surrounded, but continued to fight. Stephen himself was prominent in the vicious hand-to-hand fighting that followed. Henry of Huntingdon vividly describes the desperate scene as 'the battle raged terribly round this circle; helmets and swords gleamed as they clashed, and the fearful screams and shouts re-echoed from the neighbouring hill and city walls.'[25] The rebel cavalry charged into the royal forces killing many, trampling others and capturing some. King Stephen was deep in the midst of the fighting:

> No respite, no breathing time was allowed, except in the quarter in which the king himself had taken his stand, where the assailants recoiled from the unmatched force of his terrible arm. The Earl of Chester seeing this, and envious of the glory the king was gaining, threw himself upon him with the whole weight of his men-at-arms. Even then the king's courage did not fail, but his heavy battle-axe gleamed like lightning, striking down some, bearing back others. At length it was shattered by repeated blows, then he drew his well-tried sword, with which he wrought wonders until that, too, was broken.[26]

According to Orderic Vitalis and the *Gesta Stephani*, it was the king's sword that broke first, before he was passed a battle-axe by one of the fighting citizens of Lincoln, in order to continue the fight.[27] Whatever the order, the king's weapons were now useless and the king 'fell to the ground by a blow from a stone.'[28] Stephen was stunned and a soldier named William de

Cahaignes then rushed at him, seized him by his helmet and shouted, 'Here! Here! I have taken the king!'[29] The king's forces being completely surrounded, flight was impossible. All were killed or taken prisoner, including Baldwin fitz Gilbert, the man who had given the rousing pre-battle speech to the men. In the immediate aftermath of the fighting, Lincoln was sacked, buildings set alight, valuables pillaged, and its citizens slaughtered by the victorious rebels. Defeated, Stephen was first taken to Empress Matilda and then to imprisonment at Bristol Castle. A victorious Matilda was recognised as sovereign by the English people; the people of London being among the first to accept her. By February 1141, the empress had accepted to the submission of Cirencester en route to Winchester, where she met with King Stephen's brother, Henry of Blois, Bishop of Winchester and papal legate. Torn between family and church, and the reality of the situation at the time, Bishop Henry agreed to meet with the empress.

They met on open ground outside Winchester on Sunday 2 March, where empress and bishop came to an agreement, in which the empress promised to consult with Bishop Henry on all important matters of government and to allow him control of the appointment of all bishops and senior churchmen. In return, Bishop Henry agreed to swear allegiance to the empress and to hand over the royal treasury, which was based in Winchester.[30] After a ceremonial procession the next day to Winchester Cathedral, Empress Matilda then moved on to Oxford, while Bishop Henry called a council of prelates to mark a more official acceptance of Empress Matilda's new position. It was at this council that Bishop Henry first proclaimed Matilda *domina Anglorum*, 'lady of the English'.[31]

With Stephen imprisoned and the church behind her, Empress Matilda was now in command of England. In May 1141, she visited her father's tomb at Reading Abbey and there accepted more submissions from Stephen's supporters. The leading magnates of the land did not come over to Matilda as speedily, or in as great numbers, as Matilda had expected or hoped for. While Roger de Beaumont, Earl of Warwick, did go over to Matilda, his cousin Waleran, Count of Meulan and Earl of Worcester, still held for Stephen as did Waleran's younger, half-brother, William de Warenne, Earl of Surrey. By mid-June, the empress was at Westminster, outside the city walls of London, where she received the oath of Geoffrey de Mandeville, castellan of the Tower of London. Not recognising Stephen's appointment of Geoffrey as earl of Essex, Empress Matilda had granted Geoffrey the same earldom by charter.[32]

Empress Matilda was now at the height of her success. Her rival was in her custody, the church was on her side and she had the keys to the royal treasury. She was about to make a ceremonial entry into London, her capital, with the support of her uncle David, King of Scots, and her half-brothers, Robert of Gloucester and Reginald de Dunstanville, now Earl of Cornwall. It was at this point that Bishop Henry petitioned the empress to allow King Stephen's son, Eustace, to receive his father's personal estates, the counties of Boulogne and Mortain. Perhaps remembering how William Clito had been a thorn in her father's side after he had inherited the lands of his father, Robert Curthose, the empress refused. While her approach may be justified and appear as common sense to the casual onlooker, to the barons of England it set a dangerous precedent over the rules of inheritance. If the empress could so easily disinherit the captured king's son, what was there to prevent her from doing the same to the heirs of any of her barons? Matilda appeared to be blaming a child for the acts of his father and as a consequence alienated England's most powerful churchman, Henry of Blois.

The empress's success had turned sour. According to Henry of Huntingdon, she was 'elated with insufferable pride at the success of her adherents in the uncertain vicissitudes of war, so that she alienated from her the hearts of most men.'[33] The *Gesta Stephani* claimed Matilda 'at once put on an extremely arrogant demeanour instead of the modest gait and bearing proper to her gentle sex, began to walk and speak and do all things more stiffly and haughtily than she had been wont … she actually made herself a queen of all England and gloried in being so called.'[34] The *Gesta* goes on to claim that Matilda began acting in an arbitrary manner, taking lands and honours from those who supported Stephen and handing them out to her own supporters. Stating that she acted in 'extreme haughtiness and insolence', the *Gesta Stephani* says Empress Matilda 'arranged everything as she herself thought fit and according to her own arbitrary will.'[35] While such actions would be acceptable in a king, a woman was expected to take the advice and direction of the men around her.

In the meantime, Stephen's queen, Matilda of Boulogne, aided by William of Ypres, had established a secure base in Kent, from where the queen had sent messages to Empress Matilda, petitioning for her to release Stephen and return him to the throne. She now raised an army in Kent and marched on London, burning and ravaging the countryside surrounding the capital. It became apparent to all that the struggle was far from over.

On the eve of the empress's ceremonial entrance into the capital, the city's church bells rang out, a prearranged signal for the citizens to rise against the empress and open the gates to the queen's approaching army. The empress was still at Westminster, an unfortified palace that was not easily defensible.

She had no choice but to flee the approaching forces. Matilda and her half-brother, Robert of Gloucester, and her uncle David, the king of Scots, rode for Oxford. Bishop Henry fled in the opposite direction and shortly afterwards renounced his allegiance to the empress, once again declaring for his brother Stephen. Although things appeared precarious, all was not lost, Queen Matilda now held London, but the empress still had Stephen in her custody and room for manoeuvre. By the end of July, the empress and her army were riding south, to take Winchester, home of the royal treasury. As she approached Winchester, the empress sent a message to Bishop Henry, to meet her outside the city; Henry fled to join with Queen Matilda at Guildford.

Winchester had two castles; the royal one, which held for the empress and Wolvesey, a palatial castle that was the residence of Bishop Henry of Winchester, located in the south-east corner of the city. Empress Matilda arrived at the royal castle of Winchester on 31 July 1141 and began the siege of Wolvesey on 1 August. In their defence, the garrison of the bishop's castle threw burning material from the ramparts, which, in the summer heat, quickly set the whole city ablaze. The stone cathedral survived, but much of the town, built in wood with thatched roofs, was lost. The devastation meant the city's population had lost their homes and livelihoods, and the empress's army were deprived of shelter and provisions. Worse, Queen Matilda was now approaching with an army of her own, which included, among others, Bishop Henry, William of Ypres, the mercenary, and William de Warenne, Earl of Surrey. Empress Matilda's army, besieging Wolvesey Castle now found themselves in a fire-ravaged city and were themselves besieged by the queen's army, camped outside the walls of Winchester. The empress's army was trapped.[36]

Her enemies closed in, tightening the trap. Andover and the surrounding area were burned and the nearby abbey at Wherwell was attacked and burned. The garrison at Wherwell sought shelter in the abbey church, which was also set alight. While many of the empress's soldiers were captured fleeing the burning church, John Marshal, the father of William Marshal, the future regent of England under Henry III, remained inside even as the lead roof of the church fell in upon him. Marshal was badly wounded and lost an eye to the molten lead. Nevertheless, he waited until the queen's army had assumed that he was dead and moved on before emerging from the building and making his painful way home. Things were not going well for the empress, the siege of Wolvesey was at an impasse, supplies were running short and she was left with just three options; starve, surrender or force a breakout of the city. She settled on the latter and they planned a withdrawal for Sunday 14 September.

Matilda led the withdrawal, her uncle, the king of Scots and half-brother Reginald of Cornwall with her; Robert of Gloucester commanded the rearguard. All went well until the army reached the ford of the River Test at Stockbridge. So many men trying to cross caused a bottleneck and the queen's army closed in: 'The king's troops poured in upon them from all sides in countless numbers with so much impetuosity that they were routed and dispersed.'[37]. Robert of Gloucester made a stand at the ford, trying to give the empress, and main body of the army, time to make their escape. According to William of Malmesbury the earl of Gloucester 'himself retreated gently, with a chosen few, who had spirit enough not to be alarmed at a multitude. The earls immediately pursuing him, as he thought it disgraceful, and beneath his dignity to fly, and was the chief object of universal attack, he was made captive.'[38] Robert of Gloucester was captured by William de Warenne, in command of a party of Flemish mercenaries, perhaps redeeming himself for his flight from the Battle of Lincoln. Earl Robert had achieved his purpose; the empress had got away, making first for Ludgershall and then to Devizes, riding astride like a man, before finally arriving at Gloucester, totally exhausted.

Thanks to William de Warenne's capture of Robert, Earl of Gloucester, the empress's half-brother and the commander of her armies, the royalists now had a valuable bargaining chip which they would use to negotiate for the release of King Stephen. As Henry of Huntingdon tells us, his capture 'secured the king's release, by a mutual exchange. Thus the king who, by God's judgement, had been exposed to a painful captivity, was by God's mercy liberated; and the English people greeted him with great rejoicings.'[39] William de Warenne's capture of Earl Robert of Gloucester had been fortuitous indeed for King Stephen. By November 1141 the king was back in control and holding council in London, where Bishop Henry had an uncomfortable time, explaining himself and his actions to his brother. Although his claims that he had acted under duress were accepted by the king, his reputation and influence had suffered severely. William de Warenne, 3rd Earl Warenne, was with Stephen's court when it moved to Canterbury for Christmas, 1141, where the king was symbolically re-crowned, by Archbishop Theobald of Canterbury, on Christmas Day. The earl appears alongside seven other earls, including Simon de Senlis and William of Aumale, who had both been at the Battle of Lincoln, in a charter granted to Geoffrey de Mandeville by the king.[40] He was witness to another of Stephen's charters, at Ipswich, shortly afterwards.[41]

Barely two years later, in September 1143, Earl Warenne was with the king at St Albans when Geoffrey de Mandeville, Earl of Essex, was arrested. Though the reason for his arrest is not entirely certain, it may have something to do with Mandeville's detention of Constance, Stephen's daughter-in-law, when Queen Matilda had been forced to abandon London in 1141. The queen and princess had been staying at the Tower of London when the empress approached the capital. Although the queen had been allowed to leave, Geoffrey de Mandeville had insisted that Constance, the teenage bride of Stephen's son and heir, Eustace, stay behind. Whatever the reason for the arrest, Mandeville was forced to relinquish the Tower of London and his castles at Pleshey and Walden in order to gain his freedom. This sent Mandeville into open rebellion for the remainder of his life; he died a year later while besieging the royal garrison at Burwell.[42] During Mandeville's revolt, William de Warenne was also involved in an expedition against St Albans, in which he and three other of Stephen's military captains were prevented from burning the town by a large bribe from Geoffery, abbot of St Albans.[43] It is notable that Earl Warenne's twin half-brothers, Robert and Waleran de Beaumont, are missing from the Canterbury charter; the empress's recent success had caused them to waver in their support of Stephen. Another factor affecting the Beaumont brothers was the success of the empress's husband, Geoffrey of Anjou, in Normandy, where they each had extensive lands.

By 1143 Geoffrey of Anjou's five-year campaign in Normandy was coming to its inevitable conclusion. He was welcomed into Rouen, the duchy's capital, in January 1144. Rouen Castle, however, held out. Defended by the men of William de Warenne, the castle endured a three-month siege that lasted until 23 April, when their supplies ran out and the defenders had no choice but to surrender. Count Geoffrey was aided in the siege by Rotrou, Count of Perche, who was killed during the siege, and Waleran de Beaumont, William de Warenne's older brother. Concerned for his lands in the Vexin, where he was count of Meulan, Waleran may have wavered in his support of Stephen following the Battle of Lincoln. When he returned to Normandy at the end of 1141, he and his twin brother, Robert, Earl of Leicester, appear to have come to an agreement. They divided their lands and their interests based on each other's main area of influence. Waleran, with his lands in the Vexin, agreed to come to terms with Geoffrey of Anjou while Robert returned to England to take care of the brothers' interests there.[44] Conversely, their half-brother, William de Warenne, fought in Normandy for King Stephen for some of the time in 1142 and 1143 where he appears to have been Stephen's sole commander, though he was still only in his 20s.[45]

With the fall of Rouen, Geoffrey finally assumed the title of Duke of Normandy, and was formally recognised as such by his overlord, King Louis of France. Nevertheless, pockets of resistance still held out, including Earl Warenne's men at Drincourt, now known as Neufchâtel-en-Brai, which he would surrender later in the year.[46] It is not recorded whether the earl was actually present during the siege, though it is noted that it was to his own half-brother, Waleran that the castle was finally surrendered.[47]

Earl Warenne was back in England before the end of 1144 and was at court on at least two occasions in 1144 and 1145.[48] Although the conflict between Stephen and Matilda was still not resolved, Earl Warenne and his half-brother, Waleran de Beaumont, appear to have wanted to get away from the constant unrest of the cousins' war and looked to join a more noble enterprise. On 24 March 1146, Palm Sunday, near Vézélay, and perhaps motivated by the example of his royal cousin, Louis VII of France, William de Warenne took the cross and committed himself to the Second Crusade. From this moment on, the earl's time was taken up with preparations for the expedition and making arrangements to ensure the security and administration of his earldom during his absence. Among others, he confirmed grants to Castle Acre Priory of the land of Thexton in Norfolk which Osmoda de Candos had given with the consent of her husband Philip: William's brother Reginald is named in the charter and his brother Ralph, as well as his wife, Countess Ela, are both listed among the witnesses.[49] He also confirmed a gift made to his brother Reginald whereby William son of Philip, gave his land of Harpley in Norfolk.[50] During the winter of 1146–47, the earl granted to the monks of Castle Acre, a confirmation of any acquisitions which they might make, 'from my fee of whatever tenancy within my *tenseria* [authority], whether by way of gift or purchase.'[51]

In 1147, before leaving England's shores, the earl, his family and leading magnates congregated at Lewes Priory for the dedication of the new priory church. Most of the royal court were present, as were Ralph and Reginald de Warenne, the earl's brothers; four leading church prelates attended, including Theobald, Archbishop of Canterbury and Henry of Blois, Bishop of Winchester as well as the bishops of Rochester and Bath. Also present were the abbots of Reading and Battle, the prior of Canterbury and William d'Aubigny, Earl of Sussex.[52] Earl Warenne used the occasion to confirm to Lewes Priory 'all of its lands, churches and tithes of his fee (specified in detail), including in Yorkshire the church of Conisbrough with its other churches, chapels, lands, and tithes, and the churches of Wakefield and Dewsbury.'[53] Ralph and Reginald, the earl's two brothers, were both witnesses to this charter and a second one which confirmed to the priory 'the church of Conisbrough with the churches, chapels, lands and tithes belonging thereto, namely the churches of Braithwell, Dinnington, Harthill, Fishlake, Hatfield with the chapel of Thorne, and Kirk Sandal with the chapel of Armthorpe; also the churches of Wakefield with the chapel of Horbury, Dewsbury with the chapel of Hartshead, Kirkburton, and Sandal Magna.'[54]

The most significant charter issued on this occasion added to the endowment of Lewes' priory church and promised that the earl would pay the taxes that the priory would ordinarily owe to the king. In it, the earl confirmed 'all its lands of his fee, undertaking to acquit it of danegeld and all other services due to the king; and gift of tithe of corn, etc., from all his demesne lands and a full tenth penny of all his rents in England. He issued the charter when he caused the priory church to be dedicated and endowed it with the tenth penny of his rents, giving it seisin thereof by hair from his own head and that of Ralph de Warenne his brother, cut with a knife by Henry, bishop of Winchester, before the altar.'[55] The locks of hair of Earl William and his brother Ralph, ceremoniously cut off by Bishop Henry before the altar, would afterwards have been placed on the altar, alongside the knife used in the ceremony, and may have later been 'filed' within the charter when it was sealed.[56]

His affairs in order, the earldom was placed under the supervision of his very capable brother, Reginald de Warenne. The pope stipulated that church sanctions should not be invoked, 'in respect of those men whom our beloved son Stephen the illustrious king of the English or his adversaries disinherited on the occasion of the war held for the realm before they took the cross.'[57] In a time of continued civil war, this guaranteed protection of a crusader's lands was a necessity. Earl William was now able to depart on crusade, secure in the knowledge that the family and lands he left behind were well protected from anyone wishing to take advantage of his absence:

> At Whitsuntide Lewis [Louis], king of France, and Theodorie, earl of Flanders, and the count of St Egidius, with an immense multitude from every part of France, and numbers of the English, assumed the cross and journeyed to Jerusalem, intending to expel the Infidels who had taken the city of Rohen. A still greater number accompanied Conrad, emperor of Germany; and both armies passed through the territories of the emperor of Constantinople, who afterwards betrayed them.[58]

There were, in fact, two crusades that departed England's shores in 1147. Some of the crusaders, an Anglo-Flemish force, went to Portugal and successfully captured Lisbon from the Muslims. Earl William de Warenne and his older brother Waleran de Beaumont joined their cousin King Louis VII of France and set out for the Holy Land. Taking the overland route, they followed in the footsteps of the German emperor, Conrad III, who had left Germany in May and arrived in Constantinople in September. Louis, accompanied by his wife Eleanor of Aquitaine, arrived in Constantinople with his army, on 4 October.

Tensions ran high from the start. On initially hearing of the proposed crusade, Byzantine emperor Manuel Comnenus, afraid of losing local trading connections, made a truce with the Turkish sultan of Rum in 1146 to protect Constantinople's Asian lands from attack. To the Western crusaders, this was more proof of the apostasy of the Eastern church. The more fervent of Louis' followers accused Emperor Manuel of treason and urged Louis to attack the emperor. Louis, on the other hand, was persuaded to appease the emperor by his less volatile advisers and the king promised to restore any imperial lands they may capture.[59]

The German and French contingents met at Nicaea in November, with the Germans having already suffered a defeat at Dorylaeum on 25 October, after taking the inland route towards the kingdom of Jerusalem. The two armies combined now set off on the coastal route, following the path of the first crusaders' advance into Philadelphia in Lydia.[60] By the time they reached Ephesus, Conrad was seriously ill and returned to Constantinople to recover. The French king and his army continued on to Antioch; marching through difficult terrain in mid-winter proved particularly harrowing. The Seljuk Turks waited for the crusaders on the banks of the river Meander, but Louis' army forced their way through. On 6 January 1148, they reached Laodicea and from there marched into the mountains that separate the Phrygia of the Pisidia. It was here that the army met with disaster.

As they crossed Mount Cadmus, the vanguard advanced too far ahead under the leadership of Geoffrey de Rançon, thus becoming detached from the main body of the army. As the vanguard progressed across Mount Cadmus, the French column followed behind, secure in the knowledge that the vanguard occupied the high ground to their front. William de Warenne was in the king's bodyguard, towards the rear of the column, as they advanced. When the Turks appeared, the French broke their ranks and rushed upon them with swords drawn; the disorder in the ranks handing the advantage to their enemy. Retreating, the French found themselves in a narrow gorge, with a steep precipice on one side and crags on the other. Horses, men and baggage were forced over the precipice by the advancing

Turks. King Louis' bodyguard was cut down in the fighting and William de Warenne was among the fallen. Louis himself was able to escape the carnage, standing alone against a number of attackers. As the night drew in, the king and survivors were able to take advantage of the darkness to reunite with the vanguard, which had been believed lost.[61] In one of his letters to Abbot Sugar, King Louis wrote of the disaster on Mount Cadmus, explaining how he had been separated from the vanguard and his escort had been cut down, with the loss of his cousin, William de Warenne. He was too upset to give any more details and Mount Cadmus remains a battle of which very little is known beyond the basic details.[62]

Despite the heavy losses, King Louis' crusade continued, reuniting with the German contingent between March and June 1148. They failed to take Edessa and were forced to withdraw from Damascus after a week of heavy fighting, when fresh Muslim forces arrived. The crusade ended in failure and the French king, who blamed Emperor Manuel Comnenus for the fiasco, accepted the aid of Manuel's enemy Roger of Sicily, who sent ships to take the French forces home. Of the English forces, while William de Warenne was lost at Mount Cadmus, his brother Waleran de Beaumont, Count of Meulan and Earl of Worcester, made it back to England's shores, narrowly surviving a shipwreck along the way; he founded a monastery in gratitude. Of the two Anglo-Norman bishops who accompanied the crusade, Roger of Chester died at Antioch and was buried there, whereas Arnulf of Lisieux, who had served as one of the leading diplomats, returned but with his reputation faded.

Perhaps it was always on the cards that Earl William de Warenne's unspectacular military career would end with his death in battle. He was only 28 years old and had held the earldom for just over nine years. The earl had been a stalwart supporter of King Stephen, not once wavering in his allegiance, despite his failures in Normandy and at Lincoln early on in his career. He had done extensive work on the family's property at Castle Acre, reinforcing the castle and replanning the town, building the ramparts that now surround it. The new fortifications had three purposes. The first and obvious one being for defence, especially in the uncertain times of civil war and a disputed crown. The second purpose was financial; the gates of a walled town made the collection of tolls far easier and more efficient, and more difficult for traders to avoid. The third and final reason was status, giving the impression of power, riches and authority, over the Warenne lands.

William de Warenne, the third earl, had been a generous benefactor to the church, especially the Warenne foundations at Lewes and Castle Acre.

Among his grants were included permissions to the infirmarer at Lewes Priory to 'take venison outside the parks' and a licence to 'fish in all his fisheries and waters of Lewes for the use of their sick, an official of the earl being present.'[63] The canons of Thetford Priory were given permission to hold a fair for two days. To the abbey of St Mary's in York, the earl gave 'Haines [in Hatfield] with the moor and marsh surrounding it and "Munkeflet" with its fisheries; also at the feast of the Assumption 3 good pike and 12 breams in Bradmere.'[64] To Castle Acre Priory, Earl William issued a writ to 'Robert de Freville and all his barons of Norfolk in favour of Castle Acre priory, directing that the monks should hold their tenure in Massingham [Norfolk] as they held it on the day when he gave the vill to Robert de Freville the younger.'[65] Sometime before he left on crusade, the earl also made a gift 'to the Templars of 40s yearly from his rents of Lewes.'[66] Even in his absence on crusade, the earl was still technically in charge; his brother, Reginald, issued a number of charters, each with the proviso that 'if Jesus Christ brought back the earl [from the crusade] he would cause him to confirm it' or 'do his best to obtain the earl's confirmation.'[67]

The death of the third earl of Warenne and Surrey brought an end to the senior male line that had been founded with the creation of the earldom for William (I) de Warenne in 1088. The earl was survived by his wife, Ela de Talvas, still a young woman, and his daughter, Isabel de Warenne, who was now the richest heiress in England. The earl's estates were left in the capable hands of his youngest brother, Reginald de Warenne, Baron of Wormegay.

Chapter Nine

The Warennes of Wormegay

Reginald de Warenne was one of the three sons of William de Warenne, 2nd Earl Warenne and Isabel de Vermandois. Through his mother, he was a second cousin of King Louis VII of France and half-brother to the Beamont twins, Waleran and Robert, earls of Worcester and Leicester respectively. In the genealogical notes of the Lewes Cartulary he is given as a younger son of the second earl, though in a senior position to his brother Ralph. However, in the charters of their brother, the 3rd earl, in which both appear as witnesses, it is Ralph who appears first, in the place of seniority.[1] Moreover, it is Ralph who appears, alongside their brother William, in a number of charters of the second earl, in which the two boys appear alongside their parents as grantors of Warenne land and rents to the priory at Lewes.[2] This charter evidence suggests, therefore, that the order of birth was William and then Ralph, with Reginald being the youngest son. Reginald's parents did not marry until June 1118, so, with two older brothers, the earliest date of birth for Reginald would be 1121: as he was of age by 1147, when he was left in charge of the Warenne estates on the third earl's departure on crusade, his latest possible date of birth is 1126. In addition to his brothers William, the third Earl Warenne, and Ralph, Reginald had two sisters, Gundreda, Countess of Warwick and Ada, Countess of Huntingdon and Northumberland, one or both of whom may have been older than him. Reginald was, therefore, born sometime between 1121 and 1126, but without further evidence it is impossible to narrow this down.

From the time that William became the third Earl Warenne, in 1138, Reginald appears as a regular witness in his brother's charters, though he was still only a teenager. As we have seen, he was at the dedication ceremony of the new church for Lewes Priory in 1147, acting as witness on the charters in which his brother, the earl, confirmed his donations to the Priory as part of his preparations for the crusade.[3] Even before Earl William's departure for the Holy Land, Reginald was active in the estate management of the family's holdings in Norfolk. Although only a younger son, Reginald was enfeoffed of many lands belonging to the vast honour of Warenne, including the manors of Plumpton and Barcombe in Sussex and a large estate in Norfolk. Between 1159 and 1164 he was also enfeoffed of the manor of Hartshill, in the honour of Conisbrough, which he and his descendants held as an under-tenancy of the honour. He gave the church at Plumpton to the priory of St Mary Overie at Southwark and he gave his tenement of Shernborne, Norfolk, to Lewes Priory.[4] He also made gifts to Carrow, Clerkenwell and Binham priories, and a quitclaim to Battle Abbey.[5]

Between 1138 and 1147, the earl confirmed a number of grants made by his younger brother, including 'the gift made by Reginald de Warenne to Lewes priory of a messuage in the borough [of Lewes] and "Pilecestrete" which adjoined.'[6] In another, the earl confirmed a gift by Reginald to Lewes priory 'of the mill of Attlebridge [Norfolk], and of a sokeman named Turold de Scottow, rendering half a mark of silver.'[7] Just before leaving on crusade, in either 1146 or 1147, the earl confirmed 'the gift which William son of Philip [de Burnham] made to Reginald his brother of his land of Harpley [Norfolk].'[8] Such charters serve to demonstrate that Reginald was actively involved in the administration of the Warenne's Norfolk estates. Moreover, the charters issued by Reginald during the earl's absence serve to demonstrate that the younger brother was always aware that the earl was still ultimately in command, and that he acted in expectation that his brother would approve of his actions. One charter was a notification 'by Reginald de Warenne to William, prior of Lewes, that he confirmed the hide of land in Rottingdean given to the priory by Ralph d'Angiens, and that if Jesus Christ brought back the earl [from the crusade] he would cause him to confirm it.'[9] It is a testament to the trust that the earl had placed in Reginald, and also to Reginald's loyalty, that he always seems to have acted as he thought his brother would expect. It is also a clear indication of the close family bonds that all three brothers appear to have held.

Another charter was a notification:

> to the sheriff and all the barons of the earl [de Warenne] that by the counsel of the prior of Lewes and the earl's barons he had restored to the burgesses of Lewes the gild-merchant as they had had it in the time of his grandfather and his father, rendering 20s yearly to the prefecture of Lewes; undertaking that if God should bring back the earl [from the crusade] he would do his best to obtain the earl's confirmation, or otherwise that of his lord earl William, the king's son.[10]

This last charter was issued in 1148 or soon after and confirms that news of the earl's death at Mount Cadmus in January 1148 had not yet reached

England. This causes some confusion, however, as William of Blois is named as 'lord earl William, the king's son', which suggests that the young prince, married to the earl's daughter, had already been recognised as earl of Warenne and Surrey. It may be that calling young William 'earl' was a courtesy title to give the prince some authority, or may suggest that while they had not had confirmation of the third earl's death, the family were already aware that there was a strong possibility of it. Alternatively, it could suggest that the third earl had settled the succession of the earldom on William and Isabel, even before his departure for the Holy Land, just in case, though the wording of the charter appears to contradict such a suggestion. One final option is that King Stephen had bestowed an earldom on his youngest son, in addition to the Warenne earldom he was set to inherit, although this is mere conjecture as there is no surviving charter evidence to confirm this.[11]

Reginald proved to be a most able administrator of the Warenne estates, working on his brother's behalf during the latter's absence on crusade and, later, on behalf of William of Blois, the young husband of the third earl's daughter, Isabel de Warenne, for whom Reginald became principal adviser.[12] William of Blois was the youngest son of King Stephen and, though still only a child, was married to the Warenne heiress probably before Earl Warenne departed on crusade. With the protection of the king, the marriage not only guaranteed the security of the Warenne lands but also ensured the vast Warenne holdings would not fall into the hands of the king's enemies. Stephen was still, after all, in the midst of a long-running civil war, with the end still several years in the future and this ensured that the Warenne affinity of knights and men-at-arms would remain at the king's disposal.

The extent of Reginald de Warenne's influence is indicated in the fact that he appears in the terms of the treaty between King Stephen and Henry, Duke of Normandy and Count of Anjou. The 1153 Treaty of Winchester was drawn up to bring an end to the conflict that had ravaged England for almost two decades, the conflict in which Henry's mother, Empress Matilda, had fruitlessly wrestled to take the throne from her cousin, King Stephen. In it, perhaps in recognition for Reginald's continued administration of the Warenne lands for Stephen's youngest son, William of Blois, now earl of Warenne and Surrey by right of his wife, Reginald was given the option of having the custody of the castles of Bellencombre and Mortemer in Normandy:

> the agreement being that Reginald de Warenne shall, if he wish, keep the castle of Bellencombre and the castle of Mortemer, giving the duke hostages in respect of them; but if Reginald does not wish to do so then other liegemen of the earl of Warenne acceptable to the duke shall keep the said castles.[13]

These two castles were the centre of the Warenne holdings in Normandy and had belonged to the first earl long before he had joined the invasion of England in 1066.[14] Reginald was even among the thirty-seven witnesses to the Westminster charter, the king's notification of the treaty, perhaps a recognition of his vital role in the administration of the vast Warenne holdings and his extensive administrative experience. Thirteen bishops and twelve earls were also witness to the charter. Given that he was one of only eight laymen of lower rank who attested the charter, it is possible that he played an active role in its creation.[15] It is interesting to note that, according to *The Chronicle of Battle Abbey*, in the uncertain times that marked the end of the reign of King Stephen and the accession of Henry II, Reginald de Warenne made an agreement of mutual support with Richard de Lucy, a favourite of Henry II, and his half-brother Robert of Leicester, whereby each would look after the others' interests wherever they could.[16]

Early in his career, Reginald had married Alice, or Adeliza, daughter and heir of William of Wormegay in Norfolk. Just six miles south of Kings Lynn, Wormegay was only fourteen miles west of the Warenne castle and village at Castle Acre. Reginald became baron of Wormegay by right of his wife on William's death in 1166. Alice's parentage is given in a charter to Southwark Priory, which was issued by Reginald de Warenne. Alice's father, William de Wormegay had succeeded to the barony sometime before Michaelmas (29 September) 1160, when he not only paid £100 for his land but also assumed the responsibility for a debt in Norfolk and Suffolk which had previously been owed by Richard de Wormegay.[17] In 1161, William made a payment towards the debt of £20. In 1165 he paid £15 5s for scutage for the army of Wales. According to the details of his *carta*, drawn up in 1166, the barony was comprised of fourteen and a quarter knights' fees of old feoffment, and a quarter of a knights' fee of new feoffment made by his father, who is likely to have been the Richard de Wormegay who was still living in 1159. This meant the barony of Wormegay held a total of fourteen-and-a-half knights' fees on William's succession in 1160. When he inherited the barony, before Michaelmas 1166, Reginald de Warenne owed £466 13s 4d for a fine of the land of William de Wormegay. The debt appears in the Pipe Rolls and Reginald made no payments towards it until Michaelmas 1176, when he paid £166 13s 4d, leaving a balance of £300. In the following year, Reginald paid a further £133 6s 8d towards the debt, leaving a balance of £166 13s 4d which was due at Michaelmas 1178.[18]

The year after he became baron of Wormegay, in 1168, Reginald paid £9 10s for the aid for the marriage of the king's daughter, Matilda. The aid was a mark per fee, with Reginald's assessment being fourteen-and-a-quarter fees of old feoffment and one quarter fee of new feoffment; these fees corresponding exactly with the fees recorded in the *carta* by William de Wormegay in 1166. As baron of Wormegay he was also included among the escort that accompanied Matilda to Saxony for her wedding to Henry the Lion, Duke of Saxony and Bavaria. In the same year, Reginald is recorded as owing 3s 4d in respect of a new feoffment; the debt is included in the ensuing Pipe Rolls and was still due at Michaelmas 1178. In addition to this, Reginald owed £14 10s at Michaelmas 1172, for the honour of Wormegay; 5s was included in respect of a new feoffment, for the scutage of Ireland. Of this debt, he had paid the £14 by Michaelmas 1176, but still owed the remaining 10s at Michaelmas 1178. At Michaelmas 1179, the year after Reginald's death, his wife Alice is recorded as owing 200 marks for a fine of her land of Wormegay and £166 13s 4d (the balance of the fine owed by Reginald on his accession to the barony in 1166). Poor Alice also owed the 3s 4d and 10s that had been due from Reginald in the preceding year.[19]

For a younger son, Reginald had an impressive administrative career in the reign of King Henry II, son of Empress Matilda, who acceded to the throne on the death of King Stephen in 1154. Reginald held a number of positions under the first Plantagenet king. In 1164 he was present at the Council of Clarendon, at which the Constitutions of Clarendon were produced, comprising sixteen articles aimed at curbing the privileges and power of the church, and the extent of papal authority in England. Between 1168 and 1176, Reginald was a justice itinerant in several counties, in September 1169 he was one of the barons of the Exchequer and from Easter 1170 to Michaelmas 1178, he was sheriff of Sussex.[20] He witnessed a large number of charters, and not just for his brother the earl. Sometime between 1146 and 1154, he witnessed several charters for King Stephen, in 1157 and 1165, he witnessed charters for King Henry II and in 1158 he witnessed a charter for the queen, Eleanor of Aquitaine.[21] Reginald de Warenne was in attendance on the king in 1157, at Battle Abbey, when Henry II acted as judge in a dispute between Archbishop Theobald of Canterbury and Abbot Silvester of St Augustine's Abbey, Canterbury, and the abbot of Battle Abbey.[22]

As you would expect, Reginald witnessed many charters for his niece, Isabel, and her second husband, Hamelin; he also witnessed a charter issued to May priory by Duncan, Earl of Fife, who may have been his son-in-law. In 1170, perhaps as a result of Thomas Becket's refusal to allow the proposed marriage between his niece, Isabel, and Henry II's brother, William of Anjou, Reginald was among those who opposed the archbishop of Canterbury's landing in England.

Reginald and Alice had a number of children, including three or four daughters. Although their identities are not known with certainty, it is likely that they were Gundreda, Alice, Muriel and Ela. One daughter, Gundreda de Warenne, married three times: first to Peter de Valognes, then William de Curcy III and finally to Geoffrey Hose. It seems likely that Gundreda and Peter de Valognes were married as children, with Gundreda's father having acted as Peter de Valognes' guardian after he succeeded to his father's estates as a minor. Reginald had close associations with the Valognes family, having given grants to the priory of Binham, a Valognes foundation; moreover, the Valognes held a tenancy of the honour of Warenne. This would explain the connection with the Valognes which saw Gundreda receive Little Fakenham as her *maritagium*, which was a Valognes under-tenancy. Gundreda's marriage to Peter de Valognes is mentioned in a case of 1234–35 in relation to the descent of land in Dersingham, Norfolk, which formed part of Peter's barony of Valognes. In it, it is stated that Peter was the oldest of three brothers, and he had died without an heir of his body. His wife is named as Gundreda de Warenna, who had held the land at Dersingham for the rest of her life as her dower. According to the judgement, the land had descended to the children of Robert, Peter's next brother, and then to the ultimate heirs, the granddaughters of Philip, the third and youngest brother.[23]

Peter was dead by 1160, when his brother Robert had rendered account of 200 marks for his land. In his *carta* of 1166, Robert stated that Gundreda had been given a knights' fee of new feoffment for life by Peter. A return of 1219 states that Gundreda was in the king's gift and held Dersingham, valued at £30. Gundreda's second husband, William de Curcy III, died in 1171. Although Gundreda had no children with her first husband, with William she had a son, William de Curcy IV, who appears to have come of age in 1189, and a daughter, Alice, who inherited the honour of Curcy on her brother's death in the 1190s. As William de Curcy's widow, Gundreda held a dower property in Nuneham Courtney, Oxfordshire, which in 1219 was worth £15, yearly. In 1194, an assize of darrein presentment was called relating to the church at Nuneham Courtney, in which Gundreda de Warenne claimed the advowson of the church against the abbot of Abingdon.[24]

Gundreda's third husband was Geoffrey Hose, or de la Huse. He was the sheriff of Oxfordshire from 1179 to 1182 and died sometime between September 1192 and September 1193, when Gundreda's brother William de Warenne of Wormegay paid £22 17s in Wiltshire for the issue of the land which had belonged to Geoffrey Hose, and which William held in his custody. The custody of the land then passed to Robert de Tresgoz.[25] On

11 June 1199, at Canterbury, King John granted 'to Gundreda de Warenne, widow of Geoffrey Hose, that she may have the custody of Geoffrey Hose son and heir of her late husband, with all his lands until he comes of age, and the right to decide his marriage, and for this concession she has given the king 200 marks.'[26] Gundreda completed the payment of the 200 marks at Michaelmas 1202.

Gundreda de Warenne died in 1224, over sixty years after the death of her first husband, Peter de Valognes, and over fifty years after the death of her second husband. It was in December 1224 that the daughters of Gundreda's daughter, Alice, claimed the vill of Nuneham, Gundreda's dower land from her second husband, as their inheritance. Alice was the heiress of her brother, William de Curcy IV. Her daughters were Joan, wife of Hugh de Neville, who was chief forester and one of King John's hated councillors, and Margaret, who married in turn Baldwin de Redvers, son of the 5th earl of Devon, and then Faulkes de Bréauté, another of King John's adherents; he also fought at the 1217 Battle of Lincoln.

Reginald de Warenne, Baron of Wormegay, had a second daughter, Alice de Warenne, who was described as the widow of Peter the Constable in an assize in 1213 in which the prior of Wormegay had given a palfrey for having a writ of this assize. This Peter is identified as Peter de Mealton or Meltone, sheriff of Norfolk and Suffolk from 1200 to 1203. In 1214, Alice was the defendant in an assize of darrein presentment to the church of East Tuddenham, Norfolk, brought by the prior of Wormegay. A darrein presentment is a legal action brought to determine who was the last patron to appoint to a vacant church benefice and therefore who could make the next appointment. East Tuddenham was a part of the honour of Wormegay, where in 1232–33 the constable Peter de Meltone held a knights' fee. This would suggest that Peter the Constable had acquired the knights' fee through his wife as her *maritagium* and it then passed down through Peter's family.[27]

It seems likely that Reginald de Warenne had two further daughters. One named Muriel, who became a nun at Carrow Priory when William de Warenne of Wormegay, her brother, made a gift to that house of land in Stow Bartolph. A fourth daughter is thought to be Ela, or Adela, who married Duncan, Earl of Fife, and who was a companion of her aunt, Ada de Warenne, Countess of Huntingdon and Northumberland.[28] Reginald and Alice also had one son, Reginald's heir, William. In a charter issued by William, it is stated that Reginald de Warenne became a monk at Lewes Priory, sometime in 1178. Having pursued a lifetime of service, both to his family and the Crown, Reginald died at the priory of St Pancras, Lewes, before Michaelmas 1179 and was buried there. William de Warenne succeeded as baron of Wormegay, rendering account at Michaelmas 1180 of 200 marks for the fine of the land of Wormegay, made by his mother with the king in 1179. He also rendered account for the fine of £166 13s 4d for the fine made by his father; a total of £300 of which he paid £55 11s. He was also responsible for the smaller sums of 3s 4d and 10s which his father had still owed at his death. William paid the outstanding sums in instalments, which were completed by Michaelmas 1189. The smaller sums, however, were still due at Michaelmas 1203. At Michaelmas 1190, William owed a scutage of £7 2s 6d in Norfolk and Suffolk for knights of the honour of Wormegay, a holding of fourteen-and-a-half knights' fees; the same number as his father had held. This remained consistent in subsequent years.[29]

As well as inheriting Wormegay from his mother, William de Warenne also inherited his father's holdings of the honour of Warenne, including the under-tenancy at Harthill, Yorkshire. He quitclaimed to Lewes Priory the advowson of Harthill in exchange for a quitclaim of Portslade, Sussex. He also gave the priory land at Brighton in exchange for the mill of Newhaven, which his father had given to the priory when he became a monk at Lewes. William married, as his first wife, Beatrice, thought to be the daughter of Hugh de Pierrepont, a member of the Warenne affinity. The couple had one daughter, Beatrice, who survived into adulthood; the younger Beatrice mentions a brother and sister, Reginald and Isabel respectively, in a charter to Southwark priory, who appear to have died before their father.[30]

William married again in 1203, this time to Milisent, the widow of Richard de Montfichet, sheriff of Essex and Hertfordshire from 1200. At Michaelmas 1203 he owed 500 marks, 400 marks for her as his wife and 100 marks for her dower but was pardoned 200 of the 400 marks and made a payment on account at Michaelmas 1208. Milisent's son by Richard, also Richard, and his lands were given in wardship to Roger de Lascy, constable of Chester. In October 1203, the king ordered that, as William had made the fine of 100 marks in respect of Milisent's dower, she should receive custody of it as soon as de Lascy returned to England, if not before.[31]

William de Warenne of Wormegay continued the tradition of service that his father had started. As king's justice, he served as a justice itinerant and at Westminster from 1192 onwards. He was appointed justice of the Jews in 1200, overseeing the debts of Christians to Jews and is last referred to as such on 24 March in either 1207 or 1208; the New Year was traditionally marked on 25 March, rather than 1 January, and so it is often unclear as to which year an entry refers. Between 1194 and 1196 he held a part of the honour of Gloucester and appears as a witness on charters of both King Richard I and King John. William de Warenne was still living in 1208 but died before Michaelmas 1209. He gave his body to the priory of Southwark, along with sixty acres of land at Foots Cray in Kent, called Wadeland, for the souls of Reginald his father, Alice his mother, Beatrice his wife, Reginald their son and Beatrice and Isabel their daughters. William's second wife, Milisent, outlived him at least until 1234–35, when an inquisition was ordered in Norfolk, of the knights' fees which had belonged to William de Warenne and which had been assigned to her in dower.[31]

William was succeeded as baron of Wormegay by his sole surviving child, his daughter Beatrice. Beatrice had been married to a man named Doun Bardolf, who died on 13 March in either 1204 or 1205, when Ruskington, Lincolnshire, was assigned to her in dower. Beatrice had at least one son by Doun, William Bardolf, who is recorded as owing one knights' fee of old feoffment for Ruskington in 1242–43. Her second marriage was to a man named Ralph, sometime in the year before Michaelmas 1209. We know of this marriage from a Pipe Roll entry and Beatrice's charter, issued to Southwark Priory, confirming her father's gift of sixty acres of land in Foots Cray. This charter was issued in her widowhood after the death of her husband, Ralph, and after her father's death; it was issued 'for the health of Reginald de Warenne her grandfather, Alice her grandmother, William her father, Beatrice her mother, Reginald her brother, whose body rested at Southwark, Isabel her sister, and her own.'[32]

Beatrice was not a grieving widow for very long as, soon afterwards, she was married for a third and final time to Hubert de Burgh, King John's justiciar, who came from a gentry family rather than the higher echelons of the nobility. The origins of Hubert de Burgh are quite obscure. His mother's name was Alice, as evidenced by a grant he made to the church of Oulton in about 1230, stating the gift was 'for the soul of my mother Alice who rests in the church at Walsingham.'[32] Hubert de Burgh's father may have been the Walter whose daughter Adelina owed 40 marks in the Pipe Rolls of Henry II, for recognition of a knights' fee at Burgh in Norfolk, although this is little more than a possibility.[33] De Burgh was the younger brother of William de Burgh who had accompanied King Henry II's youngest son, John, to Ireland in 1185; he eventually became lord of Connacht. Hubert de Burgh also had two younger brothers. Geoffrey became archdeacon of Norwich in 1202 and then bishop of Ely in 1225. A third brother, Thomas, was castellan of Norwich Castle in 1215–16.[34]

A self-made man, coming from a family of minor landowners in East Anglia centred on the manor of Burgh in Norfolk, Hubert de Burgh first appears in official records on 8 February 1198, when he witnessed a charter of John, as count of Mortain, at Tinchebrai in Normandy. In a charter of 12 June in the same year, he was identified as chamberlain of John's household and in 1199, when John succeeded to the throne, he was created chamberlain of the royal household.[35] Hubert de Burgh's career in royal service developed rapidly. In December 1200 he was made custodian of two important royal castles, Dover and Windsor. In 1201 he was sheriff of Dorset and Somerset and when John departed for France in June 1201, along with the two senior Marcher lords, the earl of Pembroke and constable of Chester, de Burgh was created custodian of the Welsh Marches with 100 men-at-arms at his disposal. He was also given the castles of Grosmont, Skenfrith and Whitecastle 'to sustain him in our service.'[36]

Further grants followed, making Hubert de Burgh a significant and powerful figure in the royal administration by 1200. In that year, Hubert de Burgh was one of the ambassadors despatched to Portugal to negotiate a possible marriage between John and a daughter of Portugal's king, but the embassy was abandoned after John married Isabelle d'Angoulême. Later, in 1202 Hubert de Burgh was sent to France and made constable of Falaise Castle in Normandy, where he was entrusted with guarding Arthur of Brittany following the latter's capture at Mirebeau in August. Hubert was given the order to have Arthur blinded and castrated but refused to carry out the punishment, claiming that the king had given the order in anger and would come to regret it – and lay the blame on the one who carried it out.[37] The fact Hubert de Burgh faced no repercussions on refusing the order suggests that he had read the situation perfectly. Moreover, given the persecution John later inflicted on William de Braose, following his complicity in Arthur's murder at Rouen the following year, it is clear that Hubert de Burgh knew John well.

In 1204 Hubert de Burgh was entrusted with the defence of Chinon, against the king of France. He held out for a year, until the summer of 1205, when the walls of the castle were practically levelled. In a last desperate engagement, de Burgh and his men rushed from the castle to confront the French. A fierce fight followed in which de Burgh was wounded and captured; he was held for two years. King John helped with his ransom, with writs to the treasurer and chamberlain, in February 1207, ordering them to pay William de Chayv 300 marks 'for the pledge of Hubert de Burgh.'[38] De Burgh returned to England before the end of 1207 and again began to accumulate land and offices. In May 1208 he was given custody of the castle and town of Lafford in Huntingdon and in the following year he married Beatrice de Warenne, who had succeeded her father in the barony of Wormegay; de Burgh became guardian of William, Beatrice's young son by her first husband, Doun Bardolf. Beatrice was the mother of at least one son by Hubert, John, who was probably born before 1212. It is possible another son, named Hubert, from whom the Burghs of Gainsborough were descended, was born in 1213 or 1214. In the same year, de Burgh returned to France in royal service, first as deputy seneschal of Poitou and then as seneschal in association with Philip d'Aubigny and Geoffrey de Neville. After the French defeated the English at Bouvines in 1214, de Burgh was one of the witnesses to the truce with King Philp II of France, which agreed that John should keep all his lands south of the River Loire.[39]

The fine assigned to Beatrice on her father's death in 1209, is referred to in a charter of 12 July 1227, to Hubert de Burgh, then earl of Kent, acquitting him of the £684 6s 8d owed.[40] The outstanding sum was to be recovered from Beatrice's heir, after de Burgh's death. The heir in question was William Bardolf, Beatrice's son by her first husband. On 29 August 1215, the sheriff of Nottinghamshire was ordered to give young William seisin of the lands and tenements of his inheritance from his father, though he would not receive his inheritance from his mother until after Hubert de Burgh's death in 1243. It was on 7 July of that year that the king restored the honour of Wormegay, which had been held by Hubert de Burgh for life, to William.[41] William Bardolf died in 1275; his descendants continued to hold Wormegay, in Norfolk, and the under-tenancy at Harthill in present-day South Yorkshire, until the fifteenth century.

Beatrice and Hubert's son, John, was knighted on 3 June 1229, but was specifically excluded from inheriting the earldom of Kent, bestowed on his father on 19 February 1226 or 1227. This earldom was created following Hubert de Burgh's third marriage, to Princess Margaret of Scotland, daughter of William I the Lion and therefore granddaughter of Ada de Warenne. The earldom of Kent was to descend exclusively through his children by the Scottish princess. In 1241 John owed relief on the manor of Portslade which had been given to him by his half-sister, Margery – the daughter of Hubert de Burgh by his third wife, Margaret of Scotland. Margery had received the manor from her father, who had held it of Earl Warenne. When John died on 7 January in 1273 or 1274, he held the manor of his older half-brother, Sir William Bardolf.[42] John de Burgh was succeeded by his son, also John, who was married to Cecily, daughter of John Balliol and his wife

Dervorguilla; she was also the sister of John Balliol, King of Scots, who was himself married to Isabella de Warenne, daughter of John de Warenne, sixth Earl Warenne.

Beatrice de Warenne died sometime before 18 December 1214. As we have seen, Hubert de Burgh retained Beatrice's lands at Wormegay throughout his lifetime and they only passed to her eldest son, William Bardolf, on de Burgh's death in May 1243.[43] William Bardolf's inheritance of Portslade and Harthill, both held from the honour of Warenne, serve to demonstrate the continued connections that this junior branch of the family held with the powerful Warenne earls throughout the thirteenth century. A remarkable expert in administration and estate management, Reginald de Warenne had spent a lifetime serving the interests of his family and the Warenne earldom. His son William and granddaughter Beatrice had continued in that tradition, maintaining the family links and ensuring the continued prestige of the Warenne name and the earldom of Surrey.

Chapter Ten

The Prince and the Countess

The Warenne earls of Surrey had been stalwart supporters of the Crown since William de Warenne, the first earl, had fought alongside William the Conqueror at the Battle of Hastings. The family held a total of sixty knights' fees in England. They had lands stretching from Lewes in Sussex to Sandal Castle in West Yorkshire, with their main landholdings at Castle Acre in Norfolk; they also had extensive estates in Normandy, including Mortemer and Bellencombre.[1] In January 1148 the third earl had been killed at Mount Cadmus, close to Laodicea in modern-day Turkey, fighting in the rearguard of France's King Louis VII during the Second Crusade.[2]

The third earl left behind a wife, Ela de Talvas, and young daughter, Isabel, now the fourth countess of Warenne and Surrey. The earl's widow, Countess Ela, was still a young woman and, although she and the earl had only one living child, she was still of child-bearing age. A short time after the death of her husband, Ela received a letter from Theobald, Archbishop of Canterbury, admonishing her for her failure to pay 'to Lewes priory the tithe money from the demesne lands which formed her dower.'[3] The archbishop's letter is recorded as 'containing a very strong complaint against her, for withdrawing from the monks of Lewes, the tithes of that part of her husband earl Warren's [sic] estate, which was appropriated to her dower and threatening to do justice to the monks if she withheld them any longer.'[4] These tithes had formed part of the donation granted to Lewes Priory by the earl, prior to his departure for the Holy Land. Unfortunately, we do not have Countess Ela's response, but one can imagine that she rectified the situation as there are, apparently, no further letters on the subject. The letter is dated to sometime between 1149 and 1152.

The year 1152 is the probable date for Ela's second marriage, to Patrick, Earl of Salisbury. Ela was to have at least four further children with Patrick, all boys: William, Patrick, Philip and Walter. Given that her eldest son, William, attained his majority in 1174, it can be surmised that he was born in 1153 and that Ela had married Earl Patrick by 1152, at the latest. Ela's eldest son, William, was himself the father of Ela of Salisbury, Countess of

Salisbury in her own right and wife of King John's illegitimate half-brother, William Longespée. Earl Patrick was also uncle to the young William Marshal, later earl of Pembroke and regent for King Henry III: William's mother, Sybilla, was Earl Patrick's sister. Ela's marriage to Earl Patrick, therefore, gave her daughter, Isabel, an extended family with royal and noble connections that would prove useful in the future.

Countess Ela is believed to have died on 4 October 1174; her place of burial is unknown and not recorded in the Lewes Cartulary, suggesting she was not buried at Lewes Priory among the previous Warenne earls and countesses.[5] Earl Patrick had been killed six years before in an ambush perpetrated by the Lusignan brothers who had attempted to kidnap Eleanor of Aquitaine, Henry II's wife and queen; Earl Patrick was in command of Queen Eleanor's escort. William Marshal was wounded in the ambush and captured; Queen Eleanor paid the ransom to have the young knight released.

Isabel de Warenne was the only child of William de Warenne, 3rd Earl Warenne, and his sole heiress, making her one of the most prized heiresses in England and Normandy. As Rev John Watson argued, the fact that the earldom passed in its entirety to Isabel and, as a consequence, her two husbands, confirms that she was the earl's only child to survive infancy; had Isabel had younger sisters, the lands would have been divided equally between all co-heiresses.[6] The earl had been a strong supporter of King Stephen; he had fought alongside the king during the Anarchy and supported his wife, Queen Matilda, after King Stephen was captured at Lincoln. This affinity with Stephen's regime helps to explain why, in the same year that her father died, or maybe before his departure on crusade, and as part of Stephen's attempts to control the vast Warenne lands, Isabel was married to Stephen's younger son, William of Blois, who became earl of Surrey, by right of his wife. William's exact date of birth is unknown, though it is thought he was born sometime between 1132 and 1137.

It has been suggested that Isabel was in her mid teens at the time of her marriage. It seems more likely that she was only 11 or 12 years old, and possibly even younger. Isabel's father had been born in 1119, a year after his parents' marriage. He was, therefore, only 29 years old when he died in the Holy Land in January 1148. Given that the youngest age permitted by the church for a boy to marry was 14, the oldest Isabel could possibly be when she married William of Blois is 14. However, Isabel's mother, Ela de Talvas, was the youngest of her parents' twelve children.[7] Given that her parents, William of Ponthieu and Ela of Burgundy did not marry until 1112, the earliest Ela could have been born was 1124, and that is if her mother gave birth to a living child every single year after her marriage. Ela de Talvas was, therefore, likely to have been born sometime between 1124 and 1130. She would have been legally allowed to marry at the age of 12, though not all parents married their daughters off so young and it was rare for girls to have children of their own at such a young age. It seems probable that William and Ela were married sometime in the late 1130s, with Isabel born a year or two later. Isabel, therefore, was probably aged somewhere between 8 and 12 when she and William were married.

The date of Isabel's marriage to William is not known, though it seems possible that it happened before her father left on crusade. To have Isabel married and settled before his departure would have been a sensible precaution for both the earl and the king. A rich heiress with lands stretching from Yorkshire to the south coast, would have been a big attraction for any ambitious magnate, and not necessarily one who was loyal to the king. Marrying Isabel to his own son ensured the Warenne lands stayed loyal to Stephen and guaranteed to the earl that the king would look after Isabel's interests and the interests of the Warenne earldom. A charter issued in 1148 by the earl's brother, Reginald, when the earl was away in the Holy Land lends weight to the theory the children were already married as it mentions the earl's absence and refers to William of Blois as 'his lord, earl William, the king's son'.[8] For Stephen, William's marriage to Isabel gave the king the assurance that his youngest son would be well provided for, with the wealth, lands and influence appropriate to his status; it would also ensure that the prince would be in a strong position to support his elder brother's kingship when the time came.

As the younger son of Stephen and Matilda, William was probably born shortly after his father ascended the throne in 1135. William's older brothers, Eustace and Baldwin, both bore names representative of the county of Boulogne, whereas William was named for his great-grandfather, William the Conqueror, king of England, suggesting – though not conclusive – that Stephen was already king when his youngest son was born. William's older brother, Eustace, was probably born sometime between 1129 and 1131. William also had a sister, Mary, who survived infancy and was pledged as a nun to a convent at Stratford in Middlesex when still a child. Two other children, Baldwin and Matilda, died in infancy. Matilda had been married as a toddler, c. 1136, to Isabel de Warenne's half-uncle, Waleran de Beaumont, Count of Meulan, who was over thirty years the young child's senior. She died within a year, aged 4.

Eustace was groomed to be Stephen's successor and according to Henry of Huntingdon, Eustace performed homage for Normandy to the king of France in 1136, as Stephen's heir.[9] He was married to Constance of France, daughter of King Louis VI and sister of Louis VII, in 1140, when he was still only a teenager of 13 or 14. Eustace was knighted in 1147, and the following year

> in his seventeenth year [Stephen] wished to have his son Eustace crowned, and he required Theobald, archbishop of Canterbury, and the other bishops whom he had assembled with that design, to anoint him king and give him their solemn benediction; but he met with a repulse, for the pope had by his letters prohibited the archbishop from crowning the king's son, because King Stephen appeared to have broken his oath of fealty in mounting the throne.[10]

By many accounts, despite his youth – he was 17 or 18 when he was knighted – Eustace had a ruthless streak that endeared him to few. In 1140, the *Anglo-Saxon Chronicle* said of him 'he had little success, and with just cause, because he was an evil man, because wheresoever he came he did more evil than good; he robbed the lands and laid great taxes on them.'[11] Henry of Huntingdon, moreover, described him as 'a good soldier, but an ungodly man, who dealt harshly with the rulers of the church, being their determined persecutor.'[12] The *Gesta Stephani*, however, paints a picture of 'a young man of high character ... his manners were grave; he excelled in warlike exercises and had great natural courage ... he was courteous and affable ... and possessed much of his father's spirit ... ever ready to draw close the bands of peace' but he 'never shrank from presenting a resolute and indomitable front to his enemies.'[13] Eustace inherited the county of Boulogne on his mother's death in 1152, though he had borne the title for several years.

In the latter years of Stephen's reign, Henry had taken over from his mother in the wars against the king. His father, Geoffrey of Anjou, had conquered Normandy and was invested as its duke in 1144, giving Henry a strong power base from which to pursue the main prize: England. In 1147, aged only 14, Henry made his first expedition to England, though his campaign achieved little success and his men soon demanded money which Henry didn't have. With no money or aid forthcoming from his mother or his uncle, Robert of Gloucester, Henry turned to the only other person who could help him, King Stephen himself. It surprised many that Stephen complied, paying off Henry's mercenaries and allowing his reckless young rival to return home to Normandy. The *Gesta Stephani* defends Stephen's kindness, saying he did it 'from wise and noble views; for the more kindly and humanely a man treats his adversary, the more he humbles him and lessens his power.'[14]

It was in the aftermath of Henry's failed invasion that Eustace was knighted and Stephen's younger son, William, was married to Isabel de Warenne. The promise of wealth and power that the marriage brought was realised when the third earl died on crusade and William of Blois, still little more than a child, became one of the greatest magnates in England. Henry was back in England within two years and at the age of 16 was knighted at Chester by his uncle David I, King of Scots. By 1151, Henry's father was dead and the young contender for England's throne was now duke of Normandy and count of Anjou. His presence continued to put pressure on Stephen and was a constant reminder to England's barons that there was a strong alternative royal line just waiting in the wings. While none would seek to displace Stephen, what would come after him was still up for discussion. Henry kept up the pressure, taking Stamford and Nottingham by force in 1153.

Following the unexpected death of Eustace earlier in the year, the way was now clear for King Stephen, urged on by Theobald, Archbishop of Canterbury, to make a pact with Duke Henry that would see the throne returned to the grandson of Henry I. William of Blois, it seems, was not considered as a possible heir to his father, with many claiming that he did not want to be king. Following a meeting with Henry at Colchester in September or October of 1153, William waived his own rights to the throne; whether he did so willingly or was persuaded by others is not known.[15] He would, however, feature strongly in the settlement agreed between Stephen and Henry. The terms of the agreement were determined through the autumn of 1153 and ratified at Winchester on 6 November, the same year. By this treaty Henry was formally established as Stephen's heir 'by hereditary right'.[16] Henry did homage to King Stephen and swore to accept him as his liegeman, promising to honour and protect the king in accordance with the terms of their agreement. In return Stephen undertook to govern with the advice of Henry, in all parts of the kingdom. Stephen's son, William, did homage to Henry in his turn. Henry of Huntingdon described the scene:

> What boundless joy, what a day of rejoicing, when the king himself led the illustrious young prince through the streets of Winchester, with a splendid procession of bishops and nobles, and amidst the acclamations of the thronging people; for the king received him as his son by adoption, and acknowledged him heir to the crown! From thence he accompanied the king to London, where he was received with no less joy by the people assembled in countless numbers, and by brilliant processions, as was fitting for so great a prince.[17]

The effusive Henry of Huntingdon went on to sum up the mood brought on by the last eighteen years of warfare: 'Thus, through God's mercy, after a night of misery, peace dawned on the ruined realm of England.'[18] By the terms of the treaty, all the lands would return to the control of whoever had owned them on the day of Henry I's death, 1 December 1135. All castles constructed in the intervening time, including temporary fortifications, were to be demolished, all hostages to be released. No one pursued the cause of Stephen's sole surviving son, William, a youth of 18 who had lived his life in his older brother's shadow. By the Treaty of Winchester, he would succeed Eustace in inheriting their mother's county of Boulogne; he would also inherit the honours that Stephen had held before becoming king, including the county of Mortain, the honour of Eye and the honour of Lancaster. In addition, William was confirmed in his possession of the castle of Norwich and a large interest in the *comitatus* of Norfolk, given him by his father, and the castle and honour of Pevensey on the Sussex coast.[19] These lands, added to those he had taken possession of on marrying Isabel de Warenne, would make him the foremost magnate in England and Normandy. Based on enfeoffments alone, William would be lord over more than 600 knights.[20] The idea was to make William's holdings so substantial that he would not want to make a bid for the crown. The charter, issued at Westminster in December of 1153, detailed the settlement that was agreed concerning William of Blois, whose rights as Stephen's sole surviving son and heir were recognised:

> William my son has done liege homage and given surety to the duke of Normandy, and the duke has granted him to hold from him all the lands which I held before I acquired the kingdom of England, whether in England or in Normandy or in other places. He is also to hold whatever came with the daughter of the earl of Warenne, whether in England or in Normandy, and whatever pertains to those honours. And the duke will put William, my son, and the men of that honour into possession of all the lands, villages and boroughs and revenues which the duke has now in his demesne, and especially those which pertain to the honour of the earl of Warenne, particularly the castle of Bellencombre and the castle of Mortemer: the agreement being that Reginald de Warenne shall, if he wish, keep the castle of Bellencombre and the castle of Mortemer, giving the duke hostages in respect of them; but if Reginald does not wish to do so, then other liege men of the earl of Warenne acceptable to the duke shall keep the said castles, likewise giving the duke good hostages. The duke shall return to him the other castles which belong to the count of Mortain, at my pleasure, when he can, for safeguard and with safe hostages, it being understood that all hostages

shall be returned without dispute to my son when the duke comes into possession of the kingdom of England.[21]

William may not have been as satisfied with the outcome of negotiations as was expected of him, however. His name is noticeably missing among the witnesses of the treaty. Moreover, in the early months of 1154, William was implicated in an incident in which a Flemish plot to assassinate Henry was uncovered. Possibly the brainchild of William of Ypres, the plot was thwarted when Henry hastily left for Rochester and then to safety in Normandy.[22] The plot may have arisen from a visit by Thierry, Count of Flanders, who met with the king and Duke Henry at Dover. Although it is not known for certain, it is possible that William was asked to do homage to Count Thierry, for the county of Boulogne. The plot was discovered after the count had left, and once the king and duke had returned to Canterbury. According to Gervase of Canterbury, 'the Flemings wished to kill the duke, since they hated both him and the peace'.[23]

Although it is by no means certain that William was involved, he appears to have known about it and it remains conceivable that William sought to undermine the Treaty of Winchester, or that the Flemings sought to advance William's cause. Nothing came of the plot as shortly afterwards, during a meeting with Henry at Barham Down, William fell from his horse and broke his leg rather badly, 'to the great distress of his followers.'[24] William stayed with the monks at St Augustine's Abbey in Canterbury to convalesce; Henry, perhaps, feeling a little insecure in the king's heartland of Kent, sought permission to leave court and returned to Normandy.

King Stephen died on 25 October 1154; in less than three years William had lost his mother, brother and father. The king was buried with his wife, Queen Matilda, and son, Eustace, at the monastery founded by Stephen at Faversham in Kent. Besides his wife, the only close family left to William now was his sister, Mary, who had been dedicated to convent life since early childhood. No one thought to back William's claim to the throne, least of all William, it seems, and Duke Henry succeeded to the throne without opposition.

Now in an unassailable position as king of England, duke of Normandy and Aquitaine and count of Anjou, Henry was able to discard some of the generosity towards William that had been sealed in the Treaty of Winchester. In 1157 the king took advantage of a dispute between William and Hugh Bigod, the other powerful magnate in the region of East Anglia, to confiscate all of William's lands and estates in Normandy. The king did return all William's paternal and maternal inheritances, but without the castles that went with them. William went so far as to appeal to the pope, Adrian IV, the only English pope there has ever been, complaining of mistreatment, but it availed him nought.[25] Henry did make some concessions, allowing the earl exemptions from past gelds afterwards; now that the teeth had been taken out of his young rival and William no longer posed a threat.

We know nothing of Isabel and William's married life. Countess Isabel is little more than a shadow on the pages of history during this time. Indeed, she appears as a witness on only one of William's known charters; a charter dated between 1153 and 1159, in which William gifts to his kinsman Faramus of Boulogne and his heirs, 'the manor of Martock, Somerset [honour of Boulogne], to hold by the service of one knight; addressed to all his barons, ministers and faithful men of the honour which had belonged to count Eustace, his grandfather, in England or outside; first witness Isabel the countess, his wife.'[26]

On 24 June 1158, and now in his early 20s, William was knighted by the king at Carlisle. He then probably accompanied Henry to Normandy in August, in view of a charter William issued at Tinchebrai that is dated 1158.[27] The following year William joined King Henry on his expedition to Toulouse. It was the largest gathering of nobility from Henry's dominions and allies since his coronation. It is likely William was included in the expedition so the king could keep him close. For William himself, a young man approaching his mid-20s and recently knighted, it would have been an adventure he needed little persuading to join. He may well have seen it as an opportunity to ingratiate himself with the king and to establish his status as one of the foremost barons of the realm, both through his blood and his landed status. It was not to be, however, for on the journey home, William succumbed to the illness that had ravaged Henry's troops before the gates of Toulouse. He died shortly afterwards and was buried at the abbey of Montmorillon in Poitou. King Henry issued a charter to the house 'for the soul of William count of Boulogne, whose body lay there, giving 10 marks worth of land in the vill of Ickleton [co. Cambridge], in accordance with the bounds set by Turold de Boreham, the count's steward, at the order of Reginald de Warenne.'[28]

William was aided in his administrative duties by his wife's uncle, Reginald de Warenne, not just with matters pertaining to the Warenne lands, but also with the lands William had inherited from his father, including the county of Mortain and the honour of Lancaster. William was also supported by a man named Eustace the Chancellor, who witnessed many of the young earl's charters. In 1148 he witnessed a charter by Reginald de Warenne as Eustace '*clericus comitis Willelmi filii regis*' ('clerk to Earl William, the king's son').[29] It is rare for a tenant-in-chief to have a chancellor in twelfth century England; that William had one is more likely due to his royal status as a king's son, than his vast landholdings. William appears in his charters using various styles, for example in a charter for a gift of land he made for the building of Croxton Abbey in Leicestershire he refers to himself as '*comes Bolonie et Moretonie et Warennie.*'[30] Whilst in his charters relating to the Warenne lands, which may have been issued prior to William inheriting Boulogne, William styled himself *comes Warennie* or *de Warenna*; he appears as '*Willelmus comes Warennie*' on a confirmation charter of between 1154 and 1159 to 'Nostell priory of the gifts which Elias de Bosville had made, namely 50 acres of land in Barnborough, the mill of Harlington, except 10s 8d retained by him therein, and a bovate of land with a toft adjacent to the mill as William the miller had held it.'[31] Another charter issued by William was a gift 'to Lewes priory of the land of Burchard for a hospice for the use of the priory, 20s being deducted from the tithe money of the rent of his manor of Betchworth [Surrey].'[32] The witnesses to this charter included William de Pierrepont and Drew de Freville, both of whom had been regular witnesses for the third earl and whose enduring appearances after his death demonstrate a continuity in the administration of the earldom. Isabel herself issued a charter in confirmation of William's gift 'in accordance with the charter of William earl de Warenne, her husband, on the same condition as affecting tithe from her manor of Betchworth.'[33]

Although they had been married for over ten years, Isabel and William had remained childless, a fact that must have pleased Henry; children of William of Blois would have had a claim to the throne and offered the English a rival dynasty should they tire of the Angevins. It was a threat Henry did not need. It is possible that Henry kept William with him, at Carlisle and then at Toulouse, to hinder the couple's chance of becoming parents, though that is merely conjecture. What is certain is that William had been just a handful of steps from the throne and, had events played out differently in 1153/1154, William and Isabel may well have become king and queen, thus paving the way for a Warenne heir to rule England. A man of ambition such as Henry II was, could never forget that. As it was, William's death conveniently removed that threat, leaving Isabel without the consolation of children but a very wealthy young widow, still only in her early 20s and with an earldom to bestow on any future husband.

William was succeeded in the county of Boulogne by his sister, Mary, the only surviving child of Stephen and Matilda. Mary was born around 1136 and placed in a convent at an early age, first at Stratford in Middlesex, with some nuns from St Sulpice in Rennes. After some discord with the nuns there, she moved to the Priory of Lillechurch, Kent, founded for her by her parents in 1150–52. She later moved to Romsey Abbey, where she was elected abbess sometime before 1155. Shortly after William's death, Mary was abducted by Matthew of Alsace, second son of the count of Flanders, and forced to marry him.

There was outrage among the clergy – the incident was even discussed by the pope who imposed an interdict on Matthew – but the marriage was allowed to stand. Mary and Matthew had two children, Ida and Mathilde, and it was after the birth of Mathilde that the couple were divorced, in 1170. There is some suggestion that Matthew was pressured into accepting the divorce by his dying father and the emperor, Frederick Barbarossa, in order to have the interdict that had been imposed on him when he married Mary lifted. Matthew would continue to rule Boulogne and be succeeded by Ida on his death in 1173. Mary was finally allowed to return to the convent life, becoming a Benedictine nun at St Austrebert, Montreuil. She died there in July 1182, aged about 46.

The abduction and forced marriage of Mary may well have been a political move. Although there does not appear to be any proof that Henry II sanctioned it, he certainly benefited from Mary being safely married to a loyal vassal. She was, after all a great heiress and, through her father, a rival claimant to the throne of England.

Isabel's marriage to William of Blois had fulfilled a purpose in 1147. It had guaranteed the security of the earldom at a time when it was most vulnerable; left in the hands of a young girl. The marriage had also ensured the full might of the earldom would stand behind the king, offering support and security to a regime that had been under constant threat since Stephen ascended the throne in 1135. It also served to fulfil the ambition of Isabel's grandfather, the second earl, whose aspirations had included a royal bride. Isabel had married her prince. It must be conceded, however, that the marriage did not fulfill its potential on several levels. Although the earldom remained with a steady hand on the helm, its future was threatened by the lack of an heir, even after over ten years of marriage. William's own potential went unfulfilled when he was passed over as a candidate for the crown in favour of Henry, Duke of Normandy and Count of Anjou, who already had an heir in the cradle. Had William had the driving ambition of Henry, and the support his father had enjoyed from the barons of England, Isabel may well have worn a crown. Unfortunately, it was not to be.

Chapter Eleven

Hamelin and Isabel

With the death of William of Blois, as the county of Boulogne passed to his sister, the county of Mortain and the honours of Lancaster and Eye, would be kept by the king. The earldom of Surrey, which had belonged to William only by right of his wife, remained with Isabel de Warenne. Isabel was still only a young woman, 25 years old at the most but more likely somewhere between 21 and 23. King Henry II was faced with a new problem, which was to find a suitable husband for the widowed countess; a man who would be a custodian for the great and powerful earldom of Surrey, while remaining loyal to the king.

A charter issued sometime between 1159 and 1164, during Isabel's widowhood is testament to the fact that Isabel had personal control of her earldom. It was by:

> Elias son of Hugh [de Bosville] to Reginald de Warenne, for his service and 100*li*. sterling, of all his land of Harthill, to hold for him and his heirs of the grantor and his heirs by the service of a quarter of a knight as freely as the grantor and his father had held it of earl de Warenne. Reginald and William his son had sworn to be faithful to the grantor and his heirs as lord of the fee. The grantor and Lettice his daughter and heir had sworn to warrant the gift to Reginald and his heirs; this they had done in the presence of Isabel countess of Warenne, their lady, and of their peers; and they had pledged the countess to warrant the gift.[1]

As countess, Isabel's was the first name on the witness list as '*Isabel comitissa*'.

Though recently widowed, Isabel would have been well aware that she was expected to remarry, just as her mother had done. The fact she held the mighty earldom of Surrey would have made settling her future even more pressing; the earl of Warenne had contributed knights and men from his own lands to the armies of both King Stephen and Henry II. This was expected to continue, but Isabel could not be expected to lead men into battle. It is all the more surprising, therefore, that Isabel was allowed some respite in the marriage market and the prospect of a husband is not mentioned until 1162.

By this time Henry II's youngest brother, William FitzEmpress, was seeking a dispensation to marry her. The dispensation was refused by Thomas Becket, Archbishop of Canterbury, on the grounds of consanguinity. The objection was not due to a blood relationship between Isabel and William, but between William and Isabel's first husband, William of Blois, who were second cousins. It has often been suggested that this was a love-match rather than an arranged marriage. We will, of course, never know how Isabel felt but William died shortly afterwards, at Rouen on 30 January 1164, whilst visiting his mother, possibly seeking her assistance in the matter. Many of his friends claimed that he died of a broken heart after being disappointed in his desire to marry Isabel. He was 27.

One of William's knights, Richard Brito, was among the quartet who murdered Thomas Becket in December 1170. The knights had travelled from Normandy to demand that the archbishop restore the English bishops who had been suspended from their offices, and to absolve those under sentence of excommunication. Becket refused, saying that it was not 'for a lesser judge to dissolve the sentence of a superior, and that it was not for any man to undermine what had been decreed by the apostolic see.'[2] According to William FitzStephen the knights attempted to arrest the archbishop and a struggle ensued after he refused to go with them. The archbishop's companion, Master Edward Grim, stepped into the path of the first stroke meant for Becket. The archbishop then gave thanks to God,

> saying, 'Into thy hands, O Lord, I commend my spirit.' As he knelt down, clasping and stretching out his hands to God, a second stroke was dealt him on the head, at which he fell flat on his face hard by an altar there dedicated to St Benedict ... On the right hand he fell, as one proceeding to the right hand of God. While he lay there stricken, Richard Brito smote him with such force that the sword was broken against his head, and the pavement of the church: 'Take that,' said he, 'for the love of my lord William, the king's brother.'[3]

Beyond the reaction of William's knight, there is little evidence that the proposed marriage between William and Isabel was a true love match, and we have no indication of Isabel's thoughts on the matter. Even without the love angle, for William, marrying Isabel would have been an attractive prospect and would have given him position in England, not only as the king's brother but also as one of the foremost magnates in England and Normandy. It was, for King Henry, a very practical match and would have been the perfect solution; to bring the vast Warenne holdings into the royal family and to have them held by the king's own brother. Henry II was not to be so easily thwarted, and indeed did not object to Thomas Becket's ruling. He came up with a solution that would achieve the same end, while satisfying the restrictions of the church: his brother Hamelin.

Hamelin Plantagenet was an illegitimate son of Henry's father, Geoffrey of Anjou, by an unnamed woman. He was likely conceived a year after Geoffrey had married Henry I's daughter, Empress Matilda, when the couple were separated. Never a happy marriage, Matilda had left her husband and returned to Normandy in the autumn of 1129. Geoffrey had not chased after his wife, but remained in Anjou, apparently in the company of a mistress; Hamelin was born in 1130.[4] Hamelin's father had been 14 years old when he was married to 26-year-old Matilda. The marriage started off badly, with Matilda resenting being married to a count who was not just her junior in years, but also in status. It was a marriage that she was forced to endure and though it was no love match, Geoffrey and Matilda had one thing in common, protecting their sons' interests. And so, while Matilda chased the Crown in England, Geoffrey successfully pursued the duchy of Normandy, which gave their eldest son, Henry, a strong powerbase to press his own claims to England when the time came. The identity of Hamelin's mother remains open to conjecture; she may have been Adelaide of Angers, or a woman named Matilda.[5] Geoffrey also had two illegitimate daughters, either by the same mistress or other women, Emma and Mary. Emma of Anjou would become one of the ladies of the bedchamber of Eleanor of Aquitaine. She married Welsh prince Davydd ab Owain Gwynedd in the summer of 1174. Mary became a nun and eventually rose to be abbess of Shaftesbury Abbey.[6]

Little is heard of Hamelin prior to his marriage to Countess Isabel, though it can be assumed that he was in the entourage of his half-brother, King Henry, who obviously depended on Hamelin's loyalty, given that he was entrusted with the rich Warenne earldom. Unlike Isabel's first husband, Hamelin had no pretensions or rights to the throne, nor did he have any claims on the Angevin patrimony, due to his illegitimacy. He was entirely dependent on Henry's generosity to get ahead in the world, and Henry was generous toward Hamelin. Even before he was given the hand of Countess Isabel, Hamelin had been given lands in Touraine, along with the title of 'Vicomte de Touraine'.[7] Touraine was a sensitive area of Normandy, a border region between the counties of Blois and Anjou and was perhaps a demonstration of the trust which Henry had in his older half-brother. Hamelin was to later exchange his lands in Touraine for Thetford in Norfolk, valued at £35 a year. If the estate made a profit, the excess was to be handed to the Exchequer, but if it made less than £35 a year, the Crown was to make up the difference.[8]

Acceding to the mighty earldom of Warenne and Surrey, however, was probably more than he had ever hoped for or expected. Isabel owned substantial lands in Yorkshire, East Anglia and Sussex; at the time of the Domesday Book in 1086, the lands were valued at £1,140, with sixty knights' fees, and among the five wealthiest baronies in the country, after the king. By the mid-twelfth century, the honour of Warenne held over 140 knights' fees in England, with sixty in Sussex alone, along with castles at Lewes, Castle Acre, Conisbrough, Reigate and Sandal in Wakefield.[9] Hamelin was married to Isabel in 1164. The couple wed in April; Isabel's trousseau cost an impressive £41 10s 8d.[10] Hamelin became the fourth earl of Surrey by right of his new wife. It is with Hamelin's tenure on the earldom that the numbering of the earls can get confusing. Both Isabel's first husband, William of Blois, and Hamelin can be counted as the fourth earl, as they each held the title through Isabel, the fourth countess; however, some writers, in order to avoid confusion, count them as the fourth and fifth earl. (We will count them both as the fourth earl, as it was Isabel's earldom, not theirs). In an unusual step for the time, Hamelin took his wife's surname, so that he was known from henceforth as Hamelin de Warenne, rather than Hamelin Plantagenet.

In the same year as he was married, Hamelin supported his brother the king in the contest of wills that Henry was engaged in with his archbishop of Canterbury. Henry's friend and chancellor, Thomas Becket, had been promoted to the senior post in the English church, at Henry's insistence, in 1162. However, once in the post, Becket had essentially abandoned Henry's policies and sought to defend and extend the influence and rights of the church in England, while Henry sought to curb them. A clash was inevitable and came about when Henry sought to extend the jurisdiction of secular courts over English clergymen and to protect the traditional rights of royal government in regard to the church. In January 1164 Henry had issued the Constitutions of Clarendon. The sixteen constitutions were intended to curb clerical independence and weaken the connection of the English church with Rome. Becket consented to the Constitutions, but disputes continued throughout 1164. Henry called for the archbishop to appear at a great council at Northampton Castle on 12 October 1164, to answer to the charges laid against him.[11] Among numerous other issues, Becket was called to account for his behaviour concerning land disputes between the church and crown, contempt of royal authority and malfeasance in the chancellor's office: 'it seemed to most people to be consistent with the law that he should be made to account for the sum of the profits, even though, before his consecration, the archbishop had been granted by Henry, the king's son and heir, freedom and exemption from the obligation to render accounts.'[12] The bishops, earls and barons of the realm were all present, including Roger, archbishop of York, the most senior clergyman in England after the archbishop of Canterbury. Hamelin was at the trial and spoke in support of Henry. Indeed, the new earl and the archbishop appear to have started a war of words; Hamelin defended Henry's dignity and called Becket a traitor. The archbishop's retort was 'Were I a knight instead of a priest, my fist would prove you a liar!'[13] Ironically, it is thought that Hamelin's denunciation of Becket was motivated by the injury caused to the royal family in Becket's refusal to allow Henry's brother, William, to marry Isabel de Warenne; who was now Hamelin's wife.[14]

According to Ralph of Diceto,

> the archbishop was in dire straits, accused of many wrongs, wounded by many insults and bereft of the support of the bishops. He raised up the cross which he carried and left the court room. The following night, he left the town in secret. Concealing himself from the view of men by day and travelling by night, after some days he came to the port of Sandwich and crossed over to Flanders in a small boat.[15]

Hamelin's animosity to Becket was not to survive the archbishop's martyrdom and he actively participated in the cult that grew up around Thomas Becket after his violent death. In later life, the earl claimed that the cloth covering Becket's tomb had cured his blindness, caused by a cataract, in one eye.[16]

It was probably as a sign of his kinship with the royal family that Hamelin was one of only a handful of great Norman magnates in England in 1166 and in Normandy in 1172, who was not obliged to report his knights' fees and royal and ducal service. As a consequence, the Warenne fiefs are not among the two great land surveys of Henry's reign, the *Cartae baronum* and *Infeudationes militum*. We do know, however, that with over 140 knights fees that the earldom held in the second half of the twelfth century, Hamelin was the ninth greatest lord in England, as reckoned by the enfeoffments.[17] It is more difficult to ascertain his ranking in Normandy, although Countess Isabel's ancestral lands, centred around the castles of Mortemer and Bellencombre, would have made Hamelin one of the more influential landowners in Upper Normandy. At some point in his tenure of the earldom,

Hamelin rebuilt the castle at Mortemer, possibly around the same time that he built the magnificent keep at Conisbrough, which was 'an enlarged and improved version of the Mortemer design.'[18] Conisbrough Castle was rebuilt in stone sometime between 1170 and 1180.

By the time Hamelin became earl, Conisbrough already had a long and rich history. According to Geoffrey of Monmouth, Conisbrough – then known as Conigsburgh, or Cyngesburgh – belonged to the great British warrior Ambrosius Aurelianus. Geoffrey of Monmouth was not known for his historical accuracy, of course, but it is fascinating to think that this little town may once have belonged to a candidate for the legendary King Arthur. What we know, for certain, is that by 1066 the honour of Conisbrough belonged to Harold Godwinson, Earl of Wessex and later King Harold II of England. On a prominent, steep hill, it guards the main road between Sheffield and Doncaster to the east, and the navigable River Don to the north. Following Harold's defeat and death at the Battle of Hastings, it was given to one of William the Conqueror's greatest supporters, and Isabel's ancestor, William de Warenne. In those days the castle itself was probably located on the same site on which it now sits, though it would have been a wooden motte and bailey construction, surrounded by wooden palisades and earthworks.

It was Hamelin who built the spectacular hexagonal keep. The stairs to the keep were originally accessed across a drawbridge, which could be raised in times of attack. The ground floor was used for storage, with a basement storeroom below, housing the keep's well, and accessed by ladder. The first floor holds the great chamber, or solar, with a magnificent fireplace and seating in the glass-less window. This is where Hamelin and Isabel would have conducted business or entertained important guests. Henry II and King John are both known to have visited Conisbrough during Hamelin's tenure: King John even issued a charter from Conisbrough Castle in March 1201. The second floor of the keep would have been sleeping quarters for the lord and lady. Both the solar and the bedchamber have impressive fireplaces, garderobes and a stone basin, which would have had running water delivered from a rainwater cistern on the roof. On this second floor, also, built into one of the keep's buttresses is the family's private chapel, a stunning feature. This may well have been the chapel endowed by Hamelin and Isabel in 1189–90 and dedicated to St Philip and St James (although there is thought to have been a, now lost, second chapel in the inner bailey to which the endowment could refer). The chapel is well-decorated, with quatrefoil windows, elaborate carving on the columns and a wonderful vaulted ceiling. There is a small sacristy for the priest, just to the left of the door, with another basin for the priest's personal use, and cavities for storing the vestments and altar vessels.[19]

The winding stairs, built within the keep's thick walls, give access to each successive level and, eventually, to the battlements, with a panoramic view of the surrounding area. These battlements also had cisterns to hold rainwater, a bread oven and weapons storage; and wooden hoardings stretching out over the bailey to aid in defence. The keep and curtain walls – which were built slightly later, probably by Isabel and Hamelin's son William, the fifth earl – were of a state-of-the art design in their day. The barbican, leading into the inner bailey, had two gatehouses and a steep passageway guarded by high walls on both sides; an attacking force would have been defenceless against missiles from above, with nowhere to run in the cramped corridor. Although the encircling moat is, and always has been, dry, all the detritus from the toilets and kitchens drained into it; another little aid to defence – imagine having to attack through that kind of waste.[20] The inner bailey housed an extensive kitchen range, guard rooms, a great hall with a raised dais and private chambers for the earl's family. Although Conisbrough is not a large castle, the extensive range of buildings, the magnificent decorations of the fireplaces and chapel, suggest it would have been impressive in its day; and reflects the importance and status, not only of Hamelin and Isabel, but of the earldom as a whole. Earl Hamelin may also have been responsible for the building of nearby Peel Castle, Thorne, which was built in the hunting grounds of Hatfield moors, Doncaster. This castle was a smaller version of Conisbrough, built as a motte and bailey in stone. The stone tower on the motte was composed of rounded stone and had three large buttresses. Leland wrote of it in 1534, 'by the church garth of Thorne is a praty pile or castelet, well diked, now used for a prison for offenders in the forestes.'[21]

The marriage of Hamelin and Isabel appears to have been highly successful. Hamelin was loyal to his younger, royal, half-brother, Henry II. Henry himself had to face the animosity of Europe following the murder of Thomas Becket, especially in the sensitive Touraine region where Hamelin was vicomte, which bore the brunt of the hostility of the French court and Blois in particular.[22] Hamelin acted as one of the principal guardians of his brother's dominions, whilst the king rode out the backlash with a self-imposed exile in Ireland. Although he only attested ten of Henry II's royal charters, suggesting he was not among the king's inner circle at court, Hamelin appears in support of his brother at all the crucial moments of Henry II's reign.

He was at the king's side when Henry met with Raymond de St Giles, Count of Toulouse, to resolve a long-standing dispute, in February 1173. Hamelin attested the accompanying charters as 'vicomte de la Touraine'.[23] Hamelin supported the king during the conflict with his sons in 1173; when Henry, the Young King, Richard and Geoffrey rebelled against their father, with the support of their mother, Eleanor of Aquitaine, and their French and Scottish allies. Henry's decision to give his youngest son, John, the castles of Chinon and Loudun, strongholds belonging to the Young King, as a marriage portion, drove the older boys into rebellion. These castles were both in Touraine and, had the plan come to fruition, Hamelin would have been given custody of the castles until the marriage could be solemnised.

Hamelin next appears in the records as one of the nobles chosen to escort Joanna, the king's youngest daughter, on the long journey to her marriage to William, King of Sicily. The ambassadors, the bishops of Troia and Capaccio and the count of Camerota, had arrived at Henry's court in April 1176, along with Rotrou of Rouen, a kinsman of the king of Sicily, seeking a betrothal with Joanna, the youngest of the king's daughters. The ambassadors were answered,

after deliberation, on 20 May. The mention and promise of a future marriage were turned, with oaths on each king's soul, into a definite wedding. In order to bring about the alliance with the king of Sicily effectively and enter more closely and solemnly into it, the king of England sent ambassadors to Sicily who, after settling what gifts were to be made on account of the marriage, hurried back.[24]

Before leaving for the Continent in August 1176, Joanna was allowed to bid farewell to her mother at Winchester; Queen Eleanor had been held captive since aiding her sons in their failed rebellion against their father in 1173. Joanna was provided with a magnificent trousseau, similar to that of her sister Matilda, which was worth £63 and had included saddles with gilt fittings, 'two large silken cloths, and two tapestries and one cloth of samite and twelve sable skins.'[25] The princess left England's shores on 27 August 1176, sailing for Normandy:

There Henry the Younger came to meet his sister, conducting her with the greatest honour to the County of Poitiers of his brother, Richard. Thenceforth, Richard escorted Joanna through the lands he held [Aquitaine]. Then the girl traveled to Saint-Gilles with Richard of Canterbury, Geoffrey of Ely, Giles of Evreux, Hugh of Beauchamp, and Hamelin of Warenne, her father's half-brother.[26]

Some of the escort arrived back in England in December 1176, although Bishop John of Norwich reported to Henry 'that during his voyage from Messina to Saint-Gilles he had encountered a storm, and two fine galleys carrying various, precious gifts from William had sunk.'[27] Other nobles accompanying the English princess had been ordered not to return home until they had seen 'the King of Sicily and Joanna crowned in wedlock'[28] and remained in Sicily until after the wedding in February 1177. Roger of Hoveden (or Howden) described Joanna's entry into Palermo and subsequent wedding:

> When she had arrived at Palermo, in Sicily, together with Giles, bishop of Evreux, and the other envoys of our lord, the King, the whole city welcomed them, and lamps, so many and so large, were lighted up, that the city almost seemed to be on fire, and the rays of the stars could in no way bear comparison with the brilliancy of such a light: for it was by night that they entered the city of Palermo. The said daughter of the King of England was then escorted, mounted on one of the King's horses, and resplendent with regal garments, to a certain place that there she might in becoming state await the day of her marriage and coronation. After the expiration of a few days from this time, the before-named daughter of the King of England was married to William, King of Sicily, and solemnly crowned at Palermo, in the royal chapel there, in the presence of Giles, bishop of Evreux, and the envoys of the King of England, who had been sent for that purpose. She was married and crowned on the Lord's day before the beginning of Septuagesima, being the ides of February... .[29]

Ralph of Diceto also described the scene:

> The city of Palermo was resplendent with the marriage celebrations of the king of Sicily and the king of England's daughter. Archbishops and bishops, counts and barons, clergy and people, flocked at once to solemnise the marriage and crowning of the new queen, and Walter archbishop of Palermo performing the marriage ceremony on 13 February.

Hamelin, Earl of Warenne and Surrey, would have been among the throng of English nobles watching the marriage and coronation of his 12-year-old niece, now Queen Joanna of Sicily. The earl would have been the young princess's closest relative to attend the ceremony and may have been relied on, by the king, to give a more personal account of events when he returned home, later in the year.

Hamelin appears to have spent a large amount of time in the 1180s at his estates in Yorkshire, overseeing the completion of the magnificent keep at Conisbrough Castle. The Warennes were a family that prided itself on its prestigious building projects; the first earl had founded and built St Pancras Priory at Lewes, while the second earl had rebuilt Castle Acre in Norfolk with a new castle, town wall, priory and planned village. Conisbrough Castle was Hamelin's own addition to this Warenne tradition.

Hamelin continued his support of the Crown when his nephew Richard I succeeded in 1189. Although he played no ceremonial role in Richard's coronation, Hamelin was present at the ceremony and travelled widely with the new king in the first year of his reign, attesting no less than thirteen charters at Geddington, Bury St Edmunds, Canterbury, Rouen and Montrichard.[30] He played a prominent part in English politics while Richard was absent on the Third Crusade, supporting the justiciar, William Longchamp, during the chaos caused by the intrigues of the king's brother, John. It was an alliance of convenience, made due to Longchamp and Hamelin's mutual interests in curbing the power of Hugh de Puiset, Bishop of Durham, and John, the king's only surviving legitimate brother. Hamelin held great store in the rule of law, attested by the legend on his seal, 'pro lege, per lege' ('for the law, by the law').[31] This adherence to the law explains Hamelin's support for Longchamp against that of his own nephew, John, and even as the justiciar's overzealous actions alienated others. Hamelin's motivation may also have been driven by a personal animosity towards John. At some point in the early 1190s John fathered an illegitimate child, Richard, with one of Hamelin's daughters.

It was Hamelin, therefore, who was sent by Longchamp to arrest the archbishop of York, Henry II's illegitimate son Geoffrey, on his arrival at Dover and bring him to London. Geoffrey had sworn an oath to stay out of England whilst the king was away on crusade. John had sworn a similar oath, though that appears to have been revoked earlier. The archbishop was to face judgement by the barons of the realm, but the outcry at his arrest, and at Longchamp's ambition in arresting the archbishop who was the king's brother, albeit a half-brother, galvanised the baronial opposition led by John. King Richard, still en route to the Holy Land, had sent Walter de Countances, Bishop of Rouen, back to England to mediate between John and Longchamp. However, tensions still seethed, with Hamelin stalwart in his support of Longchamp. Following the death of one of John's knights in a skirmish near Windsor, and with John gaining support, the justiciar and prince met in conference at the Tower of London on 10 October. The crisis was resolved with William Longchamp's resignation as justiciar. He was replaced by Walter de Coutances himself. Coutances was no pushover and John was denied full authority, having to work alongside the new justiciar.

Hamelin appears to have suffered no repercussions from having backed the wrong horse. It may well be that his reputation for integrity stood him in good stead. When news of Richard's capture and imprisonment in Germany reached England, Hamelin was one of only two magnates entrusted with the collection and storage of the king's ransom; the other was William d'Aubigny, Earl of Arundel.[32]

After the king's return from Germany, Hamelin carried one of the three swords at Richard's second coronation at Winchester on 17 April 1194.[33] The other two sword-bearers were Ranulf, Earl of Chester, and William the Lion, King of Scots, Countess Isabel's first cousin. Hamelin was also present at the king's side later in the year, at the council held at Nottingham to deal with the insurgents who had supported John. Richard publicly forgave his brother, although his lands and castles were not returned to him. The king's forbearance did not extend to John's adherents, who lost their lands and offices.

Hamelin was approaching 70 years of age when he attended John's coronation on 27 May 1199, but still occasionally attended court duties. He witnessed the Scots king, William the Lion, perform his homage to John, on 21 November 1200, at Lincoln. In the same year, Hamelin was granted a weekly market at Conisbrough. In March 1201 the earl and countess were honoured with a visit from the king himself; John stayed at Conisbrough Castle overnight on 5 March, from where he issued a charter and a letter to the dean and chapter of York.[34] Earl Hamelin was not among the witnesses of the charter, it was witnessed by a William de Warenne; either the earl's son or, possibly, the baron of Wormegay, Countess Isabel's cousin and administrator of the Warenne lands.

Charters issued by Hamelin during his time as earl included confirmations of 'the gifts of churches and lands of his fee, with quittance and hidage or any other geld demanded by the king; and confirmation of the church of Conisbrough' to Lewes priory.[35] Other charters demonstrate Hamelin's interest and involvement in the administration of his lands and churches. One such is a letter from Hamelin to

> Guy Ruffus, saying that he had heard that the church of Braithwell belonged to the church of Conisbrough, and asking him to present master Clement to the archbishop for institution to the church of Braithwell instead of Philip, brother of the countess his wife, on whose behalf he had often made a request to Guy.[36]

Philip was Countess Isabel's half-brother, a younger son of Ela de Talvas by her second husband, Patrick, Earl of Salisbury. Philip had also witnessed a charter, alongside his sister, Countess Isabel, of Osbert, prior of Lewes in around 1180.[37] Such charters help to demonstrate the strength of continuing familial relations between the various branches of the family. Hamelin's charters also included further gifts to Lewes Priory, the Hospitallers, St Mary's Abbey in York, Nostell Priory, the chapel of St Philip and St James in Conisbrough Castle, St Katherine's Priory in Lincoln, Southwark Priory and the abbey of St Victor-en-Caux, Normandy. Earl Hamelin also revived the old Warenne interest in the abbey of Saint-Bertin at Saint-Omer, of which the second Earl Warenne and his brother, Rainald, had held the advocacy. Despite the fact the Warennes had not acted as advocates since 1096, Earl Hamelin appears around 1182, 'granting the abbey three *mensura* of land at Rocquetoire, known to have belonged to Gundrada [de Warenne]'s family until 1096.'[38] Over the ensuing years, the earl, countess and their son, William de Warenne, appear in various other transactions with the abbey of Saint-Bertin and its tenants.[39]

Many of Hamelin's charters are issued with his wife, Countess Isabel, or with her assent and that of his son and heir, William. Grants made by Hamelin and Isabel included a grant to Lewes Priory 'that the monks' men of the fens should be quit of carrying service beyond Well Stream towards Conisbrough or Wakefield, provided that they performed it on the return journey as far as [Castle] Acre or Methwold [Norfolk].'[40] One charter, which must have been very personal to Hamelin, confirmed in separate charters by Countess Isabel and their son, William, was to Lewes Priory, giving

> all the tithe of his eels in Yorkshire; for the souls of Geoffrey count of Anjou, his father, of king Henry his brother, of William [3rd] earl de Warenne, father of Countess Isabel, of all the earls de Warenne his antecessors, of Ala [Ela] countess de Warenne, and of all the countesses de Warenne; the tithe not to be farmed or sold, but the eels to be taken together to Lewes priory for the use of the convent.[41]

Another charter, issued by Hamelin sometime between 1182 and 1189, also made reference to his family and, specifically, to his father Geoffrey, Count of Anjou:

> Gift by Hamelin earl de Warenne to Lewes priory of the church of Conisbrough to be held in demesne, which church the monks had received after the death of Guy who had held it of them, and which they were holding '*in proprios usus*' by the authority of pope Lucius III

and the grace of king Henry [II], his brother, and with his own assent; together with all chapels and churches belonging to it, to be held likewise 'ad proprios usus' when they should fall vacant; for the welfare of king Henry, for his own and of countess Isabel his wife and William their son, and for the soul of Geoffrey count of Anjou, his father whose anniversary the monks would celebrate; any increment to be devoted to the alms of the poor, the entertainment of visitors on the day of his father's anniversary, and the feeding of the convent.[42]

Among Hamelin's charters are, also, those relating to the settlement of a dispute between Hamelin and Hugh, abbot of Cluny, over the appointment of a new prior to Lewes priory. Abbot Hugh was known as a man of great piety and honour; he had been prior of Lewes but was elected as abbot of Reading in 1186 and became abbot of Cluny in 1199. In 1200, Abbot Hugh appointed a monk named Alexander to the vacant position of prior of Lewes but Hamelin refused to accept the nomination. In establishing the priory at Lewes, the abbots of Cluny had apparently reserved the right to appoint the prior, and to admit all monks seeking entry into the order; however, Hamelin claimed that the patronage of the priory belonged to him, and it was his right to appoint the prior.

Initially, he was supported by some of the monks of the priory, who claimed they were independent of the mother house at Cluny, save for an annual payment of 100s. An appeal to the pope brought a decision in favour of the abbot, but Earl Hamelin appealed against it and seized the priory's possessions in Yorkshire and Norfolk. The earl went so far as to place armed guards on the priory gate, to prevent the monks from sending to Cluny for aid from the abbot. Visitors and pilgrims seeking the hospitality of the priory were searched and questioned before being admitted, to ensure they were not carrying messages from the abbot. The abbot even placed the priory under interdict, which prompted Hamelin to threaten the monks with starvation, should they observe the order.

The pope appointed the archbishop of Canterbury and the bishops of Ely and Chichester to investigate the case. The abbot himself came over to England to try and resolve the matter but was repulsed by the earl's men at the gates of both Castle Acre and Lewes priories. After intervention from King John, agreement was eventually reached whereby, should the position of prior become vacant, the earl and the monks should send representatives to the abbot, who would nominate two candidates, of whom the earl's proctors should choose one to be appointed prior.[43] The charges against Earl Hamelin were that, after the abbot of Cluny had appointed a prior to Lewes, he had oppressed the priory and its possessions for about five years. The agreement was sealed in a charter at Lambeth on 10 June 1201 'by which the procedure for the appointment of future priors of Lewes was regulated; no exaction from the priory to be made by the abbot except a payment of 100s yearly.[44]

One charter by Hamelin, a confirmation of a gift by Robert Brito of Denaby to Lewes priory 'of all his "*cultura*" adjoining the fields of Conisbrough called Rauennis Croswang' had the unusual quirk of being witnessed by the earl's goatherder, a man named Haregrim.[45]

Hamelin died on 7 May 1202 and was buried at Lewes Priory. Isabel was widowed for a second time; in the same year, she granted, for the soul of her husband earl Hamelin, 'to the priory of St Katherine, Lincoln, of similar easements for 60 beasts, namely for 40 as of his gift and 20 as of hers.[46] These grants were an addition to an earlier grant by Earl Hamelin to the priory of St Katherine

> of free entry and exit along his causeway called Cowbridge for 40 beasts to his pasture in his moor towards Thorne, and of pasture for 40 beasts in the said pasture among the beasts of his men at Hatfield. The canons had granted him two beds for the infirmary of the hospital and 300 masses in the first year of this gift and 1000 psalters, and had made him a participant in all the benefits of the order of Sempringham; as their charter bore witness.[47]

Sometime after Hamelin's death, Countess Isabel issued in a charter, a gift 'after the death of her husband earl Hamelin, to Richard son of Robert de Combe and his heirs of a virgate of land and a mill called Sidlow mill [in Horley, Surrey]; to hold; for which gift the donee gave a mark of silver.[48] The countess issued one other charter some time in 1202 or 1203, which was a confirmation 'with the assent of William her son and heir, to Lewes priory, of the tithe of her eels throughout all Yorkshire, to be received from her bailiffs of Yorkshire by the hand of the monks' bailiff of Conisbrough.[49]

Isabel and Hamelin had four surviving children. Their son and heir was William, who would become the fifth Earl Warenne. William was born in the late 1160s and was probably raised in Normandy; five days after his father's death, William was allowed to do homage for his father's estates. The couple also had three daughters. Ela married twice, first to Robert de Newburn and later to William FitzWilliam of Sprotborough. A second daughter, Isabel, was married first to Robert de Lascy, and then to Gilbert de L'Aigle, Lord of Pevensey. It has been suggested that another daughter,

Matilda, was Hamelin's daughter by a previous, unknown marriage, but this seems unlikely, and she was in fact the daughter of Hamelin and Isabel. Matilda was first married to Henry, Count of Eu, who died in 1191 and secondly to Henry d'Estouteville, lord of Valmont in Normandy.[50] From the late 1180s or early 1190s onwards, Hamelin's relationship with King John was complicated by the fact that John had a brief affair with one of Hamelin's daughters, though it has been impossible to determine which. The result of the affair was an illegitimate son, named Richard, after John's older brother. Known in various guises as Richard of Chilham, Richard of Dover, Richard fitzRoy, he was also known as Richard de Warenne, which is the name he used on his seal.[51]

Isabel de Warenne did not long outlive her second husband and died on 12 July 1203; the date is known as it is the day on which she was commemorated by the monks of Beauchief Abbey, Sheffield.[52] She was buried beside Hamelin in the chapterhouse at Lewes Priory. Isabel was, after all, a great heiress who had held the earldom of Surrey for over fifty years, from 1148 until her death in 1203. She had been married first to the son of a king and then to the brother of a king, albeit an illegitimate half-brother. Isabel and Hamelin had been married for almost forty years, had raised four children together and taken care to continue the Warenne tradition of supporting the Crown twinned with the sound administration of their lands and generous support of their chosen religious institutions. Hamelin had continued the Warenne building programme by adding the impressive cylindrical keep at Conisbrough Castle in Yorkshire, as well as the smaller keeps at Mortemer and Thorne. The couple passed on an earldom as strong as, if not stronger than, it had ever been, to their only son, William de Warenne, the fifth Earl Warenne.

Chapter Twelve

The Fifth Earl: William de Warenne
and the First Barons' War

C ountess Isabel and her first husband, William of Blois, had no children. With her second husband, Hamelin, the countess bore four surviving children, three girls and a boy. Their son and heir was William, who would become the fifth earl of Warenne and Surrey; although it is from William onwards that the numbering of the earls can get confusing. Some secondary sources count William as the sixth earl if they count William of Blois and Hamelin as the fourth and fifth earls, respectively. I have chosen to go with the *Oxford Dictionary of National Biography*, which counts William of Blois and Hamelin, both, as the fourth Earl Warenne.

William was born in the late 1160s and was probably raised in Normandy. In 1194, he was among those who interceded with King Richard to plead a license to reopen the English tournament circuit.[1] He came of age sometime in the late 1180s and appears as a witness on a charter of Richard I at Rouen in September 1197. Before 1202, he appears on several of his father's charters, as having given his consent to donations. One such charter was a

> Confirmation by Hamelin, earl de Warenne, with the assent of countess Isabel his wife and of William his son and heir, to Lewes priory of all the gifts of his predecessors, including in Yorkshire the churches of Conisbrough, Wakefield, Halifax, Dewsbury, Sandal Magna, Kirkburton, Hatfield with the chapel of Thorne, Fishlake, Harthill, Kirk Sandal, and Dinnington; also gift of tithe of money from his rents everywhere and grant of several privileges; also confirmation of all the tithe of [?] shingle of 'Rigeburg,' and the mills of Meeching [modern Newhaven] and 'Higardeseya,' in view of the exchange of Barcombe [Sussex] and Meeching which he had made.[2]

William de Warenne is mentioned in some of Hamlin's charters and referred to as '*Willelmi filii et heredis mei*' ('William my son and heir').[3]

William appeared in Hamelin's charter which had granted a tithe of eels in Yorkshire to Lewes priory, for the souls of Hamelin's father and brother and

Countess Isabel's parents and Warenne ancestors. William then appeared in his mother's accompanying charter as giving consent to her confirmation of Hamelin's charter. In addition, William then issued his own charter as a 'Confirmation by William de Warenne, son of earl Hamelin, of his father's grant to Lewes priory of the tithe of his eels in Yorkshire.'[4] And sometime between 1188 and 1202, a charter was issued which was a gift by

> Hamelin earl de Warenne, countess Isabel his wife and William their son to each of their free burgesses of Wakefield of a toft of one acre of land in their town of Wakefield, to hold in free burgage for 6d yearly, free from all customs of sale and purchase throughout their lands of Yorkshire; and grant of dead wood in their wood of Wakefield for burning. For this the burgesses gave to earl Hamelin 100s sterling, to countess Isabel 20s and to William 20s.[5]

We have no details of William's whereabouts or actions before his father's death in 1202. It is clear, from the charters, that Hamelin involved his son in the management of the Warenne estates, and in the family's religious benefactions. From his witnessing of a charter by King Richard, in Rouen, we may also assume that William spent some time with the king and may have been involved in Richard's campaigns against France. Richard was William's first cousin, and probably about ten years his senior. The king's wars would have certainly proved to be an ideal training ground for a young lord learning the art of war and command.

On 10 June 1201, William was present with his parents at Lambeth to settle the long running dispute between Hamelin and Hugh, Abbot of Cluny over the appointment of priors at Lewes priory in Sussex, a Warenne foundation. The issue first appears to have arisen in 1181, when Earl Hamelin and Theobald, then abbot of Cluny, had agreed a procedure for the appointment of priors. The question arose again when Abbot Hugh appointed one Alexander as the new prior at Lewes. Earl Hamelin had insisted that Lewes priory was independent of the abbey of Cluny and that, as the priory's patron, he had the right to appoint its priors. Whereas Hugh, abbot of Cluny, who was himself a former prior of Lewes, insisted that it was his right to appoint the prior, and insisted that the monks at Lewes obey Alexander, under threat of interdict. The compromise which was eventually reached, allowed for representatives of the monks and the earl to attend on the abbot at Cluny, when a new prior was to be chosen, and the abbot would suggest two suitable candidates, from which the earl would make the final choice. The agreement at Lambeth was made 'in the presence of Isabel countess de Warenne and William her son and heir.'[6]

For William de Warenne, the 1201 agreement was not the end of the matter. Cluny did not find the arrangement satisfactory, nor see it as a final settlement. On 25 October 1228, Pope Gregory IX granted the abbot of Cluny a faculty to appoint the prior of Lewes notwithstanding the composition between Earl Warenne, the patron, and the abbot's predecessor of thirty years before, which he declared was '*juri contrariam et ecclesie ipsi damnosam*' ('right contrary and damaging to the church').[7] The pope further asserted that it had given occasion for the prior and monks of Lewes to rebel against the church of Cluny, its mother house. As earl, William de Warenne appealed to the pope and in 1234 the 1201 agreement was read to the king, the archbishop of Canterbury, the bishops of London and Exeter and others, 'when it was recorded that the earl, desirous of establishing the right which he and his predecessors had in the appointment of the prior of Lewes, and which they had exercised many times in accordance with the said agreement, had appealed to the apostolic see.'[8] Later, the archbishop and archdeacon of Canterbury instructed all Cluniac monasteries in England to pay a tenth of the revenues for three years to the abbey of Cluny, but made no mention of the prior agreement with Earl Hamelin and included the priory of Lewes in the order. On 6 February 1239 or 1240, reference was made to the financial aspect of the earl's petition when the pope ordered them to cease the exactions until further orders. The earl had stated that

> his ancestors had founded and endowed the priory, where a hundred monks were living and exercising hospitality and that the abbot and convent of Cluny under pretext of spiritual jurisdiction made inroads on the priory's property, so that H[amelin] the earl's father and [Isabel] his mother made an agreement that the abbot should be content with 100s yearly from the priory.[9]

William's father Earl Hamelin died on 7 May 1202. Five days after his father's death, William was allowed to do homage to his cousin King John for his father's estates.[10] In the first eighteen months after his succession to the earldom, William was in Normandy, playing a major role in the defence of the duchy against King Philip II Augustus of France. In August 1202 he had fought alongside William Marshal and William Longespée, Earl of Salisbury, hounding the retreating forces of King Philip. The French king had withdrawn from the siege of Arques following news of John's victory over his nephew, Arthur, at Mirebeau. When King John lost the majority of his Continental possessions, in 1204, William de Warenne was refused permission to do homage to King Philip for his Norman lands, despite promising that he would remain loyal to John. In compensation for the loss of his Norman estates, William received the towns of Stamford and Grantham, in Lincolnshire.

Earl William nevertheless retained strong links with Normandy, with two of his sisters overseeing the family's interests there. Matilda, married first to Henri, Count of Eu, and then to Henry d'Estouteville, Lord of Valmont in Normandy, was joined in the duchy in 1204 by her sister Isabel, who had married Gilbert de l'Aigle. In that year, Gilbert had defected to the French and he and William had made an arrangement whereby Gilbert would look after the Warenne lands in Normandy while William watched over Gilbert's lands in England. William therefore paid a fine of £2,000 to the Crown to take possession of Gilbert's English estates on behalf of his sister, Isabel.[11]

The fine was paid in full between 1207 and 1212: after 1217 Gilbert was able to return to England and reclaim his lands. In the same year Earl William was given custody of the lands of Leonia, mother of Henry d'Estouteville, William's brother-in-law. The lands, in Yorkshire, Nottinghamshire and elsewhere, had been seized on Leonia's death.[12]

In 1206, William served on the king's expedition to Poitou, probably in the hope of regaining his French estates. The expedition was diverted to Gascony to counter a threat from Alfonso VIII of Castile. After a successful campaign against Alfonso, John's forces headed north, taking Angers. As King Philip II moved to confront John, the campaign ended in a stalemate and a two-year truce was agreed between the two kings. In the following year Earl William took part in the peace negotiations with Scotland. The two kings, John and William the Lion, King of Scots, met at York between the 26 and 28 May, although we have no record of what was discussed. William the Lion, you may recall, was a descendant of William, 2nd Earl Warenne, through his daughter Ada de Warenne, and was therefore a first cousin of Earl Warenne's mother, Countess Isabel. In 1210 the earl sent a contingent of knights to join King John's punitive expedition to Ireland, which was intended to bring recalcitrant barons to heal, and to capture William de Braose and his wife, Matilda, who had sought sanctuary with their son-in-law, Walter de Lacy, Lord of Meath, from John's vindictive pursuit of their family. John's hounding of the Braose family resulted in William de Braose's death in exile and Matilda's gruesome death by starvation, alongside their eldest son, also called William, in John's dungeons.

In the build up to the Magna Carta crisis of 1215, William de Warenne remained loyal to his cousin; in 1212 he was briefly appointed sheriff of Northumberland and given custody of several castles seized from barons suspected of plotting rebellion. In the ensuing years, he was given custody of several baronial hostages surrendered to the king. In 1213, William de Warenne was a guarantor for the peace agreement between King John and the church, which was to bring to an end the papal interdict which had been placed on England in March 1208. A papal nuncio, Pandulph, arrived in England with instructions from the pope of what John should do in order to get the interdict lifted and allow the return of the exiled English bishops. The consequences of not complying with the pope's orders were very clear:

> This was the most important part of his orders: that before 1 June four of the most important men in the kingdom should swear, on the king's behalf, he being present and ordering it, that if the pope sent the king a signed letter of agreement then the king would promise the same in his letters patent and seal the agreement with the archbishop and bishops. Otherwise the time of severest punishment had not yet come.[13]

The Barnwell Annalist continues with his narrative:

> What need for many words? Inspired, it is said, by Him in whose hand are the hearts of kings, he acquiesced in peace. And those who swore to the aforesaid written agreement of the pope were Renaud, count of Boulogne, William, earl of Warenne, William, earl of Ferrers, and William, earl of Salisbury, the king's brother. And when this had been completed the king promised the same in his letters according to the form which these four had sworn on his behalf.[14]

John went a step further and surrendered the kingdom to the papacy, promising

> he and his heirs should pay one thousand marks a year to the popes as a token of their subjection, that is seven hundred marks for England and three hundred for Ireland, not counting the payment of Peter's Pence. At the same time he swore liege homage and fealty to Pope Innocent III and to his successors. And all this was publicly proclaimed by letters patent published in the manner of charters.[15]

In 1214 William de Warenne again sent a contingent of knights with the king's army, this time to Poitou. John met with some initial success, outmanoeuvring the French forces of Prince Louis and besieging the castle of Roche-au-Moine. The expedition ended in failure, however, when John's half-brother, William Longespée, and his ally and nephew, Emperor Otto, were defeated by King Philip at the Battle of Bouvines. While Otto escaped the battlefield, Longespée was captured and held for ransom, returning to England in March 1215. John's failure in Poitou further exacerbated the situation at home. With the outbreak of civil war Earl Warenne sided with the Crown, supporting his royal cousin. He negotiated with the rebels at Northampton in May 1215: 'the king tried to win them back through many emissaries and there was much discussion amongst them, the archbishop, bishops and other barons acting as intermediaries, the king himself staying near Oxford.'[16] He was named as one of the royalists present when Magna Carta was issued at Runnymede on 15 June in the same year, 'Having agreed upon a place where the parties could conveniently gather, after many deliberations they made peace with the king, and he gave to them all that they wanted, and confirmed it in his charter.'[17]

Magna Carta proved only a temporary respite to the tensions on both sides. Within weeks, King John had written to the pope to be released from the promises he had made, and the rebel barons were once again up in arms. William de Warenne was with the king at the siege of Rochester in November, 1215, 'the besieged, being closely pressed at Rochester, urged the king to negotiate with them, but he refused to grant this request and hurled stones against them unceasingly, both day and night, with five throwing machines.'[18] John eventually set the sappers to work undermining the castle; even when half of the keep collapsed, the rebels continued their resistance in the other half. When the besiegers finally surrendered in December, John ordered that some of the captives have their hands and feet cut off, while others were thrown in chains, the king keeping the knights and nobles for himself and giving the less important prisoners into the custody of others.

After the fall of Rochester, William de Warenne served the Crown as a commander in Sussex, where he had extensive lands and influence, and on 26 May 1216, Warenne was given the charge of the Cinque Ports. However, on 6 June the rebel army led by Louis of France was allowed to enter the earl's castle at Reigate unopposed and, later in the month, Warenne submitted to Louis at Winchester, alongside his cousin, William Longespée, Earl of Salisbury, and the earl of Arundel.

It has been suggested that Warenne defected due to a personal grievance after John seduced one of his sisters in the 1190s. The girl had given birth to John's illegitimate son, Richard of Chilham, although twenty years seems like a long time to hold a grudge, and William had worked well with John since. It seems more likely that the earl had seen the way the wind was blowing and thought King John's cause doomed. Warenne's personal rebellion lasted less than a year; King John's death in October 1216 may have help to precipitate a reconciliation with the new king, 9-year-old Henry III. By March 1217 he was taking instructions from King Henry over his lands at Stamford and on 17 April, at Chichester, he was reconciled with the royalists, after a truce was negotiated by Guala, the papal legate.[19] On 17 June, eager to safeguard his interests in France, Warenne sent formal letters to Louis to notify the French prince of his decision to return to the royalists. On 9 May, a month before he officially renounced his allegiance to Prince Louis, William was given letters of safe-conduct, possibly to travel between the French and English camps, possibly as a spy but more likely to act as a go-between:

> Conduct. William, the earl Warenne, has letters of conduct of the lord king, with the stipulation that if any of his men shall have been sent on his behalf to the lord king or to his faithful men with letters patent of the said earl, they will be able to travel throughout the lord king's power. Witness the earl [of Pembroke], at Oxford, the ninth day of May, in the first year of the lord king's reign.[20]

William de Warenne was not recorded as present at the Second Battle of Lincoln in May, 1217, when the forces of William Marshal routed the French. However, in August 1217 the earl equipped a ship of knights that took part in the Battle of Sandwich against the French fleet led by Eustace the Monk. Although he did not fight himself, the earl's ship was one of the first to engage with the French fleet and took several prisoners. Eustace the Monk was taken and executed; Roger of Wendover suggested that the execution was personally carried out by Earl William's illegitimate royal nephew, Richard of Chilham.[21] After the battle, the earl paid over 1000 marks to the men of the Cinque Ports, to take custody of many of the French prisoners, in the hope of extracting large ransoms for their freedom. With the defeat of the French fleet, Louis was forced to make peace. 'From that day the cause of the king flourished while that of Louis declined. Then, with the forces of the king gathering near London, Louis did not delay to make such peace as fortune offered.'[22]

Earl Warenne was also prominent in the negotiations with Louis to bring the war to a close:

> On 12 September, terms were made, concerning the release of those who had been captured; concerning the civil customs which had been the cause of the war; and concerning the observance of the liberties which had been sought by the English nobles. A financial settlement was made for the expenses which Louis had incurred in the kingdom.[23]

Louis was paid 10,000 marks to go home. The peace settlement would cause William de Warenne problems well into the next decade; all French prisoners were to be released without ransom. The earl's fellow barons promised to refund, from the Exchequer, the 1,000 marks that William had spent on purchasing valuable prisoners. However, when the money was not forthcoming, save for an occasional payment, William was forced to borrow heavily from the justiciar, Hubert de Burgh, widower of William's cousin, Beatrice de Warenne of Wormegay.

William de Warenne, 5th Earl Warenne, served in the administration of the minority government of Henry III throughout the 1220s. He had been appointed sheriff of Surrey in 1218, a position he had pursued during the civil war, disputing it with the alien royalist Engelard de Cigogné. He remained in that post until November 1226. In 1219 he attended the funeral procession of William Marshal, Earl of Pembroke and regent for King Henry III. The solemn procession brought the great knight's body from his home at Caversham, where he had died, to the Temple Church in London, where he was to be buried. That same year, the earl aided his niece, Alice, Countess of Eu, in the recovery of her lands in both England and Normandy, including the honours and castles of Tickhill in Yorkshire and Hastings in Sussex. The earl was given custody of both on behalf of his niece, though his possession of Tickhill was challenged by Robert de Vieuxpont.

In 1220, William de Warenne joined his cousin, Ela, Countess of Salisbury and her husband, William Longespée, in laying foundation stones for the new Salisbury Cathedral. Ela and her husband were great patrons of the church, laying the fourth and fifth foundation stones.[25] William de Warenne and Countess Ela shared a grandmother in Ela de Talvas, mother of William's mother, Countess Isabel, and Ela's father, William FitzPatrick, 2nd Earl of Salisbury. In the same year, the Earl Warenne took part in the negotiations with both the French and the king of Scots, another kinsman, Alexander II, son of William the Lion and grandson of Ada de Warenne. The next year he provided a contingent of knights to aid in the recovery of Bytham Castle on behalf of Henry III. In the spring of 1223 Warenne went on pilgrimage to Santiago de Compostela in Spain but was back in England in time to join the campaign against Montgomery, providing the king's army with twenty knights and being a witness to the terms of the truce with the Welsh.[26] The earl was a staunch ally of the justiciar, Hubert de Burgh, who had been married to his cousin Beatrice de Warenne, the daughter and heir of William de Warenne of Wormegay. Their kinship had gained William de Warenne favours from the minority administration. In return, he supported de Burgh in 1223–24, when the justiciar's position was threatened by rivals at court.

King John's mercenary captain, Faulkes de Bréauté and his court allies, the earls of Chester and Gloucester, attempted to seize the Tower of London, forcing Hubert de Burgh and the king to flee the capital and seek shelter in Northampton. Stephen Langton, Archbishop of Canterbury, managed to avert civil war, but tensions still ran high. By 1224 de Burgh was back in command and ordered Bréauté to relinquish Plympton and Bedford castles. When he refused, de Burgh sent justices to accuse him of breaching the peace; they found him guilty of sixteen counts of wrongful disseisin (seizure of land). In response, Bréauté's brother seized one of the justices, Henry of Braybrooke. The king and his forces, including Earl Warenne, besieged Bréauté at Bedford castle as the archbishop of Canterbury excommunicated the brothers and the entire garrison. The siege lasted eight weeks, with over 200 royalist attackers killed by missiles launched from the castle. When Bedford castle was captured by assault, Bréauté's brother and eighty knights were refused pardon and hanged. Faulkes de Bréauté submitted to Henry III on 19 August and was escorted into exile by William de Warenne. It was possibly as reward for his continuing support that William was granted custody of the royal castle of Bramber and the castle of Hornby in Lancashire.[27]

Disappointments in later 1226 and early 1227, when he was replaced as sheriff in Surrey and forced to surrender Hornby to its rightful heir, may explain the reason behind William briefly joining the confederation against the king, led by Henry III's brother Richard of Cornwall. The disaffected barons, including the earls of Pembroke and Chester, met at William's manor of Stamford to confirm their accord. After this short-lived defiance, William de Warenne was forced to surrender custody of Tickhill, but was confirmed in his manors of Stamford and Grantham in 1228. In the same year he received the third penny of the county of Surrey for the first time; this was an honorary payment due to the earl of a county, but appears to have been previously denied to William and his father Hamelin, before him.[28] The earl's fall from grace seems to have been soon forgiven, if not forgotten.

William de Warenne continued to be a part of the royal administration throughout the 1230s. When the king went on an expedition to Brittany in 1230, Earl William was appointed keeper of the ports along the east coast of England. In the following year, he served with the army in Wales, fighting against the forces of Llywelyn ap Iorwerth – Llywelyn the Great:

In May, the Welsh burst forth from their dens like shrews from holes, raising fires everywhere. King Henry III sent Hubert de Burgh, justiciar of the realm to repress their attacks. No sooner had they heard of the king's departure, however, than the Welsh reverted to their pillaging and, infesting the provinces near Montgomery Castle, they laid them waste. When the English soldiers who were defending that famous castle realised what was afoot, they set out to teach the Welsh a lesson. The English cut off their escape route, captured many and killed even more and when they presented their prisoners to the justiciar, he ordered them to be executed and their heads taken to Henry III.[29]

Llywelyn retaliated by harassing the lands of the barons along the Welsh March, to the extent that Henry himself led an army into Wales.

In July 1232, the king relieved Hubert de Burgh of his position as justiciar and replaced him with Peter de Roches, Bishop of Winchester. In his annoyance with de Burgh, the king 'demanded an immediate account from him of the royal treasure paid into the exchequer and of the debts owed to the king from both his father's reign and his own.'[30] Hubert de Burgh was escorted to his imprisonment at Devizes Castle by four earls, including William de Warenne. Although de Burgh was no longer married to William's cousin – Beatrice de Warenne had died in 1214 – the two had remained political allies and guarding de Burgh in his imprisonment was probably an unpleasant task for Earl Warenne. He remained sympathetic to de Burgh, who had married Margaret, a princess of Scotland, as his third and final wife in 1221 and had been created earl of Kent in 1227; although it was stipulated that the earldom would descend through Hubert de Burgh's children by Margaret, rather than his eldest son by Beatrice de Warenne, John. Hubert de Burgh's connections with William de Warenne were still close as he had retained the Wormegay lands of Beatrice for life; the lands would only revert to Beatrice's eldest son, William Bardolf, on de Burgh's death.

After the fall of Hubert de Burgh's persecutors, and his return to government in 1234, William de Warenne was there in support. Warenne was the earl to accept the surrender of de Burgh's castles at Bramber and Knepp, which had been taken by the former justiciar's enemies.[31] The Earl Warenne served as ceremonial cup-bearer at the coronation of Henry III's queen, Eleanor of Provence, in January 1236 and in 1237 he was one of the few surviving barons, who had witnessed the original 1215 Magna Carta, to witness the charter's reissue. In the same year, he was admitted to the king's council and in 1238 was sent to Oxford to protect the papal legate, Otto, who was the subject of violent attacks.[32]

William de Warenne was married twice. He was first married to Matilda, daughter of William d'Aubigny, Earl of Arundel, sometime before 1207.

The marriage remained childless and Matilda died, possibly on 6 February 1215; she was buried at the Warenne foundation of Lewes Priory in Sussex.[33] William married for a second time, before 13 October 1225, Matilda Marshal, widow of Hugh Bigod, Earl of Norfolk, who had died in February of the same year. Matilda was the eldest daughter of the great William Marshal, Earl of Pembroke and regent of England during the minority of Henry III. The marriage appears to have been one of convenience, rather than genuine affection, Warenne being considerably older than his new wife.

Although we do not have a birth date for Matilda Marshal, also known as Maud or Mahelt, given that her parents married in 1189 and she had two elder brothers, she was probably born in 1193 or 1194. She was the third child and eldest daughter of William and his wife, Isabel de Clare. The *Histoire de Guillaume le Maréchale* praises Matilda saying she had the gifts of 'wisdom, generosity, beauty, nobility of heart, graciousness, and I can tell you in truth, all the good qualities which a noble lady should possess.'[34] The *Histoire* goes on to say: 'Her worthy father who loved her dearly, married her off, during his lifetime to the best and most handsome party he knew, to Sir Hugh Bigot.'[35] Of William and Isabel's five daughters, it is only Matilda who is mentioned in the *Histoire* as being 'loved dearly' by her father. Matilda had been married to Hugh Bigod in 1207, at the age of 13 or 14. Hugh had succeeded to the title of earl of Norfolk when his father died sometime between April and August 1221, probably aged well into his seventies. The new earl, however, only enjoyed his title for four years; he died suddenly in 1225, aged only 43. Hugh was succeeded by his eldest son by Matilda, Roger, then only 16 years old and therefore still a minor.

Matilda was still only 32 years old when Hugh died, with four children to care for. As a valuable marriage prize she, or her family, acted quickly to secure her future and safety and, within eight months of her husband's death, Matilda was married to William de Warenne. William was a neighbour of the Bigods in Norfolk, and he had joined the rebellion against King John at about the same time as Roger Bigod, although William was back in the Royalist camp by March 1217. The earl had purchased Matilda's marriage, essentially meaning her dower in Norfolk, before July 1225. Matilda continued to style herself as 'Matildis la Bigot' in charters, with 'Matildis de Warenne' added only as an afterthought, or not at all. For example, a charter from the early 1240s, following the death of William de Warenne, has the salutation, *'ego Matilda Bigot comitissa Norf' et Warenn.'*[36] On any charters relating to her Norfolk holdings this may have served to emphasise Matilda's rights over her dower lands. However, it may also be an indication that this marriage was not of Matilda's own choosing and that she may even have preferred to remain a widow, rather than entering into this second marriage. The continuing use of her name from her first marriage may have been her own mark of rebellion against her new situation.

As with his predecessors, William de Warenne was adept at the complex estate management needed to administer lands in Norfolk, Sussex, Yorkshire and elsewhere. A return from the rape of Lewes of 1212 shows that he held in chief a total of sixty-two knights' fees throughout his English lands; in addition, in the rape of Pevensey, he held thirty-and-a-half fees of Gilbert de l'Aigle, as a result of the fine he had made with the king for control of Gilbert's English lands. On 15 March in 1203 or 1204, he was granted permission to hold a yearly fair at Wakefield. As a widow, William's niece, Alice, Countess of Eu, gave her uncle the manor of Greetwell in Lincolnshire, in return for the annual payment of a sparrowhawk to Philippa de Tylly, whose family held the land as a fee of Countess Alice. Philippa de Tylly herself then added the lands at Mealton and Upton in Nottinghamshire for a payment of 200 marks.[37] The earl was still holding Greetwell, worth £10, at his death, along with the manors of Stamford and Grantham in Lincolnshire. The earl created an under-tenancy at Greetwell for Roger FitzWilliam, the son of his sister, Ela.[38]

The fifth earl's charters include a general confirmation to Lewes priory in memory of his predecessors from the first earl to Earl Hamelin and Countess Isabel, though it omits Isabel's first husband, William of Blois.[39] Also among the earl's charters is the confirmation of a gift of his sister, Ela, to Roche Abbey, 'which dame Ela de Warenne, his late sister, had given with her body [for burial].'[40] Roche abbey was a Cistercian monastery which had been founded in the twelfth century; although only a few miles from the family honour of Conisbrough, it had not featured extensively in the donations of earlier Warenne earls.

There is also confirmation of a gift of Reiner son of William Fleming 'made to Kirklees priory as his charter testified.'[41] Other charters by the earl included a gift to 'Richard de Cartworth of 12 acres of land in Wooldale [par Kirkburton]; rendering 2s yearly,' the counterseal being the Warenne 'shield of arms, checky.'[42] Sometime between 1210 and 1225, Earl William issued a letters patent 'ordering Sir Matthew de Shepley, his steward in Yorkshire, and John de Wakefield, clerk, to cause the tithes of his rents in their bailiwicks to be paid to Lewes priory at the fixed terms.'[43] A further charter to John de Wakefield was a 'Quitclaim by William earl de Warenne to John de Wakefield, his clerk, of a yearly rent of 2s from his messuage in Northgate [Wakefield], with power to give it in frankalmoin.'[44]

The earl issued letters patent 'to his water-bailiffs of Bradmere, ordering them to cause the monks of Roche to have a tithe of the residue of his eels from all his fisheries in the parishes of Hatfield, Thorne and Fishlake after the full tithe belonging to the monks of Lewes, in accordance with the gift which he had made.'[45] A gift was also issued to the priory of St Michael in Stamford 'of 40s of silver yearly from the rent of his mill of Wakefield, which he had assigned to the priory kitchen, for the celebration of the obit of Elias de Marvile yearly on the eve of St George's day.'[46]

William de Warenne was most likely the earl involved in an exchange with the count of Aumale to arrange a tournament between the two barons' knights, which he saw as necessary after a long period of peace and inaction:

> The earl of Warenne to the count of Aumale, greetings. That which ceases from use has prepared the way for its own retirement. We knights are being kept from action like unskilled clodhoppers; this long interval of sitting around, which prevents the practice of knightly exercise, gives one kidney stones. You will have heard that a certain tournament has been sworn between us and O, the earl of such-and-such a place. We beg you with our utmost affection to come to it. Since we are unfit, we trust in your integrity as to a city; to your triumphal banner as to a castle with its walls and surrounding moat, which is accustomed to be the refuge of the weary and of those oppressed by an adverse fate. And those who are accustomed to our protection in the best possible manner have committed themselves to being defended [by] the might of your protection. We also desire your presence there all the more because we believe it will be essential to us.[47]

The letter is dated to sometime between 1214 and 1240, between the succession of William II de Forz to the earldom of Aumale and William de Warenne's death. It may well have been sent in the 1220s, during Henry III's minority, a time when the country was relatively at peace. Apparently these events became a little too frequent and a second letter, probably sent by Earl Warenne sometime after the first, requests a break from tournaments:

> An earl to an earl, greetings. An assembly for the practice of knightly skills is refreshed by a modest suspension. One should not cancel it, but let it be interrupted for a brief time. For who can fight without a pause? That which lacks daily rest cannot endure; a bow, unless you cease to draw it, will grow slack. After a break, the benefit of rest, we rise up all the keener for our knightly exercise; after a rest, with our strength renewed, we strive all the more at the delightful sport of the

tournament. We recall the deeds of our ancestors – the deeds of the duke of Macedon and the doughty deeds of the Twelve Peers – who rouse us to a gathering of knightly practice. They learned by tourneying in war. One whom fear holds back, or costs constrain, should not [?be forced] to a tournament; one who is terrified to [?hear] the sound of the charge should stay at home. *We* shall come thither to preserve our honour, [and] so that we may put ourselves to the test there. And [if] anyone is more fervent at arms, may the gout take him![48]

These two letters serve to emphasise the enthusiasm for tournaments among the knightly class, and for William de Warenne in particular. Even his request for a pause is so that his men can come back refreshed and ready to continue the fight with renewed vigour. It is a fascinating glimpse into one aspect of baronial life that obviously meant a great deal to the barons themselves, both as entertainment and as a means to training men for combat.

After an eventful life at the heart of English politics, William de Warenne, the fifth Earl Warenne, died in London on 27 or 28 May 1240, in his early seventies, and was buried before the high altar of Lewes Priory. The king, who referred to Warenne as his 'beloved and faithful Earl Warenne' ordered that a cross should be erected to his memory, on the road between Merton and Carshalton in Surrey.[49] William's death was recorded in the *Annals of Lewes Priory* though it was dated to 1242. In 1243 the same chronicle relates: 'On the anniversary day of the Lord Earl William, the foundation was laid for the new work of our church.'[50] Matilda outlived her second husband by eight years. Her son still a minor, on 7 February 1242 at Windsor, the king

granted to Matilda, Countess Warenne, all lands and tenements formerly of W., formerly Earl Warenne, in Norfolk and Yorkshire which pertain to the king by reason of the custody of the land and heir of the aforesaid earl being in his hand, namely in Yorkshire the manors of Wakefield and Conisbrough, the water of Bradmere and a certain chamber in Thorne which the king has retained to his use with their appurtenances, having retained in his hand the knights' fees, wardships, escheats and the advowsons of churches of the same manors, and also the corn now sown in the lands and in the granges, stock and all issues of the same manors until the Close of Easter in the twenty-sixth year, to have and hold at farm until the legal age of the aforesaid heir, rendering £244 15s. 8d. each year at the Exchequer for the aforesaid manors and £100 per annum for the increment of the aforesaid manors and for the manors in Norfolk. Order to the sheriff of Yorkshire to cause the countess to have full seisin of all lands and tenements aforesaid in his bailiwick.[51]

With the Warenne lands in Norfolk and Yorkshire to sustain her, Matilda had no need to seek the protection of a new husband and did not marry again after William's death. In 1246, as the last surviving child of William Marshal, and with neither of her five brothers leaving a son, Matilda was granted the Marshal's rod by King Henry III. She did, at this point, change her name on charters, to '*Martill marescalla Angliae, comitissa Norfolciae et Warennae.*'[52] Emphasising her Marshal name as her father's eldest surviving child, Matilda was, significantly, claiming the title Marshal of England as her right, thus increasing her power and prestige, and taking the authority of the marshal as her own. Matilda appears to have acted independently during her second marriage, purchasing land in the Don Valley in South Yorkshire, close to the Warenne stronghold of Conisbrough Castle, in her own name. After the queen she was 'undoubtedly the most powerful and wealthy woman in England from 1242 onwards.'[53]

Matilda Marshal, Countess of Norfolk, Warenne and Surrey, died in March 1248 and was buried with her mother at Tintern Abbey. William and Matilda had two children together. A son and heir, John, was born in 1231 and was a prominent magnate and military commander in the reigns of Henry III and Edward I. John also had an older sister, Isabel, who we will meet in the next chapter. Isabel was born sometime between 1226 and 1230.

Chapter Thirteen

Warenne Women: The Daughters of the Fourth and Fifth Earls

William de Warenne had three sisters, Ela, Isabel and Matilda, and a daughter, Isabel. Each of these women had their own stories to tell. Their lives serve to demonstrate the strong family links engendered by the Warennes throughout the generations, helping to promote the image of a strong, caring family in which William, as earl and patriarch, was a driving and unifying force.

Ela, or Adela, married twice, firstly to a Robert de Newburn, of whom nothing else is known, and secondly to William FitzWilliam of Sprotborough, a village just a few miles from the Warenne stronghold of Conisbrough Castle, Yorkshire. Sometime between 1238 and 1240, Ela's brother the earl issued a charter to 'Roger son of William' who is described as his nephew, and therefore Ela's son.[1] The earl had created an under-tenancy, at Greetwell in Lincolnshire, for his nephew.[2] William FitzWilliam was the son of Godric and his wife Aubreye de Lisours. He was born around 1170 and died sometime between 1219 and 1224. Ela was his second wife; his first wife was named Maud, for whom he confirmed a gift by his mother to Hampole priory, as the son and heir of Aubreye de Lisours, of 'a rent for a pittance of the nuns and for buying oil for a lamp to burn at the tomb of Maud formerly his wife.'[3] In 1253 the FitzWilliam family are recorded as owning the manor of Emley. Three carucates of this were soke of the manor of Wakefield in 1086. It is possible, therefore, that Emley was given to Ela by her father, Earl Hamelin, in frank-marriage and thereafter descended through the FitzWilliam family.[4] After she was widowed for the second time, and before her death, Ela issued a charter mentioning both of her husbands by name, and all of her children. In this charter, Ela made a gift to Roche Abbey, just a few miles south of Conisbrough, 'of five virgates of land in Rottingdean [Sussex], together with three villeins and their sequels.' Her gift was confirmed by her brother after her death, in which the earl stated that the land had been 'given with her body [for burial].'[5] Ela appears to have been the only Warenne to be buried at Roche Abbey, despite its proximity to their castle at Conisbrough. The land in Rottingdean was sold by Roche Abbey to the dean and chapter of Chichester, under whose auspices Lewes priory fell. The land was exchanged with Sele priory in 1248 for a payment towards a chantry in the cathedral.[6]

A second sister, Isabel, was given land in Sowerby and Sowerbyshire, Yorkshire, in frank-marriage, by her father, Hamelin. Isabel married, firstly, Robert de Lascy (or Lacy), who died in 1193; after his death, Isabel rendered account at Michaelmas 1194 of 80 marks for her reasonable dower from his land. Payment was completed at Michaelmas 1196.[7] Isabel was married for a second time, to Gilbert de L'Aigle, Lord of Pevensey, no later than the spring of 1196. In 1200 she was involved in a dispute with Roger de Lascy, constable of Chester and lord of Pontefract, cousin of Isabel's first husband, Robert. Isabel complained that Lascy had disseised her of part of her dower from her first marriage, whereas Lascy claimed that Isabel's dower was excessive. In 1201, as part of the case, Gilbert de L'Aigle stated that Isabel had been married in another county in the time of Robert de Lascy's father, Henry de Lascy, and that Robert had dowered Isabel with a third of his prospective inheritance and that, after his father's death in 1177 or 1178, Robert had assigned Isabel's dower in a third of 100 librates of land. Roger de Lascy argued that she was dowered in specified lands and the service of five knights' fees.[8] I was unable to discover the final outcome of the legal proceedings, although it does seem that the two families may have resolved their disagreement with a marriage, arranged between Roger's son, John de Lacy, and Alice de L'Aigle, the daughter of Gilbert, in 1214. However, there is scant evidence for this marriage, and if it did take place, it was short-lived and childless. John de Lacy married Margaret de Quincy in 1221, so poor Alice must have died before then. Isabel also held the manor of Northease in the rape of Lewes from her brother, William, and, as a widow after the death of her second husband, she gave a third of it to Michelham priory, which she had founded with Gilbert de L'Aigle in 1229; the priory later held the same land from earl Warenne, who, as Isabel's brother, was also her heir.

Earl Warenne looked out for his sisters. When the king confiscated the vills of Westcott and Witley from Gilbert de L'Aigle, after he had gone to Normandy without the king's permission in 1204, to protect his Norman lands after John had lost the duchy to the French, the earl made a fine on his sister's behalf, as Gilbert's wife, for these vills. Westcott was, in fact, part of Isabel's dower. In 1207 the earl paid 3,000 marks, in instalments, for Gilbert's entire estate, for the use of his sister.[9] By 1216, Gilbert's English lands were back in his own hands, with King John writing that he 'had restored his rights to Gilbert de Laigle some time ago.'[10] Despite the restoration of his lands, Gilbert still joined the baronial rebellion against the king. The regency council of Henry III, however, were prepared to be lenient with some rebels and wrote to Gilbert in December 1216, commanding that he return to his allegiance. They promised that he would be restored to all the lands he held before the civil war, making specific mention of his castle at Pevensey; the regents were eager to prevent the castle from falling into the hands of Prince Louis and the rebel barons. The letter sent to Gilbert promised that 'we will show you full justice regarding that castle.'[11] Gilbert died shortly before 19 December 1231 and in January 1232 his lands were assessed in Sussex, Surrey and Southampton, in order that a reasonable dower could be assigned to Isabel. Isabel died sometime before 30 November 1234, leaving no surviving children by either marriage. Her brother, William, Earl Warenne, was named as her heir.[12]

One of the sisters of William, 5th Earl Warenne – although it is not clear which – bore an illegitimate son, Richard FitzRoy (also known as Richard de Chilham or Richard of Dover), by her cousin, John (the future King John). Richard was probably born in the 1190s and was the only one of John's illegitimate children to gain honorific title, following his marriage to Rose of Dover in 1214, by which he became lord of the castle and honour of Chilham, in Kent.[13] Richard's lordship held in the region of fifteen knights' fees, in Kent and Essex. Richard served his father and, subsequently, his royal half-brother, Henry III, as a royalist captain and administrator during the First Barons' War of 1215–17. From 1216 he was constable of Wallingford Castle and custodian of the honour of Wallingford; it was a strategically important castle and the honour held some 120 knights' fees. In May 1218, he was granted the honour at royal pleasure and held it until 1227. Between 1217 and 1221 he was also sheriff of Berkshire, though it appears he had little involvement in the day-to-day duties of the position; Henry Saccario did the accounting for him at the exchequer, with Richard always finding reason to be elsewhere.[14]

Richard distinguished himself at the Battle of Sandwich on 24 August 1217, the sea battle in which the English naval forces intercepted the French bringing equipment and supplies to Prince Louis, the dauphin of France, who had invaded England in 1216 and made a bid for the throne. The dauphin's French forces and baronial allies had been defeated at the Battle of Lincoln in May but were still causing trouble in other parts of England. Richard commanded one of the ships in the battle: 'On 24 August, the whole enemy fleet joined battle with the king's men, not far from the Isle of Thanet. Many of their ships and some of the leaders of the French party were captured, but the rest were able to evade capture by flight; many of the lesser men were killed. Scattered in confusion, the enemy could not regroup.'[15] Richard brought his own ship alongside the French flagship, the most formidable of the enemy's vessels, commanded by Eustace the Monk. Richard and his men boarded the ship. Roger of Wendover suggests that it was Richard himself who beheaded Eustace the Monk after his capture, though other sources disagree with this, none deny that Richard's actions in the battle were significant.[16] The Battle of Sandwich was an important action in that it forced Prince Louis to come to terms with the regency government of King Henry III. As a consequence, Louis agreed to a settlement of £10,000 as an inducement to go home.

In 1218 Richard left to join the fifth crusade in Egypt. He returned home in 1220 or, more likely, 1221. He is known to have reached the crusader camp at Damietta as he borrowed money whilst there, 20 marks from an Italian cardinal, and was pressured for its repayment in 1228.[17] Henry III eventually repaid the loan for him. Richard was perhaps as much as seventeen years older than his half-brother, King Henry III, and does not appear to have had a close relationship with him. He never appeared on the king's witness lists. Richard did receive some gifts, though nothing extravagant from the king but, despite the trust his father had held in him, he played a limited role in affairs after his return from crusade. He fought against the Welsh in 1223 and in the same year accompanied Alexander II, King of Scots, his second cousin once removed through his Warenne family, on pilgrimage to Canterbury. Though it has to be said that the records are unclear, and the Richard involved in either, or both, of these events could have been Richard of Cornwall, the full brother of Henry III and half-brother of Richard of Chilham. It was certainly Richard of Chilham who was one of the tax collectors for Kent in 1225, when the fifteenth was granted for Henry III's campaign to Poitou.

Most of the evidence of Richard of Chilham comes from the debts and lawsuits held against him. Indeed, one of the advantages of his joining the fifth crusade was that it resulted in the deferment of a court case in which he was the defendant. His debts to the Crown started with the scutage of 1217, a tax of 2 marks per fee on the fourteen knights' fees of his Chilham barony.[18] The debts piled up through the 1220s, with Richard failing to appear when summoned. He was threatened with having his land taken into the king's custody. The debts he owed to one William Scissor (or the tailor) were to be recovered by distraint of land and chattels, with his land to be

Warenne shield. 'Plate 102: N. Aisle of Nave. Shields in Spandrels', in *An Inventory of the Historical Monuments in London, Volume 1, Westminster Abbey* (London, 1924), p. 102. (*British History Online*) http://www.british-history.ac.uk/rchme/london/vol1/plate-102 [accessed 4 June 2019])

Frinton Church. Arms of Elderbeke and Warenne. In North Window of Chancel; 14th-century. 'Plate 95: Glass', in *An Inventory of the Historical Monuments in Essex, Volume 3, North East* (London, 1922), p. 95. (*British History Online*) http://www.british-history.ac.uk/rchme/essex/vol3/plate-95 [accessed 4 June 2019])

Lewes Castle, Sussex. (*Author collection*)

Lewes Priory, Sussex. (*Author collection*)

Tomb of Gundrada de Warenne, Trinity Church, Southover. (*Photo by the author and published with the kind permission of the rector of Trinity Church, Southover*)

Window of William de Warenne, Trinity Church, Southover. (*Photo by the author and published with the kind permission of the rector of Trinity Church, Southover*)

Window of Gundrada de Warenne, Trinity Church, Southover. (*Photo by the author and published with the kind permission of the rector of Trinity Church, Southover*)

Conisbrough castle, South Yorkshire. (*Author collection*)

Conisbrough Castle, South Yorkshire. (*Author collection*)

Donjon of Conisbrough Castle, South Yorkshire. (*Author collection*)

St Peter's Church Conisbrough. (*Photo by Andrea Houlbrook*)

Detail of a marginal drawing of Hubert de Burgh kneeling at an altar in Matthew Paris' Chronica Maiora. (*Courtesy of the British Library Catalogue of Illuminated Manuscripts*). http://www.bl.uk/catalogues/illuminatedmanuscripts/ ILLUMIN.ASP?Size=mid&IllID=43410

Seton armorial image of John Balliol and his wife, Isabella de Warenne (*Wikimedia Commons*)

Sandal Castle, Wakefield. (*Author collection*)

Warenne Shield, Trinity Church, Southover. (*Photo by the author and published with the kind permission of the rector of Trinity Church, Southover*)

Seal of John de Warenne, earl of Surrey, Howard de Walden, 1904. (*Wikimedia Commons*)

Peel Castle, Thorne, South Yorkshire. (*Author collection*)

Roche Abbey, South Yorkshire. (*Author collection*)

Miniature of busts of Geoffrey, Duke of Ardenne; William, Count of Warenne; Godfrey, 'Erle of Arigy'; and Eric, Count of Bigorre; each with their arms and at the beginning of a branch of the genealogical tree. (https://www.bl.uk/catalogues/illuminatedmanuscripts/ILLUMIN.ASP?Size=mid&IllID=2513)

Detail of miniature of busts of Geoffrey, Duke of Ardenne, and William, Count of Warenne. (https://www.bl.uk/catalogues/illuminatedmanuscripts/ILLUMIN.ASP?Size=mid&IllID=3463)

Castle Acre, Norfolk. (*Author collection*)

Castle Acre Priory, Norfolk. (*Author collection*)

Town Gate, Castle Acre, Norfolk. (*Author collection*)

Warenne Tomb, Southwark Cathedral. (*Photo by Andrea Raee. With the kind permission of the Dean and Chapter of Southwark Cathedral*)

Harley 2110. ff. 1-152 Castle Acre cartulary, England (Castle Acre, Norfolk; 2nd quarter if the 13th century. (*Courtesy of the British Library Catalogue of Illuminated Manuscripts*) http://www.bl.uk/catalogues/illuminatedmanuscripts/ILLUMIN.ASP?Size=mid&IllID=23790

Pevensey Castle, Sussex. (*Author collection*)

Memorial to the 1264 Battle of Lewes, Lewes Priory Gardens, Sussex. (*Author's collection*)

Tickhill Castle, South Yorkshire. (*Author collection*)

Tickhill Castle gatehouse, South Yorkshire. (*Author collection*)

returned when he paid his debts. The king stepped in at this point, though for the sake of his siter-in-law, Rose, rather than his half-brother. Henry III ordered the sheriff of Kent to prevent Richard from wasting, selling or damaging the manor of Northwood, which was assigned to Rose for her maintenance.[19] Richard and Rose were also locked in a long-running dispute with Robert fitz Walter and Richard de Montfichet over Rose's right to the manor of Lesnes. The eyre in Kent in 1227 decided that the dispute should be settled by a duel, with each side nominating champions, which Richard and Rose won. After the duel, Robert fitz Walter recognised Rose's right to Lesnes and quitclaimed to Richard, Rose and their heirs, for which Richard and Rose gave him 40 marks, which they had to borrow for the purpose.[20]

Their debts thus increased further, in 1229, sheriffs were ordered to take possession of all the manors of Richard and Rose, save Lesnes, which Rose was to keep for her maintenance. Richard joined Henry III's forces sailing for Brittany, which put two pending court cases against him into abeyance and he was granted respite from his debts. Later in the 1230s, sheriffs were ordered to prevent the sale of lands and woods by Richard, lands which formed part of Rose's inheritance.[21] By 1242 Richard was back in the king's favour and was advanced 20 marks to buy equipment and supplies for an expedition to Lundy, although it is possible that this was Richard's son, also called Richard, who would join the king's expedition to Gascony that same year, receiving an annual fee of 50 marks. He and William Bardrolf led the seaborne operations against the notorious outlaw and pirate, William de Marisco. In 1238 the would-be assassin of Henry III, whose attack was foiled by the king spending the night with the queen instead of in his own bed, claimed that Marisco was behind the plot. Marisco had based himself on the island of Lundy in the Bristol Channel, from where he attacked shipping, taking ransoms and plunder. Richard successfully captured Marisco and his accomplices, after scaling the island's cliff to reach them, most of them were later executed in London.[22]

In 1243 Richard was granted a pardon for £100 for a debt to the moneylender Benedict Crispin. This seems to have come about, not by Richard's actions, but by the affection the king held for Richard's son, King Henry's nephew, Richard, who is referred to in the fine roll, alongside the payment of his fee for the Easter term, as 'our beloved and faithful Richard of Dover'.[23] Richard of Chilham died in 1246, leaving his wife, Rose of Dover, still burdened by her husband's debts, his son Richard and a daughter, Isabel, who eventually inherited the honour of Chilham. One argument for the identity of Richard's mother is in the naming of his daughter. It has been suggested that Richard named his daughter after his mother, Isabel, but this is hardly incontrovertible proof; he could have named her after his grandmother, Countess Isabel. It could just as easily have been Ela, whose marriages were that bit less prestigious than her sisters', being to men we know little-to-nothing of beside their names, perhaps suggesting a scandalous past. Unfortunately, a strange entry in the *Annales Cestriensis* only adds to the confusion. In an entry for 1200, it records the death of *'W. de Waren meunch fil Regis'* ('W. de Warenne mother of the king's son'). However, Earl Hamelin and Countess Isabel are not known to have had a daughter with the initial 'W' and neither did any of their known children die in 1200. In the chronicle of Robert of Gloucester, Richard's mother is merely identified as 'the erles daughter of Wareine'.[24] The entry in the *Annales Cestriensis* is, therefore, either a red herring or referring to a daughter of Hamelin and Isabel who is previously unknown – and not mentioned elsewhere. With such little information to go on, we can only speculate.

William's third sister, Matilda or Maud, married Henry, Count of Eu and Lord of Hastings, who died around 1190. It has been suggested that Matilda was a daughter of Earl Hamelin by a previous relationship. This was based on the fact that Henry's year of death has been noted at one point as 1172, which would mean that Matilda could not have been a daughter of the marriage of Isabel and Hamelin, who were married in 1164, as she would have been too young to have married and borne children with Henry.[25] The *Chronicle of the Counts of Eu* records Henry's death as 1183, which also appears to be an error as Henry was assessed for scutage of Wales at Michaelmas 1190; with this later death date it was entirely possible, and indeed likely, that Matilda was the legitimate daughter of both Hamelin and Countess Isabel.[26]

Matilda de Warenne and Henry had four children, two sons and two daughters. Alice was the eldest of the daughters, her sister Jeanne being younger. Sadly, both sons, Raoul and Guy, died young and in consecutive years, with Guy dying in 1185 and Raoul in 1186, leaving Alice as heir to her father's lands.[27] Very little is known of Alice's early years; we do not even have a year for her birth. Given that her grandparents did not marry until 1164, her parents would not have married until the early 1180s, at least, which would mean it is likely that Alice was born sometime around the mid-1180s. On her father's death in 1191, she came into possession of lands in both England and Normandy and became *suo jure* Countess of Eu and Lady Hastings.

As Alice's mother, Matilda, had married again to Henry d'Estouteville of Eckington, Lord of Valmont and Rames in Normandy, and had a son, John, by d'Estouteville it was John, Alice's half-brother, therefore, who became the heir to all the Warenne lands Matilda held in her own right. At the death of Robert d'Estouteville in 1306, he held a capital messuage and land in Gresham, Norfolk, of the heir of John de Warenne, Earl Warenne, by the service of two knights' fees. This was likely passed down through the family from the time of Matilda; it may have been her *maritagium*, given to her by her father, Hamelin.[28] In 1212 Matilda made a donation to the abbey at Valmont. She died sometime before 13 December 1228 as on that day her husband, Henry, made a donation to the same abbey for lights in the church on the anniversary of the death of his wife Matilda, Countess of Eu.[29]

With Matilda's Warenne inheritance going to her son by her second marriage, Alice was left solely with the inheritance from her father, the county of Eu, in Normandy, and the lordship of Hastings in England. The struggle to obtain and hold on to this inheritance would be the driving force in Alice's adult life, complicated by England's loss of Normandy and rival claimants to her English lands. Alice's uncle, William de Warenne, the fifth earl, actively supported his niece in her fight to retain her paternal inheritance. In August 1209, Alice officially received the Comté of Eu from Philip II Augustus, King of France, when she also made a quitclaim of all rights to Neufchatel, Mortemer and Arques. Mortemer was a part of the de Warenne ancestral lands in Normandy, given to William I de Warenne by William the Conqueror, but lost to the family with King Philip's conquest of Normandy in 1202; suggesting that Alice was renouncing her own rights to the French de Warenne lands, as a granddaughter of Isabel de Warenne, Countess of Surrey.[30]

Alice had been born into two of the great noble families of England and France and married into a third. The daughter of Henry, Count of Eu and Lord Hastings, and Matilda de Warenne made a prestigious marriage to Raoul de Lusignan, the second son of Hugh de Lusignan, a powerful Poitevin lord. It was Raoul's brother, Hugh IX, who was the intended husband of Isabelle d'Angoulême, until King John claimed her as his bride. Alice and Raoul married sometime in the 1190s, possibly in 1191.[31] Alice lost her lands in 1201–02, when John married Isabelle, causing a rift with the Lusignan family. Raoul and Alice had two children together; a son, Raoul and a daughter, Mathilde. Their son, Raoul II de Lusignan, Count of Eu and Guînes, was married three times and had one daughter, Marie de Lusignan, by his second wife, Yolande de Dreux. Raoul II died sometime between 1245 and 1250 and was buried at the Abbey of Foucarmont. Mathilde married Humphrey de Bohun, 2nd Earl of Hereford and Earl of Essex, and they had seven children together, including four boys. Their eldest son, also Humphrey, was killed fighting for Simon de Montfort at the Battle of Evesham, 1265. Mathilde died in August 1241 and was buried in Llanthony Secunda Priory, Gloucester. Her husband was buried beside her when he died in September 1275.

In 1139, the honour of Tickhill in Yorkshire had been granted to Alice's grandfather John, Count of Eu, by King Stephen, after John had proved his rights as heir to the original owners, the de Busli family, through Beatrice, the sister of Roger de Busli, who died in 1102.[32] However, in 1141, Empress Matilda captured the castle after Count John was taken prisoner at the Battle of Lincoln. The castle was not returned to Count John's son, Henry, and seems to have stayed in royal hands for many years afterwards, with Richard I taking possession on his accession; he then gave it to his brother John, as part of his holdings. As a consequence, the castle was besieged by the bishop of Durham when John rebelled against Richard in 1194; it was surrendered only when the king returned to England following his capture and imprisonment in Germany, three years after Henry of Eu's death.

In 1214 Alice, as Countess of Eu, was restored to the honour of Tickhill by King John, as part of the conditions of an agreement with her husband's family, the de Lusignans. However, Robert de Vieuxpont, who was in physical possession of the castle, refused to relinquish it, and claimed the castle in his own right. In 1219, Earl Warenne managed to arrange for the restoration of the estates to his niece. Alice recovered her lands in both England and Normandy, including the honours and castles of Tickhill in Yorkshire and Hastings in Sussex. The earl was given custody of both on behalf of his niece, though his possession of Tickhill was challenged by Robert, leading to a court case and, for a time, to threats of violence and unrest. Alice won the court case, defending her claim to Tickhill Castle, in 1220 and appears in an entry dated 19 May 1221 in the Fine Rolls of Henry III concerning Tickhill:

> Order to the sheriff of Nottinghamshire to place in respite the demand that he makes from the men of the countess of Eu of the honour of Tickhill for suits of wapentake, amercements and defaults, until the king's first arrival in those parts. Witness H. etc. By the same.[33]

After many years and much litigation, Alice finally took possession of Tickhill Castle in 1222.

Alice's husband, Raoul had died on 1 May 1219 and was succeeded as count of Eu by their son, Raoul II, who was still only a child. It was left to

Alice, now dowager countess, to administer the Eu inheritance. She paid 15,000 silver marks to the French king to receive the county of Eu in her own name and regained control of her English lands, entrusted to her uncle, the Earl Warenne, as her representative, following her husband's death.[34] Alice was a shrewd political survivor and may well have used the clauses of Magna Carta, which safeguarded the lands of widows, to press her case for the restoration of Tickhill. However, with lands in France and England, two countries often at war, she found herself caught between a rock and a hard place. In 1225 she handed Tickhill Castle to Henry III, until the end of hostilities with France, as a means of safeguarding her lands. Nevertheless, this did not save her when she was ordered to levy troops for the French king, Louis IX, as countess of Eu, and send her forces to fight for him. As a consequence, Henry III seized Tickhill Castle, although it was only permanently attached to the English Crown after Alice's death.

Alice had considerable resources and was renowned for her wide patronage, both secular and religious, and has left numerous charters as testament. She was a benefactor of both French and English religious houses, including Battle Abbey and Christ Church, Canterbury in England as well as Eu and Foucarmont, where her son would be laid to rest, in France. Alice issued a charter in 1219, to Roche Abbey, which was witnessed by her uncle William, Earl de Warenne. She also granted an annual allowance to Loretta de Braose, Countess of Leicester, and daughter of Matilda de Braose, the victim of King John who was starved to death in his dungeons in 1210. The widow of Robert de Breteuil, a renowned crusader, Loretta lived as an anchorite at Hackington, near Canterbury. Alice also granted several lands to others, such as Greetwell in the county of Lincoln, which had previously been held by Walter de Tylly in Alice's name and was given to her uncle, Earl Warenne, in August 1225; the earl was to annually render a sparrowhawk to Philippa de Tylly in payment.[35] In 1232 Alice issued a charter to Malvesin de Hersy, of Osberton in the county of Nottingham, providing him with all customs due to Tickhill in return for two knights' fees. Malvesin had been constable of Tickhill in 1220–21 and his brother Sir Baldwin de Hersy was constable of Conisbrough Castle, seat of earl Warenne. Around 1220, she lent 140 marks to the count of Aumale, who still hadn't repaid her in 1223.[36]

Having spent most of her life fighting for the rights to her lands in England and France, caught between two great nations whose relations were acrimonious to say the least, Alice appears to have conducted herself admirably throughout. Her connections to the powerful Lusignan and Warenne families could not have harmed her situation. Having been a widow for almost thirty years, Alice died sometime in May 1246 (probably between the 13 and 15), aged in her sixties, at La Mothe St Héray in Poitou, France, apparently leaving a will in which she bequeathed land to the abbey at Foucarmont. It seems likely, though not certain, that she was buried at her husband's foundation of Fontblanche Priory in Exoudon; it seems just as possible that she was buried at Foucarmont, where her son would later be laid to rest.[37]

Alice was not the only Warenne daughter capable of fighting for her rights. Her cousin, Isabel, was an equally strong character who was not afraid to challenge the highest in the land to recover what was hers. Isabel was the only daughter of William de Warenne, 5th Earl Warenne, and his second wife, Matilda Marshal. She was, therefore, a granddaughter of William Marshal, Earl of Pembroke and regent of Henry III, and niece to William II Marshal, 2nd Earl of Pembroke. Through her paternal grandparents, Countess Isabel and Earl Hamelin, Isabel was also a cousin to both Ela, Countess of Salisbury, and King Henry III. With her impeccable parentage and family connections, it is no surprise that she made a suitably prestigious marriage. In 1234, at no older than 8 years of age, and possibly a little younger, Isabel was married to 20-year-old Hugh d'Aubigny, 5th Earl of Arundel. Hugh's father, William, 3rd Earl of Arundel, had died in 1221 on his way home from the Fifth Crusade. William had been succeeded as fourth earl by his oldest son and namesake, who died three years after his father, aged just 21, leaving the earldom to his younger brother, Hugh.[38]

On their marriage, Isabel's father granted the couple a manor at Marham in Norfolk, worth £40 a year in rent. Isabel later founded an abbey at Marham for nuns of the Cistercian order. The charter for this grant offers the only details available for the marriage:

> This abbey of Cistercian nuns was founded by Isabel, widow of Hugh de Albini, earl of Arundel. It was dedicated to the honour of the Blessed Virgin, St. Barbara, and St. Edmund, on 27 January, 1249, by Richard, bishop of Chichester. The original endowment was the lands of the foundress at Marham, together with the manor and all its services; they were granted for the good of the souls of William Earl Warenne and Surrey her father, of Maud her mother, daughter of William Marshall, earl of Pembroke, of Hugh her husband, and of all her ancestors and successors.[39]

In 1242 Hugh accompanied the king on his expedition to Aquitaine. However, after just nine years of marriage, on 7 May 1243, Hugh died, leaving Isabel, at 17 years of age, a childless widow, with a rather large dower. Within just three weeks of her husband's death, on 29 May, Isabel's marriage was granted to Pierre de Genevre, a Savoyard favourite of the king, Henry III. However, the Patent Rolls show that provision was made for Isabel to remain unmarried should she so wish, a right guaranteed her by clause 8 of Magna Carta, although she would have to pay Pierre for the privilege. Given that she never remarried, she must have been more than happy to make the payment.[39]

The Arundel inheritance was divided between Hugh's four sisters: Mabel, Isabel, Nicholaa and Cecily. The earldom itself went to Hugh's nephew, his sister Isabel's son, John FitzAlan. As the earl's widow, Isabel was well provided for, with her dower including the hundred and manor of Bourne in Lincolnshire, the manors of Wymondham and Kenninghall in Norfolk, Stansted in Essex and several properties in Norfolk and Buckinghamshire. Suffice to say, she was a very wealthy widow and would continue to be styled countess of Arundel until her death. It was in 1249, a year after the death of her mother, that Isabel founded the only English female convent that was part of the Cistercian order at Marham. Two Cistercian abbots had inspected it in its first year. Isabel's brother, John de Warenne, 6th Earl Warenne, the bishop of Norwich and Henry III himself all issued charters confirming the abbey's foundation. Along with other endowments, Isabel herself made eleven grants to the abbey in its early years, giving it a strong economic foundation. In 1252 Isabel was granted papal permission to visit the Cistercian house at Waverley to consult with the abbot about her own convent; the Waverley annals record that she granted four marks and a cask of wine to the monks there.[40]

Isabel was very protective of her property rights and went on the offensive when they were threatened, even if that meant going against the king himself. In 1252 she did just that. One of her tenants, Thomas of Ingoldisthorpe, held a quarter knight's fee from Isabel at Fring and Snettisham; he also had property in the honour of Haughley, as an escheat from the Crown. On his death in 1252 Henry III took all of Thomas's lands in wardship until Thomas's heir was of age, including Isabel's quarter knights' fee. In March of 1252 Henry granted the wardship of the lands and marriage of the heir to his former treasurer and keeper of the king's wardrobe, Peter Chaceporc. Had Thomas held his lands in chief from the king, Henry would have been within his rights to take prerogative wardship. However, his land at Haughley was held from the honour of Haughley, which was in the king's hands as an escheat and Isabel was treated unjustly in being denied the wardship of his heirs, who held land direct from her at Fring and Snettisham.

Isabel took her grievances direct to the king himself. In an audience with Henry III, she is said to have berated him for trampling on the rights laid out in Magna Carta. She is said to have asked, 'Where are the liberties of England, so often recorded, so often granted, and so often ransomed?' According to Matthew Paris, the chronicler and a personal friend of Isabel's (though no particular fan of Henry), Henry scorned Isabel's argument, 'derisively and curling his nostrils' and asked if the nobles of the realm had given her permission to speak on their behalf.[41] Isabel argued that the king had given her the right to speak thus in the articles granted in Magna Carta and accused the king of being a 'shameless transgressor' of the liberties laid down in the Great Charter, breaking his sworn oath to uphold its principles. At the end of the audience, Henry refused to be moved, 'After listening to her [civilly] reproachful speech, the king was silent, and the countess, without obtaining or even asking for permission, returned home.'[42] Isabel was one of the great nobles of England, the daughter of one earl, sister of another and widow of a third, and was obviously undaunted by an audience with the king. Although the king did not react to her reprimand immediately, he did, eventually, admit that he may have been in the wrong, issuing a letter to her on 23 May 1253 saying:

> Since the king has learnt that Thomas of Ingoldisthorpe, whose son and heir is in the custody of Peter Chaceporc by concession of the king, did not hold from the Crown of the king in chief but from the honour of Haughley, which is in the hand of the king as his escheat, and that the same Thomas held from Hugh de Aubigny, once earl of Arundel, a quarter part of the fee of one knight with appurtenances in Fring and Snettisham and the service of which was assigned to Isabella, countess of Arundel, the widow of the foresaid earl, in dower, he has returned to the same countess custody of the foresaid quarter part of a fee with appurtenances; and the foresaid Peter is ordered to give the countess full seizin of the foresaid custody.[43]

Isabel was still unable to gain full possession of the land, however, and in late 1253, while the king was overseas in Aquitaine, she instigated legal proceedings against Peter Chaceporc 'for custody of Ingoldisthorpe.' Whether Chaceporc had not relinquished the land, or she believed she was entitled to more land than was returned to her, we do not know. Isabel in fact lost the suit and was amerced £20 (30 marks) for a false claim. The writ was witnessed by Henry III's queen, Eleanor of Provence, and his brother Richard, Earl of Cornwall. As persistent as ever, and although he was overseas, Isabel appealed directly to the king, who responded with a pardon, although it seems he still smarted from the upbraiding she had given him earlier in the year:

3 April. Meilham. Henry, by the grace of God king of England, lord of Ireland, duke of Normandy and Aquitaine and count of Anjou sends greeting to his beloved consort E, by the same grace queen of England, lady of Ireland, duchess of Normandy and Aquitaine and countess of Anjou and to his beloved and faithful brother, R. earl of Cornwall. Know that we have pardoned our beloved and faithful Isabella countess of Arundel the 30m. at which she was amerced before our justices against our beloved and faithful … Peter Chaceporc, our Treasurer, for custody of Ingoldisthorpe. We, therefore, order you to cause the same countess to be quit of the aforesaid 30m. by our seal of England provided she says nothing opprobrious to us as she did when we were at Westminster and as we have signified to her by letter. Witness myself.[44]

Isabel obviously had an eye for business, given that she could so concern herself with a quarter knight's fee out of the sixty that she held. A wealthy widow with impressive family connections, she was renowned not only for her religious endowment of the Cistercian convent at Marham, but also as a patron of religious texts, having commissioned at least two saints' lives, including the life of St Richard of Wyche by Ralph Bocking. Isabel could count among her friends Richard Wych himself, the bishop of Chichester who was later canonised, and the famed chronicler, Matthew Paris. Paris translated a life of Saint Edmund of Abingdon into Anglo-Norman verse for Isabel's personal use.

Isabel died shortly before 23 November 1282 and was laid to rest at her own foundation at Marham; her dower properties passed to her husband's great-great nephew, Richard FitzAlan, 8th Earl of Arundel. Having spent almost forty years as a childless widow, Isabel never remarried, her remarkable life was dedicated to the patronage of her convent at Marham and religious writers, such as Paris and Bocking. This incredible woman stands out as the countess who reprimanded and humbled her king for his injustices, using Magna Carta to its greatest effect.

It is notable that not one but two of the granddaughters of Isabel and Hamelin de Warenne used the clauses of Magna Carta to assert their rights, as widows, over their inheritances. The Warenne family had been at the heart of royal administration since the time of the Norman Conquest; the women were just as aware of this as were the earls who carried on the family name. Perhaps emboldened by their impressive lineage and family connections, Warenne women such as Alice de Lusignan and Isabel d'Aubigny proved the strength and determination of the family as a whole.

Chapter Fourteen

John de Warenne and the
Second Barons' War

With the death of William de Warenne, 5th Earl of Warenne and Surrey, in 1140, the vast earldom of Surrey fell to the earl's only son, John, who was then only 9 years of age. John would hold the earldom for a total of sixty-four years, much longer, even, than the second earl, who had been earl of Surrey for fifty years. John de Warenne, 6th Earl Warenne, would see the earldom through the turmoil of the Second Barons' War, led by Simon de Montfort, and the wars of Edward I against the Welsh and the Scots. Although no longer in possession of their lands in Normandy, in England the Warenne barony included Lewes in Sussex, Stamford and Grantham in Lincolnshire, Castle Acre in Norfolk, Conisbrough and Sandal in Yorkshire, Reigate in Surrey, and various other pockets of land throughout the country. Through his father, John was a second cousin to both King Henry III of England and Alexander II, King of Scots, and a distant cousin of Louis IX, King of France. Through his mother, Matilda Marshal, he was related to most of the great baronies of England, including the Marshals, the Bigods, the de Clares and others.[1] His family connections, in both England and France, were impeccable.

On his father's death, John became a ward of King Henry III and was raised at court. His lands in the south were given into the care of Peter of Savoy, Earl of Richmond and uncle of Henry's queen, Eleanor of Provence: 'it appears from a patent dated in Sep. 25 Hen. III. That the king granted all the lands of John de Warren [sic.] in Sussex, and Surrey, to this Peter, and that he was also made governor of the castle of Lewes.'[2] In 1246 Henry promised to marry John to one of the daughters of another of his wife's uncles, Amadeus of Savoy. However, the marriage never materialised and in 1247 John was married to Alice de Lusignan, King Henry's half-sister. Alice was the second eldest daughter of the second marriage of Henry's mother, Isabelle of Angoulême, Countess of Angoulême in her own right and widow of King John. Alice's father was Hugh X de Lusignan, Count of La Marche and Lord of Lusignan and Valence.

Born in around 1224, Alice was seven years older than her 16-year-old husband. The marriage was part of Henry's much-despised policy of patronising his Lusignan siblings and thus was condemned by Matthew Paris. Paris claimed that the marriage was 'beyond the bride's station.'[3] After the marriage, John received two extra robes at Christmas, and in 1248, although he had yet to reach his majority, received some of his father's lands, probably in order for John to support himself and his new wife.[4] John's mother, Matilda, had died in 1248, in her mid-fifties. Choosing to be laid to rest with her Marshal family, rather than either of her husbands, Matilda was buried at Tintern Abbey, Monmouthshire. Her three Bigod sons and their Warenne half-brother carried their mother's bier into the church, where she was laid to rest close to her mother, Isabel, two of her brothers, Walter and Ancel, and her sister, Sybil.

John and Alice had three children together. Their eldest daughter, Eleanor, married Henry Percy and was the mother of Henry de Percy, 1st Baron Percy. A second daughter, Isabella, was born around 1253 and was married to John Balliol, Lord of Bywell, sometime before 7 February 1281. There is some suggestion that Isabella was born later, not as a daughter of Alice but a second, unidentified wife, which would explain her apparently late marriage to John Balliol. Given her father's high profile in the reign of Edward I, this seems highly unlikely; someone would surely have mentioned that the powerful Earl Warenne had remarried. A more likely possibility is that Isabella herself had been married before, or was intended for another and the match fell through resulting in a marriage in her mid-20s to John Balliol. In the early 1290s, John was one of the thirteen competitors for the Scottish throne. He was the great-grandson of Ada de Warenne's youngest son, David of Huntingdon, by David's daughter, Margaret. John and Isabella were, therefore, distant cousins, both descended from William de Warenne, second Earl Warenne, and his wife, Isabel de Vermandois.

Following the tragic deaths of Alexander III of Scots and and his granddaughter Margaret, the Maid of Norway, in 1286 and 1290 respectively, Scotland was left without an outright successor to the crown. With thirteen claimants to the Scottish throne it was Edward I of England who was given the duty of selecting Scotland's next king. Isabella's close family links to the English Crown may have helped Edward decide in John Balliol's favour and he was installed as king of Scotland in November 1292. John and Isabella had at least three, but possibly four, children together. A daughter, Margaret, died unmarried. There is mention of another daughter, Anne; but there is doubt as to whether she ever existed. Their eldest son, Edward, was born around 1283. With English support, Edward made his own bid for the Scottish throne in the 1330s, and was crowned king following his defeat of David II's forces at the Battle of Dupplin Moor in 1332. David II was the young son of King Robert I the Bruce, who was 5 years old when he ascended the throne on his father's death in 1329. David's supporters and Edward struggled against each other, until David's forces eventually triumphed over Edward and he was deposed in 1336. Edward finally surrendered his claim to the Scottish throne in 1356 whilst living in English exile; he died in Wheatley, Doncaster, probably in 1363 or 1364.[5] Although his final resting place has recently been claimed to be under Doncaster Post Office, the former site of Doncaster Priory, it remains elusive.

John and Isabella's possible younger son, Henry, was killed on 16 December 1332 at the Battle of Annan, a resounding victory for supporters of David II against Henry's brother, Edward. Although Edward was briefly married to Margaret of Taranto, the marriage was annulled. Neither Edward nor Henry had any children. Very little is known of John and Isabella's life together. Her death date and final resting place are both unknown. It is by no means certain that Isabella was still alive when John became king, so she may have died before 1292, when John succeeded to the Scottish throne. She was certainly no longer living when her own father defeated John and the Scottish army at the Battle of Dunbar in April 1296; John Balliol abdicated in July of the same year and died in French exile in 1314. John's claim to the Scottish throne was supported by the Comyns, which led to the murder of John Comyn, in the church at Dumfries, by Robert the Bruce, grandson of the other leading competitor to the throne in 1290, who eventually succeeded as King Robert I and won a resounding victory over the English at Bannockburn in 1314.

The only son of John de Warenne and Alice de Lusignan, William de Warenne, was born in 1256. He married Joan de Vere, daughter of the fifth earl of Oxford, and was father to two children, a son and a daughter, John and Alice. The younger John de Warenne was the last Earl Warenne, whose marital and extra-marital situation led to the extinction of the senior Warenne line. It was through John's sister, Alice de Warenne, that the title earl of Surrey would eventually pass to her son Richard FitzAlan, 10th Earl of Arundel. Alice de Lusignan, Countess of Warenne and Surrey, died in 1256, shortly after William's birth. She was 'placed in the earth before the great altar [Lewes priory] in the presence of her brother Adelmar [Aymer], elect of Winchester.'[6] John de Warenne would never remarry, perhaps an indication of the deep affection that he held for his semi-royal wife.

He did, however, father up to six illegitimate children including two known, illegitimate sons, John and William, both of whom followed careers in the church. On 23 December 1291, they were granted a dispensation for illegitimacy by Richard de Swinefield, Bishop of Hereford. John was presented to the church of Dewsbury by the prior of Lewes, in 1293; he was a canon of York Minster by 1296. By 1300, William was rector at Nafferton (Yorkshire) and studying at Oxford when he resigned that post on 1 January 1303; William's resignation letter bears the university seal. In 1303 Robert Winchelsea, Archbishop of Canterbury, wrote to Pope Boniface VIII, asking for favours for John and William de Warenne, Masters of Arts, on account of their learning and virtuous lives. In 1306 both John and William received papal dispensations for having been ordained as priests, underage. Each brother was provided with livings from Warenne family churches in the family heartlands of Yorkshire, Norfolk and Sussex.[7]

In his late teens, but still not having reached his full majority, the king continued to show an interest in John de Warenne's affairs. On 29 November 1249, King Henry issued an order at Clarendon, concerning lands to be taken into the king's hand for a tournament: 'Order to the sheriff of Norfolk and Suffolk to take into the king's hand all lands that John de Warenne has in his bailiwick and to keep them safely until the king orders otherwise, so that he answers for the issues arising therefrom at the Exchequer.'[8] On 26 March 1251, at Walsingham, the king sent an order on behalf of the men of John de Warenne: 'Order to the sheriff of Norfolk to place in respite, until the quindene of Easter next to come, all distraints and demands that he makes by summons of the Exchequer from the men of John de Warenne of new land for their amercements before the justices last itinerant in his county.'[9]

In the 1250s, John was drawn into the court circle that centred around the Lusignans, taking the side of Aymer de Lusignan, Bishop of Winchester, in his dispute with the archbishop of Canterbury, Boniface of Savoy, in 1252 and 1253. Aymer was wholly unsuited to the position, being illiterate, unable to speak English and leading a secular lifestyle, but was preferred by his half-brother the king, and confirmed in the position by the pope. In November 1252, following an attack on the prior of the hospital of St Thomas in Southwark by an official of the archbishop, Aymer incited his own supporters to undertake a violent raid on the archbishop's houses at Lambeth and Maidstone, to arrest the official and imprison him at Farnham Castle.[10] The official was later release, but the archbishop passed a sentence of excommunication on Aymer and his followers, which was not lifted until

January 1253: 'in the same year, as we may collect from Holinshed, he was excommunicated with William de Valence, and others, for being concerned in a trifling dispute between the archbishop of Canterbury, and the bishop of Winchester, but the sentence was soon taken off.'[11]

John de Warenne came of age in 1252 and obtained the emoluments of his earldom: 'he obtained from the crown, a charter for free warren (which implied a manor) in the towns, or townships of Haldsworth, Halifax, Heptonstall, Hipperholm, Langfield, Midgley, Northouram, Ovenden, Rastrick, Rishworth cum Norland, Rowtonstall, Saltonstall, Skircoat, Soland, Stansfeld, Wadsworth, etc, all within the present vicarage of Halifax in Yorkshire.'[12] The following year, he was knighted along with the king's eldest son, Lord Edward, who was eight years his junior. That year, John served with the king in Gascony, having sailed from Dover to Bordeaux, and stood surety for Henry's debts in Bordeaux.[13] In 1254 he was overseas again, with the king's half-brother, William de Valence, Earl of Pembroke, and Richard de Clare, Earl of Gloucester. Valence was married to John's first cousin, Joan Munchensi; their mothers, Joan and Matilda, were both daughters of William Marshal, Earl of Pembroke and regent for Henry III from 1216 to his death in 1219. In the same year, John was among the barons who escorted the king of Scots, Alexander III, and his wife, Margaret, Henry III's daughter, from Edinburgh to Wark-on-Tweed to meet with King Henry. The earl was also present when a new regency council was constituted for the young Scottish king, still only 14 years of age, ousting the Comyn faction. In 1257, John travelled with the king's brother, Richard, Earl of Cornwall, to Aachen in Germany for Richard's coronation as king of the Romans.

As with most nobles of the time, John de Warenne was drawn into the political unrest of the late 1250s and 1260s, now known as the Second Barons' War. In 1255, he had been among those protesting at the large number of foreigners that Henry was patronising. By 1257, however, he was a member of Lord Edward's retinue, and in the company of his own brother-in-law, William de Valence; together, they led the opposition to the Savoyard faction of Henry III's court. Recently widowed as his wife Alice had died the previous year, John may have seen it as an opportunity to get revenge on Peter of Savoy, the queen's uncle, who had exploited his wardship of the Surrey lands during John's minority.[14] John de Warenne vacillated in his allegiance in the early days, first siding with the Crown and then the barons. However, given that his wife had been the king's half-sister, and that he himself had been raised at court, it is no surprise that John would finally come down on the side of the Crown. In 1258, at Oxford, he was among those chosen from among Henry's supporters to elect the council of fifteen that was to direct the government of the realm:

> In 1258, when the barons came with a great power to Oxford, to compel the king to submit to the provisions which they made there, he was one of the twelve lords elected on the king's part, to settle matters with the like number deputed by the barons; and for some reason or other he refused to consent to the provisions then proposed, as did the king's four half brothers, Ademar [Aymer] bishop of Winchester, Guy de Lezignan [Lusignan], Geoffry de Lezignan [Geoffrey de Lusignan], William de Valentia [Valence], and others. This gave so great an offence to the barons, that they forced the king's brothers to quit the kingdom, and having for their security obtained the king's safe conduct, bearing date July 5, 1258, earl Warren [Warenne], with other noblemen, had orders to guard them to the seaside.[15]

John de Warenne swore to uphold the Provisions of Oxford but refused to comply with the order to take back the lands and castles that Henry had given to his Lusignan favourites. John was eventually persuaded to accept the conditions, probably after seeing the futility of opposition and the Lusignans surrender to the inevitable. He was one of the barons who escorted the banished barons to Dover and exile. John was among the young lords of Edward's affinity when the heir to the throne tried to establish his political independence in 1258 and 1259, allying himself with the earl of Gloucester in March 1259. Later in the same year, John witnessed Edward's letter which gave his support to Gloucester's opponent, Simon de Montfort, Earl of Leicester.[16] By the following spring, however, John returned to Henry's side, after some persuasion or outright bribery; in March 1260, Henry authorised an annual payment to John de Warenne.[17] In the same year, John was appointed as one of the itinerant justices in Somerset, Dorset and Devon.[18] The following month, in April 1260, when it appeared that Edward was preparing to oppose his father, the king, John de Warenne was among those summoned to London, armed, and given lodgings in the city; Edward, on the other hand, was denied entry. The crisis was averted when Edward reconciled with his father, and with John, who then travelled with the king's son to the Continent, to take part in tournaments. One chronicler noting, 'Also this year John Earl Warenn twice crossed the sea for the sake of a tournament.'[19]

John was back in England by February 1261, when King Henry summoned him and twenty-six other magnates to come armed to London. Edward arrived back in April and a month later papal bulls, issued by Alexander IV, arrived in England, absolving the king, queen and the realm, of their oaths to adhere to the Provisions of Oxford. Henry published the bulls at Winchester in early June.[20] However, with Henry asserting his personal power, the young Earl Warenne joined in a new confederacy with his older half-brothers, Roger (III) Bigod, Earl of Norfolk, and Hugh Bigod, and sided with Simon de Montfort; insisting that the king adhere to the Provisions of Oxford, Montfort appealed to Louis IX of France to arbitrate in the dispute.[21] By the end of the year, resistance had collapsed and John, along with the king's other opponents, was pardoned for his actions. Simon de Montfort took his wife and children and left for the Continent. John de Warenne also went overseas, returning in March 1263 with Henry of Almain, the son of Richard, Earl of Cornwall, and Henry de Montfort, son of Simon de Montfort.

Earl Simon himself returned to England the following month and assembled a group of young councillors, including John de Warenne, Henry of Almain and Gilbert de Clare. He was now undisputed leader of the rebel faction. Meeting at Oxford, they insisted on the enforcement of the Provisions of Oxford of 1258. Many of the barons had grievances to work through, for John, it was an opportunity to pursue his vendetta against Peter of Savoy, at least against Peter's English lands as he himself had returned to Savoy the previous year.[22] John was involved in some violent clashes when Montfort's army attacked royalists and occupied the Welsh Marches. In May 1263 he was among those summoned to Worcester, by Montfort, and told to come armed for war. The king was in dire straits; his Savoyard allies were pursued and violated, the queen's barge was attacked, pelted with mud, rotten eggs and stones, as it approached London Bridge, and the king was isolated in the Tower of London, surrounded by a hostile mob; Eleanor of Provence was eventually able to reunite with the king in the Tower, but the experience had shaken her. On 15 July, Simon de Montfort's army entered London, with Montfort appearing at the Tower the next day to ask for Henry's submission; Henry had little choice but to agree. The king then rode with Simon to Windsor, where Lord Edward, now firmly on the side of his father, was continuing his resistance. The young prince relinquished the castle, if a little ungraciously, without a fight.

Simon de Monfort, earl of Leicester and the king's brother-in-law (as the husband of Henry III's younger sister, Eleanor of England), now had control of the ministries of state and the royal castles of England. After the king's capitulation to the barons, John de Warenne was given custody of Pevensey castle, Sussex, on the advice of his fellow barons and was appointed by the council to negotiate for peace with Llywelyn, Prince of Wales, with, among others, Simon de Montfort and Henry of Almain.[23] John was also involved in the provisions for Isabella de Forz, the 26-year-old heiress to the earldoms of Aumale and Devon. In August 1263, the king wrote to his escheators on both sides of the River Trent, informing them that John de Warenne, William de Valence and Hugh Bigod had all agreed to stand as sureties for Isabella de Forz, the widowed countess of Aumale:

> To William de Weilond', the king's escheator on this side of the Trent. Because John de Warenne, William de Valence, the king's [half-] brother, and Hugh Bigod have mainperned before the king (coram nobis) for Isabella des Forz, countess of Aumale, sister and heiress of Baldwin de Lisle, formerly earl of Devon, that she will come to the king in person in the next parliament that will be in London at the Nativity of the Blessed Mary next to come, ready to perform homage for all lands and tenements formerly of the aforesaid Baldwin on the day he died, and for making over her relief, the king has rendered those lands and tenements to her. Order to cause Isabella to have full seisin of all lands and tenements of which the abovesaid Baldwin was seised in his demesne as of fee in his bailiwick on the day he died.[24]

Perhaps with a view to reconciliation, Simon de Montfort and his handpicked council awarded Isabella's marriage to Henry III's younger son, Edmund, who was 18 years old at the time: Edmund would become earl of Aumale and Devon and receive a rich endowment from the accompanying lands.

It was at this point that John de Warenne once again changed sides; John, his half-brothers, Roger and Hugh Bigod, and their cousin, Henry of Almain. Henry was the son of the king's brother Richard of Cornwall, and, like John and his Bigod half-brothers, he was also the grandson of William Marshal, through his mother, Isabel Marshal. They joined Edward's ranks and on 18 September John was rewarded with a 'heritable grant of all the Norman lands that he held or that would fall to him within his estate.'[25] On 23 September, John de Warenne and his cousin, Henry of Almain, sailed with Edward, and the king and queen, to France to meet with King Louis. John spent the autumn and winter of 1264 strengthening his ties with the king and his eldest son. He served on the royal council, witnessed charters and was rewarded with various favours. On 3 December, he was with the royal army when it marched on Dover. On 24 December he was appointed to the military ward of the counties of Surrey and Sussex by the king.[26] In the same month, John de Warenne's name appears among the list of royalists in the letter submitted, by King Henry, to King Louis for the French king's adjudication over the Provisions of Oxford.

As the country descended into civil war, John de Warenne remained on the royalist side. He was given command of Rochester Castle, alongside Roger of Leybourne, and was besieged there by Simon de Montfort between 19 and 26 April 1264. Montfort was forced to withdraw to London when the royalist army arrived to relieve the castle. The king proceeded to secure the submission of the Channel ports. Simon de Montfort, with reinforcements from his son Henry and the London irregulars, marched out of London and headed south, hoping to bring the king's forces to battle.[27]

The two armies came face-to-face at Lewes in Sussex, the seat of the Warenne earldom. Edward's troops were billeted in John de Warenne's castle while Henry's forces were camped further south, around St Pancras Priory, the Warenne Cluniac foundation where John's Warenne ancestors were buried.[28] On 13 May 1264, Simon de Montfort and his men formally withdrew their homage to the king and on the morning of 14 May, the two armies arrayed themselves for battle, with Henry having the larger force, but Simon having the higher ground, on Offham Hill, just over a mile to the north-west of the royal army. Eager for battle, Edward took the field in advance of Henry and charged the left of the baronial line, comprised of the raw troops recruited in London, before the rest of the royal army was ready. Inevitably, in the face of such a ferocious attack, the Londoners broke and fled, Edward and his cavalry hot on their heels.

Henry was left with no option but to hurry to the attack, climbing the hill to engage Simon's centre. The royal left, led by the king's brother, Richard of Cornwall, engaged Simon de Montfort's right but, faced with stiff opposition, were pushed back down the hill. Despite attacking uphill, Henry's division held its own in the centre, until Simon sent in his reserve to tip the balance in the barons' favour. Simon's troops pursued the royalist forces into the town of Lewes, with Henry only just able to disentangle himself from the street fighting and seek shelter in the priory. By the time Edward and his cavalry returned to the field, the battle was lost. Edward tried to rally his forces for a fresh offensive, his leading barons thwarted his efforts by riding from the field, John de Warenne among them. Earl Warenne, his brother Hugh Bigod and his brothers-in-law, William de Valence and Guy de Lusignan fled the battle, seeking shelter at nearby Pevensey Castle.[29] Instead of pulling back and regrouping, Edward chose to fight his way to his father, who had set up a defensive perimeter at the priory.

Father and son were trapped; the next day they agreed to surrender. A monk at Lewes priory recounted a vivid account of the battle:

1264. This year, on the 14th of May, and on the day of the translation of Hugh Abbot, and of the Holy Martyrs Victor and Corona, there was a deadly battle between King Henry and Symon de Munfort and the barons, and so it was, that the greatest part of the king's army was utterly overthrown between prime and noon. Firstly, the king was much beaten by swords and maces, and two horses killed under him, so that he escaped with difficulty, and his brother Richard, king of Germany, was soon captured. Edward, the king's son, delivered over in hostage to Symon de Muntfort, and many of the greatest men of England, who held with the king, wounded in their heads and bodies even to death, the number of which dead is reckoned at 2700, more or less. All these things took place at Lewes, at the mill of the hide.[30]

The king was now firmly in Simon de Montfort's control, little more than a figurehead with Edward held hostage for his father's good behaviour.[31]

John de Warenne's unfortunate exploits at the Battle of Lewes were to later be turned into poetry:

By god that is aboven ous, he dude muche synne,
That lette passen over see the erl of Warynne:
He hath robbed Engelond, the mores, ant the fenne,
The gold, ant the selver, and y-boren henne,
For love of Wyndesore.

Sire Simond de Mountfort hath swore bi ys chyn,
Hevede he nou here the erl of Waryn,
Shud he never more come to is yn,
Ne with sheld, ne with spere, ne with other gyn,
To help of Wyndesore[32]

From Pevensey, John de Warenne and his companions took ship for the Continent. Chroniclers condemned the lords for their flight, with one laying the blame of Edward's capture squarely on the shoulders of John de Warenne.[33] The lords met with Henry's queen Eleanor, who was already in France trying to gain support for his husband's cause, and told her of the disastrous battle. The barons stayed with the queen for a time, 'mourning happier times.'[34] After advising the queen to gather a force for invasion, the exiled lords appealed to the king of France for aid for their cause. In England, John de Warenne's lands were seized. On 20 June, all, except Reigate and

Lewes, were given into the custody of Gilbert de Clare, Earl of Gloucester. The Sussex lands were given to Simon de Montfort's second son, also called Simon de Montfort.[35]

John remained on the Continent for the rest of the year, returning only at Whitsuntide 1265; he landed on the Pembrokeshire coast with his brother-in-law, William de Valence, Earl of Pembroke, and 'with a power of crossebowes and other men of warre.'[36] Warenne and Valence landed with a force of 120 men, both cavalry and infantry. They sent a plea to the king for the restoration of their lands, Warenne alleging 'that he had done nothing to deserve the forfeiture of them, and was answered, that if he could go thither in person, and submit to a trial in the king's court, he should have safe conduct so to do.'[37] It was added that he would also have to answer for certain trespasses. Perhaps suspecting a trap, Warenne stayed away, joining forces with Gilbert de Clare, Earl of Gloucester, who had recently deserted the baronial cause. On 28 May, Edward escaped his captors, slipping his guard while out riding, and rendezvoused with John de Warenne and William de Valence. On 30 May the earl of Leicester obliged the king to write letters to all his tenants, saying 'that his son Edward was gone off to John de Warren [sic], and the barons marchers rebels, and disturbers of the peace, commanding them to come with horse and arms, to go with him against them.'[38] Under Edward's leadership, they attacked several towns in the Welsh Marches and on the night of 1–2 August, having ridden through the night from Worcester, launched a surprise attack on Kenilworth Castle, Simon de Montfort's home. They captured a good number of Simon's noble commanders, men and equipment, but the earl's son, the younger Simon de Montfort, managed to escape with a sizable force.

Although the chroniclers do not mention him, it seems likely that John de Warenne was with Edward just a few days later, on 4 August, at the Battle of Evesham. The battle effectively ended Simon de Montfort's rebellion, and his life, with only small pockets of resistance holding out afterwards. On the morning of the battle, Edward appeared on the high ground, north of the town of Evesham. Mistaken in the belief that the royal army was a contingent of reinforcements being brought up by the younger Simon de Montfort, the Earl of Leicester was taken by surprise:[39]

At dawn on Tuesday, 4 August, Simon de Montfort set out towards Evesham. The king, on arriving there with his men, wished to eat breakfast; this he did, although Simon de Montfort refused to take any food. After the king had eaten, they set out together for Kenilworth.

When they arrived outside the town of Evesham, Prince Edward, the king's son, fell upon them with a large force of men. As soon as the king saw Edward, he abandoned Simon de Montfort, and fighting broke out on all sides. In the battle, the most worthy knight, Simon de Montfort, earl of Leicester, his son Henry and Hugh le Despenser, were among the many who were slain.[40]

The battle was a slaughter. Edward had decided that Simon de Montfort had to die and assigned men to the job of seeking out the rebel leader and despatching him, and rather gruesomely mutilating him afterwards:

Simon de Montfort, whose head was cut off, whose body was dismembered, and – shameful to relate – whose private parts were removed, suffered glorious martyrdom, so we believe, for the peace of the land and the restoration of the realm and our mother the Church, more especially as he could have fled easily to Kenilworth, had he so chosen.[41]

In the aftermath of the war, John de Warenne was called upon to help restore order to the country. He was despatched to the south coast, to subdue Kent and the Cinque Ports. He brought 200 archers from the weald of Sussex to intimidate London; the city had sided with the rebels and insulted the queen. With Henry of Almain, John routed the northern rebels, led by the earl of Derby. He then moved into East Anglia, attacking Bury St Edmunds with William de Valence, in an effort to bring order to the area. In 1267 John was again working with his brother-in-law, the two of them having been asked by the king to encourage the earl of Gloucester to attend parliament, which he had refused to do. In 1268 John was pardoned by the king for any rebellion against the Crown, and for the actions of his followers. The rewards he received were by no means extravagant: he received an important wardship, the London houses which had been forfeited by Hugh de Neville, a promise of £100 of land out of royal escheats, 200 marks in cash and several Jewish debts. Several gifts and pardons were issued by the Crown, at John's request.[42]

At the Northampton parliament of 1268 John, along with Edward, Henry of Almain and William de Valence, among others, took the cross, promising to go on crusade. While Edward fulfilled the promise, John remained in England. When Henry III died on 20 November 1272, John de Warenne attended his funeral four days later where, together with other leading magnates, he swore an oath of loyalty to Edward as the new king:

1272. King Henry died, to whom succeeded Edward, his first-begotten son, who at that time was in the Holy Land; and, on account of his absence, for the keeping the peace, by the assent of all the magnates, four guardians of the land were appointed, of whom the first and principal was Lord Gilbert, Earl of Gloucester, the second, Lord John Earl Warenne, the third the Archbishop of York, the fourth, Edmund, son of Richard, king of Almaine.[43]

Edward was in Sicily, on his way home from the Holy Land, when news reached him of his father's death. He would not return to England until August 1274: John de Warenne acted as one of the custodians of the realm in the new king's absence, making a new seal, appointing officials, protecting the royal treasury and preserving the king's peace.[44]

At the death of Henry III, John de Warenne had just turned 40. As a prominent baron, he had been involved in every aspect of the turbulent years that culminated in the Second Barons' War. While he could not pride himself in remaining constant to the king, neither had he been any less loyal than the majority of his fellow barons. In the end, he had chosen his side, suffered defeat and ignominy at Lewes but recovered his honour and his lands in supporting Edward through the Evesham campaign. For John, his loyalties appeared to be tied more to his family and friends, than to crown or reform. He chose his sides based on where lay the interests of his brothers, brother-in-law and cousins; in other words, his loyalties were primarily to Hugh Bigod, William de Valence, Edward and Henry of Almain. And it was to this close affinity that John looked for guidance on his political affiliations. Though a leader of men, he does not stand out, at this point in his life, as one to take the lead, or the initiative, in the wider field of national politics. He took his cues from those he trusted, and these friendships were to stand him in good stead. Forged in war, his friendship with Edward was to last throughout their lives.

Chapter Fifteen

John de Warenne and the Wars of Edward I

As one of the senior barons of England, John de Warenne had a dual responsibility. His duties were not only to involve himself in national affairs, but also to oversee and administer the vast earldom he had inherited at the tender age of 9. During his minority, many of his lands were administered by Peter of Savoy; rather badly, it seems, given John's later animosity towards him. The honour of Conisbrough was entrusted to the custody of John's mother, Matilda Marshal, until her death in 1248.

As with previous earls, John de Warenne was a generous benefactor to the church and ensured that the abbeys, priories and churches under his protection were well provided for. In 1281, he had granted the advowson of the church at Gresham to the priory of the Holy Sepulchre at Thetford.[1] In 1274, John de Warenne made a grant 'to Thomas de Walton, for life, of a messuage in Suthwerk which Henry Garland held, paying one mark yearly to the prior of Bermundesey.'[2] Also like his predecessors, he was involved in land deals, such as 'in 1260 John de Ferles and Maud his wife gave a carucate of land in Rottingdean to John de Warenne, Earl Warenne, in exchange for the manor of Twineham.'[3] Land grants and exchanges were also arranged between family members, including with John's Bigod half-brothers; 'release by Ralph le Bygot to John, Earl of Warenne, of his messuage, lands, and other possessions in Thorne, and in Balne in the parish of Fislake.'[4] John de Warenne's deeds and charters not only included the exchange of lands, but also the exchange of fealty associated with the land:

> Release by Richard de Stubbes, son and heir of Alexander de Stubbes, to Sir John, Earl of Warenne, of the homage and service of Robert Curton, by reason of the land he sold to the said Robert in Warneswurthe, with licence of the said Earl; and attornment for the same Robert to do homage and suit of court [to the Earl in his stead] for the said land.[5]

John was keen to preserve his family's traditional interests. For example, in 1278, when he was claiming the right to hold a market at Dorking, Surrey, John de Warenne asserted that the manor had been 'held by his ancestors from before legal memory.'[6]

Other charters reveal the levels of service owed to the earl in return for lands. Eleanor l'Estraunge is recorded as holding land from John de Warenne in return for the service of a part of a huntsman: 'Friday after St. Chad, 9 Edw. I. Blaminister. A fourth part of the manor held of the earl of Warenne by service of a fourth part of a huntsman to the earl at his will and at his cost.'[7] An inquisition in Essex also showed that Eleanor l'Estraunge held land there of Earl Warenne to the value of knights' fees:

> Sunday after St. Peter ad Cathedram, 9 Edw. I. Extanis ad Montem. 2 carucates land held of John de Warenn earl of Warenn (Warennye) by service of 1 knight's fee. Little Canevel. 80a. arable, 4a. meadow, 3a. pasture, 6a. wood, and 67s. rent, held of the said John earl of Warenn by service of ¼ knight's fee.[8]

John de Warenne's business dealing also extended to commercial properties, such as shops in Southwark, where a grant was made 'by John son of Robert de Coventre, to Sir John, earl of Warenne, of 5s. yearly rent from the second shop westward from the grantor's hall in which hall Henry "in the Lane" dwells, in the parish of St. Olave, Suthwerk ... Friday before Michaelmas 6 Edward I.'[9]

Unlike his predecessors, John de Warenne had a reputation for ruthlessness that seems extreme even for the violent times of the thirteenth century. He was known as a strict and unpopular landlord, with a temperament that brought him into conflict with many. In 1253 he was convicted of unjustly enclosing common land in Wakefield and ordered to tear down the fences he had only recently erected.[10] A land dispute with the Lacy lords of Pontefract was in danger of turning into physical violence, each mustering private armies, before the king himself had to intervene in 1268: royal justices determined that the pastureland in question belonged to Lacy.[11] In 1270 the earl was censured by the archbishop of York for levying unwarranted exactions on account of the Second Barons' War. And in 1274, the earl's archers and other men were reported for harassing the people and lands of Robert d'Aiguillon, and causing unrest in Sussex, so much so that Edward I himself visited Warenne at his castle at Reigate to resolve the situation.[12] To appease Warenne, Robert d'Aiguillon was deprived of his castle, but the king appointed a new sheriff in the county in order to restore the authority of the Crown. In a letter of complaint from John Pecham, Archbishop of Canterbury, John de Warenne was asked to resolve an issue whereby his well-stocked deer parks were posing a danger to the crops in adjacent fields.[13]

It is hard to ascertain how much time and interest John de Warenne had in his various estates. At Castle Acre, for example, we can assume that he was present for the king's visits to the castle, of which there were five by Edward I between 1285 and January 1297: during the last of these visits, the king received news of the clergy's refusal to pay tax without the consent of the pope, sparking a significant political crisis.[14] In 1277, in his South Yorkshire estates, the earl claimed rights that allowed him control over practically every aspect of the lives of the people within his domains. He claimed

> the right to carry out judgements involving the death sentence; the right to regulate the price and quality of bread and beer; the regulation of weights and measures; the right to settle disputes where blood had been shed, and the right to judge cases where landlords seized goods in lieu of unpaid rent.[15]

The administration of the earl's domains was handled on a daily basis by the officials at his various manors: these officials appear to have been as ruthless as their earl and between 1274 and 1276 were accused of 'diabolical and innumerable oppressions.'[16] His various stewards and bailiffs were accused of preventing royal ministers from performing their duties, levying arbitrary taxes, fines and tolls, and imprisoning those who opposed the earl or violated his rights.[17] At Conisbrough, for instance, in Yorkshire, the Warenne estates were managed by the earl's steward, Richard de Heydon, and constable, Nigel Drury. Perhaps having taken their cue from the earl himself, Heydon and Drury were highly unpopular and notorious as harsh taskmasters, so much so that the people of Conisbrough appealed to the king about their behaviour. Richard de Heydon was accused of numerous tyrannies, including the unlawful imprisonment of Beatrice, the wife of William the Taylor of Rotherham. Nigel Drury was accused of the theft of six stone of wool from one Conisbrough resident, and of a horse and a sack full of oats from another; he took them into the castle, with the earl claiming that they were taken in lieu of unpaid rent.[18]

As one of the leading magnates and close allies of Edward I, John de Warenne was also involved in administration on a national level. Between 1274 and his death in 1304, the earl was witness to 496 royal charters, that is more than a third of all Edward I's charters for his entire reign. John's friendship with Edward was not something the earl could take for granted, however, and he had fallen foul of the king even before Edward came to the throne. A dispute arose between John and Sir Alan de la Zouche in 1269; John de Warenne's ward, Isabella, was the granddaughter and heir of

David of Ashby, who had died whilst supporting the baronial cause in 1265. Although David's widow and children had been treated kindly, the family lands of Castle Ashby and Chadstone in Northamptonshire had been taken into the possession of Alan de la Zouche. An inquiry was held in 1269 to determine the status of David of Ashby at the time of the Second Barons' War, and whether or not he was in a state of rebellion against the crown at his death. The fact that the Zouche family were still in possession of Castle Ashby in the 1270s and 1280s suggests that John de Warenne and his ward lost the lawsuit as a result of Isabella's grandfather's rebellion and disinheritance.[19]

In the aftermath of the legal battle, John confronted Alan de la Zouche in front of the full court at Westminster. Matters got so heated that Earl Warenne's men drew their swords and set upon Zouche and his men. Alan de la Zouche was mortally wounded in the ensuing scuffle. John fled to his castle at Reigate and swore that he had attacked Zouche out of uncontrollable anger, rather than with any premeditation to do the baron harm.[20] Edward's subsequent pursuit of justice led to a severe punishment, if far more lenient than a commoner would expect to suffer; John was fined 10,000 marks, to be paid in instalments of 700 marks a year. He was also ordered to perform a penance barefoot. Perhaps with a view to needing John's support for future endeavours, when he became king, Edward relaxed the terms of payment for Warenne's fine and eventually forgave it altogether.[21] Justice had been seen to be done, but the punishment handed out was followed by pragmatic mercy.

John de Warenne was given various duties as a part Edward's administration, starting from the moment Edward became king, when John de Warenne was appointed as one of the guardians of the realm until Edward's return from crusade. This appointment had been made by the agreement of his fellow magnates. The four guardians, which also comprised the earls of Cornwall and Gloucester and the archbishop of York, led an executive council which itself was headed by two royal clerks, Robert Burnell and Walter Merton, Bishop of Rochester, and included Roger Mortimer of Wigmore, the Marcher baron and Edward's executor. Earl Warenne attended the king's coronation in 1274. In a story that encapsulates the sense of camaraderie that accompanied the advent of the new reign, at the coronation banquet John, Alexander III, King of Scots, and the earls of Lancaster, Cornwall, Gloucester and Pembroke, each with 100 men-at-arms, presented themselves before the newly crowned king and released 600 horses, to be claimed by any who could catch one.[22]

In 1289 Earl Warenne and the earl of Lincoln formed part of a commission established to hear complaints by the Scots of extortions committed by the northern sheriffs.[23] In 1296 John was appointed guardian of Scotland, with the title 'warden of the kingdom and land of Scotland'.[24] And in 1297 Warenne and Lincoln were again appointed to a commission, this time alongside two other barons and two bishops, to hear complaints arising from the crisis of that year, when Edward's barons bridled against heavy taxes and the king's right to demand military service. John de Warenne also took his place on the regency council of 1297, constituted to assist Edward's son and heir, who was nominal regent during the king's absence on campaign.

John de Warenne is probably best known for his reported response to Edward I's commissioners in the *Quo Warranto* proceedings of 1279:

> Here my lords, here is my warrant! My ancestors came with William the Bastard and conquered their lands with the sword, and I shall defend them with the sword against anyone who tries to usurp them. The king did not conquer and subject the land by himself, but our forefathers were partners and co-workers with him.[25]

The scene of John de Warenne's brandishing of a rusty sword and claiming his rights to his lands through the Norman Conquest is described only in one chronicle, that of Walter of Guisborough. As a consequence, there is a large question mark over whether the chronicler was sensationalising events, or whether other chroniclers just did not see the need to mention such a dramatic gesture when writing about the *Quo Warranto* proceedings. With this distance in time, it would be impossible to say for certain. What it is possible to say, is that, given what we know of the temperament of John de Warenne, it would not be out of character for him to make such a dramatic gesture when being asked to prove his right to the lands his family had held for over 200 years. The challenge to use the sword to defend against anyone who would seek to usurp his rights is certainly in keeping with the personality of the gruff earl, and his violent tendencies, of which there is ample evidence. Moreover, everything John is reported as saying in the speech is the truth. His ancestors did come to England with William the Conqueror, and did take the lands by the sword; especially seeing as many of the Warenne lands had previously belonged to King Harold, killed at the Battle of Hastings.

The *Quo Warranto* proceedings of 1279 were used by Edward I in order to challenge the usurpations of the earls of Warenne and Gloucester, who had taken liberties over their rights and franchises during the reign of Henry III. The intent of the hearings was to establish by what authority Edward's magnates held their lands and privileges: if the baron had a charter setting this out, they faced no challenge. However, many of the lands and privileges were held by tradition or had been held for such a long time that a charter had never existed or had been lost over time.

The case against John de Warenne, Earl Warenne, followed on from the 1274 incident, when the earl's archers and other men were reported for harassing the people and lands of Robert d'Aiguillon, and causing unrest in the Sussex region. In the Hundred Rolls of 1272, it was stated that the earl's father and subsequently the earl himself had taken control of the chaces and warrens throughout the whole barony of Lewes, including the lands and tenements of Robert d'Aiguillon. In addition it was stated that the earl prevented Aiguillon and others from hunting with dogs in areas in which hunting had been customary since ancient times. It was further alleged that the earl had infringed on lands to which the king himself held rights. Following on from the findings of the Hundred jury, Robert d'Aiguillon petitioned the king to resolve the issue.[26] The plea was heard in the summer of 1279 when 'the earl of Surrey was summoned to be here at this day to show by what warrant he claims to have free warren etc.'[27] Questioned before the justices itinerant in Sussex, John de Warenne is reported as claiming that he held free warren of all the lands in Sussex, with tongue firmly in cheek, I suspect, by virtue of his very name, Warenne.[28]

Despite the dramatic gestures and flippant responses, the *Quo Warranto* proceedings sought to redress the trespasses committed by the earl, and firmly establish the royal supremacy of Edward I over even his most powerful magnates. John de Warenne was required to offer proof of his rights to various lands and franchises; failure to provide adequate evidence would result in the loss of those rights. Hence John's dramatic gesture of waving a rusty sword aloft as if it belonged to the first Earl Warenne and citing his family's assistance in the conquest of England. As a consequence of the proceedings, John lost the valuable franchise of return of writs in both his Lincolnshire towns of Stamford and Grantham.[29] In other claims, the earl was confirmed in his rights. The *Quo Warranto* proceedings appear to have been an exercise in Edward I flexing his muscles, and sending a message to his barons that they should not infringe on royal rights and prerogatives. Though punishments were issued, including forfeits, they were, on the whole, lenient. Edward was using a combination of carrot and stick, to bring his barons into line and firmly put them in their place within the hierarchy of the royal administration.

King Edward I needed to be firm with his barons, but he also needed to be sure not to alienate them, nor send them into rebellion. Royal power was a delicate balancing act. The relationship between king and baron was one of mutual need and assistance. While the king governed the country, he relied on his magnates to govern the regions under their control. He also relied on the magnates to provide the soldiers with which the king defended – or extended – his borders. John de Warenne was a prominent military commander for Edward I, serving on the king's campaigns in both Wales and Scotland.

Relations between King Edward and the Welsh prince, Llywelyn ap Gruffudd, later to become known as Llywelyn the Last, gradually deteriorated after Edward's return from crusade and assumption of royal power. Llywelyn had failed to attend the king's coronation, and later, due to illness and short notice, failed to respond to a summons to pay homage to the king at Shrewsbury on 2 December 1274. At about the same time, the Welsh prince had uncovered a conspiracy to murder him, involving his own brother, Dafydd. King Edward's willingness to shelter the would-be murderers at his own court further heightened tensions between the Welsh and English rulers. Llywelyn was yet again summoned to meet the king at Chester on 22 August 1275. Although messages passed between them, the Welsh prince refused to meet the king while Edward was harbouring the men who had plotted Llywelyn's murder. As a result, on 11 November 1276, Llywelyn was declared 'a rebel and a disturber of the peace'.[30] John de Warenne sat on the court that rendered the judgement.[31] Throughout the winter, Llywelyn sent the king proposals aimed at appeasing him and averting war; but by the spring, the Welsh prince had been excommunicated and Edward was gathering his army ready for invasion.

John de Warenne would serve in this Welsh campaign, but first he joined the king and court near Northwich in Cheshire, where the king had decided to found a Cistercian abbey. Larger than its sister house at Fountains, it was to be named Vale Royal. It was intended 'that no monastery should be more royal in liberties, wealth and honour.'[32] On 9 August, on the banks of the River Weaver, amidst a grand and solemn ceremony, Edward laid the first stone on the spot that was to be the abbey's high altar. Edward's queen, Eleanor of Castile, laid the second and third stones, for herself and her son, Prince Alphonso, who died in 1284, aged 10. John de Warenne was among the great magnates who laid additional stones before Edward's chancellor, Robert Burnell, celebrated mass, emphasising God's blessing on their impending invasion of Wales.

The kings' declared aims in Wales were to occupy the whole of Gwynedd and divide it between himself and Llywelyn's younger brothers, Dafydd and

Owain, although he intended that Dafydd and Owain would attend the king's parliaments 'just like our other earls and barons.'[33] The king launched his major offensive on 23 August, with the main royal army advancing on Conwy while a smaller force occupied Anglesey; the occupation of Anglesey was a major blow for Llywelyn, it was where most of the grain in Wales was produced. Its loss meant the Welsh forces were faced with dwindling supplies and the prospect of starvation. Llywelyn had no choice but to submit to King Edward. The treaty of Aberconwy of 9 November 1277 formally ended hostilities. Llywelyn was allowed to retain the style prince of Wales, but with only the homage of five minor lords and he ceded the Four Cantrefs; his broader principality was destroyed. Llywelyn's brothers were provided for and a fine of 50,000 marks was imposed on the prince. Llywelyn swore fealty to Edward at Rhuddlan on 11 November.[34]

In 1278 John de Warenne was again in Wales, leading a contingent of soldiers to quell the uprising of Rhys ap Maredudd. Four years later, he was there for the 1282–83 campaign, in which Llywelyn was killed and his surviving brother, Dafydd, captured and, later, executed. During the campaign, John captured the castle of Dinas Brân. The king rewarded him with Bromfield and Yale, one of several new lordships sliced out of Welsh lands and handed to English lords:

Gruffyth ap Madoc tooke part with king Henry III and Edward I against the prince of North-Wales, and therefore for feare of the prince, he was faine to lye in his castle of Dinas-Bran, which standeth on the top of a very steep hill, to the which there is no way but one to come. He died, his children being within age, whereupon shortly ensued the destruction of two of them. For the said king Edward I gave the wardship of Madoc (who had for his part the lordship of Bromfield and Yale, and the said castle of Dinas-Bran, with the reversion of Maelor Saefneg, after his mother's decease, who had the fame to her jointer) to John earle Warren, and granted the wardship of Llywelyn (to whose part the lordships of Chirke and Nanheudwy came) to Roger Mortimer. These guardians, forgetting the service done by the father of the wards, to the king, so guarded their wards with small regard, that they never returned to their possessions. And shortly after, the said guardians did obtain the said lands to themselves as charters of the king. This John earle Warren began to build the Holt Castle and William his son finished the same. The lordship of Bromfield and Yale continued in the name of earle Warren three descents, John, William and John that died without issue, and then the said lordship descended to Alice, daughter of the said William earle Warren, (and sister and heir of the said last John) married to Edmund Fitzalan earle of Arundel.[35]

John, Earl Warenne, was again in North Wales in 1294, where he helped to reduce the rebellion led by Madog ap Llywelyn. During the campaign, Earl Warenne vigorously attempted to assert his rights to the temporalities of the bishopric of St Asaph which lay within his Welsh territories, unsuccessfully laying claim to their income during vacancies.[36] The earl took an active interest in his newly acquired Welsh lands. At Wrexham he constructed Castrum Leonis, or 'Chastellion', now known as Holt Castle. Built above the west bank of the River Dee, it stood guard to one of the ferry crossings into Cheshire. The castle was of a modern design, pentagonal with a tall, round tower in each of its five corners. The residential quarters were arranged around an inner courtyard, with up to three storeys above ground level and three basement levels cut into the sandstone bedrock.[37]

The Calendar of Ancient Petitions Relating to Wales demonstrates that Earl John treated his Welsh tenants in much the same manner as he treated his English ones, that is to say, rather harshly. One petition, undated, brought before the king by the men of Hopedale and Kynartone, complained that 'the earl had not allowed them to take, or make use of, anything in their own woods, except by view of foresters, whereas they had been wont to do this at their own will, and, moreover, the greater part of their sustenance is derived from the woods.'[38] The men complained that the earl 'has not allowed them to make assarts and to enclose the ground thus reclaimed within their hedges or ditches, not make their profit as they had been wont to do in the time of our aforesaid lord, the king, by petition.'[39] Earl Warenne replied that he 'knew nothing of this and confessed not to the causing of any such grievance, but said that they should be maintained in his time as they had been wont to be previously, so that they should not have reason to complain of such harshness in future.'[40] According to the petition, dated to after 1301, the complaint was not remedied and the men of Hope and Kynartone found themselves facing 'greater harshness and grievance than previously, caused by the Earl's bailiffs.'[41] Although we do not know the final outcome, the matter was passed to the king's son Edward, as prince of Wales, so that his council in Wales could investigate as to what rights the men had previously held.

Another petition against the earl was brought by Margaret, widow of Madoc Fychan:

The petitioner took the manor of Eyton at farm, for the term of life, from the wife of Griffin ab Madawe by the payment of 10 marks yearly but the Earl de Waran (Warenne) has disseised her and wrongfully holds it. Wherefore she prays the king to do her justice (*dreytur*); also concerning a vill which she held under him, for which she has good charter; and the earl holds it wrongfully. Also she prays the king to do right to Griffin the Younger (*Griffin le petit*) who held it in addition to the 2 vills, viz., Corvain (Corwen) and [Havot] Kilmainloyt (Cilymaenllwyd) for which she has good charters from the same Griffin.[42]

According to the notes attached to the petition, Margaret had so offended against the king that he was not disposed to look on her petition favourably; he did, later, send her a gift of 5 marks out of charity.[43] Margaret was sister of Llywelyn, the last prince of Wales, which may have coloured the king's relationship with her.

Earl Warenne's continued involvement in Wales and the Welsh wars did not prevent him from taking part in King Edward's dealings with Scotland. In 1278, John accompanied Alexander III, King of Scots, to London and was present in parliament when Alexander swore fealty to Edward. The earl travelled to Scotland in 1285 and in 1289–90 served as a royal envoy during the delicate negotiations for the marriage of Prince Edward and Margaret, the Maid of Norway, who was to be the queen of Scots. Margaret was the granddaughter of Alexander III through her mother, Margaret. Her father was King Erik II of Norway. Young Margaret was a month short of her third birthday when her grandfather died in an accident in March, 1286; the unfortunate king had fallen over a cliff to his death when his horse lost its footing in a stormy night time ride to visit his new bride, Yolande de Dreux.

The marriage between Edward and Margaret was intended to secure the futures of both kingdoms, whilst guaranteeing Scots independence. John de Warenne helped to negotiate the treaty of Salisbury in the autumn of 1289 and the subsequent treaty of Brigham, of July 1290, which established the terms of the marriage and of the future relationship between England and Scotland. John was also one of the prince's proctors, and one of the ambassadors sent to Norway to treat with Margaret's father, King Erik. Following little Margaret's death in September 1290, during the sea voyage from Norway to Scotland, John backed the candidacy of his own son-in-law, John Balliol, for the vacant Scottish throne. The Scots agreed to abide by the decision of King Edward, as to who would become king of Scots, with at least thirteen competitors throwing their hats in the ring. The leading candidates, however, were John Balliol, Lord of Bywell, and Robert de Brus,

Lord of Annandale; both were descendants of David, the youngest son of Prince Henry of Scotland and Ada de Warenne.

Before 7 February 1281, John Balliol had been married to Earl Warenne's youngest daughter, Isabella, by whom he had at least one child, a son named Edward, and possibly several others, including a second son, Henry and two daughters; Margaret, who died unmarried, and Anne, whose existence is doubted. It seems likely, however, that Isabella had died some years before her husband laid claim to the Scottish throne, as there is no mention of her ever being crowned queen. Balliol's claim lay through seniority, he was grandson of Margaret, the eldest daughter of David of Huntingdon. Robert de Brus's claim lay in the fact he was closer in degree to the same David, being the son of David's youngest daughter, Isobel. John Balliol was therefore David's great-grandson, whereas Robert de Brus was his grandson, though by a younger daughter. King Edward decided in favour of descent through the eldest daughter of David and awarded the throne to John Balliol. Balliol was enthroned in an inauguration ceremony on the ancient stone of Scone, as King John, on 30 November 1292.[44] Administratively, John's reign as king was distinguished; he asserted royal authority, establishing three new sheriffdoms and held four sessions of parliament between February 1293 and May 1294.[45]

King John's relationship with England, however, was to be his undoing. His reign was dominated by a series of appeals from Scottish courts to King Edward in England; of the eleven known cases, three were brought by English subjects and three by political malcontents. John's position as king was severely weakened by his barons seeking redress in England if the Scots king failed to satisfy them. In the autumn of 1293, King John appeared in the English parliament, to protest against the English claim that they had a right to hear appeals from Scotland. Faced with an uncompromising King Edward, the Scots king withdrew his protest and renewed his submission and homage to King Edward. However, when Edward summoned John and twenty-six of his magnates to undertake personal military service overseas, in June 1294, against the king of France, the Scots king stood defiant.

Growing tired of the constant humiliation of their king, the Scottish parliament established a council of twelve elected guardians to direct the government of the king, at Stirling in July 1295. In October of the same year, a treaty with France, ratified in parliament on 23 February 1296. agreed to a military alliance and was to be sealed with the marriage of John's son and heir, Edward, with a niece of King Philip V. It became known as the Auld Alliance. Almost immediately the treaty was ratified, the

Scots received a demand from King Edward that certain Scottish towns and castles be handed to English garrisons as sureties for the answering of appeals. Confident in the new Franco-Scottish alliance, the Scots refused, and war became inevitable.

John de Warenne was entrusted with the defence of English interests in Scotland; in 1295 he was named keeper of the sea-coasts and then keeper of Bamburgh Castle. He captured Dunbar Castle on 27 April 1296; though a minor battle, it was proclaimed as a great victory, with as many as 10,000 Scotsmen killed.[46] King John retreated northwards but was suing for peace by late June. John's submission and surrender to Edward are recorded in three separate documents: at Kincardine on 2 July, John confessed his rebellion; at Strathcathro on 7 July he renounced the French treaty and at Brechin Castle on 10 July John resigned his kingdom and royal dignity.[47] The public removal of the royal blazon from John's surcoat led to the derogatory nickname of 'Toom Tabard', meaning 'empty surcoat' by which he is still known today. John was sent south and by August of 1296 was installed in comfortable confinement in the Tower of London, although he was later moved between the Tower, Hertford (where he was allowed to hunt) and elsewhere.

An incident from 1296 demonstrates the contrast between momentous national events and the mundane, everyday life that continued apace, even for the great personalities of the realm. The plea rolls of that year record a complaint made by John de Warenne whilst in the recently captured town of Berwick:

> The earl of Warenne by his attorney presented himself against Thomas Havard in a plea of trespass. Whereon he complains that Thomas illegally withholds a black horse and a basket filled with 10 shillings' worth of bread which Warenne bought on Friday in Easter Week [30 March] in Berwick, and that he still withholds [them] to the earl's great damage etc. Thomas, who is present, says with respect to the horse that he bought it from a certain John the tailor, whom he calls to warranty. And because he does not have John he is sent to prison.
>
> Concerning the bread he now says that he is in no wise guilty. He asks for enquiry to be made, as does the earl. Later they are agreed by licence. Thomas puts himself [on the country] and makes a fine of shillings. (amercements 2 shillings, paid).[48]

It is interesting to note that a man involved in the subjugation of Scotland can have paid such interest in the theft of bread. It is a demonstration, perhaps, of the fact noblemen had to have their fingers in many pies, paying attention to national and international events whilst keeping one eye on their own estates and interests. Having dispensed with John Balliol, King Edward proceeded on a victorious summer march through Scotland, accompanied by John, Earl Warenne, who was appointed custodian of Scotland on 3 September. By this point, John was 65 years old. He had been earl of Surrey for fifty-six years. And he did not like Scotland. Finding the climate inhospitable to his ageing bones, the earl returned to northern England, leaving officials in charge of the day-to-day government of Scotland, led by Hugh de Cressingham, the treasurer appointed by King Edward:

> Earl Warenne, to whom the king had entrusted the care and protection of the whole kingdom of Scotland, as his own deputy, complained about the dreadful climate there, and said he could not remain there without damage to his health. So he went to live in England, albeit in the north, and was only half-hearted in his pursuit of exiled Scots there, which was the source and origin of our troubles thereafter.[49]

John de Warenne even refused to return to Scotland when the Scots rose in revolt with William Wallace at their head in 1297; until King Edward specifically ordered him to proceed to Scotland and lead the fight. The earl sent his grandson, Henry Percy, on ahead as he slowly made his way northward, reaching Berwick in July. Although Percy met with some success, a frustrated Edward attempted to replace Earl Warenne as keeper of Scotland, with Brian fitzCount; but pleading poverty, Brian claimed he was too poor to take on such an expensive responsibility. In the end, Edward managed to persuade John to remain in Scotland and deal with the Wallace rebellion: 'Now that the king was ready for the crossing to Flanders he put Earl Warenne in charge of all military forces in the county of Yorkshire from the Trent to Scotland, and ordered him to go with all speed to crush the insolence of the Scots and punish the ringleaders as they deserved.'[50]

John de Warenne marched on Stirling, where the two armies faced each other, on the opposite banks of the Firth of Forth, on 9 September 1297. Warenne sought to negotiate but was rebuffed by Wallace, being told, 'Tell your commander that we are not here to make peace but to do battle to defend ourselves and liberate our kingdom. Let them come and we shall prove this in their very beards.'[51] John de Warenne appears to have been over confident, convinced that the defeat of Wallace and his comrade, Andrew Murray, would be a matter of a simple campaign, given the Scottish army was comprised of common soldiers, with no heavy cavalry to speak of and few lords not on the English side or in English custody. The Scottish set up a defensive position on the high ground at the Abbey of Craig, overlooking the bridge. In order to attack, the English had to cross the narrow Stirling bridge, wide enough to allow only two horses riding abreast, and then navigate a narrow causeway through boggy terrain. Battle began on 11 September amid some confusion; Earl Warenne had given orders for the men to prepare to cross the bridge that morning, but had overslept. His infantry mobilised, ready to cross the bridge, without the earl's authority, and had to be called back. When the earl was finally ready for battle, he ordered Hugh de Cressingham to lead the cavalry over the bridge and crush the Scots.[52]

Only able to ride two abreast, the column of English cavalry was soon stretched out along the bridge and causeway, presenting Wallace and Murray with their opportunity. The Scots infantry attacked the English flank, forcing knights and horses from the causeway and into the boggy fields. The horses becoming trapped in the deep mud, the English knights were massacred. As this was unfolding, a second contingent of Scots were sent to the bridge, destroying it with their axes and thus preventing Earl Warenne and the remainder of his army from crossing and coming to the aid of the beleaguered cavalry. The Scots proceeded to finish off the cavalry, inflicting a significant and shocking defeat on the English. Seeing the battle lost, Earl Warenne turned his horse and rode straight for Berwick, not stopping until he was safe in the English held town; his exhausted horse collapsed and died upon arrival.[53] Hugh de Cressingham, the English treasurer of Scotland, and hated by the Scots, was not so lucky. He was cut down and killed in the rout, his body flayed, with small pieces of his skin sent as gifts throughout the country. Wallace is said to have made a belt of Cressingham's skin, which he wore as a reminder of his great victory.[54]

John de Warenne's defeat at Stirling Bridge was a devastating blow for England and a boost for the Scottish resistance. It proved that the English war machine, so long unstoppable, was not invincible. The Scots were quick to take advantage of their victory and opened their seaports to European trade. Andrew Murray had been mortally wounded at Stirling Bridge and was dead by the end of the month, leaving Wallace to lead the country and the army. He marched south, harrying the English population along the borders and forcing them to abandon their homes. Panic spread across Northumberland:

The Northumbrians were petrified with fear and they evacuated from the countryside their wives and children and all their household goods, sending them with their animals to Newcastle and various other places. At that time the praise of God ceased in all the monasteries and churches of the whole province from Newcastle to Carlisle. All the monks, canons regular and the rest of the priests and ministers of the Lord, together with almost the whole of the people fled from the face of the Scot.[55]

The *Chronicle of Lanercost* depicts the devastation caused by the Scottish army:

After this ... the Scots gathered together and invaded, devastating the whole country, causing burnings, depredations and murders and they came almost up to the town of Newcastle; but turned away from it and invaded the county of Carlisle; there they did as in Northumberland, to devastate more fully anything they had overlooked previously; and on the feast of St Cecilia, virgin and martyr [22 November 1297], they returned to Scotland.[56]

Earl Warenne, though rattled by his defeat, rallied himself and, along with Robert de Clifford, led his men into Annandale, burning villages and tenements and further stretching the financial resources of the powerful Bruce family. In January 1298, Earl Warenne presided over a parliament at York, in King Edward's name, which confirmed Magna Carta. He then led a short campaign against Scotland, during which he reoccupied Berwick, recently abandoned by Wallace, who did not have the resources to hold it.[57]

By March 1298, William Wallace had been knighted and appointed sole guardian of Scotland. King Edward had been fighting on the Continent during the disastrous Stirling Bridge campaign but returned to England on 14 March 1298. On arriving in England, he summoned John de Warenne to discuss the Scottish situation, warmly thanking the aged earl for his services in the campaign.[58] The king set out for the north almost immediately; on 1 July, his army entered Scotland.[59] The English king had a force of 25,000 foot and 3,000 cavalry.[60] Wallace had retreated into Scotland, leaving a devastated countryside behind him, with no sustenance available for the advancing English; the threat of starvation was a real possibility for Edward's army.

John de Warenne was with the king when he brought Wallace and the Scots to battle at Falkirk on 22 July 1298. Outnumbered, Wallace deployed his spearmen in four densely packed schiltrons on the southern aspect of Callendar Wood, protected to the front by a marsh and the Westquarter burn, which stood between the two armies. His archers were placed between the rings of spearmen, with the cavalry to the rear. The English vanguard was commanded by the earls of Norfolk and Hereford, the second battle by Anthony Bek, Bishop of Durham and Edward was in command of the reserve.

As the English advanced, the van and second battle veered left and right, respectively, to avoid the marshy ground, before delivering their attack. The Scottish cavalry fled the field without even engaging with the English, leaving the infantry to their fate. The archers were ridden down but the schiltrons did their job, stopping the English and inflicting a number of casualties. Whereupon Edward brought up his archers and the schiltrons disintegrated under the hailstorm of arrows. The English cavalry charged once again, this time filing into the gaps in the schiltrons left by the rain of arrows, slaughtering the Scottish rank and file.[61] Wallace escaped, but his prestige was gone, and he took ship for France. In 1305 he would be betrayed to the English and suffer the traitor's death on the gallows at Smithfield.

After the victory at Falkirk, the English advanced into Fife, occupying St Andrews and destroying Perth. Earl Warenne returned south and in November was appointed by the king as one of the justices inquiring into the oppressions and misdeeds of forest officials throughout the kingdom. In 1299, he was summoned to military service once again and in September of the same year, he attended the banquet to celebrate the marriage of Edward I to his second wife, Margaret of France. In November, John de Warenne was entrusted with the guardianship of his own grandson, Edward Balliol, whose claim to the Scottish throne would be supported by Edward III in the 1330s. In 1300, now approaching 70, John de Warenne was again performing military service in Scotland. He was given command of the second battalion and was present at the famous siege of Caerlaverock Castle.

John de Warenne turned 70 in 1301, although his advanced age did not prevent him from campaigning in Scotland in 1301, 1302 and 1303; active almost to his last breath. John, 6th Earl of Warenne and Surrey, died on 29 September 1304 at Kennington in Kent; '1304. This year died John de Warenne, Earl of Surrey, about the feast of St Michael, at Kennington, near London.'[62] The old earl's body remained at Kennington until 1 December. After Christmas, he was buried before the altar in the priory church of St Pancras at Lewes, among his Warenne ancestors, including four Warenne earls. He was buried close to his wife, Alice de Lusignan, who had died in 1256, and their only son, William. The old earl held the reins of the earldom for sixty-four of his seventy-three years. Never remarrying, he had been a widower for almost fifty years and was succeeded as Earl Warenne by his grandson and namesake, John.

John de Warenne was probably the most colourful character to have ever held the earldom of Surrey. High-handed and impudent in his dealings with his tenants, murderous when his rights were challenged and a little dramatic in the *Quo Warranto* proceedings, he had limited successes in politics and on the battlefield, preferring to take the lead from others. He certainly had his flaws. His sense of duty and responsibility, both to his earldom and the kingdom at large, however, is demonstrated clearly by the fact that his public life continued to the very end.

Chapter Sixteen

The Last Earl

John de Warenne, the sixth Earl Warenne, had fathered one legitimate son by his wife, Alice de Lusignan. William was born in 1256, on or before 9 February, the day of his mother's death. He was married to Joan, daughter of Richard de Vere, Earl of Oxford, sometime in 1284: 'Also William de Warenne married the daughter of the Earl of Oxford.'[1] Through his mother, William was the nephew of Henry III and first cousin to Edward I. Through his father, William was descended from, among others, William Marshal, Geoffrey of Anjou and six Warenne earls of Surrey.

William was destined never to succeed his father. He was killed in a tournament at Croydon in December 1286, just six months after the birth of his only son and heir, John:

> This year, on June 30, was born the first-begotten son of Sir William de Warenn, by his wife, daughter of the Earl of Oxford, whom he had married, as appears above. He was baptised and called by the name of John, on the 7th of November, with immense rejoicing; but alas! As the prophet testifies, 'our joys are extinguished, but lamentation possesses us;' for in the same year, on the first Sunday before the feast of Thomas the Apostle, which was on December 15, the father of the aforesaid youth [Sir William, killed in a tournament at Croydon], concerning whom our gladness had been, expired, and, oh sadness! He in whom flourished entire nobility, generosity and honesty, and the beginning of the glory of all knighthood, now lies buried and covered with stones. But there was present at the entombment of this so noble a man, the lord of Canterbury, who buried him before the high altar, on the left side, near his mother, with the greatest devotion of respect, as was fitting, many nobles of the land being present. The earl marshal [Roger Bigod, Earl of Norfolk], the Earl of Oxford and several barons ... were anxiously afflicted.[2]

Some sources suggest that John was the posthumous son of William, stating that William was killed in January 1286; however, this entry in the *Annals of Lewes Priory* makes it clear that John was born almost six months before his father was killed.[3] John's sister, Alice, on the other hand, may well have been born the year after her father's death, in June 1287. Given the chronicle was written by a monk at Lewes, a priory patronised by the Warenne family, the laments and praise of William may be slightly exaggerated. However, that the archbishop of Canterbury conducted the funeral rites, and the presence of many senior nobles, suggests that William was, indeed, well thought of. This fact may give the lie to the rumours of murder that inevitably accompany a medieval death from unnatural causes. Rumours that William's enemies had taken the opportunity of the tournament to despatch the young lord appear to be without foundation.[4]

Young John suffered a further bereavement on 1293, when his mother, Joan died. Aged only 7, it seems arrangements had already been made should John still be a minor when his parents died. It had been agreed that the custody of John and his lands should go to Joan's parents, Robert de Vere and his wife, Alice de Sanford. However, Earl Robert died in 1296 and it is not known where 10-year-old John spent the remainder of his childhood. It seems likely that John was raised by his grandfather, until the sixth Earl's death in 1304. At the age of 18, John succeeded to the earldom of his grandfather as the seventh earl of Warenne, Surrey and Sussex. His vast holdings included lands and manors in Sussex, Surrey, Lincolnshire, Yorkshire, Wiltshire and Norfolk. John, Earl Warenne, was still a minor, and would be for another three years; and so, he was made a royal ward, his lands taken into the custody of the Crown. Though he and his lands were in royal custody, and managed by custodians, John lived on his own estates and in 1305 the king commanded him to provide him with forty dried and salted barrels of deer.[5] In the same year, he was sent to attend a tournament at Guildford, part of John's estates, by Edward I, who provided the young lord with considerable funds for his maintenance.[6]

On 7 April 1306, in spite of the fact he had not yet performed homage to the king, Edward granted him his grandfather's lands. It may well have been at this time that Edward Balliol was placed in John's custody. The son of John's aunt, Isabella, and King John Balliol of Scotland, the younger Balliol had been in the custody of his grandfather, the sixth Earl Warenne, from 1299 until the old earl's death in 1304. Given that it is likely his mother was no longer living when John Balliol became king, it seems probable that Edward was born sometime in the 1280s, making him of a similar age to his cousin, John de Warenne. John was Balliol's guardian until it was ordered that he be delivered into royal custody in 1310, by Edward II.[7] In May 1306, John de Warenne attended his first parliament at Westminster, an event which marked his coming of age, although he was not yet 21; in fact, he was still a month shy of his twentieth birthday.

John's early coming of age appears to have been a part of larger scheme by King Edward, as during the parliamentary session, John was brought before the king and offered Edward's granddaughter in marriage; the young earl readily agreed to the marriage, even though his bride was only 10 years old. The proposed bride was Joan, or Jeanne of Bar, Edward's granddaughter by his eldest daughter, Eleanor and her husband Henry, Count of Bar. In the week following the betrothal of John and Joan, and in anticipation of a new expedition against Scotland, on 22 May 1306, Edward I held a magnificent ceremony for the knighting of his eldest son, Edward; the king knighted the prince, who then went on to knight the other candidates, in the glorious setting of Westminster Abbey. In anticipation of the prince's knighting, and in order to gather a body of knights who would be loyal to his son, the king proclaimed that all young men of sufficient age and income should travel to Westminster, to be knighted at royal expense alongside their future king, Prince Edward.[8] The ceremony was also to bestow knighthoods on almost 300 men, John de Warenne included: 'The yong Erle of Warenne with grete nobley was thare / A wif thei him bikenne, the erles douhter of Bare.'[9]

There were so many young men to be knighted, that it was impossible to find accommodation for all, and apple trees had to be chopped down in the gardens of the New Temple to make room. The prince and his closest companions kept their vigil, the night before the ceremony, watching their arms, in the abbey church at Westminster.

> Matthew of Westminster records that there was such a noise of trumpets and pipes, and such a clamour of voices, that one side of the choir could not hear the other. The others kept their vigil at the New Temple. The King provided them the necessary scarlet cloths, fine linen and belts for their use from his own wardrobe.[10]

The following morning, the king knighted his son in the palace of Westminster, investing him with his knight's belt and spurs. The prince then crossed to Westminster Abbey, to invest the others; 'The crowd was enormous, so great indeed, that two knights were killed. Each candidate was attended by three knights, who saw and assisted him through the ceremony.'[11] The prince knighted sixty of the candidates himself, with other knights assisting with the rest. A lavish banquet – which later became known as the Feast of the Swans – followed the proceedings:

when two swans were brought in ornamented with gold network, emblematical of constancy and truth. When they were placed upon the table the King rose and made a vow to God and to the *swans*, that he would set out for Scotland and avenge the death of Comyn, and punish the treachery of the Scots … It was under these exceptionally interesting circumstances that Warenne received his knighthood.[12]

The murder of John Comyn, at the hands of Robert the Bruce in the church of the Greyfriars in Dumfries, on 10 February 1306, following an argument, had sent shockwaves through Christendom. Bruce had then raced to Scone where he was crowned King Robert I of Scots.

As the celebrations continued a number of weddings also took place, involving several barons and nobles. John's sister, Alice, married Edmund FitzAlan, 9th Earl of Arundel. Edmund had been a ward of John's grandfather. The two young men were very close in age and were political allies and friends. John de Warenne and Joan of Bar were married on 25 May in a lavish ceremony.

In the wider world, Edward I died in the summer of 1307 and was succeeded by his son, Edward II. John was not immune to the turbulence and distrust of Edward's reign and changed sides several times in the arguments between the king and his barons. Initially, John de Warenne was a supporter of King Edward; witnessing the charter which made Edward's favourite, Piers Gaveston, earl of Cornwall on 6 August 1307.[13] On 2 December 1308, John de Warenne was one of three earls who took to the field at a magnificent tournament at Wallingford, hosted by Gaveston. The other earls were Hereford and John's own brother-in-law, the earl of Arundel. Gaveston swelled his ranks with young knights as they faced the three knights and their men. Although the new earl of Cornwall was bested by the earls, he took the spoils and was declared the winner 'for it is a recognised rule of this game, that he who loses most, and is frequently unhorsed, is adjudged the more valiant and the stronger.'[14] John de Warenne was so angry at the injustice of the outcome that he showed Gaveston no favour thereafter.

In January 1308, John de Warenne accompanied the king to France to claim his bride, Isabella, daughter of Philip IV of France. He was present on 25 January when 23-year-old Edward met his 12-year-old bride at the doorway of the cathedral of Boulogne, and the couple exchanged marriage vows. Eight days of celebrations and tournaments followed the ceremony. Sometime during the celebrations at Boulogne, the earl of Lincoln and Anthony Bek, Bishop of Durham, gathered together a group of nobles, which included John de Warenne as earl of Surrey, to discuss how they could help guide the king through the reforms needed to alleviate the financial burden on the kingdom and solve the Scottish problem.[15] The Boulogne Agreement was a document to which Warenne, Bek, and the earls of Lincoln, Pembroke and Hereford all put their seals. It is seen as the first formal step in the mounting opposition to Gaveston.[16] Robert Clifford, Payn Talbot, Henry de Grey, John Botetourt and John de Berwick, also attached their seals to the document. Anthony Bek, as bishop of Durham, asked to excommunicate anyone, who put their seal to the reform document, if they failed in their duty to help the king.[17]

The parliament of April 1308, attended by John de Warenne and his brother-in-law the earl of Arundel, demanded that Gaveston be sent into exile. By June, the tide had turned against Edward II and Gaveston in particular. In order to get Gaveston out of the firing line, Edward created him Lieutenant of Ireland, giving him regal powers far above any held by predecessors; and the favourite departed for Dublin on 25 June. Edward spent the next few months working to smooth the path for Gaveston's return; he held a tournament for the earls, barons and knights of England at Kennington in the early autumn.

However, the fact that the earls failed to take part suggests they were not ready to see things the king's way. From the writs of summons issued by the king, we can assume that John de Warenne attended the parliament held at Westminster on 20 October 1308, where the earls recounted their complaints and pressed for the release of Scotland's leading prelates, Robert Wishart, Bishop of Glasgow, and William Lamberton, Bishop of St Andrews, held in captivity since 1306. Edward II was eager to appease the church in order to smooth the path for Gaveston's return from his Irish exile. The king also agreed to reforms in return for a vote of taxation, though this was not immediately granted.[18]

By February 1309, Edward was in a stronger position and may have proposed Gaveston's return to a meeting of his earls, including John de Warenne, at Westminster on 28 February. However, the earls were still not totally behind the king and met at Dunstable in late March, under the pretext of a tournament, to discuss the situation. The gathering was probably led by Thomas, Earl of Lancaster, the king's first cousin. Thomas was the most powerful nobleman in England and, significantly, the most vocal of Piers Gaveston's opponents. It was about this time that John de Warenne became a retainer of Thomas of Lancaster. John agreed to serve Lancaster with eighty men-at-arms and another earl, presumably his brother-in-law, Arundel, though this is not certain.[19]

The barons set a reform agenda, containing eleven articles, which they intended to present to the king at the parliament in April 1308. The earls complained that the king was abusing his rights of purveyance, just as Edward I had, taking goods at greatly reduced prices and, in consequence, burdening the populace. It was also argued that the jurisdictions of the steward and marshal of the royal household had been unjustly extended and that the king's use of the privy seal to offer royal protection was delaying the course of the legal process under common law. Four new complaints included in the eleven articles demanded better control of the issue of pardons to criminals, the abolition of new customs, an end to the depreciation of the coinage and the provision of receivers to deal with unheard petitions in parliament.[20]

Edward stalled by declaring that he would give his response in the next parliament. All the while, he was working behind the scenes to ease Gaveston's return from Ireland and lift the sentence of excommunication which had been imposed on Piers Gaveston by Robert Winchelsea, Archbishop of Canterbury. On 14 June 1309, keen to prevent his earls from plotting their opposition to Gaveston's return, Edward issued an order preventing the earls of Lancaster, Warenne and Hereford, among others, from engaging in tournaments; this was clearly a response to the plotting that had occurred at the Dunstable tournament in March the previous year.[21] Gaveston returned from his Irish exile on 27 July and John de Warenne again allied with the king. Henry de Lacy, Earl of Lincoln and Lancaster's father-in-law, was instrumental in persuading John to accept Gaveston's return. One chronicle goes so far as to claim that John became Gaveston's man:

> the earl of Lincoln, who the year before had been foremost of the barons in bringing about Piers' exile, now became a friendly go-between and mediator. At his repeated and anxious requests the earl Warenne who, ever since the conclusion of the Wallingford tournament, had never shown Piers any welcome, became his inseparable friend and faithful helper. See how often and abruptly great men change their sides.[22]

Piers Gaveston forged few new friendships in this time, and the king became more circumspect as to where he extended his patronage; although the perception that Gaveston was the one who directed where that patronage went, was still widespread throughout the court. The despised earl created nicknames for his detractors: Lancaster was 'the churl', Lincoln was 'burst belly' and the earl of Warwick was 'the black dog of Arden'.[23] Warwick's response to his nickname was probably indicative of the sentiment of all those opposed to Gaveston: 'if he call me a dog, be sure that I will bite him so soon as I shall perceive my opportunity.'[24] John was with Edward and Gaveston at York in October, for a secret parliament summoned by the king, but which the other earls refused to attend, on account of Gaveston's presence. The earls were in such fear of Gaveston, apparently, that they insisted on attending the parliament of February 1310 in arms, claiming that Gaveston 'was lurking in the king's chamber.'[25] For the duration of the parliament, John, alongside the earls of Gloucester and Richmond, was appointed to help keep the peace in London.[26] The three earls were instructed to provide safe conduct to those attending parliament, to arrest anyone who broke the king's commands and to settle any quarrels that broke out during the parliamentary session. Gaveston was sent away for his own safety.

The purpose of the parliament was to decide what action should be taken against Robert the Bruce and Scotland. The topic was never raised as Thomas of Lancaster dominated proceedings with a long list of grievances against the king, including that he was guided by evil counsel; that he could only maintain his household through extortion, and was consequently in breach of Magna Carta; that he was losing Scotland; that taxes previously granted in order to fight Scotland, were being wasted.[27] Lancaster also complained that the war in Scotland was not being pursued. The earl called on the king to address the concerns of the barons. Edward initially refused but eventually acceded to the demands and on 16 March issued letters patent authorising the election of twenty-one Ordainers, with the authority to introduce reforms to the government of the kingdom and to the royal household, with a proviso that the reforms were not prejudicial to his sovereignty. The term of office of the appointed Ordainers was to run for one year from 29 September 1310. The composition of the Ordainers was a balance of reformers and those sympathetic to the king. John de Warenne was one of only three earls not elected; the others being the earl of Oxford, who was a political nonentity, and, unsurprisingly, Piers Gaveston.

Meanwhile, Robert the Bruce was gaining ground in Scotland and, in March, held his first parliament. Edward needed to act; he ordered the army to assemble at Berwick-on-Tweed for 8 September. With limited finances, the army was small, only 4,700 knights, infantry and archers.[28] Of England's earls, only John de Warenne and Gilbert de Clare, 8th Earl of Gloucester answered Edward's summons. The rest, refusing to serve alongside Piers Gaveston, sent the minimum number of men they were required by law to supply in time of war. With no major successes in Scotland that autumn, the king set up his winter quarters at Berwick, Gaveston at Roxburgh, Gloucester at Norham and John de Warenne was at Wark; all on the Scottish borders.

The campaign began again in January and in February John and the earl of Gloucester were traversing Selkirk Forest, seeking out those willing to swear their allegiance to the king of England. When the earl of Lincoln, left in England to act as *custos regni* (guardian of the kingdom) died on 5 February, the king sent Gloucester south to act as his replacement. John de Warenne remained in Scotland throughout the spring and summer of 1311, with a force of knights and men-at-arms.[29] Edward had rewarded John for his continuing support with a number of gifts, including life grants of two Northamptonshire manors and, in June 1310:

> the castle and honour of High Peak, [was granted] for life, together with the entire Forest of High Peak, and the approvement of its wastes, with its knights' fees, advowsons, wardships, and other appurtenances, to hold as fully as William Peverel, sometime Lord thereof, had held the same; but subject to a yearly payment to the Exchequer of £437 6s 8d.[30]

The annual payment was to be paid in two equal instalments of 293 marks at Michaelmas (September) and Easter. In 1310 the majority of this rent was remitted and in 1311 the payment was remitted for life by the king.

Thomas of Lancaster had married the only surviving child of Henry de Lacy, Earl of Lincoln. With the earl's death Thomas now inherited two further earldoms, through his wife, Alice de Lacy; added to his existing earldoms of Lancaster, Leicester and Derby, this now gave Lancaster a total of five earldoms and a virtually unassailable power base.

Lancaster rode north to perform homage to Edward for his two new earldoms, but refused to meet the king in Scotland. Edward was therefore forced to cross the border into England to accept Lancaster's homage for the Lacy earldoms of Lincoln and Salisbury. By June, Edward was running out of money and forced to abandon his military activities in Scotland, returning south. In August 1311 parliament was called and King Edward was presented with the Ordinances.

Containing forty-one clauses, the Ordinances were aimed at curbing the power and authority of the king and included; that parliament was to meet once a year, the king was not to go to war, nor leave the country, without prior approval, the king could not appoint his own administration and all 'evil councillors' were to be removed and replaced by suitable alternatives.[31] The far-reaching clauses effectively made the king subject to the community of the realm or, rather, the nobility. In one final blow, clause twenty called Gaveston 'evil', saying he had ill advised the king, detached him from his natural and loyal lieges and his people, had robbed the kingdom and the crown of land ... assumed royal dignity, taking offices for himself and his supporters displacing men of honour...; he had taken the king to war in Scotland without the consent of all the nobles thereby endangering him....[32]

In short, Piers Gaveston had to go; he was not just to leave England, but he was to leave Edward's domains altogether.

Edward tried everything to keep Gaveston with him, refusing to accept all the demands outright, until he was advised that he did not have the money or men to fight back. He then offered to accept forty of the clauses, so long as they dropped the clause regarding Gaveston. The nobles were adamant, however, and Edward was forced to accept all forty-one Ordinances. Piers Gaveston sailed into his third exile on 4 November 1311. He was back before Christmas, however, reuniting with the king in Yorkshire, just as his wife, Margaret de Clare, gave birth to a daughter named Joan. On 16 December, a defiant Edward revoked the Ordinances, declaring them prejudicial to the Crown and saying he had been forced to accept them under duress. The king spent the opening months improving the defences of York and Scarborough, in preparation to resist whatever the Ordainers threw against them

Gaveston's return, not authorised by parliament, galvanised the opposition against him. More determined than ever to remove the royal favourite, Lancaster and his allies swore an oath that they would not rest until the Ordinances were reinstated in full and Gaveston was removed from the king. By May the king, queen and Gaveston had moved from Yorkshire to Newcastle, where they were almost captured by a force led by Lancaster. The queen had then travelled south by road to York while the king and Gaveston sailed from Tynemouth to Scarborough. Once back on dry land, the king met the queen at York, leaving Gaveston behind the sturdy walls of Scarborough Castle.

John de Warenne was persuaded, by Archbishop Winchelsea, to join in the pursuit of Gaveston. John, his cousins Aymer de Valence, earl of Pembroke and Henry de Percy were tasked with bringing Gaveston in; they commenced the siege of Scarborough Castle, with Gaveston inside, on 10 May. To avoid a protracted siege, the king himself proposed the terms of surrender. Warenne, Pembroke and Percy were to promise on oath to protect Gaveston while he was taken into their custody and escorted to meet with the king and Lancaster. If Edward was unwilling to continue the negotiations over Gaveston's future, then he was to be allowed to return to Scarborough and his guarantee of safe conduct would come to an end.

During Gaveston's absence from the castle, Scarborough was not to be regarrisoned nor restocked with supplies. In return, Warenne, Pembroke and Percy agreed to the forfeiture of their lands if Gaveston came to any harm while in their custody; Gaveston agreed not to counsel the king to alter the terms of the agreement.[33]

With the conditions agreed, Gaveston opened the gates of Scarborough Castle and surrendered on 19 May. Warenne, Pembroke and Percy, with Gaveston in their custody, reached St Mary's Abbey at York on 26 May. After a heated meeting during which the king promised to satisfy the demands of the earls at the next parliament, Gaveston was placed in the sole custody of the earl of Pembroke to be taken south. As Pembroke was escorting Gaveston to his castle at Wallingford, the party were intercepted by the earl of Warwick, who took Gaveston to Warwick Castle and imprisoned him. Eight days later, Gaveston was put on trial before the earls of Lancaster, Hereford and Arundel, accused of treason and sentenced to death. Two days after that he was led out to Blacklow Hill, two miles north of Warwick, where he was run through with a sword and then beheaded, his body left where it fell.[34]

Gaveston's murder enraged Edward. John de Warenne and his cousin, Aymer de Valence, earl of Pembroke sought out the king in July and begged his forgiveness. Although they had not been involved in Gaveston's murder, they had been unable to prevent it. Edward readily granted his forgiveness. In August, John de Warenne was appointed keeper of the peace in Sussex. In the following year, the king issued orders in January and September, specifically forbidding John from participating in tournaments; the tournament in September involved Lancaster, Arundel and three other earls.

In 1314 John de Warenne refused to join the king's campaign against Scotland, which would culminate in English defeat at the Battle of Bannockburn. John and his brother-in-law the earl of Arundel claimed that they had not been summoned in the correct way, and that the campaign had not been sanctioned by parliament. As the king had secured taxation for the expedition, this last argument was lame, to say the least. The truth was far more personal; tensions between the king and John were fraught due to John's attempts to seek an annulment of his marriage to Edward's niece, Joan, but more on that later.

Despite his failure to take part in the Bannockburn campaign, John de Warenne steadfastly supported King Edward throughout the political crises of the ensuing years. In 1317, he was among a small number of noblemen summoned by Edward to a colloquium at Clarendon; although we do not know what was discussed, it is possible that the continuing problems in Scotland were raised, and the possibility of an attack on Lancaster. Shortly afterwards, John de Warenne abducted Alice de Lacy, Lancaster's wife:

> In this year, on Monday preceding the Ascension of our Lord, the Countess of Lancaster, the lawful wife of the noble man, Lord Thomas, Earl of Lancaster, was seized at Cranford, in Dorset, by a certain knight of the house and family of John, Earl Warenne, with many English retainers called together for the detestable deed, as it is said, with the royal assent. And she was conducted, with not a little pomp, to the said Earl Warenne, to his castle of Reigate. And while the lady was so conducted, behold during the journeying among the woods and fences, between Haulton and Farnaham, the leaders saw at a distance flags and banners, for the priests were going with the people, making processions in the usual manner about the fields (Rogation days). The conductors, therefore, of the countess, struck with sudden fear and terror, thinking that the Earl of Lancaster, or some people sent by him to obtain the said lady, and vindicate themselves against so great an injury, fled with all celerity, leaving the countess almost alone. But when the truth of the affair was discovered, they returned with threats and bluster. With them was a certain man of miserable stature, lame and hunchbacked, called Richard de S. Martin, exhibiting and declaring constantly his evil intentions towards the lady, so miserably led away. He, puffed up by great encouragement, demanded her as his wife, firmly declaring that he had known her carnally before she married the Earl of Lancaster. Also he stated that she publicly acknowledged it, and admitted it to be true … Therefore the said Richard, exalting himself above himself, dared to claim in the King's Court the earldom of Lincoln and Salisbury, in the name of his wife – *jure uxoris* – but in vain.[35]

Alice was kidnapped in 1317 from her manor in Canford, Dorset, by John de Warenne's man, Sir Richard de St Martin, supposedly with the king's knowledge. Several reasons for the abduction have been put forward; one is, of course, that Alice and St Martin were having an affair while another is that the affair was between Alice and John de Warenne, Earl of Surrey, himself. Given the king's involvement, it may have been an attempt to antagonise the earl of Lancaster; something John would have been happy to do, given Lancaster's recent obstruction of John's divorce attempts. Alice was held at Reigate Castle, Surrey. Her abduction set off a private war between the two magnates, although Lancaster seems to have made little effort to actually rescue his wife and there is no record of how and when she was eventually released.

In the escalating feud, and unable to strike against the king directly, for fear of being charged with treason, Lancaster attacked John de Warenne's Yorkshire estates, which were close to his own castle at Pontefract, in October and November, sending forces to seize the Warenne castles at Sandal and Conisbrough. Lancaster's men found the gates of Conisbrough closed to them. The castle was defended by only six men, including the town miller and three brothers, Thomas, Henry and William Greathead, who were men-at-arms.[36] The siege lasted less than two hours and the defenders appear to have relinquished the castle after apparently putting up a token resistance; the three brothers were fined for drawing blood.[37] The chapel in the castle's inner bailey may have been damaged in the brief altercation, as the following year, Lancaster sent orders to his castellan at Conisbrough, John de Lassell, to *repailler la couverture de la chapele de Conynggesburgh*. ('repair the roof of Conisbrough's chapel').[38]

Edward tried to stop the fighting, sending messages to Lancaster:

> The King has lately heard that the earl has, with a multitude of armed men, besieged and captured divers castles of John de Warenne, Earl of Surrey, in the county of York, and that he still detains them; and has done many other things in those parts to the disturbance of the King's peace. Wherefore, the King orders him to desist entirely from these proceedings; and if he have done any such things to cause them to be amended in due form: and forbids him to go armed, or to assemble men-at-arms: or to do anything else to this disturbance of the King's peace. The King is prepared to do justice in his Court concerning the things that the earl has to prosecute against the Earl of Surrey and certain others.[39]

Lancaster was relentless, even ejecting John's mistress, Maud de Nerford, from her property. In June 1318, Lancaster attacked John's Welsh lands at Yale and Bromfield; again, these lands were in close proximity to Lancaster's own property. John de Warenne wrote to the king, complaining of Lancaster's actions on his Welsh estates:

> The Earl Warenne to the King: The Earl offers reverence and all honour to his most noble and most honourable Prince and most dear lord and wishes the king to understand that news comes to him out of Wales, in haste, day and night, from his people of Bromfeud and Ial [Bromfield and Yale], that the Earl of Lancaster has ... [in] his letters

to them bid them attourn themselves to him, and that he wishes by all means to have such lands and he has menaced the Earl's said people to the effect that they shall attourn themselves to him in one manner or another, which fact the king may more fully see by the transcript of the letter which they have sent to the petitioner, which he sends to the king enclosed within this. It is great marvel that the Earl of Lancaster wishes to move in such manner upon the petitioner more than he has done, since good peace and agreement were lately made between the king and him, the Earl of Lancaster, on all points. In this agreement the petitioner intends that the business between the Earl and himself shall be brought to good end by means of the king's good lordship, and by his aid and counsel. Wherefore petitioner prays and demands of his highness that on these things he will, if it is his pleasure, take counsel and good advice and will send his letters to the Earl, ordering him to surcease from making or commending such threats against the peace, to the dishonour of the king and the grave loss of the petitioner; and that the king, if it please him, may send other letters to his justices of Wales and Chester and to the sheriffs of those parts, that if any people come in force to enter the petitioner's lands, that they, the officers mentioned, may take action, that the king's people in those same parts may be ready with all their power, well and openly to withstand, and to defend the petitioner's lands. May the king command these things to be done in the greatest haste possible... .[40]

In response to John's desperate letter, it was agreed in council that the earl should be ordered to proceed to Bromfield to protect his territories and ascertain what could be done. It was also decided that the earl of Lancaster should be ordered not to do anything which disturbed the peace. Given that Lancaster gained control of both Bromfield and Yale, it is obvious that he chose to ignore the king's commands. Shortly afterwards, the king and Lancaster temporarily resolved their differences, meeting somewhere between Loughborough and Leicester on 7 August, when they exchanged the kiss of peace in front of the court. Within two days of the meeting, 'Roger Damory and the rest, except Hugh le Despenser the Elder and the Earl Warenne, humbly presented themselves before the earl, [and] were received into his grace.'[41] John de Warenne, it seems, was abandoned by the king in the interests of peace, leaving Lancaster to pursue his personal feud with the earl. John was hunted down and imprisoned in Lancaster's castle at Pontefract. Beaten into submission, he was forced to come to terms with Lancaster, coming to an agreement in 1319 which meant giving up most of his Yorkshire estates and some of his lands in Wales and Norfolk, in exchange for land in Devon, Wiltshire and Somerset. Edward, perhaps feeling guilty on how John had been hung out to dry for the sake of national harmony, altered the grant so that Lancaster could only hold the lands during John's lifetime; they would revert to John's heirs on his death. John also acknowledged that he owed Lancaster a debt of £50,000, an astronomical sum, though none of it was ever collected.[42]

John de Warenne attended a muster in 1319 and went on campaign in Scotland, even if little was achieved. In 1321 the barons again united against the king's new favourites, this time it was Hugh le Despenser, father and son. In July, with Lancaster at Pontefract, the Marcher lords, with a force of 5,000 men, marched on London. Hugh le Despenser the Younger had escaped to France, but the rebels were demanding the permanent exile of the Despensers. When they entered the city on 29 July, Edward refused to meet them. Pembroke, John de Warenne and the remaining earls loyal to the king met with the Marcher barons, who attempted to persuade Pembroke to their side. The earls took an oath with the Marcher lords, agreeing to defend their grievances against the Despensers. Pembroke made it clear to the king that he was at risk of losing his throne, and that he himself would withdraw his homage if the king continue in his refusal to change his mind. The barons drew Warenne, Arundel and Pembroke into the attempts to have the Despensers banished at a parliament in August. The Despensers, father and son, were to be permanently exiled by 29 August, their children disinherited. On 20 August, Edward and his council caused a 'Pardon to be issued to John de Warenne, Earl of Surrey, pursuant to the agreement lately made in Parliament, last midsummer, of any actions by reason of anything done against Hugh le Despenser the son, and Hugh le Despenser the father, between March 1 and August 19, last.'[43]

John de Warenne was back at the king's side when, in September 1321, Edward began plotting not only for the return of Hugh le Despenser, but also for his revenge against Thomas of Lancaster. Intensely unpopular with Lancaster, John knew he had a stronger position with the king. Edward ordered that the Despenser lands taken by the rebels be returned to the Crown. Bartholomew Badlesmere refused to relinquish Tonbridge Castle and placed his castles at Chilham and Leeds, Kent, on a defensive footing. In early October the king and queen went on pilgrimage to Canterbury, with Queen Isabella seeking shelter at Leeds Castle *en route*. Not only was she refused entry by Badlesmere's wife, but her party were fired on, with six of the queen's men killed by arrows. Furious, the king ordered that the castle be placed under siege on 16 October. John de Warenne was with the king when the castle fell on 31 October, having suffered heavy bombardment. The following day, twelve of the garrison were hanged and the castle commander was taken to Winchelsea and publicly executed. Badlesmere's wife and children were sent to imprisonment in the Tower of London.

John de Warenne marched with the king into the Welsh Marches in 1322, where Roger Mortimer of Wigmore and his uncle, Roger Mortimer of Chirk, had risen in rebellion. John, Pembroke, Arundel and Richmond, were deputed to talk with Mortimer at Shrewsbury on 17 January, which resulted in the Mortimers being taken into custody. On 13 February, John and Roger le Ewer were ordered to escort the Mortimers to imprisonment in the Tower.[44] Lancaster, meanwhile, was in the process of besieging Tickhill Castle, once in Warenne hands but now belonging to Edward: this gave the king the excuse to confront Lancaster directly. On 1 March at Tutbury, the king issued a writ of aid to his brother, Edmund of Kent, and to John de Warenne, to besiege the earl of Lancaster's castle at Pontefract. John had also been charged with the task of arresting Lancaster.[45] At Pontefract, Lancaster's retainer, Robert Holland, abandoned the rebellious earl, leaving Lancaster unable to mount an effective defence.

The earl abandoned his castle, fleeing north. The rebels were confronted at Boroughbridge by Andrew Harclay, commanding a force of 4,000 men on 17 March and defeated. Lancaster was taken first to York Castle and then to Pontefract, where he was brought before the king on 21 March. The next day, he was tried, in his own castle, before Edward, the Despensers and the earls of Kent, Pembroke, Richmond, Warenne, Atholl and Angus. The indictment was long and included, among other charges, bringing armed men to parliament, the siege of Tickhill, and treasonable correspondence with the Scots; an indenture had been found on the body of Lancaster's ally, the earl of Hereford, after Boroughbridge, in which Robert the Bruce promised to aid the two earls.[46] Lancaster was found guilty and sentenced to be hanged, drawn and quartered; the sentence was commuted to beheading in deference to his royal blood. The vanquished earl was taken from the castle to a nearby hill, mounted on a mule, where he was given into the custody of an executioner. Forced to kneel facing Scotland, as a reminder of his treason, he was beheaded, rather clumsily; it took two or three blows from the sword to complete the sentence.

Afterwards, John de Warenne sat in the parliament at York which repealed the 1311 Ordinances. Lancaster's lands were forfeit to the Crown and on 27 May the king surrendered the castle of Holt (Castrum Leonis) and the lands of Bromfield and Yale to be returned to John.[47] The castles of Conisbrough and Sandal, for the moment, remained in the king's hands. Earl Warenne spent the summers of 1322 and 1323 campaigning in Scotland. In February 1325 he was appointed, alongside the earl of Atholl, to lead the expedition to Aquitaine, following the French invasion of the duchy in the summer of 1324. John de Warenne covenanted with the king

> to go with 100 men-at-arms at his wages, in the said fleet, to stay for half a year from the day of landing. On March 2 the King at the tower of London granted to Earl Warenne that this covenant should not be to his prejudice, or drawn into a precedent. He further granted that the earl should not be bound to stay there beyond the half year, unless he – the King – should come to the duchy in person.

The army embarked in May, but the infantry had not been paid and had become restless; they had taken to rioting and looting around Portsmouth before their departure, and this had continued when they reached Bordeaux. John was in Aquitaine for a year, returning in 1326 to be appointed captain of the army in the north in May and again in July. In the same year, Edward restored some of the lands taken from him by Lancaster. And yet, despite his support for Edward over the years, John was forced to surrender one of his manors to Hugh le Despenser the Elder in order to save himself from destruction. The situation became desperate for Edward and the Despensers, however, when Queen Isabella, having separated from Edward and remained in France since the end of 1324, landed in England in September 1326. John de Warenne adroitly shifted his allegiance to Isabella; his brother-in-law Edmund, Earl of Arundel was not so perceptive of the situation, remained loyal to Edward and was executed in the aftermath of Isabella's coup. In December, Arundel's lands in the Isle of Axholme, Lincolnshire, were given into John's custody.[48] In January 1327, John de Warenne was a member of the delegation tasked with appealing to Edward, now imprisoned, to abdicate in favour of his son, 14-year-old Edward.[49]

A month later, on 1 February 1327, Earl Warenne attended the coronation of the new king, Edward III. He was appointed to the regency council established to counsel and advise the young king until he reached his majority. John de Warenne was now 41 years of age and had weathered the storms of Edward II's reign, if not without some loss of land, at least with his life. He remained an important figure at court, though he never became a political figure as powerful or outspoken as his great enemy, Lancaster, he was always at the centre of the action. His constancy towards Edward

II stood him in good stead at the start of the new reign. In 1327, he was named as overseer of the keepers of the peace in Oxfordshire; he was also appointed to a number of judicial commissions between 1327 and 1332. In the spring of 1327 he was on military service in Scotland and in November of the same year, was appointed to negotiate with the Scots. John was again serving in Scotland in 1330, and in 1333 was at the siege of Berwick and the Battle of Halidon Hill, when Archibald Douglas led a large force to relieve the siege and was defeated by the English archers. The Scots lost about 10,000 men, including Douglas, while English losses were no more than 100. Berwick also fell to the English.[50] The English victory effectively placed John de Warenne's cousin, Edward Balliol, on the Scottish throne, in place of Robert the Bruce's son, David II. The Scottish throne was to swap between Edward and David several times over subsequent years; Edward Balliol eventually surrendered his claim to the Scottish throne to Edward III in 1356 and died at Wheatley, Doncaster, in 1367.

Later in 1333, after rumours of unrest in the Welsh Marches, John de Warenne was sent to restore order. In the following year, he supplied the king with a sizeable force for the 1334 Scottish campaign, though did not participate himself; he was at Newcastle, however, on 12 June 1334, when his cousin, Edward Balliol, ceded to King Edward much of Scotland south of the Firth of Forth.[51] Also in 1334, John finally recovered the castles of Sandal and Conisbrough.[52] John was again campaigning in Scotland, with Balliol, in 1335 and in 1336, he was appointed one of the defenders of the realm in England, while the king was away fighting in Scotland.

Earl Warenne was generously compensated for his service to the Crown. In 1329, he had been granted 2,000 marks from the Exchequer, out of the first profit of wardships, marriages and escheats. On 5 May 1330 he was granted Swanscombe in Kent for life, 'in consideration of his agreement to stay always with the king.'[53] In 1331 the king granted various manors which had previously belonged to the king's uncle Edmund, Earl of Kent, recently executed for treason. Later in the year, he was granted Doncaster for life and in 1333 he was pardoned all debts owed by himself and his ancestors and granted 200 marks as a gift from the king. The earl was also rewarded by his cousin, the Scottish king, and granted the earldom of Strathern, forfeited by Malise, who had been on the losing side at Halidon Hill. The award did not come without its problems, however, and on 2 March 1334 Edward III wrote to the Earl of Buchan from York to explain them:

Edward, King of Scotland, granted the county of Strathern, then in the royal hand, by the forfeiture of Malisius [Malise], the late earl, a rebel, to John de Warenne, Earl of Surrey, in recompense for his expenses in the war of Scotland; but now, as is said, Malisius [Malise] is striving for the recovery of this county and the revocation of his forfeiture, to be made by persons well disposed to him and suspect of the other side; and it is not right that what has been ordained by the council of the chief men should be so lightly revoked by suspect men. Wherefore the king has written to the King of Scotland requesting him to order the said affair to be treated by the peers and other chief men of Scotland, not suspect, and the King trusts that the earl will use his best endeavours to prevent a sudden process being made before him, or before him who supplies his place.'[54]

The dispute rumbled on for several years, though Warenne seems to have eventually prevailed and from then on styled himself earl of Surrey and Sussex and earl of Strathern.

Throughout the 1330s John de Warenne served the king, sitting on various commissions in Surrey and overseeing the army in the southern counties. In 1339 he was acting sheriff of Surrey and Sussex. He was generously rewarded for his faithful service. In 1338 and 1340, when the king went overseas, John was named alongside the king's eldest son, also Edward, as keeper of the realm. And in 1345 he was one of the councillors appointed to advise the king's second son, Lionel of Antwerp, when he was made regent. In 1342 John de Warenne had been summoned to serve on Edward III's campaign in Brittany, though he failed to participate, perhaps indicating that, at the age of 56, he was getting a little old to be involved in the actual fighting; this is confirmed in the same year, by the fact he was excused from participating in a tournament at Dunstable due to age and infirmity.[55] John de Warenne appears to have suffered from declining health from that point on and in July 1346 the earl was excused from attending parliament, and performing other services, due to his frailty.

Just like his ancestors, John de Warenne fulfilled his duties to the religious institutions patronised by the Warenne family, as well as giving lands to various monastic houses and endowing a chantry. He entered the confraternity of Durham Priory and is known to have possessed a bible in French. He continued to look to the interests of the priory of Lewes, where generations of his family were buried, and defended the priory to King Edward when he took it into his own hands, as an alien foundation, during his war with France. On April 16, 1340, at Westminster, he issued a letter in respect of the priory:

Whereas the king lately took into his hands, among other alien priories, the priory of Lewes, and committed the same to the custody of the prior of a certain farm; and afterwards, on the petition of his kinsman, John de Warenne, Earl of Surrey, setting forth that the priory was founded by his ancestors, that from the time of foundation the priors paid no tribute without the realm, save 100s yearly to the abbot of Cluny of the alms of the founders; and that when Edward II took into his hands the alien priories, restitution to the prior of the lands of that priory, for causes shown before the Council; the King granted to the prior respite of all sums due for the custody until a date now past. And whereas the earl has now made petition for removal of the King's hands from the priory, with the knights' fees, advowsons and other appurtenances: the King, desiring to safeguard the liberties of the church and for the causes aforesaid, as well as at the renewed request of the earl, has restored to the prior the priory, with its appurtenances, and released all arrears of the said farm, as well as the contingent due to him, as well of the tenth for three years, lately granted by the clergy, as of the wool lately granted by the Parliament of Westminster. By the King.[56]

John de Warenne died at Conisbrough Castle between 28 and 30 June 1347; he was 61 years old and the last of his line. Although he had played an active part in the upheavals of the reign of Edward II, and steadfastly supported Edward III since his accession, the earl is best remembered not for his political and military contributions, but for the complications of his personal life and the fact that he was the last earl of Warenne and Surrey as a consequence.

Chapter Seventeen

A Disastrous Marriage and
the End of a Dynasty

Despite the political upheavals that had dominated his adult life, John de Warenne is perhaps best known for his domestic situation, which would lead to the extinction of the Warenne line, after almost 300 years of loyal service to the Crown.

John's early coming of age in 1306 appears to have been a part of a larger scheme by King Edward; during the parliamentary session, John was brought before the king and offered Edward's granddaughter in marriage; the young earl readily agreed to the marriage, even though his wife-to-be was only 10 years old. The proposed bride was Joan, or Jeanne, of Bar, the young daughter of Edward's eldest daughter, Eleanor and Henry, Count of Bar. Eleanor of England had been born in June 1264 and was married to Alfonso III, King of Aragon, by proxy on 15 August 1290 at Westminster Abbey. Unfortunately, the groom died before the marriage could be consummated so Eleanor married again at Bristol on 20 September 1293, to Henry III, Count of Bar. Henry and Eleanor had at least two children. Their son, Edward, and daughter, Joan, were born in successive years, in 1294 and 1295, although there seems to be some confusion about who was the eldest.[1] A possible third child, Eleanor, is said to have married Llywelyn ap Owen of Deheubarth; but her existence seems to be in question.

As is usual with medieval women, even royal ones, we know very little of Joan's childhood beyond the international events of the time. Joan's father had joined King Edward's war against France, in 1297, leaving Eleanor in charge of Bar, with her two young children in tow. An army led by the Constable of France invaded Bar whilst Henry was fighting in Champagne: 'By force and by fire [the French forces] devastated the land of the Count of Bar.'[2] Eleanor had hastily recalled Henry and the count returned to drive off the French army, then headed north to help fight off the French invasion of Flanders, leaving Eleanor in charge of Bar once again. Count Henry was captured by a French raiding party at Comines, near Lille, leaving Eleanor with the informal regency of Bar, looking after her children, and raising the ransom that would inevitably be demanded for Henry's release. Henry was still languishing in his French prison when Eleanor died on 29 August, of some unrecorded injury or illness.[3] The body of the English princess was brought back to England and buried in Westminster Abbey, London. Joan and her brother remained in Bar, in the charge of Henry's councillors, who were still negotiating for their count's release.

Count Henry was eventually released in June 1301, following the intercession of an English embassy to France; under the terms of his release, the count was required to pay a hefty ransom, to relinquish parts of his province and to place the county under French feudal lordship.[4] The count returned to his two children, now 6 and 7 years old, and to his disgruntled councillors, angry at the terms to which the count had had to agree to obtain his freedom. The count's reunion with his children was brief, however, as he departed on crusade the same year, never to return.

Henry, Count of Bar, died in 1302, possibly as a result of injuries received in battle while fighting in Sicily. The count was succeeded by his only son, Edward, who was then only six or seven years old. The children were placed in the guardianship of a council of elders.[5] During little Count Edward's minority, the County of Bar was to be run by his grandfather, Edward I, with the child's uncle John of Puisaye and the bishops of Liège and Metz acting as governors. It is likely the children came to live at the English court, or at least spent some time there. By 1310, aged 14 or 15, Edward's majority was declared and he married Mary, daughter of Robert II, Duke of Burgundy, in that year.

On 15 March, 1306 King Edward had offered Joan's hand in marriage to 19-year-old John de Warenne, 7th Earl of Warenne and Surrey, who had recently been granted his grandfather's lands, despite the fact he had not yet reached the required age of 21. Once the betrothal was finalised, Joan was sent for and arrived in England, landing at Dover on 13 April: 'For the expenses for the daughter of the Count of Bare coming from Dover to the king xx*li* [£20].'[6]

In the spring of 1306, Joan was in Winchester with three of her maternal aunts, Elizabeth, Mary and Margaret, and her cousin, Eleanor de Clare, who was also soon to be married; to Hugh le Despenser the Younger. Joan and her cousin Eleanor were in Winchester when their aunt, Margaret, gave birth to a daughter, Eleanor, on 6 May, before they travelled to the court at Westminster for their weddings.[7] John de Warenne was not without his own royal connections. His aunt Isabella had been married to Scots king John Balliol, and their son, John's cousin, was Edward Balliol; Edward would be, briefly, king of Scots in the 1330s, but would eventually lose out to his rival,

David II, son of Robert the Bruce. John de Warenne was the grandson of Edward I's good friend, also named John de Warenne, 6th earl of Warenne and Surrey and former Warden of Scotland.

John de Warenne and Joan of Bar were married on 25 May, 'before an altar spread with glittering cloths-of-gold.'[8] Barely 10 years old, Joan was escorted to the palace at Westminster with great pomp and she and John were married in the presence of the ageing king. The Wardrobe Accounts bear witness to the extravagance of the ceremony and celebrations: '1306. May 25. In money lent and dispersed in the presence of the King, at the nuptials celebrated in the King's chapel at Westminster, between John, Earl de Warenne, and the Lady Joanna, daughter of the Count de Barr, xls [40s].'[9] Other money was paid out 'for diverse minstrels', and 'for letting fly the king's gyrfalcon.'[10] More extravagance was expended to Thomas the coachbuilder, 'advanced on making a chariot for the Earl de Warenne, June 28, lxs [60s],' and to Walter de Bardeney, 'advanced on harness being made for the said Earl, on the same day, cs [100s].'[11] While Walter de Bedewynde was commissioned 'for a new carriage for the use of the Countess de Warenne, by order of the Treasurer.'[12]

Given Joan's tender age, it is highly unlikely that the marriage was consummated immediately; indeed, John would have expected to wait at least three years before his bride was physically mature enough to become his wife in every way. This is borne out by the fact that Joan spent the second night of her married life in the royal household, with her aunts and cousins rather than with her new husband.[13] Following the wedding John and his child-bride lived on the Warenne's Yorkshire estates, sharing their time between their castles at Conisbrough and Sandal. In January 1308, Joan may have accompanied John de Warenne and her cousin, the king, to France for the marriage of Edward II to Isabella, daughter of Philip IV of France. John was present on 25 January when 23-year-old Edward met his 12-year-old bride at the doorway of the cathedral of Boulogne, and the couple exchanged marriage vows. Although she is not named, it is possible that John's young wife, of a similar age to Isabella, was also present; many of the royal family attended the ceremony, including King Edward's sister Margaret and his step-mother, Queen Marguerite.[14] Joan was certainly present at Westminster Abbey on 25 February, with her royal aunts, Margaret, Mary and Elizabeth, and her cousins, to witness the joint coronation of Edward and Isabella.[15]

The uncertainty of Edward's reign cannot have helped the marriage of John and Joan, but neither, it seems, did John. The couple was soon estranged; Joan was half John's age when they married, and not yet old enough to consummate the marriage. This must have put an incredible strain on the relationship. There had been indications of problems as early as 1309, when the king had given John permission to name whoever he wished as his heir, as long as any children he may have by Joan were not disinherited. By 1311 John was living openly with his mistress, Maud de Nerford. The adultery had come to the attention of the church and on 22 November, when John failed to appear before Archbishop Winchelsea over the matter, the archbishop wrote to the bishop of Salisbury with instructions to excommunicate the earl.[16] The sentence of excommunication was not published, however, and the matter was still unresolved in 1313 when, on 21 May, the king asked for the sentence to be postponed until he returned to England, as John de Warenne had been charged with keeping the peace in the realm during the king's absence; a job he could not perform as an excommunicate.[17]

In the spring of that year, Edward sent his yeoman, William Aune, to bring Joan to the king. She was taken from Warenne's castle at Conisbrough and lodged in the Tower of London, at the king's expense. Apparently the locals were unaware of the reasons behind Joan's removal from Conisbrough and the king issued a mandate on 7 May 1314, at Windsor, stating the facts, with the addition: 'Now, as the King understands that divers persons, on account of this, endeavour to disturb the said William de Aune, he grants him indemnity.'[18] The sentence of excommunication was finally carried out by the bishop of Chichester when Edward's attempts to prevent it failed.

Maud, or Matilda, de Nerford was probably the daughter of Sir William Nerford and his wife, Petronilla, daughter of Sir John Vaux. The family were neighbours of the Warenne's Norfolk estates. According to a letter of the archbishop of Canterbury, at the time that the scandal broke, Maud was the wife of one Simon de Driby; there was a king's yeoman of that name at the time. Driby appears to have been granted a divorce by Winchelsea, on account of Maud's adultery, and was given permission to remarry. He died in 1322, leaving no surviving issue; the post mortem inquisition refers to a wife, named Margery, suggesting he did take another wife.[19]

On 26 May 1314, the archbishop of Canterbury and eleven of his bishops formally informed John de Warenne that the 'Countess Joanna, that good lady, his consort, who languished in expectation of his good pleasure and favour, was nevertheless his true and lawful wife and that he could never be legally separated from her while she lived, for any reason that they had heard.'[20] The church council registered disapproval of John and Maud's relationship; as did a council of nobles, which included the king's cousin and most powerful nobleman in the land, Thomas, Earl of Lancaster. It was agreed among them that the earl, who was 'unlike a true Christian, or son of Holy Mother Church, had no ways blushed to lead such an odious and execrable life, disregarding all good counsel, and *had broken into parks &c.*[21] On 10 June, Earl Warenne wrote to the archbishop of Canterbury, Walter Reynolds, from Sandal Castle:

> To the honourable Father in God and our dear friend Walter by the grace of God Archbishop of Canterbury, Primate of All England, his son John de Warenne, Earl of Surrey, greeting and due honour. Sire, in respect to that which we have learnt by your order, be pleased to understand that we are and shall be ready to do everything that Holy Church can demand by law and in reason; and upon divers other points we will answer you in time, in such a manner that no man shall be able to blame us rightfully or with reason: and, Sire, if you wish us to do anything that we can, be pleased confidently to command us, and we will do it to the utmost of our power. Adieu, Sire, and may God preserve you. Given at our castle of Sandale the 10th day of June.[22]

A long legal battle followed. Eager to marry Maud and legitimise his two sons by her, John attempted to dissolve his marriage to Joan on a number of occasions. His first attempt went before William Greenfield, Archbishop of York, who clearly laid out John's claims in a letter to the official of the Archdeacon of York, on 8 September:

> John, Earl of Surrey, has told us that when under age, and in charge of Lord Edward, formerly King of England, of illustrious memory, at the compulsion of certain nobles and magnates of the kingdom, he was compelled to marry the noble woman, the lady Johanna, daughter of the late Earl de Barro, though within the grade of consanguinity, *i.e.* in the third and in the fourth: he was entirely ignorant of this impediment when he contracted marriage, under force and fear; but when it was done, so soon as he was able and he dare, he opposed it: and afterwards having knowledge of the said impediment, for the relief of his conscience he made frequent and urgent applications to us to provide a remedy ... We therefore command you to cite peremptorily the said lady Johanna, in the castles of Conyngesburgh and Sandale, where she is known to have her domicile, if she can there be found, or her proctor, if she has left one there; if she has not, then on some Lord's Day or solemn day, whilst mass is sung in the parish churches of the said towns, and in other important and solemn places of the said archdeaconry, or where it appears to you expedient, by the publication of this citation, and by the proclaiming of it to her relations, acquaintances, and friends, she

may not have any excuse of ignorance: that she appear herself, or by a proctor sufficiently instructed, before us, or our commissaries in this matter, in our Cathedral of York, on Wednesday next after the coming Feast of S. Michael, with the said earl, to have the matter gone into and settled: announcing publicly that they will proceed whether she be there or not. Report to us by your letters patent that this has been done. Cawood, 6 id. Sep. and the 9th of our pontificate.[23]

The archbishop appointed William de Rothwell, rector of Normanton and a professor of civil law, and Henry de Wylton, rector of Corney, to hear the case and summoned Joan to appear before them. Although we do not have Joan's response, the archbishop later wrote to the bishop of Durham instructing him to deliver the citation to Clifton, a manor of the abbot of Byland, where Maud de Nerford was meant to be staying, though he was prevented from seeing her in person by retainers of Earl Warenne.[24] The archbishop's instruction was to

cite or cause to be cited, in manner and ways as you best are able, Matilda de Neyrford, that she appear personally before us, or our commissaries, in our church of Blessed Peter of York [York Minster], on Wednesday next after the Feast of S. Luke, Evang. (Oct.), upon certain articles affecting the health of her soul, concerning which she before others has better known the truth, to be laid canonically before her from our office: that the truth may be stated and sworn to: and that justice may be done. Concerning the manner and the day when the citation was made, and in what manner this our mandate shall have been executed, ye shall certify us distinctly by your letters patent. York, Oct 2, 1314.[25]

The bishop of Durham replied the next day, pointing out to the archbishop, that he was not bound to act as the matter was not brought within his diocese but continued:

Nevertheless, at the urgency of your demand and the request of certain princes and magnates, who in the presence of our lord the King urgently requested us upon this matter to go to the manor of the Abbot of Byland, in Clyfton by York, where the said Matilda was entertained both then and previously, as was commonly said, and remained. Going personally on the same day, we sought from Sir Alex de Montfort, knight, and Robert de Reppes, servant, attendants of the noble man, the Earl Warenne, then present in the hall of the same manor, that we might have access to the said Matilda. And when after waiting a long time we were not able to gain her presence, showing your citation to the said knight and servant, Mr Andrew Tange and Mr Rich. de Ganio, notaries public, and many others standing by, we cited Matilda herself according to the force and effect of the same as much as we were able, to the said day and place, in the presence of the same; offering a copy of the citation to the said knight and servant, which in the presence of many they expressly refused to attend to... .[26]

The seriousness by which the church took the petition for divorce is clearly indicated by the fact the bishop of Durham himself went to present the citation to Maud de Nerford. The petition to divorce was not granted, John's claims of compulsion and consanguinity being easily rebuffed. John was 19 when he married Joan, and though not legally of age to inherit his lands, he was well beyond the age of consent for marriage, which was 14 for boys. On the matter of consanguinity, church law specifically forbade men to bring divorce proceedings based on consanguinity; also, a dispensation to within the fourth degree of consanguinity had been obtained at the time of the marriage from Pope Clement V.[27] Clearly unhappy with John's treatment of his cousin, Edward II also ordered the confiscation of High Peak, the castle, town and manor the king had given to John in gratitude for the earl's services in the Scottish campaign of 1310.[28]

In 1315, John confirmed his and his ancestors' donations to the priory at Thetford for his own soul and the souls of his ancestors and heirs, and also for the soul of Maud de Nerford and their children. No mention was made of his wife, Joan.[29] Maud added her own voice to the proceedings. On 8 March, before the archdeacon of Norwich, Thomas Gerdeston, she petitioned for the divorce of John, Earl of Surrey, and Joan of Bar on the grounds of pre-contract. Robert, chaplain of Yaxley, was deputed to deliver notice to Joan that she was required to appear before the archdeacon. The citation was served to Joan when she was in attendance on the queen, a breach of protocol which saw the archdeacon and one of his officials brought before parliament and committed to the Tower of London.[30] The case was still ongoing the following year, when in February 1316, the king granted protection to Maud, her advocates and witnesses in the case of the pre-contract; he granted the same protection to John de Warenne and his men, advocates, proctors and witnesses in the divorce between him and Joan of Bar.

In the meantime, Joan had left England for France, accompanying the king and queen. Being of a similar age to the young queen, Joan and Isabella of France were close friends. For practical reasons, in view of his absence from England, Edward II ordered the bishop of Norwich to defer excommunicating John de Warenne, so that he could act as keeper of the peace during Edward's absence.[31] On 23 February 1316, perhaps confident of success, John agreed to pay Joan a sum of £200 annually while the suit was ongoing, and to provide Joan with lands, in Graham and Greetwell, worth 740 marks once the marriage was dissolved.[32] On 24 February John was granted licence to bring his suit for divorce to the ecclesiastical court, before Masters Gilbert de Middleton and William de Bray, canons of St Paul's in London, and the prior of the Trinity, London. On the same day, Maud de Nerford was granted permission to withdraw her petition before the archdeacon of Norwich and 'commence proceedings anew against the said earl and Dame Joan, touching such pre-contract, before the above-named judges and others.'[33]

Although we do not have the specific outcome of the case, future events serve to demonstrate that no annulment was granted. As to Maud de Nerford's specific claim of pre-contract, it has been noted that 'there is no mention of a previous contract in the Lambeth Registers.'[34] At about the same time, in June 1316, John rearranged his estates, surrendering them to the king to have them re-granted with specifications that some of the lands could pass to his sons by Maud de Nerford on his death, first to the eldest, John, and then to his brother Thomas:

10 Edw. II., pt 1, m. 28. 1316. Aug 4. Lincoln. Regrant to John de Warenne, Earl of Surrey, for his life, with *remainder to John de Warenne son of Matilda de Neirford*, and the heirs male of his body; and failing such issue, *to Thomas de Warenne, son of the said Maud de Neirford*, and the heirs male of his body; with final remainder, failing such issue, to the heirs of the body of the said earl; of the undermentioned castles, manors, and lands, and towns, which the earl had surrendered to the King, and his heirs (the manor of Kenyngton, co. Surrey, excepted, which the King has retained to himself and his heirs), viz. the castle and town of Reygate, and the manors of Dorkyng, Kenyngton and Bechesworth, county of Surrey. The castle and town of Lewes, and the manors of Cokefield, Cleyton, Dychenyng, Machyng, Peckham, Brightelmeston, Rottyngdene, Houndene, Northern, Radmeld, Kymere, Middleton, Alynton, Worth, and Picoumbe, and the towns of Ilford, Pydinghowe, and Seford, county of Sussex. And all other manors, hamlets, and lands in those counties. And the castle of Dynasbran, and Holt Castle (Castro-Leonis), and the lands of Brumfeld, Yale, and Wryghtlesham, in Wales. With knights' fees, advowsons of churches, abbies, priories and other religious houses, homages and other services of free tenants,

villeins, with their villeinages and issue, warrens, chaces, parks, woods, stews, ponds, marshes, fisheries, feedings, pastures, hundreds, liberties and royalties.[35]

This regranting of lands effectively mounted to a recognition by Edward II that John's marriage to the king's cousin was irretrievable. Edward, therefore, was allowing John to redistribute his lands in favour of his natural, illegitimate sons by Maud de Nerford, John and Thomas, perhaps in anticipation of a divorce being granted and John and Maud finally being married. Any future children John and Maud had, once married, would be covered by the stipulation of the reversion to the heirs male of the body of the earl.

Joan was desperately upset by events and in August the king allowed her to leave England and return to her brother's court in Bar, paying her expenses of £166.[36] As the hopes of an annulment faded, John enlisted the help of Aymer de Valence, Earl of Pembroke, who was on an embassy to Avignon for Edward II, in presenting a petition to the pope, seeking a papal annulment. Pembroke was abducted by Jean de Lamouilly while crossing the county of Bar, on his return journey. Lamouilly was a vassal of the count of Bar and it seems likely – though there is no proof – that Pembroke's capture and imprisonment was ordered by Joan's brother, Edward, Count of Bar, unhappy with John's mistreatment of his sister. Joan was among a number of high-profile nobles, including the kings of England and France, who successfully petitioned the Count of Bar to release Pembroke. The earl was freed in early June 1317, after the payment of a ransom of £10,400; £2,500 of which was provided by King Edward II himself.[37]

In the same year, smarting from the public opposition to his divorce by Thomas, Earl of Lancaster, John de Warenne had kidnapped the earl's wife and kicked off a private war which saw John lose his Yorkshire lands, including Conisbrough and Sandal castles, and his Welsh lands at Yale and Bromfield. Moreover, with the failure of this last attempt to obtain a divorce appealing direct to the papacy, the relationship between John and Maud appears to have broken down. The strain on the couple, over so many years, must have been immense. In 1320 John de Warenne appealed to the king to suspend a commission that was sitting against some of the earl's retainers. The plaintiff was Maud's son John and the earl claimed it had been brought to do him harm after he had 'ouste de sa companye Maud de Nerforde.'[38] In the suit it was alleged that four of the earl's men had broken the close of John de Nerford, presumably Maud's brother, at Wesenham, Norfolk, and carried away his goods.

While the troubles in England intensified, John's marriage troubles seem to have somewhat abated. In 1325, John de Warenne was appointed captain of an English expedition to Aquitaine and was away from home for the next year. Joan of Bar had been in France at the same time, having accompanied Edward II's queen, Isabella, on her diplomatic mission to her brother the king of France, to discuss peace. Joan remained with the queen when she refused to return to England because of her husband's infatuation with Hugh le Despenser the Younger. Indeed, Joan was one of the people to whom Edward II wrote in the hope of persuading the queen to return home.[39]

In 1326, John arranged for a redistribution of his estates. His sons by Maud de Nerford, John and Thomas, had joined the Order of St John of Jerusalem – the Knights Hospitallers. John, therefore, once again, surrendered his estates to the king, so that he may regrant them, with Conisbrough and Sandal finally returned following the earl of Lancaster's downfall:

1326. May 17. Marlborough. 19 Edw. II. Memb. 8. Grant for life to John Warenna, Earl of Surrey, in consideration of his quitclaim to the King of his castles, manors, &c., in the county of York: Of his manors and towns of Staunford and Grantham, co. Lincoln, to wit: – Whatever he had in demesnes, lordships and services in these counties: and by way of acting graciously towards him, of the castles, towns and manors of Conyngesburgh and Sandale, and the manors of Wakefield, Souresby, Braithewell, Fisshelak, Dewesbury and Halifax, and all other lands late of the earl in the county of York, before they came to the King's hands: *except the manors of Thorne and Haitfield:* to hold for life, with knights' fees, reversions, advowsons, homages and other services of free tenants, villeins, with their villeinages, chattels and issues, fairs, markets, warrens, chaces, parks, woods, stews, stanks, marshes, fisheries, feedings, pastures, wapentakes, liberties, and other appurtenances, in the same manner as before they came to the King's hand, with reversion to the King.[40]

The earl did similar with his lands in Sussex and Surrey, though these were not to revert to the king on his death:

the King wishing to act graciously towards the earl, and in consideration of the earl's quitclaim and warranty to the King, of all his castles, towns, manors and lands in the counties of York and Lincolnshire, was granted to the earl, and Joan his wife, all the said premises in the counties of Surrey and Sussex, and in Wales, to hold to them and the heirs males of his body, with knights' fees, advowsons, regalities, &c., to hold by the same services as were due before the said quitclaims; with remainder to Edmund, Earl of Arundel and Alesia [Alice] his wife, and Richard son of the same earl, and Isabel his wife, and the heirs of their bodies, with remainder to the right heirs of the said Earl of Surrey; notwithstanding that the reversion of the premises might belong to the King as aforesaid.

But the King is not willing, nor does he intend that by the said grant he or his heirs shall be bound to warranty of the premises, or be held to make any value of them, or any part thereof to my person.[41]

Following Edward II's downfall, the new king, Edward III, in gratitude for her service to his mother, Queen Isabella, settled lands on Joan for life, and granted her some of the goods forfeited by Edmund FitzAlan, Earl of Arundel; John's brother-in-law, Arundel had been executed in the aftermath of Isabella and Mortimer's coup in 1326.[42] John's erstwhile brother-in-law had been caught up in the turbulence of Edward II's downfall and executed. Joan had been with the queen and Prince Edward when they landed in England on 27 September.[43]

John de Warenne proved a faithful servant to Edward III, acting as keeper of the realm, jointly with young prince Edward, during the king's absences in 1338 and 1340. In February 1327, John went abroad on the king's business, apparently taking Joan with him.[44] Joan was in John's company and treated as his wife in the years between 1331 and 1337. In 1331 John gave grants to the priory at Lewes, a Warenne foundation, witnessed by Joan and her chaplain, 'for his own soul and that of the countess, Joan of Bar, his consort.'[45] This was in stark contrast to the 1315 confirmation to Thetford Priory, in which Joan was omitted, in favour of Maud de Nerford. In 1335, John de Warenne resettled more of his estates, that of Castle Acre in Norfolk in favour of Richard FitzAlan, Earl of Arundel, son of his sister, Alice.[46] However, Joan went abroad with her entire household in 1337 shortly after her brother's death; Edward, Count of Bar, had died in a shipwreck on his way to the Crusades and it is possible that Joan had returned to Bar to act as regent or guardian for her nephew, Henry IV, Count of Bar.

By the 1340s Maud de Nerford was dead and her sons had both joined the Knights Hospitallers, but John had a new lover in Isabella Holland, daughter of Sir Robert Holland, a leading retainer of Thomas of Lancaster. And it seems he was again contemplating divorce, when the queens of England and France asked the papacy to intercede on Joan's behalf:

1344. Clement VI. 5 kal. March. V., by Avignon. To the Bishop of Winchester. Mandate at the request of the Queen of France and

Philippa, Queen of England, to warn and compel John, Earl of Warenne, to receive and treat with marital affection his wife, Joan de Barre, whom he married by virtue of a dispensation (indult) granted by Clement V. (they being related in the fourth degree), and having lived together for thirty-two years; notwithstanding his pretence that the said dispensation was surreptitious, inasmuch as they are related respectively in the third and fourth degrees from a common stock.[47]

Curiously, at the same time as the pope was writing about Earl Warenne's marriage difficulties, the earl himself petitioned the pope 'for plenary indulgence at the hour of death for himself, his wife, his son William de Warenne, knight, and Margaret, his wife; and for Robert de Lynne, his chaplain, monk, of Castle Acre.' The petition was granted.[48]

By this time, Joan was abroad again, possibly acting as regent for her great-nephew, Edward II, Count of Bar. Amid fears that John de Warenne would try to take Joan's lands, Edward III acted to guarantee them in her absence, taking her lands into his own custody.[49] By 1345, in one final attempt to dissolve his marriage John was claiming that he had had an affair before marrying Joan, with his wife's maternal aunt Mary of Woodstock, when he was 19 and Mary 27 years of age. This was indeed a drastic claim, as Mary had been a nun since she was about 7 years old, and it was probably born out of desperation; John was becoming increasingly infirm and still had no heir to succeed him. It was a last-ditch attempt to marry Isabella and have legitimate children. It failed, though the earl's confession was presented to Pope Clement VI who,

on 15 May, 1345, issued a mandate to the Bishop of S. Asaph to absolve John de Warenne, Earl of Surrey and Stratherne, Lord of Bromfeld and Yale, from excommunication, which he has incurred by inter-marrying with Joan, daughter of Henry, Count de Barre, whose mother's sister, Mary, he had carnally known. A penance is to be enjoined; and as to the marriage, canonical action is to be taken.[50]

No further action seems to have been taken with regards to the marriage. John's penance, however, appears to have been the generous donation of the manor of Hatfield to Roche Abbey:

1345. November 22. Westminster. Whereas the King's kinsman, John de Warenna, Earl of Surrey, holds the manor of Haytfield for life of the grant of Edward II, with successive remainders to Maud de Neyrford for life, to John de Warenna her son, in tail male, to Thomas his brother, in tail male, and to the heirs of the body of the said earl, and reversion to the said King and his heirs, as in the letters patent is more fully contained; the earl has now made petition that – Whereas the said Maud is dead, and John son of Maud and Thomas have taken the religious habit in the Order of the Brethren of the Hospital of S. John of Jerusalem in England, at Clerkenwell, he may have licence to grant for his life to the abbot and convent of Roche, the advowson of the church of Haytfield, held in chief, which church is extended, of the value of 70 marks yearly; and the King has assented to his petition. Also, as a further grace, the King has granted that the abbot and convent shall retain in frankalmoign the said advowson, which should revert to him on the death of the earl; and may appropriate the church whenever they deem it expedient to do so, to find thirteen monks as chaplains to celebrate divine service daily for ever in the abbey for the King, Queen Philippa, and their children, and for the earl; also for the soul of William, the King's son, who lately died in the said manor; also the souls of the progenitors of the King and of the earl.[51]

It is touching that John's penance also served as a means for the king and queen to remember their infant son, William, who had been born and died at the manor of Hatfield, Doncaster, in 1337. It seems that John de Warenne was again anticipating a successful divorce petition in 1346, when he resettled his lands, once again; this time in the hope of producing an heir by Isabella Holland:

and if God should please to send him an heir, by Isabel de Houland then his wife (?), should the same heir be male or female, it should be joined in marriage to some one of blood royal, whom the King should think fittest; so that the whole inheritance of this earl, with the name and arms of Warenne, should be preserved by the blood royal in the blood of him, the said earl. And in case he should depart this life without such issue, begotten on the body of her the said Isabel, that then all castles, manors, lands and tenements, in Surrey, Sussex, and Wales, should after such his decease remain to the King, to be bestowed upon some one of his own sons, on whom he should think fit; on condition that in the person of such son and his heirs, the name, honour, and arms of Warenne should be for ever maintained and kept.[52]

It appears that Joan of Bar returned to England at this time, perhaps to add her own voice to the complaints of Richard, Earl of Arundel, who saw himself disinherited with this last ploy of Earl Warenne. It is not hard to imagine how desperate the earl felt, seeing his health failing rapidly and knowing that the family name would die with him. He was making every effort to ensure that the Warenne name continued, but it was not enough. The king, in need of Arundel's support, acquiesced to his arguments and revoked the arrangement.

John de Warenne, seventh and last Earl of Warenne, Surrey, Sussex and Strathern died at Conisbrough Castle between 28 and 30 June 1347, possibly even on his sixty-first birthday (30 June). He asked to be buried at St Pancras Priory, Lewes, in an arch near the high altar. His will, dated 24 June 1347, left various gifts to his illegitimate children and to Isabella, to whom he left plate, jewels, cows, horses and other beasts, 'and after that my debts and devises be made, I give to my said "compaigne" all the residue of all my goods and chattels, and whatsoever things they find.'[53] To Joan, his wife of forty years, he left nothing.

Warenne left several illegitimate children, including at least three boys and three girls, who survived him. These six are named in his will, though their mothers remain unidentified, a number of them are likely to have been the children of John and Maud de Nerford. To Sir William de Warenne, he left 100 marks and a hure (a hat worn over a helmet) of silver gilt and all the earl's jousting armour. Sir William's wife was bequeathed a jewelled clasp. Of two other sons, Edward de Warenne received £20 and William de Warenne, prior of Castle Acre, received a bible in French. Three daughters are named in the will; Joanne de Basing was bequeathed a silver cup, Katherine 10 marks and Isabel, a nun at Sempringham Priory, was left £20.[54]

Joan de Bar was abroad when her husband died, receiving John's Lincolnshire lands as her dower. She lived for another fourteen years, retaining the title of countess of Surrey until her death. Richard FitzAlan, John's heir, took possession of the Warenne estates on John's death, but did not use the title earl of Surrey until after Joan died. The king granted Joan an annual income of £200 as her dower; in 1350 she was granted a safe-conduct by Edward III, to go on pilgrimage on the Continent, visiting several shrines. In the 1350s Joan is said to have often visited the French king, Jean II, who was a prisoner of Edward III in London; she was also a regular visitor at court, dining with the queen, on occasion, and with other members of the royal family. After a long and turbulent life, and at around 66 years of age, Joan died in London on 31 August 1361. She was not buried in England, however; her body was conducted to France by her valet, where she was buried at Sainte-Maxe Collegiate Church in Bar-le-Duc in October 1361.[55]

Joan's marriage must have been one of the most miserable of the medieval era. At a time of great upheaval, Joan did not even have the comfort and security offered by a faithful husband. Nevertheless, she found a life and a purpose in her home county of Bar, and in supporting her nephew during his minority. She also had the trust and friendship of Queen Isabella and later, Edward III and Philippa of Hainault, who recognised and valued her loyalty and support. As for John, he had remained steadfastly loyal to Edward II almost to the very end. Only when he saw the king's cause was hopeless did he turn from him and look to the future and the next reign. And one thing that can be said of John de Warenne is that he always had one eye on the future. Acutely aware that the earldom would die with him, John de Warenne did all he could to extricate himself from an unhappy, childless marriage. Unfortunately for him, and for the earldom of Surrey, nothing could be done.

Epilogue

The Warenne Family

A lthough the last Earl Warenne died in the reign of Edward III, his honours titles and lands passed, through his sister, to the earls of Arundel and eventually to the Howard dukes of Norfolk, whose arms, to this day, include the Warenne checks, of blue and gold, in one quarter. Warenne descendants are still living, scattered throughout the world. The most prominent of these is Queen Elizabeth II of the United Kingdom, who can trace her descent through the Scottish royal line back to Ada de Warenne, daughter of the second earl.

It is, perhaps, a shame that such a great family and earldom came to a rather sad end; foiled by the failure of a marriage. That they died out in the fourteenth century has meant the family are little known today, their story always a small part of the greater history of England, rather than a story in itself. This should not overshadow the great achievements made in the 300 years of their existence. The earldom created in the aftermath of the Norman Conquest, the Warenne earls earned a reputation of loyalty to the Crown almost unequalled among their peers; the handful of slips in loyalty far overshadowed by their steadfast support in even the most dire circumstances. When King Stephen was in the hands of his great rival, Empress Matilda, it was the Earl Warenne who provided the solution to Stephen's predicament, by capturing Matilda's indispensable military commander, Robert of Gloucester. And when all others deserted Edward II, it was the last earl, John, who's backing the king came to rely on.

The few instances of disloyalty are understandable, and each, to some extent, justifiable. The indecision of the second earl, of whether to support Robert Curthose or Henry I was experienced by many Anglo-Norman barons. Having lands in England and Normandy was never going to be easy with two different rulers. The oath of fealty that accompanied landholding was a further complication; no one can serve two masters. The simple solution was for one brother to have it all; the problem for the barons was in deciding which brother, Robert or Henry. That Henry married the woman on whom William, 2nd Earl Warenne had set his heart was probably a deciding factor in the earl throwing his support behind Robert. However, Henry's magnanimity and political acumen gave Earl Warenne a way back to his side, when it became apparent where the better prospects lay. That William's brother, Rainald, remained with Robert longer suggests the Warennes were not without their own measure of political common sense, hedging their bets by supporting both sides.

As for William, the fifth earl who abandoned King John and pledged his allegiance to the dauphin, Prince Louis, it is hard to blame a man for looking to the interests of his own lands and family, or for abandoning an obviously sinking ship, as John's reign had become. Further, the king's own brother, William Longespée, had turned his back on John, so it is hardly surprising that practically the entire baronage followed suit. By the time of his death, John could count on the support of few senior nobles.

The Warenne family were not without their ambitions, as demonstrated by the second earl's search for a royal bride. They married into the senior families of the Anglo-Norman realm, their daughters marrying even higher; with daughters of the second and third earls marrying the sons of kings. When Malcolm IV sat on the Scottish throne, he surpassed even the ambitions of his grandfather, the second earl. To have a royal bride was one thing, to have your own blood sitting on a throne was quite another. Such royal links served the family well. As did the marriages of Countess Isabel, the first to a king's son and the second to a king's brother: William of Blois and Hamelin Plantagenet, respectively. These marriages saw the family moving in exalted circles and extending their own patronage and influence in consequence.

The Warennes were a family of builders, leaving behind them the great castles at Conisbrough, Sandal, Lewes and Castle Acre in England and Bellencombre and Mortemer in Normandy. Conisbrough itself stands as an example of the grandeur of the family, with its innovative keep, built to the most modern castle designs of the time, still standing sentinel over the Don Valley over 850 years after it was built. Similarly, Lewes Castle still dominates the Sussex skyline, looking down upon the remains of Lewes Priory, where so many of the Warennes found their final resting place. The priory at Castle Acre also attests to the family's penchant for building; its beautiful façade stands as a reminder of the elegance and splendour of medieval monastic buildings. While St Pancras Priory at Lewes, the first Cluniac foundation in England, remains the final resting place of five Warenne earls and many of their countesses and wider relations. The first earl and his wife, Gundrada, now rest in the church just along from the priory, in a chapel dedicated to Gundrada. Only two earls, William of Blois, who is buried in France, and the third Earl, who died in the Holy Land, are buried elsewhere. Eight generations of Warennes, and more, therefore, lie united in the grounds of Lewes priory.

Beyond the desire to extend the earldom, in influence and land, each earl had his own distinct character and agenda. They epitomise the medieval barony of the post-Conquest years, serving the Crown not just as administrators but, invariably, as soldiers. Counted among the richest landholders in England and Normandy, each earl provided, not only his own service, but also the service of his knights and men-at arms, in wars in France, Scotland, Wales and England. Admittedly, they were not always successful in war, their abilities as generals could be brought into question, especially with the third earl and his flight from the field at Lincoln in 1141. However, one must allow that death in the heat of battle, and in the heat of the Holy Land, vindicates him.

From the first to the last, each earl added his own unique personality and experiences to the Warenne story: whether it was the loyal first earl fighting alongside the Conqueror at Hastings; the second earl, caught in the fight for supremacy between Robert Curthose and Henry I; the third earl, the crusader; the heiress Countess Isabel and her two semi-royal husbands; the fifth earl, caught up in the First Barons War and the birth of Magna Carta; the brash and brutal sixth earl, who spent a lifetime fighting; or the seventh and last earl, who lived through the tumultuous reign of Edward II but failed to provide the heir to continue the family line.

Having been at the centre of English politics for generations, I had expected the overriding theme of this book to be the power and influence exerted by the various Warenne earls, not just on their own lands, but also on the nation at large. What came as a complete surprise was the sense of family that accompanied every generation of Warennes. Sibling rivalry does not appear to have risen its ugly head, unlike in the Norman and Plantagenet royal families that they served. There were no black sheep in this family, except, maybe Richard of Chilham, the illegitimate son of King John and one of the daughters of Countess Isabel and Earl Hamelin. That family loyalty extended to the stepfamilies and half-siblings of the Beaumonts, Salisburys and Bigods; as demonstrated by the second earl's presence at Henry I's deathbed, his son and stepsons beside him. Time and again, the larger interests and connections demonstrate the deep bonds forged by these family ties. The Warenne earls, especially William, 3rd Earl Warenne, and John, the sixth earl, allowed themselves to be guided by their older and more experienced half-brothers.

The Warenne earls, to a man, looked after their relations, both near and far. In the story of a family, it is quite fitting that the Warenne earls appear to have always put family first.

Appendix

The Mysterious Knight

Whilst researching the Warennes, my cousin, who lives in Conisbrough, passed on a story of the discovery of a knight to me. Whether he has any relation to the Warenne family is open to conjecture, of course, although it is entirely possible. I had no way of incorporating the discovery into the main part of the book but did not want to leave it out entirely.

The story starts in 1955, with a road widening programme that was carried out along Church Street in Conisbrough. Conisbrough was a tightly packed village, with the road so narrow in places that cars had to mount the pavement if they met oncoming traffic; this was particularly the case outside the parish church of St Peter's. As a consequence, Conisbrough Urban District Council started work to widen the road where Church Street meets Church Yard. As this was church property, and graves would have to have been disturbed, strict rules were put in place to allow the work to proceed. The then vicar, Rev. G.F. Braithwaite, allowed that the boundary wall be removed and rebuilt a metre further into the churchyard. It was stipulated, however, that no photographs or archaeological examinations could be undertaken during the works. They expected to find twelve lots of human remains in the area to be excavated, and these were to be removed and reinterred speedily, and with reverence and solemn prayer, elsewhere within the churchyard.

When the boundary wall was removed, the stones were carefully stacked for reuse. One stone proved particularly interesting. It was a large stone which had been situated close to the base of the wall, was about a metre long and half a metre wide, with the image of a sword blade carved into the façade; the part of the stone which would have shown the hilt was missing. The stone carving of the sword was merely the first exciting discovery in the excavations. Work then began on excavating the area of the church yard that was to make way for the widened road. It was expected that twelve graves, dating from Victorian times, would need to be removed. The remains were removed only a short distance and reinterred in an area which is now the memorial garden. As work continued, however, the number of graves had been sorely underestimated, and several dozen more were uncovered. It was discovered that graves had been stacked, one on top of another, going back through the years.

Among the remains found was a man who had been buried with a small shield. The shield was about 60cm long and 50cm wide, decorated with a lion rampant (where the lion is stood on his two back legs). It was, therefore, assumed that the remains were that of a knight; although the stipulation that there could be no archaeological investigation, nor photographs taken, means that we know nothing beyond this. The knight did not belong to the household of the Warenne earls, who had owned Conisbrough and its castle since the time of the Normans; their coat of arms was a shield of blue and gold checks, adopted by the second earl in the first half of the twelfth century. Although the colour of the lion was black, this is unlikely to have been the original colour; several hundred years in the ground had erased any indication of the original colours of the lion or the background (field) of the shield, thus making it impossible to identify the coat of arms. The remains were reinterred along with the others, according to the conditions imposed for the road widening scheme. The work was then continued, the road widened and a new boundary wall built, with steps into the church yard and a memorial park marking where the disturbed remains had been reburied.

The incident was then forgotten about with the passage of time. Indeed, when I came to look into it, few had heard of the mysterious knight buried in Conisbrough church yard. Internet searches brought up nothing. The story re-emerged in 1990, when Conisbrough Castle installed new floodlights and hosted a grand 'switch on' ceremony for the residents of Conisbrough. An article sent to me by a Conisbrough resident talks of meeting re-enactors at the ceremony, who were dressed as knights of the earl of Norfolk, with a lion rampant on their shields. It was then suggested that Earl Hamelin's daughter Isabel had married Roger Bigod, the first earl of Norfolk, who died in 1221. Unfortunately, this relationship is not supported by history; Earl Roger was, in fact, the second earl of Norfolk and married to Ida de Tosny, former mistress of Henry II. However, Earl Roger's son, Hugh, who died in 1225, was married to Matilda Marshal, the eldest daughter of William Marshal, Earl of Pembroke and regent for Henry III. On Hugh's death, Matilda had married William de Warenne, Earl Hamelin's son and fifth earl of Warenne and Surrey. It is entirely possible that Matilda was accompanied by knights of her first husband when she visited Conisbrough, or was visited there by a Norfolk knight who then perished and was buried in the church yard of St Peter's at Conisbrough. The emblem of the earls of Norfolk, in Matilda's time, however, was a red cross on a yellow background. The red lion rampant, on a field of gold and green, originally the coat of arms of Matilda's father, William Marshal, was not adopted until 1269, when Roger Bigod, 5th Earl of Norfolk and Matilda Marshal's grandson, inherited the title of Marshal of England, which had passed to the family through his grandmother. This also means that it is just as likely, or even more so, that the shield belonged to a Marshal retainer who was visiting Matilda, or in Matilda's employ.

There are several other possibilities for a Warenne connection to the knight in the churchyard. The emblem of the lion rampant was not an uncommon feature among medieval heraldry in England and Scotland. The royal arms of Scotland, for example, are of a red lion rampant on a yellow field. Edward Balliol, king of Scots at various points in the 1330s, was a grandson of John de Warenne, 6th Earl of Warenne and Surrey, through his mother, Isabella de Warenne. Edward did not officially relinquish his claim to the Scottish throne until 1356 and died near Doncaster in around 1367. The mysterious knight may have been one of his household retainers. Another daughter of the sixth earl, Eleanor, married Henry Percy, the son of a cadet branch of the earls of Northumberland. The Percy family arms are a yellow lion rampant on a blue field. Other families associated with the Warennes also used the lion rampant on their shields, not least being the d'Aubigny earls of Arundel, whose arms were a yellow lion rampant on a red field; Isabel, daughter of William, the fifth earl of Warenne and Surrey, married Hugh d'Aubigny, the fifth Earl of Arundel. Hugh's successors, FitzAlan earls of Arundel adopted the d'Aubigny lion as their own emblem; it was to Richard FitzAlan, son of the last earl's sister, Alice de Warenne, that the Warenne earldom descended.

One final possibility is that the knight was a natural son of the last earl. As we have seen, John de Warenne, 7th Earl of Warenne and Surrey, had no legitimate children, but fathered a number of illegitimate children by his mistress, Maud Nerford. Maud was from a knightly family in Norfolk; their coat of arms was a lion rampant. It is known that at least one of their sons, Edward, used the Nerford arms as his own. Further, the arms of John's last mistress, Isabella Holland, who he called 'ma compaigne' in his will, was a white lion rampant on a blue field, surrounded by white *fleur de lys*.[1]

As to the stone mentioned earlier with the carving of a sword blade upon it, it was suggested that it was previously a grave marker for the mysterious knight and was found lying in the church grounds sometime in the early

1800s. There was extensive building going on in Conisbrough between 1800 and 1810 and it is assumed that the stone was used to rebuild the boundary wall of the churchyard. The fact that the two were found in the vicinity of each other is no suggestion of a link. As archaeologist James Wright explained to me, such stones were often used to decorate churches, castles and important buildings, then repurposed elsewhere once those buildings fell into disuse. The stone could have come from anywhere, and was not necessarily a grave marker at all. The stone in question can still be seen at St Peter's church, to the side of the church porch.

Although we have no definitive answers as to the identity of the mysterious knight who rests in the grounds of St Peter's Church, Conisbrough, there are many possibilities that suggest a familial link with the Warennes. As we have no archaeological survey or photographs to aid the investigation, definitive identification is impossible. Indeed, we do not even have any useful dates through which we can narrow down the possibilities. Although the last earl of Warenne and Surrey died in 1347, it seems unlikely that the knight is from a later period and had no relationship whatsoever with the Warenne earls. Conisbrough Castle passed into royal hands after the earl's death and was given to Edward III's fourth surviving son, Edmund of Langley, Duke of York; the arms of Edmund and his sons were derived from the royal arms of England, which are three lions passant quartered with the *fleur de lys* of France.

It seems likely, therefore, that the knight died sometime during the 300 years that the Warenne family held the castle and honour of Conisbrough – though it is impossible at this point to identify what century – and there are several possible explanations for his association with the family, through their many and varied prestigious marriage alliances. There is also a possibility that the knight was a Warenne himself, as the illegitimate son of the seventh and final earl, John de Warenne, and his mistress, Maud de Nerford.

The possibilities may not be endless, but they are numerous; without further information, however, it is impossible to narrow it down.

Notes

Foreword
1. Steven Brindle and Agnieszka Sadraei, *Conisbrough Castle*, English Heritage Guidebook (2015), p. 23.

Chapter 1: The Warenne Origins
1. William Farrer and Charles Travis Clay, editors, *Early Yorkshire Charters, Volume 8: The Honour of Warenne* (Cambridge: Cambridge University Press, 2013) [first published in 1949]; and John Watson, *Memoirs of the Ancient Earls of Warren and Surrey, and Their Descendants to the Present Time*, Volumes I and II (Michigan: Gale research Inc., 1782).
2. L.C. Lloyd, 'The Origin of the Family of Warenne', *The Yorkshire Archaeological Journal*, Vol. XXXI (1934), p. 98
3. C.P. Lewis, 'Warenne, William de, first Earl of Surrey [Earl Warenne] (d. 1088)', *Oxford Dictionary of National Biography* (Oxford: Oxford University Press, 2004); online edition (hereafter *ODNB*).
4. Watson, *Memoirs of the Ancient Earls of Warren and Surrey* (Michigan: Gale Research Inc., 1782), p. 2.
5. Lloyd, 'The Origin of the Family of Warenne', p. 100.
6. *The Gesta Normannorum Ducum of William of Jumièges, Orderic Vitalis and Robert of Torigni*, edited by E.M.C. van Houts, 2 volumes (Oxford: Oxford University Press, 1992–95), pp. 234–235.
7. Ordericus Vitalis, *The Ecclesiastical History of England and Normandy*, edited by H.G. Bohn (London, 1853), Vol. 3, p. 237.
8. Alfred S. Ellis, 'Biographical Notes on the Yorkshire Tenants Named in Domesday Book', *The Yorkshire Archaeological Journal*, Vol. IV (1877), p. 149.
9. Lloyd, 'The Origin of the Family of Warenne', p. 99.
10. Ellis, 'Biographical Notes on the Yorkshire Tenants', p. 149.
11. Lloyd, 'The Origin of the Family of Warenne', p. 98.
12. Ibid.
13. Farrer and Clay, *Early Yorkshire Charters*, p. 2.
14. Ibid.
15. Lewis, 'Warenne, William de, first Earl of Surrey [Earl Warenne]'.
16. *Gesta Normannorum Ducum*, p. 106.
17. Ordericus Vitalis, *The Ecclesiastical History of England and Normandy*, Vol. 4, p. 88.
18. *Gesta Normannorum Ducum*, pp. 102–105.
19. Lloyd, 'The Origin of the Family of Warenne', p. 101.

Chapter 2: William and Gundrada
1. Farrer and Clay, *Early Yorkshire Charters*, p. 3.
2. Lloyd, 'The Origin of the Family of Warenne', p. 107.
3. *The Gesta Guillielmi of William of Poitiers*, edited by R.H.C. Davis and Marjorie Chibnall (Oxford: Oxford, 1998) p. 135; and Ordericus Vitalis, *The Ecclesiastical History of England and Normandy*, pp. 121–122.

4. Ordericus Vitalis, *Histoire de Normandie, seconde partie*, (Du Bois, 1826). Translated from the French by the author, p. 115.
5. Text D of *The Anglo-Saxon Chronicles*, edited and translated by Michael Swanton (London: Phoenix Press, 2000), p. 176.
6. Elisabeth Waugaman, 'The Meaning of "Mora": The Flagship Matilda of Flanders gave William the Conqueror', https://thefreelancehistorywriter.com/2014/09/12/the-meaning-of-mora-the-flagship-matilda-of-flanders-gave-william-the-conqueror-a-guest-post-by-elisabeth-waugaman/, [accessed 2 February 2020].
7. Ordericus Vitalis, *The Ecclesiastical History of England and Normandy*, p. 140.
8. *The Norman Conquest* by Marc Morris (London: Windmill Books, 2013), pp. 175–6.
9. *Gesta Guillielmi of William of Poitiers*, pp. 166–167.
10. Text D of *The Anglo-Saxon Chronicles* edited by Swanton, p. 199.
11. Ibid.
12. Henry of Huntingdon, *The Chronicle of Henry of Huntingdon*, edited and translated by Thomas Forester (London: H.G. Bohn, 1853), pp. 210–211.
13. Ibid.
14. Text E of *The Anglo-Saxon Chronicles*, edited by Swanton, pp. 197–198.
15. Ordericus Vitalis, *Histoire de Normandie, seconde partie*. Translated from the French by the author, p. 142.
16. Farrer and Clay, *Early Yorkshire Charters*, pp. 3–4.
17. Ibid.
18. Lewis, 'Warenne, William de, first Earl of Surrey [Earl Warenne]'.
19. Marc Morris, 'Castle Acre and the Warennes', marcmorris.org.uk [accessed 30 June 2016].
20. Text D of *The Anglo-Saxon Chronicles* edited by Michael Swanton, p. 202.
21. Lois Huneycutt quoted in *Queens Consort: England's Medieval Queens* by Lisa Hilton (London: Phoenix, 2009), pp. 38–9.
22. 'for the health of my mistress Queen Matilda, mother of my wife'. My translation from quote in George Floyd Duckett, *Observations on the Parentage of Gundreda, the Daughter of William Duke of Normandy, and Wife of William de Warenne* (Whitefish: Kessinger Legacy Reprints, 1878), p. 6.
23. 'William de Warenne, whose wife Gundrada was sister of Gerbod, was given Surrey'. My translation from Orderic Vitalis quoted in Duckett, *Observations on the Parentage of Gundreda*, p. 5.
24. Farrer and Clay, *Early Yorkshire Charters*, p. 41.
25. Ibid, p. 40.
26. Ibid, p. 41.
27. W.H. Blaauw quoted in Duckett, *Observations on the Parentage of Gundreda*, p. 6.
28. Ibid.
29. 'William de Warenne and his wife Gundrada, my daughter'. My translation from quote in ibid, p. 7.
30. Farrer and Clay, *Early Yorkshire Charters*, p. 43.
31. Elisabeth M.C. Van Houts and Rosalind C. Love (eds and trans), *The Warenne (Hyde) Chronicle* (Oxford: Clarendon Press, 2013), p. 90.
32. Farrer and Clay, *Early Yorkshire Charters*, p. 45 and Douglas, *William the Conqueror*.
33. C.P. Lewis, 'Warenne, Gundrada de (d.1085)', *ODNB*.
34. Elisabeth Van Houts, 'The Warenne View of the Past', in *Proceedings of the Battle Conference 2003*, edited by John Gillingham (Suffolk: Boydell Press, 2004), pp. 103–122.
35. Lewis, 'Warenne, Gundrada de (d.1085)'.
36. Van Houts, 'The Warenne View of the Past', pp. 103–122.

Chapter 3: William and Gundrada and the Foundation of a Dynasty

1. Lewis, 'Warenne, William de, first Earl of Surrey [Earl Warenne]'.
2. Hunter, quoted in Ellis, 'Biographical Notes on the Yorkshire Tenants', p. 150.
3. Watson, *Memoirs of the Ancient Earls of Warren and Surrey*, p. 24.
4. Ellis, 'Biographical Notes on the Yorkshire Tenants', p. 150.
5. Farrer and Clay, *Early Yorkshire Charters*, p. 44.
6. Lewis, 'Warenne, William de, first Earl of Surrey [Earl Warenne]'.
7. Farrer and Clay, *Early Yorkshire Charters*, pp. 2–4.
8. Elisabeth Van Houts, 'Hereward and Flanders', *Anglo-Saxon England*, 28 (1999): 201–223.
9. Ibid.
10. Van Houts and Love, *The Warenne (Hyde) Chronicle*, p. 27.
11. Ibid.
12. Van Houts, 'Hereward and Flanders', pp. 201–223.
13. *Liber Eliensis* quoted in John C. Appleby and Paul Dalton, *Early Modern England: Crime, Government and Society, c. 1066–c. 1600* (Abingdon: Routledge, 2016), p. 29.
14. Van Houts and Love, *The Warenne (Hyde) Chronicle*, p. 27.
15. Ibid.
16. Jeffrey James, *The Bastard's Sons: Robert, William and Henry of Normandy* (Stroud: Amberley Publishing, 2020), pp. 95–96.
17. Ellis, 'Biographical Notes on the Yorkshire Tenants', p. 150.
18. Ordericus Vitalis, *Histoire de Normandie, seconde partie*. Translated from the French by the author, pp. 253–254.
19. James, *The Bastard's Sons*, pp. 90–92.
20. Sharon Bennett Connolly, *Silk and the Sword: The Women of the Norman Conquest* (Stroud: Amberley, 2018), p. 175.
21. Van Houts and Love, *The Warenne (Hyde) Chronicle*, p. 25.
22. Ibid.
23. W. Page, ed., *A History of the County of Sussex: Volume 2* (London, 1973); *British History Online*, http://www.british-history.ac.uk/vch/sussex/vol2 [accessed 4 September 2020].
24. Lewes Cartulary quoted in W.H. Blaauw, 'On the Early History of Lewes Priory, and its Seals, with extracts from a MS. Chronicle', *Sussex Archaeological Collections*, vol. 2 (1849): 7–37.
25. Blaauw, *On the Early History of Lewes Priory*.
26. Bullarum. Rom. Pontiff. Collection, t.l. Roma, 1739–62 quoted in Blaauw, *On the Early History of Lewes Priory*, p. 9.
27. Edward Impey, *Castle Acre Priory and Castle* (London: English Heritage, 2016), p. 37.
28. *Lanfranci Sentntiæ*, in Spicileg. D'Archery, 1,442 summarised in Blaauw, *On the Early History of Lewes Priory*, pp. 9–10.
29. Blaauw, *On the Early History of Lewes Priory*, pp. 8–12.
30. Van Houts, 'Hereward and Flanders', and Van Houts and Love, *The Warenne (Hyde) Chronicle*, p. 33.
31. James, *The Bastard's Sons*, p. 144.
32. Farrer and Clay, *Early Yorkshire Charters*, pp. 6–7.
33. Ibid.
34. Ibid, pp. 3–4.
35. Van Houts and Love, *The Warenne (Hyde) Chronicle*, p. 33.
36. James, *The Bastard's Sons* p. 111; Farrer and Clay, *Early Yorkshire Charters* p. 4; and Morris, *Castle Acre and the Warennes* http://www.marcmorris.org.uk/2016/06/castle-acre-and-warennes.html [accessed 20 November 2019.

37. Watson, *Memoirs of the Ancient Earls of Warren and Surrey*, p. 61; and Van Houts and Love, *The Warenne (Hyde) Chronicle*, pp. 33–34.
38. Van Houts and Love, *The Warenne (Hyde) Chronicle*, pp. 33–34.
39. Lewis, 'Warenne, Gundrada de (d.1085)'.
40. Van Houts and Love, *The Warenne (Hyde) Chronicle*, p. 91.
41. Ibid.
42. 'brother of Countess de Warenne'. Farrer and Clay, *Early Yorkshire Charters*. p. 5
43. James, *The Bastard's Sons* p. 95; Farrer and Clay, *Early Yorkshire Charters*, pp. 5–6.
44. Lewis, 'Warenne, Gundrada de (d.1085)'.
45. Van Houts and Love, *The Warenne (Hyde) Chronicle*, p. 93.
46. Ibid.

Chapter 4: The Second Earl and the Norman Kings

1. Farrer and Clay, *Early Yorkshire Charters*, pp. 62–81.
2. Cluny, Tome IV quoted in *Foundations for Medieval Genealogy*, fmg.ac/Projects/ Medlands.English [accessed 6/2/20].
3. Van Houts and Love, *The Warenne (Hyde) Chronicle*, p. 35.
4. C. Warren Hollister, 'The Taming of a Turbulent Earl: Henry I and William of Warenne', *Historical Reflections / Réflexions Historiques*, vol. 3, no. 1 (1976): 83–91; www.jstor.org/stable/41298676 [accessed 15 Jan. 2020].
5. C. Warren Hollister, 'Warenne, William de, second earl of Surrey [Earl Warenne] (d. 1138)', *ODNB*.
6. Impey, *Castle Acre Priory and Castle*, p. 36.
7. Ibid, p. 1.
8. Ibid, p. 35.
9. Ibid, pp. 39–40.
10. Hollister, 'Warenne, William de, second earl of Surrey'.
11. Ordericus Vitalis, *Histoire de Normandie, Tome 3*, edited by M. Guizot (Paris, 1827), pp. 277–278. Translated from the French by the author.
12. Teresa Cole, *After the Conquest: The Divided Realm* (Stroud: Amberley Publishing, 2018), pp. 43–45 and James, *The Bastard's Sons*.
13. Orderic Vitalis quoted in Cole, *After the Conquest*, p. 53.
14. Cole, *After the Conquest*, p. 53.
15. Orderic Vitalis quoted in Cole, *After the Conquest*, p. 54.
16. Ordericus Vitalis, *Histoire de Normandie, Tome 3*, p. 351. Translated from the French by the author.
17. Hollister, 'Warenne, William de, second earl of Surrey'.
18. Cole, *After the Conquest*, pp. 100–101.
19. Hollister, 'The Taming of a Turbulent Earl'.
20. Van Houts and Love, *The Warenne (Hyde) Chronicle*, p. 49.
21. James, *The Bastard's Sons*, pp. 250–251.
22. Van Houts and Love, *The Warenne (Hyde) Chronicle*, p. 50.
23. Hollister, 'The Taming of a Turbulent Earl'.
24. Orderic Vitalis quoted in Cole, *After the Conquest*. p. 143.
25. Hollister, 'The Taming of a Turbulent Earl'.
26. Van Houts and Love, *The Warenne (Hyde) Chronicle*, p. 53.
27. Hollister, 'The Taming of a Turbulent Earl'.
28. Cole, *After the Conquest*, p. 151.
29. Ibid, p. 152.
30. Van Houts and Love, *The Warenne (Hyde) Chronicle*, p. 53.
31. Ibid.

32. Wace's *Roman de Rou* quoted in James, *The Bastard's Sons*, p. 257.
33. Hollister, 'The Taming of a Turbulent Earl'.
34. Van Houts and Love, *The Warenne (Hyde) Chronicle*, p. 55.
35. Farrer and Clay, *Early Yorkshire Charters*, p. 7.
36. Orderic Vitalis quoted in Hollister, 'The Taming of a Turbulent Earl'.
37. Farrer and Clay, *Early Yorkshire Charters*, p. 7 and note.
38. Hollister, 'The Taming of a Turbulent Earl'.
39. Hollister, 'Warenne, William de, second earl of Surrey'.
40. Farrer and Clay, *Early Yorkshire Charters*, p. 7.

Chapter 5: The Second Earl and the Last Norman King
1. Van Houts and Love, *The Warenne (Hyde) Chronicle*, pp. 75–77.
2. Ibid, p. 77.
3. Ibid.
4. Ibid.
5. Ibid.
6. Henry of Huntingdon, *Chronicle*, p. 247.
7. Van Houts and Love, *The Warenne (Hyde) Chronicle*, pp. 82–83.
8. Henry of Huntingdon, *The History of the English People 1000–1154*, p. 103.
9. Ibid, p. 103.
10. David Crouch, 'Beaumont, Robert de, count of Meulan and first earl of Leicester (d. 1118)', *ODNB*.
11. Henry of Huntingdon, *Chronicle*, p. 247.
12. Crouch, 'Beaumont, Robert de, count of Meulan and first earl of Leicester'.
13. Farrer and Clay, *Early Yorkshire Charters*, p. 12.
14. Ibid, charter nos. 20, 23 and 29, pp. 76–82.
15. Ibid, charter no. 28, p. 80.
16. Ibid, charter no. 33, p. 85.
17. Ibid, charter no. 32, p. 84.
18. Ibid.
19. Ibid, charter nos. 44 and 46, pp. 93–94.
20. Ibid, pp. 10–11.
21. Ibid.
22. *Gesta Stephani* quoted in David Crouch, 'Roger, second earl of Warwick (d. 1153)', *ODNB*.
23. Henry of Huntingdon, *Chronicle*, p. 109.
24. *Gesta Stephani* quoted in Crouch, 'Roger, second earl of Warwick'.
25. Farrer and Clay, *Early Yorkshire Charters*, p. 10.
26. Ibid, p. 10.
27. Ibid, p. 11.
28. J. Sharpe (trans.), *The History of the Kings of England and of His Own Times by William Malmesbury* (Seeleys, 1854), p. 517.
29. Van Houts and Love, *The Warenne (Hyde) Chronicle*, pp. 80–81.
30. J.F.A. Mason, 'William [William Ætheling, William Adelinus, William Adelingus] (1103–1112)', *ODNB*.
31. Ibid.
32. Orderic Vitalis, *The Ecclesiastical History of England and Normandy*, edited by H.F. Bohn (London, 1853), Vol. IV, p. 35.
33. Orderic Vitalis quoted in Edmund King, *King Stephen* (New Haven: Yale University Press, 2010), p. 42.

34. David Crouch, *The Reign of King Stephen 1135–1154* (Harlow: Longman, Pearson Education, 2000), p. 30.

35. Hollister, 'Warenne, William de, second earl of Surrey'.

36. Swanton, *The Anglo-Saxon Chronicles*, p. 265.

37. Hollister, 'Warenne, William de, second earl of Surrey'.

39. Farrer and Clay, *Early Yorkshire Charters*, p. 9.

40. Ibid, charter no. 35, p. 87.

Chapter 6: Ada de Warenne, Queen Mother of Scotland

1. Victoria Chandler, 'Ada de Warenne, Queen Mother of Scotland (c. 1123–1178)', *The Scottish Historical Review* vol. 60, no. 170, Part 2 (Oct. 1981): 119–139; jstor.org/stable/25529417 [accessed 28 Nov. 2019].

2. G.W.S. Barrow, 'David I (c. 1185–1153)', *ODNB*.

3. David Williamson, *Brewer's British Royalty* (London: Cassell, 1996), p. 100.

4. Barrow, 'David I'.

5. Keith Stringer, 'Henry, earl of Northumberland (c. 1115–1152)', *ODNB*.

6. Matthew Lewis, *Stephen and Matilda's Civil War: Cousins of Anarchy* (Barnsley: Pen & Sword, 2019), p. 59.

7. Ibid. p. 60.

8. Henry of Huntingdon, *Chronicle*, p. 268.

9. Ibid, p. 269.

10. Ibid.

11. Ibid, pp. 269–70.

12. Lewis, *Stephen and Matilda's Civil War*.

13. Henry of Huntingdon, *Chronicle*, p. 270.

14. Lewis, *Stephen and Matilda's Civil War*, p. 75.

15. Keith Stringer, 'Ada [née Ada de Warenne], countess of Northumberland (c. 1123–1178)', *ODNB*.

16. Chandler, 'Ada de Warenne, Queen Mother of Scotland'.

17. Ibid.

18. Stringer, 'Henry, earl of Northumberland'.

19. Ibid.

20. Ibid.

21. Stringer, 'Ada [née Ada de Warenne], countess of Northumberland'.

22. Chandler, 'Ada de Warenne, Queen Mother of Scotland'.

23. Ibid, nos. 4, 6, and 8.

24. Ibid, no. 9.

25. Ibid, no. 11.

26. Ibid, no. 25.

27. Ibid., no. 27.

28. Ibid.

29. Ibid, nos. 10, 12, 13, and 29.

30. Ibid, no. 17.

31. Ibid, nos. 3 and 4.

32. Stephen Spinks, *Robert the Bruce: Champion of a Nation* (Stroud: Amberley, 2019), p. 64.

Chapter 7: Warenne Blood on Scotland's Throne

1. David Ross, *Scotland: History of a Nation* (Broxburn: Lomond Books Ltd., 2014), p. 68.

2. Chandler, 'Ada de Warenne, Queen Mother of Scotland'.

3. Ibid.

4. W.W. Scott, 'Malcolm IV (c. 1141–1165)', *ODNB*.

5. The *Melrose Chronicle* quoted in Scott, 'Malcolm IV'.
6. Scott, 'Malcolm IV'.
7. Ross, *Scotland*, p. 68.
8. Scott, 'Malcolm IV'.
9. Chandler, 'Ada de Warenne, Queen Mother of Scotland'.
10. Ibid.
11. W.W. Scott, 'William I [known as William the Lion] (c. 1142–1214)', *ODNB*.
12. Ibid.
13. Ibid.
14. Ibid.
15. Ross, *Scotland*. p. 69.
16. Chandler, 'Ada de Warenne, Queen Mother of Scotland'.
17. ???? NOTE MISSING
18. Ibid.
19. Ibid.
20. Scott, 'William I'.
21. Ibid.
22. Ibid.
23. Ross, *Scotland*, p. 69.
24. Ibid.
25. W.W. Scott, 'Ermengarde de Beaumont (1233)', *ODNB*.
26. Ibid.
27. Ibid.
28. Anderson quoted in Scott, 'Ermengarde de Beaumont'.
29. Scott, 'William I'.
30. Ibid.
31. Ibid.
32. Ibid.
33. Ibid.
34. Scott, 'Ermengarde de Beaumont'.
35. Bower quoted in Scott, 'Ermengarde de Beaumont'.
36. Scott, 'William I'.
37. Ross, *Scotland*, p. 70.
38. 'Alexander II (1198–1249)', *ODNB*.

Chapter 8: The Crusading Earl

1. Orderici Vitalis, *Historiae ecclesiasticae libri tredecim*, translated by Auguste Le Prévost (*Société de l'histoire de France*, 1838), vol IV, p. 150.
2. Farrer and Clay, *Early Yorkshire Charters*, charter nos. 20, 23, pp. 76–78.
3. Ibid, charter no. 20, p. 76.
4. Victoria Chandler, 'Warenne, William de, third earl of Surrey [Earl Warenne] (c. 1119–1148)', *ODNB*.
5. Orderic Vitalis quoted in Chandler, 'Warenne, William de'.
6. Farrer and Clay, *Early Yorkshire Charters*, p. 12.
7. Chandler, 'Warenne, William de'.
8. James, *The Bastard's Sons*, p. 257.
9. King, *King Stephen*, p. 138.
10. Lewis, *Stephen and Matilda's Civil War*, pp. 97–98.
11. Henry of Huntingdon, *Chronicle*, pp. 276.
12. David Smurthwaite, *The Complete Guide to the Battlefields of Britain* (London: Mermaid Books, 1984), pp. 68–9.

13. Henry of Huntingdon, *Chronicle*, p. 274.
14. Ibid, p. 274.
15. Ibid, pp. 274–276.
16. Ibid, pp. 277–278.
17. Ibid, p. 278.
18. Ibid.
19. Ibid.
20. Ibid.
21. Ibid, p. 279.
22. Ibid.
23. Ibid.
24. Catherine Hanley, *Matilda: Empress, Queen, Warrior* (New Haven: Yale University Press, 2019), p. 140.
25. Ibid, p. 279.
26. Ibid.
27. Hanley, *Matilda*, p. 141.
28. Sharpe, *The History of the Kings of England*, p. 588.
29. Henry of Huntingdon, *Chronicle*, p. 280.
30. Hanley, *Matilda*, pp. 147–148.
31. Ibid, p. 150.
32. Ibid, p. 152.
33. Henry of Huntingdon, *Chronicle*, p. 280.
34. *Chronicles of the Reigns of Stephen, Henry II and Richard I* (Milton Keynes: Nabu Press, 2012), p. 76.
35. Ibid, p. 73.
36. Hanley, *Matilda*, p. 164.
37. *Chronicles of the Reigns of Stephen, Henry II and Richard I*, pp. 82–83.
38. Sharpe, *The History of the Kings of England*, p. 597.
39. Henry of Huntingdon, *Chronicle*, p. 281.
40. Hanley, *Matilda*, p. 172.
41. Farrer and Clay, *Early Yorkshire Charters*, p. 12.
42. King, *King Stephen*, p. 199.
43. Chandler, 'Warenne, William de'.
44. Donald Matthew, *King Stephen* (London: Hambledon, 2002), p. 116.
45. Teresa Cole, *The Anarchy: The Darkest Days of Medieval England* (Stroud: Amberley Publishing, 2019) p. 203.
46. Farrer and Clay, *Early Yorkshire Charters*, p. 12.
47. Chandler, 'Warenne, William de'.
48. Ibid.
49. Farrer and Clay, *Early Yorkshire Charters*, charter no. 44, p. 93.
50. Ibid.
51. BL Harley MS 2110, fo. 4r, quoted in King, *King Stephen*, p. 208.
52. King, *King Stephen*, pp. 232–233.
53. Farrer and Clay, *Early Yorkshire Charters*, charter no. 33, p. 85.
54. Ibid, charter no. 34, p. 86.
55. Ibid, charter no. 32, p. 84.
56. King, *King Stephen*, pp. 232–233.
57. *Epistolae Pontificum Romanorum ineditae* quoted in King, *King Stephen*, p. 233.
58. Henry of Huntingdon, *Chronicle*, p. 285.
59. 'Battle of Mount Cadmus', *World Heritage Encyclopedia*, Gutenberg.org, http://worldheritage.org/article/WHEBN0028326272/Battle%20of%20Mount%20Cadmus [Accessed 28 Jan. 2021].

60. Ibid.
61. Ibid.
62. King, *King Stephen*, p. 233.
63. Farrer and Clay, *Early Yorkshire Charters*, charter nos. 37 and 38, p. 89.
64. Ibid, charter no. 30, pp. 82–83.
65. Ibid, charter no. 43, pp. 92–93.
66. Ibid, charter no. 46, pp. 94.
65. Ibid, charter nos. 49 and 50, pp. 97–98.

Chapter 9: Wormegay
1. Farrer and Clay, *Early Yorkshire Charters*, p. 26.
2. Ibid, charter nos,. 20 and 23, pp. 76–78.
3. Ibid, charter nos. 32, 33 and 34, pp. 84–87.
4. Ibid, p. 28.
5. Victoria Chandler, 'Warenne, Reginald [Rainald] de (1121x6–1178/9)', *ODNB*.
6. Farrer and Clay, *Early Yorkshire Charters*, charter no. 39, pp. 89–90.
7. Ibid, charter no. 40, pp. 90–91.
8. Ibid, charter no. 47, p. 95.
9. Ibid, charter no. 49, p. 97.
10. Ibid., charter no. 50, pp. 97–98.
11. King, *King Stephen*, pp. 238–9.
12. Chandler, 'Warenne, Reginald [Rainald] de'.
13. *Regesta Regum Anglo-Normannorum* translated and quoted King, *King Stephen*, p. 283.
14. Farrer and Clay, *Early Yorkshire Charters*, p. 26.
15. King, *King Stephen*, pp. 289–90.
16. Ibid, p. 338 note 215.
17. Farrer and Clay, *Early Yorkshire Charters*, p. 26.
18. Ibid, p. 27.
19. Ibid, p. 26.
20. Ibid, p. 27.
21. Chandler, 'Warenne, Reginald [Rainald] de'.
22. Ibid.
23. Farrer and Clay, *Early Yorkshire Charters*, pp. 28–9.
24. Ibid.
25. Ibid.
26. *The Cartae Antiquae Rolls* 1–10, ed. L. London, Pipe Rolls Society, quoted in The Magna Carta Project http://magnacartaresearch.org/read/newly_discovered_charters/Notification_of_the_King_s_grant_to_Gundreda__widow_of_Geoffrey_Hose__of_custody_of_Geoffrey_Hose_her_son.
27. Farrer and Clay, *Early Yorkshire Charters*, p. 30.
28. Chandler, 'Warenne, Reginald [Rainald] de'.
29. Farrer and Clay, *Early Yorkshire Charters*, p. 32.
30. Ibid.
31. Ibid.
32. Ibid.
33. BL Cotton MS Nero E, vii, fol. 91, quoted in F.J. West, 'Burgh, Hubert de, earl of Kent (c. 1170–1243)', *ODNB*.
34. Henry II (1179/80) quoted in West, 'Burgh, Hubert de'.
35. West, 'Burgh, Hubert de'.
36. Ibid.

37. Ralph of Coggeshall quoted in Elizabeth Hallam, *The Plantagenet Chronicles* (Twickenham: Tiger Books, 1995), p. 276.
38. Ibid.
39. West, 'Burgh, Hubert de'.
40. Farrer and Clay, *Early Yorkshire Charters*, p. 34.
41. Ibid.
42. Ibid.
43. Ibid.

Chapter 10: The Prince and the Countess

1. Nicholas Vincent, 'Warenne, William de, fifth earl of Surrey [Earl Warenne]', *ODNB*.
2. Farrer and Clay, *Early Yorkshire Charters*, p. 13. Through his mother, Isabel de Vermandois, granddaughter of Henry I of France, William de Warenne was a second cousin of Louis VII.
3. Ibid, charter no. 48, pp. 95–7.
4. Watson, *Memoirs of the Ancient Earls of Warren and Surrey*, p. 139.
5. Farrer and Clay, *Early Yorkshire Charters*, p. 13; and Watson, *Memoirs of the Ancient Earls of Warren and Surrey*, p. 138.
6. Watson, *Memoirs of the Ancient Earls of Warren*, p. 137.
7. I owe a debt of gratitude to historian Catherine Hanley for helping me to flesh out the likely age of Isabel on her wedding day.
8. Farrer and Clay, *Early Yorkshire Charters*, charter no. 50, pp. 97–98.
9. Henry of Huntingdon, *Chronicle*, p. 265.
10. Ibid, pp. 288–9.
11. The Peterborough Manuscript (Text E), *The Anglo-Saxon Chronicles* edited by Swanton, p. 267.
12. Henry of Huntingdon, *Chronicle*, p. 293.
13. *Gesta Stephani* quoted in Cole, *The Anarchy*, p. 227.
14. Ibid.
15. Robert Bartlett, *England Under the Norman and Angevin Kings, 1075–1225* (Oxford: Oxford University Press, 2000), p. 15
16. Cole, *The Anarchy*, pp. 255–6.
17. Henry of Huntingdon, *Chronicle*, p. 294.
18. Ibid.
19. Farrer and Clay, *Early Yorkshire Charters*, pp. 15–16.
20. Thomas K. Keefe, 'William [William of Blois], earl of Surrey [Earl Warenne] (c. 1135–1159)', *ODNB*.
21. *Regesta Regum Anglo-Normannorum* quoted in and translated by King, *King Stephen*, pp. 282–283.
22. Keefe, 'William [William of Blois], earl of Surrey'.
23. Gervase of Canterbury quoted in King, *King Stephen*, p. 293.
24. Ibid.
25. Keefe, 'William [William of Blois], earl of Surrey.
26. Farrer and Clay, *Early Yorkshire Charters*, p. 48.
27. Ibid, p. 17.
28. Ibid, pp. 17–18.
29. Ibid, p. 50.
30. Ibid, p. 49.
31. Ibid, charter no. 51, pp. 98–9.
32. Ibid, charter no. 52, pp. 99–100.
33. Ibid, charter no. 53, p. 100.

Chapter 11: Isabel and Hamelin

1. Farrer and Clay, *Early Yorkshire Charters*, charter no. 111, pp. 158–159.
2. Ralph of Diceto quoted in Hallam, *The Plantagenet Chronicles*, p. 118.
3. Ibid. Richard Brito struck his blow with the words '*Hoc habeas pro amore domini mei Willelmi fratris regis.*' Quoted from *Vita S. Thomae, Cantuariensis Archepiscopi et Martyris*, edited by James Robertson, Materials for the Life of Thomas Becket, 7 vols. (London: Rolls Series, 1875–1885), p. 142.
4. Hanley, *Matilda*, p. 70.
5. Elizabeth Chadwick, 'Hamelin de Warenne *"Pro Lege per Lege"*', http://livingthehistoryelizabethchadwick.blogspot.com/2013/04/hamelin-de-warenne-par-lege-per-lege.html , 27 January 2016.
6. Ibid.
7. Ibid.
8. Farrer and Clay, *Early Yorkshire Charters*, charter no. 82, p. 20.
9. Susan M. Johns, 'Isabel de Warenne, suo jure Countess of Surrey (d. 1203)', *ODNB*.
10. Ibid.
11. Bartlett, *England Under the Norman and Angevin Kings*, p. 404.
12. Ralph of Diceto quoted in Hallam, *The Plantagenet Chronicles*, p. 112.
13. Chadwick, 'Hamelin de Warenne *"Pro Lege per Lege"*'.
14. Thomas K. Keefe, 'Warenne, Hamelin de, earl of Surrey [Earl Warenne] (d. 1202) magnate', *ODNB*.
15. Ralph of Diceto quoted in Hallam, *The Plantagenet Chronicles*, p. 112.
16. Chadwick, 'Hamelin de Warenne *"Pro Lege per Lege"*' and Keefe, 'Warenne, Hamelin de'.
17. Keefe, 'Warenne, Hamelin de'.
18. Harold Sands and Hugh Braun, 'Conisbrough and Mortemer', *The Yorkshire Archaeological Journal*, vol. XXXII (1936), p. 149.
19. Brindle and Sadraei, *Conisbrough Castle*, p. 12.
21. John Leland quoted in 'Peel Hill Motte', http://historyofthorne.com/peel_hill.html.
22. Keefe, 'Warenne, Hamelin de'.
23. Ibid.
24. Ralph of Diceto quoted in Hallam, *The Plantagenet Chronicles*, p. 146.
25. Weir, Alison, *Eleanor of Aquitaine: By the Wrath of God, Queen of England* (London: Jonathan Cape, 1999), p. 175.
26. Benedict of Peterborough quoted in Jacqueline Alio, 'Betrothal of Joanna of England to William II of Sicily', https://www.academia.edu/39276317/Betrothal_of_Joanna_of_England_to_William_II_of_Sicily, 2016 [accessed January 2020].
27. Farrer and Clay, *Early Yorkshire Charters*, p. 19.
28. Benedict of Peterborough quoted in Alio, 'Betrothal of Joanna of England'.
29. *The Annals of Roger de Hoveden: Comprising the History of England and of other Countries of Europe from A.D. 732 to A.D. 1201*, edited and translated by Henry T. Riley (London: H.G. Bohn, 1853), p. 413.
30. Keefe, 'Warenne, Hamelin de'.
31. Meaning 'for the law, by the law'. Farrer and Clay, *Early Yorkshire Charters*, p. 19.
32. Keefe, 'Warenne, Hamelin de'.
33. Farrer and Clay, *Early Yorkshire Charters*, p. 19.
34. Ibid.
35. Ibid, charter no. 54, pp. 101–102.
36. Ibid, charter no. 57, pp. 103–104.
37. Ibid, p. 104.

38. Van Houts and Love, *The Warenne (Hyde) Chronicle*, p. 107.
39. Ibid, p. 108.
40. Farrer and Clay, *Early Yorkshire Charters*, charter no. 62, p. 109.
41. Ibid, charter nos. 64, 65 and 66, pp. 110–111.
42. Ibid, charter no. 58, pp. 104–105.
43. Page, *A History of the County of Sussex*, pp. 64–71; https://www.british-history.ac.uk/vch/sussex/vol2/pp64-71.
44. Farrer and Clay, *Early Yorkshire Charters*, charter nos. 78 and 79, pp. 119–23.
45. Ibid, charter no. 124, p. 172.
46. Ibid, charter no. 85, pp. 127–128.
47. Ibid, charter no. 76, pp. 117–119.
48. Ibid, charter no. 86, p. 128.
49. Ibid, charter no. 87, p. 129.
50. Johns, 'Warenne, Isabel de'.
51. Richard Cassidy, 'Rose of Dover (d. 1261), 'Richard of Chilham and an Inheritance in Kent', *Archaeologica Cantiana*, Vol. cxxxi (2011), pp. 305–19.
52. Farrer and Clay, *Early Yorkshire Charters*, p. 19.

Chapter 12: The Fifth Earl: William de Warenne and the First Barons' War

1. Martha Carlin and David Crouch (eds and trans), *Lost Letters of Medieval Life: English Society, 1200–1250* (Philadelphia: University of Pennsylvania Press, 2013), p. 211.
2. Farrer and Clay, *Early Yorkshire Charters*, charter no. 59, pp. 105–107.
3. Ibid, charter no. 63, pp. 109–110.
4. Ibid, charter nos. 64, 65 and 66, pp. 110–111.
5. Ibid, charter no. 75, pp. 116–117.
6. Ibid, charter no. 79, pp. 120–123.
7. Ibid, p. 122.
8. Ibid.
9. Ibid.
10. Vincent, 'Warenne, William de'.
11. Ibid.
12. Ibid.
13. The Barnwell Annalist quoted in Hallam, *The Plantagenet Chronicles*, p. 300.
14. Ibid, pp. 300–301.
15. Ibid, p. 301.
16. Ibid, p. 308.
17. Ibid, p. 312.
18. Ibid, p. 314.
19. Vincent, 'Warenne, William de'.
20. Rich Price, 'King John's Letters', Facebook Study Group, 20 June 2016.
21. Simon Lloyd, 'Chilham, Sir Richard of (d. 1246)', *ODNB*.
22. The Barnwell Annalist quoted in Elizabeth Hallam (ed.), *Chronicles of the Age of Chivalry* (Twickenham: Tiger Books, 1995), p. 29.
23. Ibid.
24. Vincent, 'Warenne, William de'.
25. Farrer and Clay, *Early Yorkshire Charters*, charter no. 59, pp. 105–107.
26. Vincent, 'Warenne, William de'.
27. Ibid.
28. Ibid.
29. Roger of Wendover quoted in Hallam, *Chronicles of the Age of Chivalry*, p. 44–45.

30. Ibid, p. 48.
31. Vincent, 'Warenne, William de'.
32. Ibid.
33. Ibid.
34. Anthony J. Holden and David Crouch (eds), *History of William Marshal: Text & Translation (vol. II. 10032–end)*, translated by S. Gregory (London: Anglo-Norman Text Society, 2002).
35. Ibid.
36. Chadwick, Elizabeth, 'Clothing the Bones: Finding Mahelt Marshal', livingthehistory elizabethchadwick.blogspot.com, 7 September 2008.
37. Farrer and Clay, *Early Yorkshire Charters*, pp. 24–25.
38. Ibid, p. 25.
39. Ibid, charter no. 88, pp. 129–30.
40. Ibid, charter no. 97, pp. 135.
41. Ibid, charter no. 89, pp. 130–1.
42. Ibid, charter no. 90, p. 131.
43. Ibid, charter no. 91, pp. 131–2.
44. Ibid, charter no. 92, p. 132.
45. Ibid, charter no. 95, p. 134.
46. Ibid, charter no. 93, p. 133.
47. Carlin and Crouch, *Lost Letters of Medieval Life*, p. 210.
48. Ibid, p. 213.
49. Farrer and Clay, *Early Yorkshire Charters*, p. 25.
50. Blaauw, *On the Early History of Lewes Priory*, p. 24.
51. 26 Henry III, Fine Rolls of Henry III Project, Finerollshenry3.co.uk. https://finerollshenry3.org.uk/content/calendar/roll_038.html#it137_010
52. Chadwick, 'Clothing the Bones'.
53. David Crouch, quoted in ibid.

Chapter 13: Warenne Women: the Daughters of the Fourth and Fifth Earls

1. Farrer and Clay, *Early Yorkshire Charters*, p. 20*n*.
2. Ibid, p. 25.
3. Ibid, p. 20*n*.
4. Ibid, p. 20*n*.
5. Ibid, charter nos. 96 and 97, pp. 134–136.
6. Ibid, p. 135.
7. Ibid, p. 21.
8. Ibid.
9. Ibid, p. 22.
10. *PR16 John pp. 37, 166–7, Rott. Lit. Pat* quoted in Bartlett, *England Under the Norman and Angevin Kings*, p. 16.
11. *Pat. Rolls, Henry III* quoted in Bartlett, *England Under the Norman and Angevin Kings*, p. 16.
12. Farrer and Clay, *Early Yorkshire Charters*, p. 20.
13. Keefe, 'Warenne, Hamelin de'.
14. Cassidy, 'Rose of Dover', pp. 305–19.
15. The Barnwell Annalist quoted in Hallam, *Chronicles of the Age of Chivalry*, p. 29.
16. Lloyd, 'Chilham, Sir Richard of (d. 1246)'.
17. Cassidy, 'Rose of Dover', pp. 305–19.
18. Lloyd, 'Chilham, Sir Richard of (d. 1246)'.

19. Cassidy, 'Rose of Dover', pp. 305–19.
20. Ibid.
21. Ibid.
22. Ibid.
23. Ibid.
24. *Annales Cestrienses: Chronicle of the Abbey of S. Werburg*, at Chester, ed. Richard Copley Christie (London, 1887), pp. 36–49. *British History Online*, http://www.british-history. ac.uk/lancs-ches-record-soc/vol14/pp36-49 [accessed 1 May 2019].
25. Fmg.ac/Projects/MedLands/English, *Foundation for Medieval Genealogy*.
26. *Pipe Roll 2 Ric* 1, quoted in Farrer and Clay, *Early Yorkshire Charters*, p. 130.
27. Ibid, p. 23.
28. Ibid.
29. Ibid.
30. Susan M. Johns, 'Alice [married name Alice de Lusignan] suo jure countess of Eu (article)', *ODNB*.
31. Ibid.
32. Tickhill Castle Guide Leaflet, 'Lords of the Honour of Tickhill', 2017.
33. finerollshenry3.org.uk content/calendar/roll_015.html#it158_006, 19 May 1221.
34. Johns, 'Alice de Lusignan'.
35. Farrer and Clay, *Early Yorkshire Charters*, p. 23.
36. Johns, 'Alice de Lusignan'.
37. Ibid.
38. Ralph V. Turner, 'Aubigny, William d', [William de Albini], third earl of Arundel', *ODNB*.
39. 'House of Cistercian nuns: The Abbey of Marham', in *A History of the County of Norfolk: Volume 2*, ed. William Page (London, 1906), pp. 369–370; *British History Online* http://www.british-history.ac.uk/vch/norf/vol2/pp369-370 [accessed 26 May 2020].
40. John A. Nichols, 'Warenne, Isabel de [married name Isabel d'Aubigny], countess of Arundel', *ODNB*.
41. Ibid.
42. Matthew Paris quoted in Susan Annesley in finerollshenry3.org.uk content/month/ fm08-2009.html, August 2009.
43. Ibid.
44. Ibid.
45. Ibid.

Chapter 14: John de Warenne and the Second Barons' War

1. Scott L. Waugh, 'Warenne, John de, seventh earl of Surrey [earl of Surrey and Sussex, Earl Warenne] (1286–1347)', *ODNB*.
2. Watson, *Memoirs of the Ancient Earls of Warren and Surrey*, p. 228.
3. Waugh, 'Warenne, John de, seventh earl of Surrey'.
4. Ibid.
5. G.P. Stell, 'John [John de Balliol] (c. 1248x50–1314)', *ODNB*.
6. 'Annals written by a certain monk of Lewes, from the birth of Christ to the year 1312' quoted in Blaauw, *On the Early History of Lewes Priory*, pp. 26–27.
7. Helen Matthews, *The Legitimacy of Bastards: The Place of Illegitimate Children in Later Medieval England* (Barnsley: Pen & Sword, 2019), pp. 32–33.
8. 34 Henry III, Fine Rolls of Henry III Project, https://finerollshenry3.org.uk/content/ calendar/roll_047.html#it051_016.
9. 35 Henry III, Fine Rolls of Henry III Project, https://finerollshenry3.org.uk/content/ calendar/roll_048.html#it398_015.

10. Nicholas Vincent, 'Lusignan [Valence], Aymer de (c. 1228–1260)', *ODNB*.
11. Watson, *Memoirs of the Ancient Earls of Warren and Surrey*, p. 229.
12. Ibid.
13. Waugh, 'Warenne, John de, seventh earl of Surrey'.
14. Darren Baker, *The Two Eleanors of Henry III: The Lives of Eleanor of Provence and Eleanor de Montfort* (Barnsley: Pen & Sword History, 2019), p. 114.
15. Watson, *Memoirs of the Ancient Earls of Warren and Surrey*, p. 229.
16. Waugh, 'Warenne, John de, seventh earl of Surrey'.
17. Ibid.
18. Watson, *Memoirs of the Ancient Earls of Warren and Surrey*, p. 229.
19. 'Annals written by a certain monk of Lewes, from the birth of Christ to the year 1312' quoted in Blaauw, *On the Early History of Lewes Priory*, p. 27.
20. Baker, *The Two Eleanors*, p. 139.
21. Waugh, 'Warenne, John de, seventh earl of Surrey'.
22. Baker, *The Two Eleanors*, p. 148.
23. Waugh, 'Warenne, John de, seventh earl of Surrey'.
24. 47 Henry III, Fine Rolls of Henry III Project, https://finerollshenry3.org.uk/content/calendar/roll_060.html#it713_003.
25. Waugh, 'Warenne, John de, seventh earl of Surrey'.
26. Ibid.
27. Baker, *The Two Eleanors*, pp. 158–9.
28. Smurthwaite, *The Complete Guide to the Battlefields of Britain*, pp. 70–71.
29. Waugh, 'Warenne, John de, seventh earl of Surrey'.
30. 'Annals written by a certain monk of Lewes, from the birth of Christ to the year 1312' quoted in Blaauw, *On the Early History of Lewes Priory*, p. 28.
31. Baker, *The Two Eleanors*, p. 160.
32. From Thomas Percy's *Relique of Ancient English Poetry* quoted Watson, *Memoirs of the Ancient Earls of Warren and Surrey*, p. 235.
33. Waugh, 'Warenne, John de, seventh earl of Surrey'.
34. Thomas Wykes quoted in Baker, *The Two Eleanors*, p. 160.
35. Waugh, 'Warenne, John de, seventh earl of Surrey'.
36. Holinshed, *Chronicles of England and Ireland* (6 volumes) (London; Routledge, 2013) Vol. 1, p. 466.
37. Watson, *Memoirs of the Ancient Earls of Warren and Surrey*, p. 236.
38. Ibid.
39. John Laffin, *Brassey's Battles: 3,500 Years of Conflict, Campaigns and Wars from A-Z* (London: Brassey's, 1995), p. 162.
40. The Waverley Annals quoted in Hallam, *Chronicles of the Age of Chivalry*, p. 98.
41. Ibid.
42. Waugh, 'Warenne, John de, seventh earl of Surrey'.
43. 'Annals written by a certain monk of Lewes, from the birth of Christ to the year 1312' quoted Blaauw, *On the Early History of Lewes Priory*, p. 30.
44. Waugh, 'Warenne, John de, seventh earl of Surrey'.

Chapter 15: John de Warenne and the Wars of Edward I

1. 'Houses of Austin canons: The Priory of the Holy Sepulchre, Thetford', in *A History of the County of Norfolk: Volume 2*, ed. William Page (London, 1906), pp. 391–393. *British History Online* http://www.british-history.ac.uk/vch/norf/vol2/pp391-393 [accessed 28 May 2020].
2. A. 40470 'Deeds: A.4001 – A.4100', in *A Descriptive Catalogue of Ancient Deeds: Volume 3*, ed. H.C. Maxwell Lyte (London, 1900), pp. 19–30. *British History Online* http://www.british-history.ac.uk/ancient-deeds/vol3/pp19-30 [accessed 28 May 2020].

3. 'Parishes: Rottingdean', in *A History of the County of Sussex: Volume 7, The Rape of Lewes*, ed. L.F. Salzman (London, 1940), pp. 232–38. *British History Online* http://www.british-history.ac.uk/vch/sussex/vol7/pp232-238 [accessed 28 May 2020].

4. A.313 in 'Deeds: A.301–A.400', in *A Descriptive Catalogue of Ancient Deeds: Volume 1*, ed. H.C. Maxwell Lyte (London, 1890), pp. 33–47. *British History Online* http://www.british-history.ac.uk/ancient-deeds/vol1/pp33-47 [accessed 28 May 2020].

5. A.305 in ibid.

6. 'Parishes: Dorking', in *A History of the County of Surrey: Volume 3*, ed. H.E. Malden (London, 1911), pp. 141–150. *British History Online* http://www.british-history.ac.uk/vch/surrey/vol3/pp141-150 [accessed 28 May 2020].

7. 'Inquisitions Post Mortem, Edward I, File 27', in *Calendar of Inquisitions Post Mortem: Volume 2, Edward I*, ed. J E E S Sharp (London, 1906), pp. 223–30. *British History Online* http://www.british-history.ac.uk/inquis-post-mortem/vol2/pp223-230 [accessed 28 May 2020].

8. Ibid.

9. A. 40472 'Deeds: A.4001– A.4100', in Lyte, *Descriptive Catalogue of Ancient Deeds 3*.

10. Waugh, 'Warenne, John de, seventh earl of Surrey'.

11. Brindle and Sadraei, *Conisbrough Castle*, p. 30.

12. Waugh, 'Warenne, John de, seventh earl of Surrey'.

13. Ibid.

14. Impey, *Castle Acre Priory and Castle*, p. 40.

15. Brindle and Sadraei, *Conisbrough Castle*, p. 29.

16. *Rotuli hundredorum* quoted in Waugh, 'Warenne, John de, seventh earl of Surrey'.

17. Ibid.

18. Brindle and Sadraei, *Conisbrough Castle*, p. 29.

19. Louise Wilkinson, *Women in Thirteenth-Century Lincolnshire* (Suffolk: Boydell, 2007), p. 90.

20. Waugh, 'Warenne, John de, seventh earl of Surrey'.

21. Andrew M. Spencer, *Nobility and Kingship in Medieval England* (Cambridge: Cambridge University Press, 2014), p. 67.

22. Ibid, p. 38.

23. Ibid, p. 63.

24. Waugh, 'Warenne, John de, seventh earl of Surrey'.

25. *Chronicle of Walter of Guisborough*, quoted in ibid.

26. G. Lapsley, 'John de Warenne and the '*Quo Warranto*' Proceedings in 1279', *The Cambridge Historical Journal*, Vol. 2, no. 2 (1927): 110–132; jstor.org/stable/3020694 [accessed Dec. 2019].

27. Ibid.

28. Dr Round, quoted in ibid.

29. Spencer, *Nobility and Kingship*, p. 74.

30. Marc Morris, *A Great and Terrible King: Edward I and the Forging of Britain* (London: Windmill Books, 2009), p. 143.

31. Waugh, 'Warenne, John de, seventh earl of Surrey'.

32. *The Ledger of the Book of Vale Abbey* quoted Morris, *A Great and Terrible King*, p. 153.

33. Ibid, p. 155.

34. Waugh, 'Warenne, John de, seventh earl of Surrey'.

35. David Powel's *History of Wales* quoted in Watson, *Memoirs of the Ancient Earls of Warren and Surrey*, p. 266.

36. Waugh, 'Warenne, John de, seventh earl of Surrey'.

37. Rick Turner, 'Looking Inside the Medieval Holt Castle', https://www.historyextra.com/period/norman/looking-inside-the-medieval-holt-castle/, 4 September 2015.

38. William Rees (ed.), *Calendar of Ancient Petitions Relating to Wales (Thirteenth to Sixteenth Century)* (Cardiff: University of Wales Press, 1975), No. 2598, 1301–07, pp. 74–75.
39. Ibid.
40. Ibid.
41. Ibid, No. 8393B, 1278, p. 287–288.
42. Ibid.
43. Ibid, p. 288.
44. Stephen Spinks, *Robert the Bruce*, p. 64.
45. Stell, 'John [John de Balliol]'.
46. Laffin, *Brassey's Battles*, p. 151.
47. Stell, 'John [John de Balliol]'.
48. Cynthia J. Neville (ed.), 'A Plea Roll of Edward I's Army in Scotland, 1296', https://deremilitari.org/2014/04/a-plea-roll-of-edward-is-army-in-scotland-1296/ [Accessed 26 April 2020]
49. Walter of Guisborough quoted in Hallam, *Chronicles of the Age of Chivalry*, p. 142.
50. Ibid, p. 144.
51. *Chronicle of Walter of Guisborough* quoted in Spinks, *Robert the Bruce*, pp. 84–85.
52. Spinks, *Robert the Bruce*, p. 85.
53. Ibid, p. 85.
54. Ibid.
55. Walter of Guisborough quoted in Colm McNamee, *Robert Bruce: Our Most Valiant Prince, King and Lord* (Edinburgh: Birlinn, 2018), p. 73.
56. *Chronicle of Lanercost* quoted in ibid.
57. Waugh, 'Warenne, John de, seventh earl of Surrey'.
58. Ibid.
59. Spinks, *Robert the Bruce*, p. 86.
60. Ibid, p. 86.
61. Smurthwaite, *The Complete Guide to the Battlefields of Britain* p. 75 and McNamee, *Robert Bruce*, pp. 77–80.
62. 'Annals written by a certain monk of Lewes, from the birth of Christ to the year 1312' quoted in Blaauw, *On the Early History of Lewes Priory*, p. 37.

Chapter 16: The Last Earl

1. 'Annals written by a certain monk of Lewes, from the birth of Christ to the year 1312' quoted in Blaauw, *On the Early History of Lewes Priory*, p. 35.
2. Ibid, pp. 35–6.
3. F. Royston Fairbank, 'The Last Earl of Warenne and Surrey, and the Distribution of his Possessions', *The Yorkshire Archaeological Journal*, vol. XIX, (1907), p. 193.
4. 'William de Warenne (1256–1286)', https://en.wikipedia.org/wiki/William_de_Warenne_(1256–1286) [accessed 2 May 2020].
5. Waugh, 'Warenne, John de, seventh earl of Surrey'.
6. Ibid.
7. Ibid.
8. Kelcey Wilson-Lee, *Daughters of Chivalry: The Forgotten Children of Edward I* (London: Picador, 2019), p. 264 .
9. Langtoft quote in Fairbank, 'The Last Earl of Warenne and Surrey', p. 194.
10. Ibid.
11. Ibid.
12. Ibid.
13. Stephen Spinks, *Edward II The Man: A Doomed Inheritance* (Stroud: Amberley, 2017), p. 63.

14. *Vita Edwardi Secundi* quoted in Spinks, *Edward II The Man*, p. 66.
15. Spinks, *Edward II The Man*, p. 74.
16. Waugh, 'Warenne, John de, seventh earl of Surrey'.
17. Spinks, *Edward II The Man*, p. 74.
18. Ibid, p. 82.
19. Waugh, 'Warenne, John de, seventh earl of Surrey'.
20. Ibid.
21. Ibid.
22. *Vita Edwardi Secundi* quoted in Spinks, *Edward II The Man*, p. 88.
23. Ibid.
24. *The Chronicle of Lanercost* quoted in Spinks, *Edward II The Man*, p. 88.
25. *Vita Edwardi Secundi* quoted in Spinks, *Edward II The Man*, p. 89.
26. Waugh, 'Warenne, John de, seventh earl of Surrey'.
27. Spinks, *Edward II The Man*, p. 89.
28. Ibid, p. 91.
29. Waugh, 'Warenne, John de, seventh earl of Surrey'.
30. *Calendar of Patent Rolls, 1307–1313* (p. 283) quoted in Fairbank, 'The Last Earl of Warenne and Surrey', p. 195.
31. Spinks, *Edward II The Man*, pp. 94–95.
32. Ibid, p. 95.
33. Ibid, pp. 101–102.
34. Ibid, p. 103.
35. Thomas of Walsingham, *Thomae Walsingham Historia Anglicana*, edited by H.T. Riley, in part one of *Chronica Monasterii Sancti Albani*, pp. 148–9.
36. Brindle and Sadraei, *Conisbrough Castle*, pp. 30–31.
37. Conisbrough Court Rolls, *dhi.ac.uk/conisbrough/index.html*
38. Hunter's *South Yorkshire II: Deanery of Doncaster II* quoted in Fairbank, 'The Last Earl of Warenne and Surrey', p. 213.
39. *Calendar of Close Rolls, 1313–18, p. 575* quoted in ibid, p. 195.
40. Rees, *Calendar of Ancient Petitions*, No. 8830, 14 June 1318, pp. 296–297.
41. *Vita Edwardi Secundi* quoted in Spinks, *Edward II The Man*, p. 149.
42. Ibid, pp. 149–50.
43. *Calendar of Patent Rolls, 1321–24* (p. 15) quoted in Fairbank, 'The Last Earl of Warenne and Surrey', p. 195.
44. Spinks, *Edward II The Man*, p. 173.
45. Fairbank, 'The Last Earl of Warenne and Surrey', p. 214.
46. Spinks, *Edward II The Man*, p. 176.
47. Fairbank, 'The Last Earl of Warenne and Surrey', p. 215.
48. Ibid.
49. Waugh, 'Warenne, John de, seventh earl of Surrey'.
50. Smurthwaite, *The Complete Guide to the Battlefields of Britain*, pp. 80–81.
51. Ibid.
52. Fairbank, 'The Last Earl of Warenne and Surrey', p. 229.
53. Ibid.
54. *Calendar of Close Rolls, 1333–1337* (p. 301) quoted ibid, p. 233.
55. Waugh, 'Warenne, John de, seventh earl of Surrey'.
56. *Calendar of Patent Rolls, 1338–1340* (p. 505) quoted in Fairbank, 'The Last Earl of Warenne and Surrey', p. 240.

Chapter 17: A Disastrous Marriage and the End of a Dynasty

1. Mary Anne Everett Green suggests 1295 as Joan's date of birth. *Lives of the Princesses of England from the Norman Conquest*, Vol. 2 (London: Longman, 1857), pp. 310–311.
2. Wilson-Lee, *Daughters of Chivalry*, p. 145 .
3. Ibid, p. 192.
4. Ibid, p. 208.
5. Ibid, pp. 232–233.
6. Wardrobe Accounts quoted in Fairbank, 'The Last Earl of Warenne and Surrey', p. 193.
7. Wilson-Lee, *Daughters of Chivalry*, p. 261.
8. Ibid, p. 264.
9. Wardrobe Accounts quoted in Fairbank, 'The Last Earl of Warenne and Surrey', p. 193.
10. Ibid.
11. Ibid.
12. Ibid.
13. Wilson-Lee, *Daughters of Chivalry*, p. 264
14. Ibid, p. 286
15. Ibid, p. 290.
16. Matthews, *The Legitimacy of Bastards*, p. 34.
17. Ibid.
18. *Calendar of Close Rolls, 1313–1317* (pp. 45–6) quoted in Fairbank, 'The Last Earl of Warenne and Surrey', p. 198.
19. Matthews, *The Legitimacy of Bastards*, p. 34.
20. Fairbank, 'The Last Earl of Warenne and Surrey', p. 199.
21. Ibid, p. 200.
22. Ibid.
23. *Letters and Papers from the Northern Registers* quoted in ibid, p. 201.
24. Matthews, *The Legitimacy of Bastards*, p. 35.
25. *Letters and Papers from the Northern Registers* quoted in Fairbank, 'The Last Earl of Warenne and Surrey', p. 203.
26. Ibid, pp. 203–204.
27. Matthews, *The Legitimacy of Bastards*, p. 35.
28. Fairbank, 'The Last Earl of Warenne and Surrey', p. 199.
29. Ibid, p. 230.
30. Ibid, p. 199.
31. Kathryn Warner, *Isabella of France: The Rebel Queen* (Stroud: Amberley, 2016), pp. 76–77.
32. Fairbank, 'The Last Earl of Warenne and Surrey', p. 205.
33. Ibid.
34. Ibid, p. 206.
35. *Calendar of Patent Rolls, 1313–1317* (p. 528) quoted in ibid, pp. 208–209.
36. Spinks, *Edward II The Man*, p. 138.
37. Ibid, p. 138.
38. Matthews, *The Legitimacy of Bastards*, p. 36.
39. Fairbank, 'The Last Earl of Warenne and Surrey', p. 219.
40. Ibid, p. 220.
41. Ibid, p. 221.
42. Ibid, p. 226.
43. Ibid.
44. Ibid, p. 227.
45. *Chartulary of Lewes Priory* quoted in ibid, p. 230.

46. Matthews, *The Legitimacy of Bastards*, p. 38.
47. *Calendar of Papal Registers, Papal Letters* (p. 116) quoted in Fairbank, 'The Last Earl of Warenne and Surrey', p. 242.
48. Ibid, p. 243.
49. Ibid, p. 243.
50. Ibid, p. 245.
51. Ibid, p. 246.
52. Ibid, pp. 249–50.
53. Ibid, p. 254.
54. Matthews, *The Legitimacy of Bastards*, p. 41.
55. Waugh, 'Warenne, John de, seventh earl of Surrey'.

Appendix A: The Mysterious Knight

1. Katheryn Warner, *Philippa of Hainault: Mother of the English Nation* (Stroud: Amberley, 2019) p. 149.

Bibliography

Primary Sources

Ancrene Wisse: Guide for Anchoresses, translated by Hugh White (Harmondsworth: Penguin, 1993)

The Anglo-Saxon Chronicle, edited and translated by James Ingram (London, 1823, reprint)

The Anglo-Saxon Chronicle, edited and translated by D. Whitelock, D.C. Douglas and S.I. Tucker (London: Cambridge University Press, 1961)

The Anglo-Saxon Chronicle, edited and translated by Michael Swanton (London: Phoenix Press, 2000)

Annales Cestrienses, Chronicle of the Abbey of S. Werburg, at Chester, edited by Richard Copley Christie, London, 1887, pp. 36–49; British History Online: http://www.british-history.ac.uk/lancs-chesrecord-soc/vol14/pp36-49

'Annales monasterii de Bermundesia (A.D. 1042–1432)', *Annales Monastici*, edited by Henry Richards Luard (London: Longmans, 1866)

'Annales prioratus de Dunstaplia (A.D. 1–1297)', *Annales Monastici*, edited by Henry Richards Luard (London: Longmans, 1866)

'Annales prioratus de Dunstaplia (A.D. 1–1297)', translated by Rich Price, *King John's Letters*, Facebook Study Group, 20 June 2016 onwards

The Annals of Roger de Hoveden: Comprising the History of England and of other Countries of Europe from A.D. 732 to A.D. 1201, edited and translated by Henry T. Riley (London: H.G. Bohn, 1853)

The Autobiography of Giraldus Cambrensis, edited and translated by H.E. Butler (London: Jonathan Cape, 1937)

'The "Barnwell" Annals', (anon.), in *The Historical Collections of Walter of Coventry*, edited by W. Stubbs (London: Rolls Series, 1873)

Carlin, Martha and David Crouch (eds and trans), *Lost Letters of Medieval Life: English Society, 1200–1250* (Philadelphia: University of Pennsylvania Press, 2013)

The Carmen de Hastingi Proelio of Guy, Bishop of Amiens, edited by Catherine Morton and Hope Muntz (Oxford: Clarendon Press, 1972)

Charter of the Forest, 1225, The National Archives, C71/1; nationalarchives.gov.uk/education/resources/magna-carta/ charter-forest-1225-westminster/

The Chronicle of John Florence of Worcester with the two Continuations, edited and translated by Thomas Forester (London: Henry G. Bohn, 1854)

The Chronicle of John of Worcester, edited by R.R Darlington and P. McGurk, 2 Vols. (Oxford: Clarendon Press, 1995)

Chronicle of Melrose 731–1270, edited by Dsuvit Broun and Julian Harrison (Suffolk: Boydell Press, 2001)

Chronicles of the Reigns of Stephen, Henry II and Richard I (Milton Keynes: Nabu Press, 2012)

Crawford, Anne (ed. and trans.), *Letters of Medieval Women* (Stroud: Sutton Publishing, 2002)

Dronke, Peter, *Medieval Testimonies* (Glasgow: University of Glasgow Press, 1976)

Florentii Wigorniensis monachi chronicon ex chronicis, edited by B. Thorpe, vol. 2, English Historical Society, 10 (1849)

Fine Rolls of Henry III Project, Finerollshenry3.co.uk

Gervase of Canterbury, *The Deeds of Kings*, in *The Historical Works of Gervase of Canterbury*, edited by W. Stubbs (London: Rolls Series, 1880)

The Gesta Guillielmi of William of Poitiers, edited by R.H.C. Davis and Marjorie Chibnall (Oxford: Oxford, 1998)

The Gesta Normannorum Ducum of William of Jumièges, Orderic Vitalis and Robert of Torigni, edited by E.M.C. van Houts, 2 Vols. (Oxford: Oxford University Press, 1992–95)

Gesta Regis Henrici Secundi Benedicti Abbatis: The Chronicle of the Reigns of Henry II and Richard I A. D. 1169–1192: Known Commonly Under the Name of Benedict of Peterborough, edited by William Stubbs (Longmans, 1867)

Giraldus Cambrensis, *The Conquest of Ireland*, translated by Thomas Forester, Medieval Latin Series (Ontario: In Parentheses Publications, 2001)

Henry of Huntingdon, *The Chronicle of Henry of Huntingdon: Comprising the History of England, from the Invasion of Julius Caesar to the Accession of Henry II. Also, the Acts of Stephen, King of England and Duke of Normandy*, edited and translated by Thomas Forester (London: H.G. Bohn, 1853), archive.org

Henry of Huntingdon, *The History of the English People 1000–1154*, translated by Diana Greenway (Oxford: Oxford, 2002)

The Historie and Cronicles of Scotland ... by Robert Lindesay of Pitscottie, 3 Vols., edited by A.J.G. Mackay, Scottish Text Society, 3 volumes (1899–1911)

History of William Marshal: Text & Translation (vol. II. 10032–end), edited by Anthony J. Holden and David Crouch, translated by S. Gregory (London: Anglo-Norman Text Society from Birkbeck College, 2002)

Holinshed, *Chronicles of England and Ireland* (6 volumes) (London; Routledge, 2013) Vol. 1: England

John of Salisbury, *The Letters of John of Salisbury*, edited by W.J. Miller, S.J. Butler, H.E. Butler and revised by C.N.L. Brooke (London: Thomas Nelson and Sons, 1955)

Magna Carta, British Library, transcript from bl.uk

Magna Carta, translated by D. Carpenter (London: Penguin Random House, 2015)

Ordericus Vitalis, *The Ecclesiastical History of England and Normandy*, edited by H.G. Bohn (London, 1853)

Ordericus Vitalis, *The Ecclesiastical History of England and Normandy by Orderic Vitalis, volume IV*, translated, with notes and the introduction of Guizot by Thomas Forester, M.A. (London: H.G. Bohn, 1856)

Orderici Vitalis, *Historiae ecclesiasticae libri tredecim*, translated by Auguste Le Prévost (*Société de l'histoire de France*, 1838); archive.org

Ordericus Vitalis, *Histoire de Normandie, seconde partie*, translated by L.F. Dubois (Caen: Mancel, 1826)

An Outline Itinerary of King Henry I, edited by William Farrer (Oxford, 1861–1924), archive. org

Paris, Matthew, *Flores Historiarum*, volume III, edited by Henry Richards Luard, (London: H.M. Stationary Office, 1890)

Ralph of Coggeshall, *The English Chronicle*, edited by J. Stevenson, in *Chronicon Anglicanum* (London: Rolls Series, 1875)

Richard of Devizes, *Chronicle* (Objective Systems, ebook, 2008)

Richard of Devizes, *The Chronicle of Richard of Devizes: Concerning the Deeds of Richard the First King of England also Richard of Cirencester's Description of Britain*, edited and translated by J.A. Giles (London, 1841)

Ralph of Diceto, *Images of History*, edited by W. Stubbs, in *The Historical Works of Master Ralph of Diceto* (London: Rolls Series, 1876)

Roger of Wendover, *Roger of Wendover's Flowers of History: Comprising the History of England from the Descent of the Saxons to A.D. 1235*, volume II, edited by J.A. Giles (London: H.G. Bohn, 1849)

Rotuli parliamentorum ut et petitiones, et placita in parliamento, 6 vols, edited by J. Strachey (1767–77)

Rymer, T. (ed.), *Foedera, conventions, literae, etc.* (London: Record Commission, 1816–69)

Sawyer, P.H., *Anglo-Saxon Charters: An Annotated List and Bibliography*, Royal Historical Society Guides and Handbooks (1968)

Shirley, W.W. (ed.), *Royal and other Historical Letters*, Chronicles and Memorials (London, Rolls Series, 1862–66)

Stow, John, *The Annales of England: The Race of the Kings of Brytaine after the received Opinion since Brute, &c.* (London: G. Bishop and T. Adams, 1605)

Thomas of Walsingham, *Thomae Walsingham Historia Anglicana*, in part one of *Chronica Monasterii Sancti Albani*, edited by H.T. Riley, Vol. 4 (London: Rolls Series, 1863–64)

Trivet, Nicholas, *Annales Sex Regum Angliae*, edited by T. Hog (1845)

The Warenne (Hyde) Chronicle, edited and translated by Elisabeth M.C. Van Houts and Rosalind C. Love (Oxford: Clarendon Press, 2013)

William of Malmesbury, *Chronicles of the Kings of England, From the Earliest Period to the Reign of King Stephen, c. 1090–1143*, edited by John Sharpe and J.A. Giles (London: H.G. Bohn, 1847)

William of Malmesbury, *Chronicles of the Kings of England, From the Earliest Period to the Reign of King Stephen, c. 1090–1143* (Perennial Press, ebook, 2016)

William of Malmesbury, *The History of the Kings of England and of His Own Times by William Malmesbury*, translated by J. Sharpe (Seeleys, 1854)

Yonge, C.D. (trans.), *Medieval Sourcebook: Matthew of Westminster: Simon de Montfort's Rebellion 1265*, excerpt from Matthew Paris, *The Flowers of History*, sourcebooks. fordham.edu

Secondary Sources

'6 Facts about Magna Carta', https://www.historyextra.com/period/medieval/facts-magna-carta-when-signed-why-significant-law-today-what-king-john/, 22 August 2018

Adams, George Burton, *The History of England from the Norman Conquest to the Death of John* (public domain ebook, 1930)

Alio, Jacqueline, 'Betrothal of Joanna of England to William II of Sicily', academia.edu, 2016

Ambler, Sophie, 'Advisers of King John', *Oxford Dictionary of National Biography* (Oxford: Oxford University Press, 2004); online edition

Ambler, Sophie, 'Henry III's Confirmation of Magna Carta in 1265', https://magnacarta. cmp.uea.ac.uk/read/feature_of_the_month/Mar_2014, March 2014

Ambler, Sophie, 'Simon de Montfort's 1265 Parliament and Magna Carta', https:// thehistoryofparliament.wordpress.com/2015/01/20/simon-de-montfort-1265-parliament-and-magna-carta/, 20 January 2015

Amt, Emilie, 'Salisbury, Patrick, first Earl of Salisbury [Earl of Wiltshire]', *Oxford Dictionary of National Biography* (Oxford: Oxford University Press, 2004); online edition

Andrews, J.F., *Lost Heirs of the Medieval Crown: The Kings and Queens Who Never Were* (Barnsley: Pen & Sword History, 2019)

Appleby, John C. and Paul Dalton, *Early Modern England: Crime, Government and Society, c. 1066–c. 1600* (Abingdon: Routledge, 2016)

Asbridge, Thomas, *The Greatest Knight: The Remarkable Life of William Marshal, the Power behind Five English Thrones* (London: Simon & Schuster, 2015)

Ashley, Maurice, *The Life and Times of King John* (London: George Weidenfield and Nicolson, 1972)

Ashley, Mike, *A Brief History of British Kings and Queens* (London: Constable & Robinson Ltd., 2014)

Ashley, Mike, *The Mammoth Book of British Kings & Queens* (London: Robinson, 1998)

Baker, Darren, *The Two Eleanors of Henry III: The Lives of Eleanor of Provence and Eleanor de Montfort* (Barnsley: Pen & Sword History, 2019)

Baker, Darren, *With All For All: The Life of Simon de Montfort* (Stroud: Amberley, 2015)

Barrow, G.W.S., 'David I (c. 1185–1153)', *Oxford Dictionary of National Biography* (Oxford: Oxford University Press, 2004) [online edition: Oxforddnb.com]

Bartlett, Robert, *England Under the Norman and Angevin Kings, 1075–1225* (Oxford: Oxford University Press, 2000)

Bartlett, W.B., *Richard the Lionheart: The Crusader King of England* (Stroud: Amberley, 2018)

Bateson, Mary, *Medieval England 1066–1350* (Lecturable, e-book, 2014)

'Battle of Mount Cadmus', *World Heritage Encyclopedia*, http://worldheritage.org/article/WHEBN0028326272/Battle%20of%20Mount%20Cadmus

Bémont, Charles and Gabriel Monod, *Medieval Europe, 395–1270* (Lecturable, e-book, 2012)

Bibliography – Lewes Priory, Lewes, Sussex, sussexrecordsociety.org, https://www.sussexrecordsociety.org/dbs/biblio/authors/B/BlaauwWH

Blaauw, W.H., 'On the Early History of Lewes Priory, and its Seals, with extracts from a MS. Chronicle', *Sussex Archaeological Collections*, vol. 2 (1849), pp. 7–37

Blackburn, Robert, 'Britain's Written Constitution', https://www.bl.uk/magna-carta/articles/britains-unwritten-constitution, 13 March 2015

Bloks, Moniek, 'Matilda of Flanders: Queen of the Conqueror', https://www.historyofroyalwomen.com/the-royal-women/matilda-flanders-queen-conqueror/, 29 December 2017

Borman, Tracy, *Matilda, Wife of the Conqueror, First Queen of England* (London: Vintage Books, 2012)

Boyd, Douglas, *Eleanor, April Queen of Aquitaine* (Stroud: Sutton Publishing, 2004)

Brand, Paul, 'Bigod, Hugh (b. in or before 1220, d. 1266)', *Oxford Dictionary of National Biography* (Oxford: Oxford University Press, 2004) [online edition: Oxforddnb.com]

Brindle, Steven and Agnieszka Sadraei, *Conisbrough Castle* (London: English Heritage, 2015)

Brooks, Richard, *The Knight who Saved England, William Marshal and the French Invasion, 1217* (Oxford: Osprey Publishing, 2014)

Burke, John and John Bernard Burke, *A Genealogical and Heraldic Dictionary of the Peerages of England, Ireland and Scotland* (London: Henry Colburn, 1846)

Campbell, Bruce, 'Britain 1300', *History Today*, Vol. 50, no. 6 (June 2000), pp. 10–17

Cannon, John, ed., *The Oxford Companion to British History* (Oxford: Oxford University Press, 1997)

Carol, 'Eleanor of Leicester: A Broken Vow of Chastity', https://www.historyofroyalwomen.com/eleanor-of-leicester/eleanor-leicester-broken-vow-chastity/, 28 February 2017

Carpenter, David, 'Revival and Survival: Reissuing Magna Carta', https://www.bl.uk/magna-carta/articles/revival-and-survival-reissuing-magna-carta, 13 March 2015

Cassidy, Richard, 'Rose of Dover (d.1261), Richard of Chilham and an Inheritance in Kent', *Archaeologica Cantiana*, Vol. cxxxi (2011), pp. 305–19

Castor, Helen, *She-Wolves: The Women who Ruled England before Elizabeth* (London: Faber and Faber, 2010)

Chadwick, Elizabeth, 'Clothing the Bones: Finding Mahelt Marshal', livingthehistoryelizabethchadwick.blogspot.com, 7 September 2008

Chadwick, Elizabeth, 'Hamelin de Warenne *Pro Lege per Lege*'', https://elizabethchadwick.com/blog/hamelin-de-warenne-pro-lege-per-lege/ [accessed 2 February 2020.

Chadwick, Elizabeth, 'Isabel de Warenne: An Exercise in Joining the Dots' http://the-history-girls.blogspot.com/2015/04/isabel-de-warenne-exercise-in-joining.html,   24 April 2015

Chadwick, Elizabeth, 'Roger Bigod Earl of Norfolk circa 1140–1221', http://the-history-girls.blogspot.com/2018/11/roger-bigod-earl-of-norfolk-circa-1140.html, 24 November 2018

Chadwick, Elizabeth, 'Roger Bigod II Earl of Norfolk', https://elizabethchadwick.com/roger-bigod-ii/, 12 June 2009

Chandler, Victoria, 'Ada de Warenne, Queen Mother of Scotland (c. 1123–1178)', *The Scottish Historical Review* vol. 60, no. 170, Part 2 (Oct. 1981), pp. 119–39; jstor.org/stable/25529417

Chandler, Victoria, 'Warenne, Reginald [Rainald] de (1121x6–1178/9)', *Oxford Dictionary of National Biography* (Oxford: Oxford University Press, 2004) [online edition: Oxforddnb.com]

Chandler, Victoria, 'Warenne, William de, third earl of Surrey [Earl Warenne] (c. 1119–1148)', *Oxford Dictionary of National Biography* (Oxford: Oxford University Press, 2004) [online edition: Oxforddnb.com]

Chibnall, Marjorie, *The Empress Matilda: Queen Consort, Queen Mother and Lady of the English* (Oxford: Blackwell, 1999). Reprint

Church, Stephen, *King John: England, Magna Carta and the Making of a Tyrant* (London: MacMillan, 2015)

Cockerill, Sara, *Eleanor of Castile: The Shadow Queen* (Stroud: Amberley, 2014)

Cole, Margaret Wren, *Llywelyn ab Iorwerth: The Making of a Welsh Prince* (PhD thesis, St. Andrews, 2012)

Cole, Teresa, *After the Conquest: The Divided Realm* (Stroud: Amberley Publishing, 2018)

Cole, Teresa, *The Anarchy: The Darkest Days of Medieval England* (Stroud: Amberley Publishing, 2019)

Cole, Teresa *The Norman Conquest: William the Conqueror's Subjugation of England* (Stroud: Amberley, 2016)

Conisbrough Court Rolls, *dhi.ac.uk/conisbrough/index.html*

Connolly, Sharon Bennett, *Heroines of the Medieval World* (Stroud: Amberley, 2017)

Connolly, Sharon Bennett, *Ladies of Magna Carta: Women of Influence in Thirteenth Century England* (Barnsley: Pen & Sword, 2020)

Connolly, Sharon Bennett, *Silk and the Sword: The Women of the Norman Conquest* (Stroud: Amberley, 2018)

Corvi, Steven J., *Plantagenet Queens and Consorts: Family, Duty, Power* (Stroud: Amberley, 2018)

Crouch, David, 'Beaumont, Robert de, count of Meulan and first earl of Leicester (d. 1118)', *Oxford Dictionary of National Biography* (Oxford: Oxford University Press, 2004) [online edition: Oxforddnb.com]

Crouch, David, 'Breteuil, Robert de, fourth earl of Leicester', *Oxford Dictionary of National Biography* (Oxford: Oxford University Press, 2004) [online edition: Oxforddnb.com]

Crouch, David, 'Marshal, William [called the Marshal], fourth earl of Pembroke (c. 1146–1219)', *Oxford Dictionary of National Biography* (Oxford: Oxford University Press, 2004) [online edition: Oxforddnb.com]

Crouch, David, *The Reign of King Stephen 1135–1154* (Harlow: Longman, Pearson Education, 2000)

Crouch, David, 'Robert [Robert de Beaumont], second earl of Leicester (1104–1168)', *Oxford Dictionary of National Biography* (Oxford: Oxford University Press, 2004) [online edition: Oxforddnb.com]

Crouch, David, 'Roger, second earl of Warwick (d. 1153)', *Oxford Dictionary of National Biography* (Oxford: Oxford University Press, 2004) [online edition: Oxforddnb.com]

Crouch, David, 'Waleran [Walern de Beaumont}, count of Meulan and earl of Worcester (1104–1166)', *Oxford Dictionary of National Biography* (Oxford: Oxford University Press, 2004) [online edition: Oxforddnb.com]

Crouch, David, *William Marshal* (Abingdon: Routledge, 3rd ed., 2016)

Daniel-Tyssen, John Robert, 'Documents Relating to Lewes Priory, with Translations and Notes', *Sussex Archaeological Collections*, vol. 25 (1873, pp. 136–151; archive.org

Danziger, Danny and John Gillingham, *1215: The Year of Magna Carta* (London: Hodder & Stoughton, 2004)

Davis, H.W. Carless, *England under the Normans and Angevins 1066–1272* (Lecturable, ebook, 2013)

Davis, William Stearns, *A History of France from the Earliest Times to the Treaty of Versailles* (Cambridge, M.A.: The Riverside Press, 1919)

Doherty, Paul, *Isabella and the Strange Death of Edward II* (London: Constable, 2003)

Douglas, David C., *William the Conqueror* (New Haven: Yale University Press, 1999)

Douglas, David C., *William the Conqueror: The Norman Impact Upon England* (Los Angeles: University of California Press, 1964)

Duckett, George Floyd, *Observations on the Parentage of Gundreda, the Daughter of William Duke of Normandy, and Wife of William de Warenne* (Whitefish: Kessinger Legacy Reprints, 1878) [originally published in Vol. III of the *Cumberland and Westmoreland Archaeological Society*]

Duducu, Jem, *Forgotten History: Unbelievable Moments from the Past* (Stroud: Amberley, 2016)

Duruy, Victor, *History of the Middle Ages* (Lecturable, e-book, 2012)

Eales, Richard, 'Ranulf III [Ranulf de Blundeville], sixth earl of Chester and first earl of Lincoln', *Oxford Dictionary of National Biography* (Oxford: Oxford University Press, 2004) [online edition: Oxforddnb.com]

'Ela, Countess of Salisbury', https://www.medievalwomen.org/ela-countess-of-salisbury.html [accessed 3 Marsh 2020]

Ellis, Alfred S., 'Biographical Notes on the Yorkshire Tenants Named in Domesday Book', *The Yorkshire Archaeological Journal* vol. IV (1877), pp. 215–48

Epistolae, 'Eleanor of England', https://epistolae.ctl.columbia.edu/woman/25295.html [accessed 23 March 2020]

Epistolae, 'Isabel of Angoulême', https://epistolae.ctl.columbia.edu/woman/71.html [accessed 24 March 2020]

Fairbank, F. Royston, 'The Last Earl of Warenne and Surrey, and the Distribution of his Possessions', *The Yorkshire Archaeological Journal*, vol. XIX, (1907), pp. 193–266

Farrer, William and Charles Travis Clay, editors, *Early Yorkshire Charters, Volume 8: The Honour of Warenne* (Cambridge: Cambridge University Press, 2013) [first published in 1949]

Faulkner, Kathryn, 'Beauchamp, de, family', *Oxford Dictionary of National Biography* (Oxford: Oxford University Press, 2004) [online edition: Oxforddnb.com]

Flanagan, M.T., 'Clare, Isabel de, suo jure countess of Pembroke (1171x6–1220)', *Oxford Dictionary of National Biography* (Oxford: Oxford University Press, 2004) [online edition: Oxforddnb.com]

Foundation for Medieval Genealogy, Chapter7: Surrey Fmg.ac/Projects/MedLands/English, *Foundation for Medieval Genealogy* [accessed 6 February 2020]

Fraser, Antonia, *The Warrior Queens: Boadicea's Chariot* (London: George Weidenfeld & Nicolson Ltd., 1993)

Gardiner, Juliet and Neil Wenborn (eds), *History Today Companion to British History* (London: Collins & Brown, 1995)

Gesta Herewardi, World Heritage Encyclopedia, http://www.gutenberg.us/articles/gesta_herwardi [accessed 21 February 2020]

Gillingham, John, 'John (1167–1216)', Oxford *Dictionary of National Biography* (Oxford: Oxford University Press, 2004) [online edition: Oxforddnb.com]

Given-Wilson, C., 'Fitzalan, Edmund, second earl of Arundel (1285–1326)', *Oxford Dictionary of National Biography* (Oxford: Oxford University Press, 2004) [online edition: Oxforddnb.com]

Given-Wilson, C., 'Fitzalan, Richard, third earl of Arundel (c. 1313–1376)', *Oxford Dictionary of National Biography* (Oxford: Oxford University Press, 2004) [online edition: Oxforddnb.com]

Gladwin, Irene, *The Sheriff: The Man and his Office* (London: Victor Gollancz, 1974)

Goubert, Pierre, *The Course of French History* (London: Routledge, 1991)

Green, Mary Anne Everett, *Lives of the Princesses of England from the Norman Conquest*, 2 Vols. (London: Longman, 1857)

Grey, Madeleine, 'Four Weddings, Three Funerals and a Historic Detective Puzzle: A Cautionary Tale' *Transactions of the Anglesey Antiquarian Society*, Vol. 2014, 2014, p. 31–46. https://pure.southwales.ac.uk/files/386714/BeaumarisEffigy_CorrectedText_Photos.pdf

Hallam, Elizabeth (ed.), *Chronicles of the Age of Chivalry* (Twickenham: Tiger Books, 1995)

Hallam, Elizabeth, 'Eleanor, Countess of Pembroke and Leicester (1215?–1275)', *Oxford Dictionary of National Biography* (Oxford: Oxford University Press, 2004) [online edition: Oxforddnb.com]

Hallam, Elizabeth, ed., *The Plantagenet Chronicles* (Twickenham: Tiger Books, 1995)

Hanley, Catherine, *Matilda: Empress, Queen, Warrior* (New Haven: Yale University Press, 2019)

Hanley, Catherine, 'Nichola de la Haye', http://www.catherinehanley.co.uk/historical-background/nicola-de-la-haye/ [accessed 30 January 2020]

Hanley, Catherine, 'The Battle that Saved England', http://www.historiamag.com/the-battle-that-saved-england/, 20 May 2017

Hilliam, David, *Kings, Queens, Bones and Bastards: Who's Who in the English Monarchy from Egbert to Elizabeth II* (Stroud: The History Press, 2008); first published 1998)

Hilton, Lisa, *Queens Consort: England's Medieval Queens* (London: Orion Books, 2008)

Hindley, Geoffrey, *A Brief History of the Crusades* (London: Constable & Robinson, 2004)

Historic England, 'Peel Hill Motte and Bailey Castle, Thorne', historicengland.org.uk

A History of the County of Rutland: Volume 2 (London: Victoria County History, 1935)

Holbrook, Sue, *St Nicholas' Church, Thorne* (Hatfield: Heritage Inspired 2019)

Hollister, C. Warren, 'The Taming of a Turbulent Earl: Henry I and William of Warenne', *Historical Reflections / Réflexions Historiques*, vol. 3, no. 1 (1976), pp. 83–91

Hollister, C. Warren, 'Warenne, William de, second earl of Surrey [Earl Warenne] (d. 1138)', Oxford *Dictionary of National Biography* (Oxford: Oxford University Press, 2004) [online edition: Oxforddnb.com].

Huizinga, J., *The Waning of the Middle Ages*, 4th edition (London: The Folio Society, 2000)

Huscroft, Richard, *Tales from the Long Twelfth Century* (New Haven: Yale University Press, 2017)

Impey, Edward, *Castle Acre Priory and Castle* (London: English Heritage, 2016)

'In Their Own Words: 6 of History's Most Fascinating Letters', https://www.historyextra.com/period/stuart/history-fascinating-important-letters-extracts-monteagle-gunpowder-plot-warning-titanic/, 26 November 2016

James, Jeffrey, *The Bastard's Sons: Robert, William and Henry of Normandy*, (Stroud: Amberley Publishing, 2020)

Johns, Susan M., 'Alice [married name Alice de Lusignan] suo jure countess of Eu (article)', *Oxford Dictionary of National Biography* (Oxford: Oxford University Press, 2004) [online edition: Oxforddnb.com]

Johns, Susan M., 'Haie, Nicola de la (d. 1230), landowner', *Oxford Dictionary of National Biography* (Oxford: Oxford University Press, 2004) [online edition: Oxforddnb.com]

Johns, Susan M., 'Isabel de Warenne, suo jure Countess of Surrey (d. 1203)', *Oxford Dictionary of National Biography* (Oxford: Oxford University Press, 2004) [online edition: Oxforddnb.com]

Johns, Susan M., *Noblewomen, Aristocracy and Power in the Twelfth-Century Anglo-Norman Realm* (Manchester: Manchester University Press, 2003)

Jones, Dan, *The Plantagenets: The Kings Who Made England* (London: Harper Collins, Kindle edition, 2013)

Jones, Dan, *Realm Divided: A Year in the Life of Plantagenet England* (London: Head of Zeus, 2015)

Jones, Dan, 'What Was Magna Carta and Why Was it Significant?', https://www.historyhit.com/1215-signing-magna-carta/, 15 June 2018

Jones, Terry, *Terry Jones' Medieval Lives* (London: BBC Books, 2005)

Keefe, Thomas K., 'Warenne, Hamelin de, earl of Surrey [Earl Warenne] (d. 1202) magnate', *Oxford Dictionary of National Biography* (Oxford: Oxford University Press, 2004) [online edition: Oxforddnb.com]

Keefe, Thomas K., 'William [William of Blois], earl of Surrey [Earl Warenne] (c. 1135–1159)', *Oxford Dictionary of National Biography* (Oxford: Oxford University Press, 2004) [online edition: Oxforddnb.com].

King, Edmund, *King Stephen* (New Haven: Yale University Press, 2010)

Koenigsberger, H.G., *Medieval Europe 400–1500* (New York: Longman, 1987)

Lacroix, Paul, *Medieval Life: Manners, Customs and Dress During the Middle Ages* (London: Arcturus, 2011)

Laffin, John, *Brassey's Battles: 3,500 Years of Conflict, Campaigns and Wars from A-Z* (London: Brassey's, 1995)

Lapsley, G., 'John de Warenne and the '*Quo Warranto*' Proceedings in 1279', *The Cambridge Historical Journal*, Vol. 2, no. 2 (1927). pp. 110–32; jstor.org/stable/3020694

Lawless, Erin, *Forgotten Royal Women: The King and I* (Barnsley: Pen & Sword Books, 2019)

'Lewes Priory: A Brief Historical Summary', Lewespriory.org.uk

Lewis, C.P., 'The Earldom of Surrey and the Date of Domesday Book', *Historical Research* (1990)

Lewis, C.P., 'Warenne, William de, first Earl of Surrey [Earl Warenne] (d. 1088)', *Oxford Dictionary of National Biography* (Oxford: Oxford University Press, 2004) [online edition]

Lewis, Matthew, *Henry III: The Son of Magna Carta* (Stroud: Amberley, 2016)

Lewis, Matthew, *Stephen and Matilda's Civil War: Cousins of Anarchy* (Barnsley: Pen & Sword, 2019)

Leyser, Henrietta, *Medieval Women: A Social History of Women in England 450– 1500* (Phoenix, e-book, 2013)

Lloyd, L.C., 'The Origin of the Family of Warenne', *The Yorkshire Archaeological Journal*, vol. XXXI (1934), pp. 97–113

Lloyd, Simon, 'Chilham, Sir Richard of (d. 1246)', *Oxford Dictionary of National Biography* (Oxford: Oxford University Press, 2004) [online edition: Oxforddnb.com]

Lloyd, Simon, 'Longespée, Sir William', *Oxford Dictionary of National Biography* (Oxford: Oxford University Press, 2004) [online edition: Oxforddnb.com]

Maddicott, J.R., 'Montfort, Simon de, eighth earl of Leicester (1208–1265)', *Oxford Dictionary of National Biography* (Oxford: Oxford University Press, 2004) [online edition: Oxforddnb.com]

Magna Carta, https://www.salisburycathedral.org.uk/magna-carta-and-archives

Magna Carta Project, magnacartaresearch.org

Marshall, Rosalind K., *Scottish Queens 1034–1714* (Edinburgh: Birlinn, 2003)

Matthew, Donald, *King Stephen* (London: Hambledon, 2002)

Matthews, Helen, *The Legitimacy of Bastards: The Place of Illegitimate Children in Later Medieval England* (Barnsley: Pen & Sword, 2019)

McConnell, Ally, 'The Life of Ela, Countess of Salisbury', Wiltshire and Swindon History Centre, http://wshc.eu/blog/item/the-life-of-ela-countess-of-salisbury.html, 15 September 2015

McGlynn, Sean, *Blood Cries Afar: The Magna Carta War and the Invasion of England 1215–1217* (Stroud: The History Press, 2015)

McGlynn, Sean, 'King John and the French Invasion of England', *BBC History Magazine*, Vol. 11, no. 6 (June 2010), pp. 24–29

McNamee, Colm, *Robert Bruce: Our Most Valiant Prince, King and Lord* (Edinburgh: Birlinn, 2018)

Marlow, Joyce, *Kings and Queens of Britain* (London: Artus Publishing, 6th edition, 1979)

Martindale, Jane, 'Eleanor, suo jure duchess of Aquitaine (c.1122–1204,)' *Oxford Dictionary of National Biography* (Oxford: Oxford University Press, 2004) [online edition: Oxforddnb.com]

Messer, Danna, 'Joan (Siwan), princess and diplomat', Dictionary of Welsh Biography, 10 October 2018, https://biography.wales/article/s12-JOAN-TYW-1237

Messer, Danna, *Joan Lady of Wales: Power & Politics of King John's Daughter* (Barnsley; Pen and Sword, 2020)

Mooers, Stephanie Christelow, 'The Division of Inheritance and the Provision of non-inheriting Offspring among the Anglo-Norman Elite', *Medieval Prosopography*, Vol. 7, no. 2 (Autumn 1996), pp. 3–44

Mooers, Stephanie L., 'Patronage in the Pipe Roll of 1130', Speculum, Vol. 59, No. 2 (Apr. 1984), pp. 282–307

Moore, Dudley, 'Lewes Priory Burials', *Sussex Archaeological Society*, 42 (2011), pp. 2–4

Morris, Marc, *Castle Acre and the Warennes*, marcmorris.org.uk

Morris, Marc, 'From Friendly Neighbours to Bitter Enemies', *BBC History Magazine*, Vol. 9 no. 3 (March 2008), pp. 34–38

Morris, Marc, *A Great and Terrible King: Edward I and the Forging of Britain* (London: Windmill Books, 2009)

Morris, Marc, *'How Important was Magna Carta?'*, https://www.historyhit.com/how-important-was-magna-carta/, 24 September 2018

Morris, Marc, *King John: Treachery, Tyranny and the Road to Magna Carta* (London: Windmill Books, 2015)

Morris, Marc, *The Norman Conquest* (London: Windmill Books, 2013).

Morris, Marc, *William I: England's Conqueror* (London, Penguin Books, 2016)

Mason, J.F.A, 'William [William Ætheling, William Adelinus, William Adelingus] (1103–1112)', *Oxford Dictionary of National Biography* (Oxford: Oxford University Press, 2004) [online edition: Oxforddnb.com]

Moss, John, *Great British Family Names and Their History: What's in a Name?* (Barnsley: Pen & Sword, 2019)

Mount, Toni, *A Year in the Life of Medieval England* (Stroud: Amberley, 2016)

Mundy, John H., *The High Middle Ages 1150–1309* (London: The Folio Society, 1998)

Musgrove, David, *100 Places that Made Britain* (London: BBC Books, 2011)

Nichols, John A., 'Warenne, Isabel de [married name Isabel d'Aubigny], countess of Arundel', *Oxford Dictionary of National Biography* (Oxford: Oxford University Press, 2004) [online edition: Oxforddnb.com]

Norton, Elizabeth, *She Wolves: The Notorious Queens of England* (Stroud: The History Press, 2008)

Oliver, Neil, *The Story of the British Isles in 100 Places* (London: Penguin Random House, 2018)

Page, W., ed. *A History of the County of Sussex: Volume 2* (London, 1973); *British History Online* http://www.british-history.ac.uk/vch/sussex/vol2

Page, W., ed. 'House of Cistercian nuns: The Abbey of Marham', in *A History of the County of Norfolk: Volume 2*, ed. William Page (London, 1906) *British History Online* http://www.british-history.ac.uk/vch/norf/vol2/pp369-370

Patterson, Robert B., 'Isabella, suo jure countess of Gloucester (c. 1160–1217)', *Oxford Dictionary of National Biography* (Oxford: Oxford University Press, 2004) [online edition: Oxforddnb.com]

'Peel Hill Motte', http://historyofthorne.com/peel_hill.html

Neville, Cynthia J. (ed.), 'A Plea Roll of Edward I's Army in Scotland, 1296', https://deremilitari.org/2014/04/a-plea-roll-of-edward-is-army-in-scotland-1296/, 2014

Phillips, Charles, *The Illustrated Encyclopedia of Kings and Queens of Britain* (Wigston: Hermes House, 2011)

Power, Eileen, *Medieval English Nunneries c. 1275–1535* (Cambridge: Cambridge University Press, 1922)

Price, Rich, 'King John's Letters', Facebook Study Group, 20 June 2016

Rees, William (ed.), *Calendar of Ancient Petitions Relating to Wales (Thirteenth to Sixteenth Century)* (Cardiff: University of Wales Press, 1975)

Ridgeway, H.W., 'Munchensi, Warin de', *Oxford Dictionary of National Biography* (Oxford: Oxford University Press, 2004) [online edition: Oxforddnb.com]

Robertson, Geoffrey, 'Magna Carta and Jury Trial', https://www.bl.uk/magna-carta/articles/magna-carta-and-jury-trial, 13 March 2015

Ross, David, *Scotland: History of a Nation* (Broxburn: Lomond Books Ltd., 2014)

Sands, Harold and Hugh Braun, 'Conisbrough and Mortemer', *The Yorkshire Archaeological Journal*, vol. XXXII (1936), pp. 147–159

Santiuste, David, *A Brief History of Conisbrough Castle*, https://davidsantiuste.com/2017/05/20/a-brief-history-of-conisbrough-castle/, 20 May 2017

L.F. Salzman, ed. 'Parishes: Rottingdean', in *A History of the County of Sussex: Volume 7, The Rape of Lewes*, (London, 1940) *British History Online* http://www.british-history.ac.uk/vch/sussex/vol7/pp232-238

Saul, Nigel, 'Geoffrey de Mandeville', https://magnacarta800th.com/schools/biographies/the-25-barons-of-magna-carta/geoffrey-de-mandeville/

Scott, W.W., 'Ermengarde de Beaumont (1233)', *Oxford Dictionary of National Biography* (Oxford: Oxford University Press, 2004) [online edition: Oxforddnb.com]

Scott, W.W., 'Malcolm IV (c. 1141–1165)', *Oxford Dictionary of National Biography* (Oxford: Oxford University Press, 2004) [online edition: Oxforddnb.com]

Scott, W.W., 'William I [known as William the Lion] (c. 1142–1214)', *Oxford Dictionary of National Biography* (Oxford: Oxford University Press, 2004) [online edition: Oxforddnb.com]

Seward, Desmond, *The Demon's Brood* (London: Constable, 2014)

Smurthwaite, David, *The Complete Guide to the Battlefields of Britain* (London: Mermaid Books, 1984)

Southern, R.W., *The Making of the Middle Ages*, 4th Edition (London: The Folio Society, 1998)

Spencer, Andrew M., *Nobility and Kingship in Medieval England* (Cambridge: Cambridge University Press, 2014)

Spinks, Stephen, *Edward II The Man: A Doomed Inheritance* (Stroud: Amberley, 2017)

Spinks, Stephen, *Robert the Bruce: Champion of a Nation* (Stroud: Amberley, 2019)

Stacey, Robert C., 'Bigod, Roger, fourth earl of Norfolk', Oxford *Dictionary of National Biography* (Oxford: Oxford University Press, 2004) [online edition: Oxforddnb.com]

Stapleton, Thomas, 'Observations in Disproof of the Pretended Marriage of William de Warenn', *The Archaeological Journal*, Vol. 3 (March 1846), pp. 1–26

Starkey, David, *Magna Carta: The True Story Behind the Charter* (London: Hodder, 2015)

Stell, G.P., 'John [John de Balliol] (c. 1248x50–1314)', *Oxford Dictionary of National Biography* (Oxford: Oxford University Press, 2004) [online edition: Oxforddnb.com]

St John Hope, W., 'A Palatinate Seal of John, Earl of Warenne, Surrey and Stratherne, 1305–1347', *Sussex Archaeological Collections*, Vol. 57 (1915), pp. 180–4

Strickland, Matthew, 'Enforcers of Magna Carta (act, 1215–1216)', *Oxford Dictionary of National Biography* (Oxford: Oxford University Press, 2004) [online edition: Oxforddnb. com]

Strickland, Matthew, 'Longespée [Lungespée], William, third earl of Salisbury', *Oxford Dictionary of National Biography* (Oxford: Oxford University Press, 2004) [online edition: Oxforddnb.com]

Stringer, Keith, 'Ada [née Ada de Warenne], countess of Northumberland (c. 1123–1178)', *Oxford Dictionary of National Biography* (Oxford: Oxford University Press, 2004) [online edition: Oxforddnb.com]

Stringer, Keith, 'Alexander II (1198–1249)', *Oxford Dictionary of National Biography* (Oxford: Oxford University Press, 2004) [online edition: Oxforddnb.com]

Stringer, Keith, Stringer, 'Henry, earl of Northumberland (c. 1115–1152)', *Oxford Dictionary of National Biography* (Oxford: Oxford University Press, 2004) [online edition: Oxforddnb.com]

The Historier, 'The Treaty of Kingston: On this Day and on this Spot?', an historiersmiscellany. com, 12 September 2017

Thompson, Kathleen, 'William Talvas, Count of Ponthieu, and the Politics of the Anglo-Norman Realm', in *England and Normandy in the Middle Ages*, edited by David Bates and Ann Curry (London: Hambledon Press, 1994)

Thompson, S.P., 'Mary [Mary of Blois], suo jure countess of Boulogne (d. 1182), princess and abbess of Romsey', *Oxford Dictionary of National Biography* (Oxford: Oxford University Press, 2004) [online edition: Oxforddnb.com].

Tickhill Castle Guide Leaflet, '*Lords of the Honour of Tickhill*', 2017

Tranter, Nigel, *The Story of Scotland* (Neil Wilson Publishing, 4th ed., 2011); e-book

Turner, Ralph V., Aubigny, William d', [William de Albini], third earl of Arundel', *Oxford Dictionary of National Biography* (Oxford: Oxford University Press, 2004) [online edition: Oxforddnb.com]

Turner, Ralph V., *Two Illegitimate Sons of King John: A Comparison of Their Careers*, Proposal for New College 2018 Conference, https://www.academia.edu/39015968/Proposal_for_New_College_2018_Conference_Ralph_V_Turner, 30 January 2020

Turner, Rick, 'Looking Inside the Medieval Holt Castle', https://www.historyextra.com/period/norman/looking-inside-the-medieval-holt-castle/, 4 September 2015

Van Houts, Elisabeth, 'Hereward and Flanders', *Anglo-Saxon England*, 28 ((1999): 201–223; jstor.org/stable/44512349. Accessed 16 January, 2020

Van Houts, Elisabeth, 'The Warenne View of the Past', in *Proceedings of the Battle Conference 2003*, edited by John Gillingham (Suffolk: Boydell Press, 2004)

Vincent, Nicholas, 'Feature of the Month: May 2015 – A Glimpse of London, May 1216', The Magna Carta Project

Vincent, Nicholas, 'From the Tower: John Sends a Coded Message to His Queen', The Magna Carta Project http://139.222.4.243/read/itinerary/From_the_Tower__John_sends_a_coded_message_to_his_queen

Vincent, Nicholas, 'Isabella [Isabella of Angoulême], suo jure countess of Angoulême (c. 1188–1246)', Oxford Dictionary of National Biography (Oxford: Oxford University Press, 2004) [online edition: Oxforddnb.com]

Vincent, Nicholas, 'King John's Evil Counsellors (act. 1208–1214)', Oxford Dictionary of National Biography (Oxford: Oxford University Press, 2004) [online edition: Oxforddnb.com]

Vincent, Nicholas, 'Lacy, John de, third earl of Lincoln', Oxford Dictionary of National Biography (Oxford: Oxford University Press, 2004) [online edition: Oxforddnb.com]

Vincent, Nicholas, 'Lusignan [Valence], Aymer de (c. 1228–1260)', Oxford Dictionary of National Biography (Oxford: Oxford University Press, 2004) [online edition: Oxforddnb.com]

Vincent, Nicholas, 'Richard, first earl of Cornwall and King of Germany', Oxford Dictionary of National Biography (Oxford: Oxford University Press, 2004) [online edition: Oxforddnb.com]

Vincent, Nicholas, 'Tournaments, Ladies and Bears', The Magna Carta Project http://139.222.4.243/read/itinerary/Tournaments__Ladies_and_Bears

Vincent, Nicholas, 'Warenne, William de, fifth earl of Surrey [Earl Warenne]', Oxford Dictionary of National Biography (Oxford: Oxford University Press, 2004) [online edition: Oxforddnb.com]

Walker, R.F., 'Marshal, William, fifth earl of Pembroke (c. 1190–1231)', Oxford Dictionary of National Biography (Oxford: Oxford University Press, 2004) [online edition: Oxforddnb.com].

Warner, Kathryn, 'Alice Fitzalan née de Warenne, Countess of Arundel', http://edwardthesecond.blogspot.com/2014/11/alice-fitzalan-nee-de-warenne-countess.html, 7 November 2014

Warner, Kathryn, 'The Amatory Adventures of John de Warenne', edwardthesecondblogspot.com, 5 April 2007

Warner, Kathryn, Edward II: The Unconventional King (Stroud: Amberley, 2017)

Warner, Kathryn, Edward II's Nieces: The Clare Sisters (Barnsley: Pen & Sword, 2020)

Warner, Kathryn, 'The Illegitimate Children of John de Warenne', http://edwardthesecond.blogspot.com/2007/04/amatory-adventures-of-john-de-warenne.html, 17 September 2009

Warner, Kathryn, Isabella of France: The Rebel Queen (Stroud: Amberley, 2016)

Warner, Kathryn, Philippa of Hainault: Mother of the English Nation (Stroud: Amberley, 2019)

Watson, Rev. John, Memoirs of the Ancient Earls of Warren and Surrey, and Their Descendants to the Present Time, Volumes I and II (1782)

Waugh, S.L., The Lordship of England: Royal Wardships and Marriages in English Society and Politics, 1217–1327 (Princeton, N.J.: Princeton University Press, 1988)

Waugh, Scott L., 'Warenne, John de, seventh earl of Surrey [earl of Surrey and Sussex, Earl Warenne] (1286–1347)', Oxford Dictionary of National Biography (Oxford: Oxford University Press, 2004) [online edition: Oxforddnb.com]

Waugh, Scott L., 'Warenne, John de, sixth earl of Surrey [earl of Surrey and Sussex, Earl Warenne] (1232–1304)', Oxford Dictionary of National Biography (Oxford: Oxford University Press, 2004) [online edition: Oxforddnb.com]

Webster, Bruce, 'Balliol, Edward (b. in or after 1281, d. 1364)', Oxford Dictionary of National Biography (Oxford: Oxford University Press, 2004) [online edition: Oxforddnb.com]

Weir, Alison, *Britain's Royal Families: The Complete Genealogy* (London: Pimlico, 2nd edition, 1996)

Weir, Alison, *Eleanor of Aquitaine: By the Wrath of God, Queen of England* (London: Jonathan Cape, 1999)

West, F.J., 'Burgh, Hubert de, earl of Kent (c. 1170–1243)', *Oxford Dictionary of National Biography* (Oxford: Oxford University Press, 2004) [online edition: Oxforddnb.com]

Wilkinson, Louise, 'Isabella of Angoulême, wife of King John', https://magnacarta800th.com/schools/biographies/women-of-magna-carta/isabella-of-angouleme-wife-of-king-john/

Wilkinson, Louise, 'Isabel of Gloucester, wife of King John', https://magnacarta800th.com/schools/biographies/women-of-magna-carta/isabella-of-gloucester/

Wilkinson, Louise, *Women in Thirteenth-Century Lincolnshire* (Suffolk: Boydell, 2007)

Wilkinson, Louise J., 'Women, Politics and Local Government in the Thirteenth Century', *Henry III Fine Rolls Project*, Related Papers https://finerollshenry3.org.uk/redist/pdf/Wilkinson_Women_Politics_Local_Govt.pdf (July 2013)

'William de Warenne (1256–1286)', https://en.wikipedia.org/wiki/William_de_Warenne_(1256–1286)

'William Marshal, Earl of Pembroke', http://www.englishmonarchs.co.uk/plantagenet_57.html

Williamson, David, *Brewer's British Royalty* (London: Cassell, 1996)

Wilson, Derek, *The Plantagenets* (London: Quercus, 2011)

Wilson-Lee, Kelcey, *Daughters of Chivalry: The Forgotten Children of Edward I* (London: Picador, 2019)

Wright, James, *A Palace for Our Kings: The History and Archaeology of a Mediaeval Royal Palace in the Heart of Sherwood Forest* (London: Triskele Publishing, 2016)

Yonge, Charlotte M., *History of France* (New York: D. Appleton and Company, 1882)

Index